60 YEARS *of* CORONATION STREET

An Hachette UK Company
www.hachette.co.uk

First published in Great Britain in 2020 by
Hamlyn, an imprint of
Octopus Publishing Group Ltd
Carmelite House
50 Victoria Embankment
London EC4Y 0DZ
www.octopusbooks.co.uk

Distributed in the US by Hachette Book Group
1290 Avenue of the Americas
4th and 5th Floors, New York, NY 10104

Distributed in Canada by Canadian Manda Group
664 Annette Street, Toronto, Ontario, Canada M6S 2C8

ISBN 978-0-60063-593-2

A CIP catalogue record for this book is available from the
British Library.

Printed and bound in China

10 9 8 7 6 5 4 3 2 1

MIX
Paper from
responsible sources
FSC® C008047

Publishing Director: Trevor Davies
Art Director: Juliette Norsworthy
Senior Editor: Pauline Bache
Designers: Tracy Killick, Jeremy Tilston and Claire Huntley
Copyeditor: Corinne Masciocchi
Illustrator: Sean Vecchione at seanvec.com
Photographer: Richard Clatworthy
Production Manager: Lisa Pinnell
Coronation Street Assistant Archivist: Dominic Khouri
ITV Head of Publishing: Shirley Patton

All images copyright ITV except for the following:
Shutterstock: 321bl, Associated Newspapers 20, Daily Sketch
19, J Smart/Daily Mail 21, Jon Super/AP 149b.
Octopus Publishing Group (photography by Richard
Clatworthy): 8a, 15, 16–17, 23, 24br, 26, 27b, 36–37, 39, 44, 45,
46, 54–55, 56, 57, 59, 61, 62, 65, 66, 70–71, 82a, 83a, 85bl, 101bl,
104t, 104bl, 104br, 105br, 108tr, 108cr, 110t, 121l, 124–125,
140b, 147bl, 148, 149bl, 149br, 151, 177tl, 256ar, 268cl, 285b,
288l, 292ar, 292br, 305r, 308c, 309r, 312, 313, 314–315.

EST. 1960

·CORONATION ST.·
™

60 YEARS *of* CORONATION STREET

The incredible story
of Britain's favourite
continuing drama

ABIGAIL KEMP

STUDIOS

hamlyn

Contents

Hair and makeup

On set and on the lot

...only a Coronation
the show's characters.

screen –
a storyline

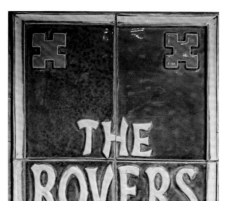

Chapter 3 – Who lives where? 69

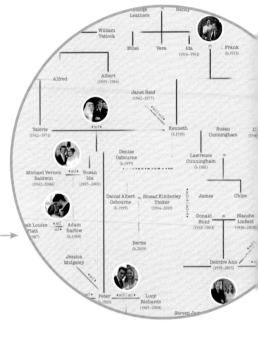

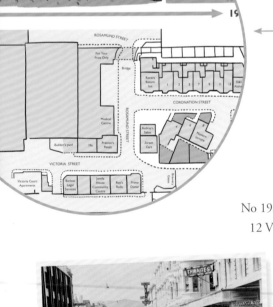

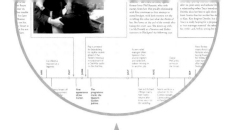

Chapter 4 – Timeline 1960–2020 125

Chapter 5 – *Coronation Street* and the wider world 315

°CORONATION ST.°

Introduction

CORONATION STREET. Just saying those two words conjures up a raft of feelings – hearth and home, growing up hearing that iconic theme tune every week, identifying with the beloved characters and their stories.

Everyone reading this book has their own connection to the *Street*. It's as much a part of British culture as a nice cuppa, a fish and chip supper or sitting down to the Queen's speech on Christmas Day.

Since 1960 this show has been part of our lives, and not just in Britain, it's loved around the world. Who would have thought, 60 years ago, that stories of the trials and tribulations of the residents of an inconsequential little back street in the north of England would provide essential entertainment for millions of viewers week in week out for decades?

The ultimate credit must go, of course, to visionary Tony Warren; he knew in his bones what would make a great TV show. Thank God he stuck to his guns and demanded to 'write about what he knew'.

What he knew was the voice of the working-class north, and he brought that to the screen with drama, sensitivity and a biting wit, traits that have been inherited and enlarged upon by some of the most talented writers in television.

And their words have been successfully transformed on screen by an ever-growing group of equally talented actors. Anyone in the business knows that soap actors are to be admired – turning out so many hours of quality drama each week is an incredible achievement and the 'inhabitants' of Weatherfield are justifiably recognised as leading the way.

But it's not just the actors. As every star appearing on screen will attest, without the skills and dedication of those behind the scenes – the storyliners and writers, the casting department, the schedulers, the designers and editors, the directors, the costume and makeup departments, the researchers, the props department, the publicity office, the office staff, builders, carpenters and electricians, the security guards and canteen staff – this juggernaut of British entertainment simply could not be produced. It's a great big family in which everyone looks out for each other; colleagues on *Coronation Street* become lifelong friends.

To still be at the top of the viewing charts after 60 years is a phenomenal achievement. This book documents the history of a TV programme that has made itself essential viewing for millions. We trace the beginnings of the show, from Tony Warren's original

Thank God he stuck to his guns and demanded to 'write about what he knew'.

concept and the bringing together of that first iconic cast, through the storylines that weaved their way into the British consciousness to the compelling episodes we love to watch today.

Thanks to actors past and present, and all the behind-the-scenes staff, this book contains in-focus sections and interviews and a timeline throughout the years that details many well-known stories, as well as others that might not, at first glance appear important, but that go on to inform subsequent plots, while production notes throughout highlight key events behind the cameras. From that first episode in December 1960 until production was temporarily halted in March 2020 due to the Coronavirus pandemic, we hope you'll be reminded, as you stroll along the cobbles, of the many fantastic *Street* stories – and also some forgotten gems.

In this Diamond Anniversary year we pay tribute to the many hundreds of actors and behind-the-scenes staff who have given us 60 years – more than 10,000 episodes – of compelling television.

And finally, what a joy it has been to research this book – it meant watching endless hours of *Coronation Street* and speaking to the best programme makers in the business. What a privilege.

Doris Speed, William Roache, Violet Carson and Jack Howarth

William Roache MBE – there from the start

WILLIAM Roache didn't want to be in *Coronation Street*. That's right, the longest-serving actor on the world's longest-running TV serial drama had to be persuaded to take the role of Ken Barlow, just for those first few trial episodes, then just for the initial contract he was offered.

In 1959, Roache was starting out as an actor. He'd landed the lead in an episode of *Play of the Week*, which went out on ITV on a Wednesday evening and was a highlight for many viewers.

'It was called *Marking Time*, about a young soldier in Germany,' recalls Roache. 'I'd done plenty of rep and some film parts and my career was just on the threshold. To get the lead in the *Play of the Week* was massive for me. I was very excited about it.'

The play happened to be filmed at Granada Television in Manchester city centre. Unknown to Roache, as he was filming it, Tony Warren took a casting director down to the studios, pointed at Roache and declared, 'He's the man I want for Kenneth Barlow'.

'He'd perhaps seen me on the monitors. We did the play and it was due to come out quite a few weeks later. In the meantime, I got a call from my agent saying, "They want you to do this thing in Manchester, I think it's a comedy…" I said I didn't want to go back up to Manchester. I had my flat in London, I'd done four film parts, things were looking really good. I had the play coming up, so no, I didn't want to do this.'

Under instruction from Warren, the programme's bosses were quite persistent, remembers Roache, so he agreed to travel back up to Manchester to do the pilot, or dry run.

'They told my agent they definitely wanted me for the part. I said no again, I didn't want to do it. My agent pointed out that it was only likely to run for 11 weeks and in the middle of that my play would be going out, then I'd only have to do three more weeks. He said a twice-weekly serial would be an even better shop window for me than the *Play of the Week*. So I said OK, I'll do it! And it was amazing, it really took off. I remember the producer saying, what have we got here? We were celebrities, instantly!'

The character of Ken Barlow was that of an intellectual young man, the first in his family to go to university. He was embarrassed by his working class 'sauce bottle on the tea table' family. Casting notes from 1960 describe Kenneth Barlow as: 'Aged 20. A Cambridge undergraduate. His looks, which are finely drawn, come from his mother. He does not speak, dress or behave like a northern working-class boy. Sometimes arrogant, he is basically likeable.' In a later brief this was changed to Ken reading English and History at a local university on a state scholarship.

Ken was, and still is, something of an idealist. And even though he's still living on that same terraced street, he remains the *Street*'s elder statesman. Nearly 60 years on from that nerve-wracking first live episode, and aged 88, Roache, who is seven years older than his character, keenly remembers the incredible impact the show had on the viewing public. Timing was everything. It was part of the new realism that was sweeping through the theatre, he explains.

'There had been John Osborne's *Look Back in Anger*, James Dean and Marlon Brando were in the cinemas and we were it, we were

Roache's original contract for the dry runs

Roache as Ken in 1963

With the cast at Christmas, 1987

the kitchen-sink drama on television. We were not a soap – I still don't like the word soap – we were a living, cutting-edge drama and we were highly respected.'

The show quickly topped the ratings and Granada was, 'totally gobsmacked by it and we were all offered longish contracts.'

'I was excited. It wasn't just another job, we were part of a whole new wave. I loved everything about the show so I thought, I'll do this and in two years I'll be able to go back to acting in other things. And here I am, still waiting to get back to my career!

'If Tony hadn't been so persistent in wanting me I'd have said no, and moved on. It's funny how fate does these things.'

Roache, as is widely documented, is the only member of the original cast still in the show. He is noted by the *Guinness Book of Records* as the longest-serving TV soap star (despite his dislike of the description 'soap'). He also holds the record for the longest time to play the same role in any TV series. 'I can't believe it's been 60 years, it's absolutely staggering. I still get nervous, you need that adrenaline pumping.'

In his autobiography, *Ken and Me*, he explains further: 'Even now, when they say, "We're going for a take. Quiet studio, ready, action!" your nerves start. If there's just two of you doing a scene, you've got the whole studio – sound, vision mixers, producers, directors – watching; over 40 people who can only operate if you're working. If you stop, the system stops. You can't be doing that and not be nervous. But I think the day you don't feel nervous is probably the day you should pack it in.'

Despite the nerves, he adds today: 'I'm extremely lucky and I appreciate that, it's been a wonderful show. I've had some great stories over the years and met some wonderful people. We've always had great actors and we do now. I still feel it's a privilege to be in it, I love it dearly.'

It's clear that Roache himself is dearly loved too. Not only by the show's millions of fans around the world, but also by his colleagues. Mention Bill, as he's known at *Coronation Street*, to anyone at the studios and the reaction is the same – he's a lovely man for whom nothing is too much trouble.

Roache, exhibiting a powerful memory people half his age would covet, recalls those early days of *Coronation Street* clearly. 'The actual format has changed dramatically,' he explains. 'When we started, we used to do the Friday night episode live and then immediately afterwards, record the one for Wednesday, but in a way that couldn't be edited so it was like doing it live. In those days a lot of things were live, even some commercials, you just accepted it.'

For today's actors, performing live to millions is an occasional event – spectacular live episodes have marked two special anniversaries for *Coronation Street*, its 40th and 50th birthdays, and also ITV's 60th anniversary in 2015. Back in 1960, many of the actors had honed their ability to perform live in repertory theatre, a training ground many of them hailed as highly beneficial.

Roache comments, 'My two years in rep – I didn't go to drama school, I'd been in the Army – was where I learned the job. In those days you had to be in (actors' union) Equity and to become a

member of Equity you had to have done a lot of theatre. You learned in front of a live audience – timing a laugh, the discipline of the theatre. I really valued that. There's no better training ground than the old rep system, which isn't there any more, sadly.'

For its first 29 years, *Coronation Street* was screened twice a week. Now there are six episodes going out each week of the year. Roache has embraced the frenetic pace of turning out three hours of quality drama week in week out, and in large part he credits his acting colleagues: 'There have been so many good people coming in, and so many good, very competent youngsters. I often feel I should go to them for advice!'

Roache's character Ken has been at the centre of many of the *Street*'s best-remembered storylines. He recalls the tremendous impact of one in particular…

'The most powerful one, and the one that set all the papers off having the soap thing, was the Ken/Deirdre/Mike (Baldwin; Johnny Briggs) love triangle. That had colossal impact and I put a lot of frustration into that. We got an award for the scene between Anne (Kirkbride, who played wife Deirdre) and myself (in which Ken argues violently with Deirdre in the hallway of No 1 as Mike Baldwin knocks on the door).

'We got flashed up at the Manchester United match at half-time – "Deirdre stays with Ken"! It hit the pulse in a most extraordinary way, the timing was right. Without any doubt, that was the one with the greatest impact for me.

Weatherfield's best-known love triangle

One of Ken and Mike's infamous punch-ups

Ken's stag night prior to his second wedding to Deirdre, surrounded by her exes

'It was good to do as well. Ken had been written in a not very interesting way for a while and I was getting a bit fed up with it. That really sorted it and I was glad about that.'

Acting in the same show for so long is certainly no mean feat, but there were always going to be downsides to living with one character for so many years. Roache admits: 'There were times I considered leaving, you have ups and downs, that's part of life.'

Before Mike Baldwin's affair with Ken's wife of just two years, Deirdre, Roache felt his character was not getting the interesting storylines he knew it deserved. The impact of the affair plot convinced him to stay and led to future storylines that the viewers – and the actors – loved. Ken and Mike were chalk-and-cheese adversaries and the writers explored this complicated relationship to great effect.

Roache says: 'That great rivalry between Ken and Mike went on and on – Ken had an affair with Mike's girlfriend, Mike married Ken's daughter. I used to say the only thing left is for Ken and Mike to have an affair! They were diametrically opposed – Ken was the idealist who wanted to write his novel and put the world to rights and Mike was the do-it-yourself businessman who would ride over anybody to make some money.'

Mike Baldwin was, of course, struck down by Alzheimer's disease and died in 2006 in his nemesis Ken's arms on the cobbles of Coronation Street.

Another storyline that was important for Roache was the Martha Fraser (Stephanie Beacham) relationship in 2009. He says: 'Ken had always dreamed about being a successful novelist attending the great literary parties in London, the world he wanted to live in, and along comes this woman offering him this life he'd always wanted, but he realised it was just too late. It wasn't fear that stopped him

but a total understanding of where and who he was and that he really loved Deirdre. It would have been a false life, a dream, not a reality.'

Roache's character Ken has had many relationships on the *Street*. They have been well documented and the most recent, with Claudia Colby (Rula Lenska), lent itself to some touching scenes, but it's that marriage to Deirdre that fans love and remember. Roache, along with the rest of the cast, was devastated to lose his on-screen wife, Anne Kirkbride, who died of cancer in 2015.

One relationship Roache looks back on equally fondly was with mother-in-law Blanche Hunt (Maggie Jones). 'I loved the humour with Blanche, the way she used to send Ken up. I'll never forget the Alcoholics Anonymous scene (in which Deirdre, Ken and a hilariously critical Blanche accompanied Peter (Chris Gascoyne) to an AA meeting during which Peter declared "Is there any wonder why I drink?"). We were so worried doing it, it's such a great organisation. It worked though, the humour came through.

'It's a tricky thing to do. If a show decides to "do something funny" often it doesn't work, that's not where the humour is. Sometimes it's at a funeral, it's remarks people make as life is going along, and the *Street* has always been good at that.

'It's part of being Lancashire as much as anything that you'll get the humour coming from within stories. The writers know how to write it and we know how to play it. It doesn't kill the moment. The humour could kill the drama or the drama could kill the humour – getting that balance of the humour within the drama and enhancing it in a way is the craft.

'You have to entertain, you have to have strong drama and you have to have humour. Those things together are the mix that has worked.

'You have to entertain, you have to have strong drama, and you have to have humour.'

'I love the humour. Ken's not one for humour sadly, I wish he was more. Anne (Kirkbride) had a brilliant, natural sense of comedic talent. I loved her comic scenes, she was such a talented actress.'

Roache says he's thankful that in every one of the 60 years he's been acting on *Coronation Street* he's had a great storyline. 'They have often been love triangles but I'm a bit past that now, thank goodness! The Sinead storyline was great – a dying young girl with a baby. It takes you down, there's no doubt you get affected by it. You do a lot of bread-and-butter stuff, ticking along, and then suddenly get those moments…' Roache was widely praised for his monologues during the harrowing storyline in late 2019 that saw Ken's daughter-in-law Sinead (Katie McGlynn) die of cervical cancer.

Reflecting on the success of *Coronation Street* over more than half a century Roache says: 'Having been on for so long is difficult in one sense but in another it means the show has its own history to call upon. I think the writers are brilliant and always have been. I have tremendous respect for the producer, the writers, everyone behind the scenes – it's a well-oiled machine.

'In terms of reference, *Coronation Street* has the widest you can have – we're not a police drama or a hospital drama, but we include those, we have everything open to us. It's about people in a little struggling back street really fighting against the odds of life. It's the underdogs' struggle. The *Street* has got something special, it has a heart, a big heart.'

And *Coronation Street* does more than entertain, says Roache, it informs, its stories are important. Alongside storylines like Sinead's cancer and Aidan's (Shayne Ward) suicide, both of which prompted a huge public reaction, there have been issues of public information.

'We're not a documentary, but we want to be as truthful as we possibly can be. I remember when the new currency came in (decimalisation occurred in the UK in 1971) the government asked us to cover it and we did, in the Rovers with Minnie Caldwell (Margot Bryant), I remember it well.'

Roache is happy with the way *Coronation Street* has changed and evolved over the years, the way it addresses current issues but still entertains. 'You sometimes get people saying the show is not what it was and they're not watching it any more and that's a sad fact,' he says, 'but it has to be that way otherwise you're not moving with the times and you're not bringing the youngsters in and that is a very tricky balance. If we're not organic, responding to society and what it is, we're not doing our job and moving forward.'

For any actor playing a part for so long, elements of their own personality must surely seep into the character they play, so how much of William Roache is in Ken Barlow?

'I am Ken's caretaker. I will defend him. I care about Ken, he's a very well-meaning guy. He wanted to be a great writer and he failed, he failed at a great many of the things he wanted to do, but he's always wanted to make the world a better place and he's a nice guy, I like him. He's a good friend to have, very loyal. I have to look after him. I'm different from Ken though, I'm sporty, he is not. And I'm not an intellectual like him. I treat him like a brother.'

And as for the future? Roache says: 'The start was incredible, but here and now is my favourite time on the show. Ken is turning into what I always wanted in a sense, to become the wise chap. Ken's been round the block. He's done it all, you name it he's done it. He's got intelligence but he's also got wisdom from experience of life.

'I love my dysfunctional family and boy, is it dysfunctional! Tracy (Kate Ford) is a murderess and a psychopath, Peter is an alcoholic bigamist… I just like being the head of my family and long may it continue.

'*Coronation Street* is a happy place to come to work, there are no big egos. I'm very grateful to the show. I look forward to coming in, and there's lots more to do! While I can do it, while I can walk and talk, and while they want me, I'll be here…'

Four generations of Barlows: Ken with his son, grandson and great-grandson, 2019

EST. 1960

60

CHAPTER I

How it all began

Before *Coronation Street* – the cultural and TV landscape

THERE was no colour, no remote control, no video. The screens were tiny and the pictures were not so much black-and-white as grey-and-white. Fast forward meant jumping out of your chair to adjust the volume and picture quality. There was 'interference' from passing traffic, resulting in a crackling, fizzing screen and temporary loss of sound. And the nightly closedown, decreed by the government, was 11pm. This was television in the late 1950s, the decade in which the upstart Independent Television (ITV) broke the BBC's monopoly and the box in the corner became a household necessity.

The event that sparked the viewer revolution was the broadcast of the coronation of Queen Elizabeth II at Westminster Abbey on 2nd June 1953. Fewer than two million British homes owned or rented a TV set at the start of 1953, living mainly in London, Manchester, Birmingham, Cardiff and Glasgow. In the build-up to the coronation, some 526,000 new sets were bought or rented. On the big day itself, an estimated 20 million people watched the broadcast, which was narrated by broadcaster Richard Dimbleby. More than half of them crowded into other people's homes and up to two million saw it in schools, cinemas, halls and pubs.

By 1959, the number of households with a set had risen to 10 million. Today, that figure is more than 27 million. TV watching in the 1950s was tightly controlled by the government. The BBC was allowed to broadcast between 9am and 11pm, with no more than two hours before 1pm. At weekends, a maximum of eight hours was allowed on Saturdays and 15 minutes fewer on Sundays. Colour? We had to wait until 1967 for that – a broadcast from Wimbledon on BBC2, which had started life in 1964.

The launch of ITV in 1955 (only in the London area at first) changed the TV scene forever. ITV had a dignified start. Its first programme was an outside broadcast from London's Guildhall of a dinner to celebrate the birth of... ITV. It was during that broadcast that the first commercial on British TV appeared – for Gibbs SR toothpaste.

The emphasis moved to focus on more 'popular' programming – quiz shows, situation comedies, variety shows, police dramas and American imports. Newscasters became stars, and the adverts (or commercials, as they were called) grew to be as familiar as the pop songs of the day. Viewers began to desert the BBC, and in late 1959 BC (Before *Coronation Street*), the five most watched shows were all on ITV. They were: US Western series *Wagon Train* (13.63 million viewers), the prize quiz show *Take Your Pick* (13.16 million), *Sunday Night at the London Palladium* (13.08 million), *Armchair Theatre* (12.74 million) and the comedy series *The Army Game* (12.6 million).

Around this time, the favourite BBC shows included *This is Your Life*, *The Grove Family*, *Dixon of Dock Green*, *Hancock's Half Hour*, *Come Dancing*, *Panorama* and *What's My Line?*. Then came along a programme that really broke the mould, a programme that the big cheeses at ITV HQ were initially hesitant about, but one that proved so popular with viewers that it was quickly extended beyond its initial 13-episode run – *Coronation Street*.

It was December 1960. The first year of that new decade was already memorable for several reasons: Princess Margaret married society photographer Antony Armstrong-Jones in the first royal wedding to be shown on television and The Beatles played their first concerts in Hamburg, Germany. Conservative Prime Minister Harold Macmillan had made his historic 'Wind of Change' speech in South Africa, and Penguin Books were prosecuted under the Obscene Publications Act for publishing D H Lawrence's *Lady Chatterley's Lover*. The company was found not guilty in the watershed obscenity trial, allowing the public to read Lawrence's final novel for the first time.

Elvis Presley spent eight weeks at No 1 in the pop charts with 'It's Now or Never', the best-selling song of 1960. The Winter Olympics took place in California (the 17-strong UK team failed to bring home a medal). Manchester City bought Denis Law from Huddersfield Town for a new British record of £55,000 and the Grand National was televised for the first time – winner Merryman II, the first clear favourite to win for 33 years. Farthings ceased to be legal tender in the UK and as post-war peace continued in Europe, National Service was scrapped.

The decade went on to see huge social change in Britain. The Swinging Sixties saw Britain, especially London, lead the world in music, fashion, theatre and film. The teenagers of the 1950s were growing up and demanding new rights at work, especially women who were no longer expected to give up their jobs when they married. Despite disquiet from some quarters and grumbles about the dangers of a 'permissive society', laws governing divorce and abortion were relaxed and the contraceptive pill was licensed for use in the United States. By the end of the 1960s the voting age had been lowered from 21 to 18.

Two decades after the end of the Second World War, people were becoming wealthier. The average annual wage was around £700, the average house price was £2,530 and a season ticket for Manchester United was just over £8. More households had cars, and families started to holiday abroad. Technologically, Britain was surging ahead – together with France it developed the first supersonic aircraft, Concorde.

Achieving the highest viewing figures, and beating the other side were the chief objectives.

The future may have been looking brighter for Britain's new middle classes, but for many communities in the north of England the pace of change was much slower. The city of Salford is part of Greater Manchester. It is situated next to the city of Manchester and is not, as is still commonly thought, part of Manchester. It's widely credited as the inspiration for *Coronation Street*. Creator Tony Warren was born in Pendlebury and went to grammar school in Eccles, both in Salford. He grew up in Swinton in a relatively middle-class semi-detached home, but his grandmother hailed from the terraced streets of Irlams o' th' Height and he knew them well. It was one of the poorest areas of the country – parts of Salford still are. By 1960 the pre-war glass-blowing industry had gone and biting poverty blighted the communities living there. The rows of back-to-back terraces on cobbled streets, a feature of so many of artist L S Lowry's famous paintings, housed proud but poor families battling to get by. Those families were often ripped apart in the late 1950s and 1960s thanks to the slum clearance programme, which saw entire streets with soot-stained brickwork, sagging roofs and pervasive damp demolished and residents rehoused often miles away from friends and neighbours.

Salford's first tower blocks had begun to spring up. The eight-storey Clement Attlee House went up in May 1956 and by the early 1960s, the first 15-floor blocks were under construction. Year on year those condemned two-up two-downs with a pokey back yard and an outside 'netty', or lavatory, which today may well be renovated and resold, were torn down. By 1971, Archie Street, on which Tony Warren and designer Denis Parkin based the look of Coronation Street, had been demolished.

Fewer of those Salford residents owned a television set than people living in the suburbs, but changes other than slum clearance and high-rise living were in the air, and television reflected that. Network bosses and programme makers realised that the televisual landscape was going to become increasingly competitive – although how many among them could have predicted the hundreds of channels on all manner of devices available to today's viewers? Although the medium was relatively new, it adapted and evolved quickly – achieving the highest viewing figures and beating the other side were the chief objectives, especially for commercial television whose income depended on this. Within weeks of *Coronation Street* airing in December 1960, it had become essential viewing, appearing in the top 10 of the TV charts week in week out, and creating income for ITV, which today is as lucrative and vital as ever. By episode 73 on 23rd August 1961, it was the best-watched programme in the UK.

This fictional northern back street, with its small terraced homes, famous cobbles and well-drawn characters reflected, for the first time on TV, the life of regular working folk with all their trials and tribulations, back at viewers and they loved it...

Tony Warren MBE (1936–2016) – the father of the *Street*

WHEN a young television scriptwriter named Tony Warren turned in the first scripts for a brand-new type of serial drama in late 1960, not even he could have imagined what a phenomenon his creation would become.

At the age of 21, the former child actor had joined the writers' pool at Granada Television in Manchester. He found himself frustrated writing for programmes he wasn't interested in, and after a couple of years he was appealing to Granada bosses to let him write what he knew about. He was given 24 hours to come up with something that would 'take Britain by storm'. Warren revisited a script he'd written several years earlier about a northern back street and its inhabitants. He spent the night honing his characters, adding new ones and giving them all an authentic northern voice. The result was *Coronation Street*, the world's longest-running TV serial drama.

As is widely documented, *Coronation Street* was originally called *Florizel Street* (after Prince Florizel in *Sleeping Beauty*, a picture of

which hung on Tony Warren's wall). Its name was changed very shortly before the first episode was broadcast live at 7pm on Friday 9th December 1960. On viewing a special screening for Granada employees, a studio tea lady named Agnes declared Florizel sounded like a disinfectant and the producers took note. Perhaps it was prophetic that a woman had such an influential say on *Coronation Street*'s name as it is the strong female characters for which the series is most famous.

Warren knew how to write women, especially working-class northern women. As a small boy he would sit on a cushion beneath his grandmother's table listening to the family gossip away, inwardly digesting their turns of phrase and caustic asides, and noting the differences between men and women. During the war, with the men often away fighting, it was women who held their families together, ran the homes and kept the wolf from the door, and nowhere was it harder than in the back streets of the industrial north. The older

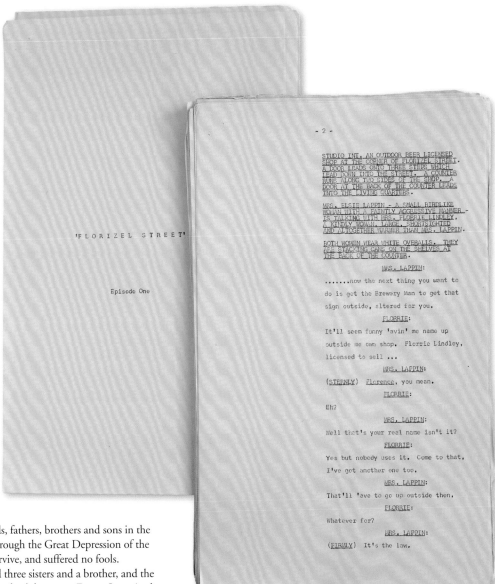

'FLORIZEL STREET'

Episode One

- 2 -

STUDIO INT. AN OUTDOOR BEER LICENSED
SHOP AT THE CORNER OF FLORIZEL STREET.
A DOOR LEADS ONTO THREE STEPS WHICH
LEAD DOWN INTO THE STREET. A COUNTER
RUNS ALONG TWO SIDES OF THE SHOP. A
DOOR AT THE BACK OF THE COUNTER LEADS
INTO THE LIVING QUARTERS.

MRS. ELSIE LAPPIN - A SMALL BIRDLIKE
WOMAN WITH A FAINTLY AGGRESSIVE MANNER -
IS TALKING WITH MRS. FLORRIE LINDLEY,
A KINDLY WOMAN, LARGE, SHORTSIGHTED
AND ALTOGETHER WARMER THAN MRS. LAPPIN.

BOTH WOMEN WEAR WHITE OVERALLS. THEY
ARE STACKING CANS ON THE SHELVES AT
THE BACK OF THE COUNTER.

                    MRS. LAPPIN:

.......now the next thing you want to

do is get the Brewery Man to get that

sign outside, altered for you.

                    FLORRIE:

It'll seem funny 'avin' me name up

outside me own shop. Florrie Lindley,

licensed to sell ...

                    MRS. LAPPIN:

(STERNLY) Florence, you mean.

                    FLORRIE:

Eh?

                    MRS. LAPPIN:

Well that's your real name isn't it?

                    FLORRIE:

Yes but nobody uses it. Come to that,

I've got another one too.

                    MRS. LAPPIN:

That'll 'ave to go up outside then.

                    FLORRIE:

Whatever for?

                    MRS. LAPPIN:

(FIRMLY) It's the law.

women had also lost husbands, fathers, brothers and sons in the
Great War. They struggled through the Great Depression of the
1930s. They knew how to survive, and suffered no fools.

Warren's mother Doris had three sisters and a brother, and the
sisters would gather at the grandma's house on Ernest Street in the
Irlams o' th' Height area of Salford, cleaning the small terraced home.
As a young boy, Warren would accompany his mother the mile down
the road from their semi-detached house on Wilton Avenue to Ernest
Street and soak up the chatter. Warren loved it. He told friends
later that he saw something a bit more alive there than in the more
middle-class cul-de-sac on which he lived with his parents. He added
that when the men got back from the war the women just raised
their voices a bit louder and carried on as before.

Born Anthony McVay Simpson in 1936, Warren was a toddler
when his father was called up. George Simpson had educated himself
at night school and was fluent in several languages. The gifted
linguist was drafted early to the Second World War because he was
considered so useful. George Simpson became a fruit importer after
the war and the family did fairly well, with mother Doris doing
piecework from home.

Warren was an only child. His cousin Roy was another only child,
and for a while they were inseparable. Roy was an art student at
Salford School of Art and through him Warren experienced a more
bohemian world than that in which he had grown up.

'He got to know a lot of artists and that was a way of being
different,' says one friend who knew Warren closely for many years.
'A lot of it was about rebelling against respectability, he didn't like
the 1950s repressed semi-detached middle classes and going back to
his grandma's, there was a certain rebellion in that too because that's
what his family had moved away from. There was an earthiness to
that, something that he saw as more "real".'

Warren attended Eccles Grammar School but frequently played
truant, preferring to spend his time in Manchester's Central Library,
reading plays. For months he would call the school secretary from a
telephone box near the library impersonating his mother and making
excuses for his absence.

As a child actor, until his voice broke at 14, he had appeared in
Children's Hour alongside future *Coronation Street* stars Doris Speed,
Violet Carson and Alan Rothwell. He went to the Shelagh Elliott-
Clarke School of Dance and Dramatic Art in Liverpool, but got
expelled from there for 'rabble-rousing' although he did maintain a

relationship with Shelagh Elliott-Clarke for several years. After his expulsion, Warren hitch-hiked to London at the age of 15 and lived in an actors' hostel, picking up acting and knitwear modelling jobs, writing cabaret and devising routines for strippers before returning north in 1958.

Warren lasted less than a morning working in the hardware department of Kendals, Manchester's famous department store. He worked in repertory theatre for a while, at venues including the Hulme Hippodrome in Manchester and at Chesterfield Theatre, before joining Granada Television, not as an actor but a scriptwriter after casting director Margaret Morris discovered he could write. He worked on *Shadow Squad* with producer Harry Elton before moving into the company's promotions department and then onto the writing team for the Elton-produced *Biggles*.

Barbara Knox (who has played Rita Tanner full-time since 1972) remembers how innovative and influential Granada Television was in those days. 'The Bernsteins (Granada founder Sydney and his brother Cecil who were not initially overly enthusiastic about Warren's proposal) knew how to do everything, they built the place. They built the wonderful studio and they looked after us, they were wonderful to work for. They were regulars at the studio, they would go round asking if everything was all right.'

Creatively frustrated at spending his time adapting W E Johns' *Biggles* adventure stories, he implored Elton to let him write about people he knew, famously jumping onto a filing cabinet and refusing to come down unless Elton agreed, a moment recreated in the Bafta-winning television play *The Road to Coronation Street* made to mark the programme's 50th anniversary. He penned five episodes, which were accepted, and he was asked to write seven more, plus an extra 'final' one in case the programme proved unpopular. Warren was closely involved in casting the original 23 roles. He had had Doris Speed in mind right from the off for Annie Walker, and when the search for his original scrawny, shrewish Ena Sharples was beginning to look fruitless, he persuaded the more comely figure of Violet Carson into the role.

Coronation Street's first script editor Harry Kershaw recalled in his book *The Street Where I Live* that Warren's scripts were a delight to read: 'The characterisation was superb and at the end of the first five episodes you *knew* Elsie Tanner and Ena Sharples and Ken Barlow and little Lucille Hewitt (Jennifer Moss). You closed your eyes and you could see the pot flight of ducks and the antimacassars and the chenille tablecloths and the newspapers stuffed under the cushion of an easy chair. You sniffed and you could smell the burning sausages and the cheap hairspray and the tang of bitter beer.'

Warren, he said, had 'a superb ear for dialogue and an undoubted devotion for the people and the streets of his native Salford', attributes that ensured *Coronation Street* immediately found its way into the hearts of the viewing public.

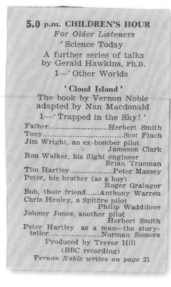

'You sniffed and you could smell the burning sausages and the cheap hairspray and the tang of bitter beer.'

William Roache adds that Warren's scripts had depth and a gritty reality. In his autobiography *Ken and Me* Roache noted: 'Many writers came in after Tony, but the *Street* was his baby. He got it off the ground, established all the characters and set the pattern for his successors to follow.'

Although Warren's original inspiration came from visiting his maternal grandmother, Coronation Street is based visually on Archie Street in Salford. Tony took designer Denis Parkin to see it as he was mapping out how Coronation Street would look. Unlike his grandmother's street it had a pub at one end, and that was the inspiration for how The Rovers Return Inn would appear on screen.

More writers were drafted in to script the increasingly successful *Coronation Street* and Warren left the show for some time. He had well-documented issues with alcohol and drugs, and spent some time in America visiting San Francisco to 'hang out with the hippies'. He returned to the UK, and after his recovery, contributed occasional scripts for *Coronation Street* as well as acting as a consultant on the programme right up to his death in 2016. He would have monthly lunch meetings with the producer to discuss the show and would be sent preview DVDs for his feedback, but he always watched each episode as it was transmitted as well. When the show moved to MediaCity, Warren would occasionally lunch in the canteen with members of the current production team to find out about them and their work too.

Throughout the 1990s Warren wrote several novels that attracted positive criticism, including *The Lights of Manchester*. In the early 1970s, he wrote a play in which he quoted from a poem by John Betjeman. He loved Betjeman's poetry. He wrote to Betjeman's agent to ask if he could use the lines and when Betjeman saw that they didn't live too far from each other in London he invited him to dinner and Warren discovered Betjeman was a *Coronation Street* fan. Sometimes the poet would invite him round to watch *Coronation Street* together and he visited the set, with Warren proudly guiding him round. The Poet Laureate and Warren exchanged fond letters and kept in touch until Betjeman's death in 1984. Betjeman is quoted as saying: 'Manchester produces what to me is the *Pickwick Papers*. That is to say, *Coronation Street*, I live for it. Thank God. Half past seven tonight and I shall be in paradise.'

Warren was also great friends with Dame Carol Ann Duffy, the first female Poet Laureate (from 2009–2019). When Warren died in 2016, aged 79, Duffy said: 'Manchester has lost its dearest son and so many of us a beloved friend. And the millions who have loved *Coronation Street* for over half a century have lost their Dickens.'

Another dear friend was Noel Streatfeild (1895–1986), the children's author whose most famous book was *Ballet Shoes* (1936). In the 1970s, when Warren lived in London, in Strutton Ground in Westminster, the church he belonged to was St Mary's Bourne Street, just off Sloane Square, in Belgravia. It was a high church,

anglo-Catholic rather than Roman Catholic, and Warren and fellow parishioner Streatfeild found they got on famously. She became what they called his 'godmother' and would address her letters to Warren 'to my godchild'.

Warren and Pat Phoenix also became great friends. She described him in her autobiography *All My Burning Bridges* as 'without a doubt, the wittiest and funniest person I know'. In the early days of *Coronation Street* they lived close to each other in the countryside village of Hayfield, near Manchester, and would enjoy walks through muddy fields together. Phoenix recalled the locals found Warren 'exotic' and his behaviour sometimes eccentric, especially when he lay on the floor of the village pub The Lantern Pike quoting the service of exorcism 'in sonorous tones'. Phoenix believed that the landlady of The Lantern Pike could have been the inspiration for Annie Walker.

When Warren relocated to Manchester after his later stint in London it was to a terraced house in Swinton, Salford, albeit a larger redbrick Edwardian property close to a park where he liked to walk his dogs and chat to neighbours. Life had come full circle, with Warren spending his final years just down the road from his childhood home.

In 2014, the main studio block at *Coronation Street*'s new home at MediaCity in Salford was named in Warren's honour, and on his death two years later stars from the show paid tribute to him, calling him 'the most inspirational man of a generation' and 'a genius of our time'. Actors past and present attended his funeral, which took place at Manchester Cathedral, a grand venue befitting his status as the father of *Coronation Street*. Perhaps Barbara Knox puts it best when she says: 'Tony Warren, what a genius he was, what a legacy he left us. We should all bow down to Tony Warren.'

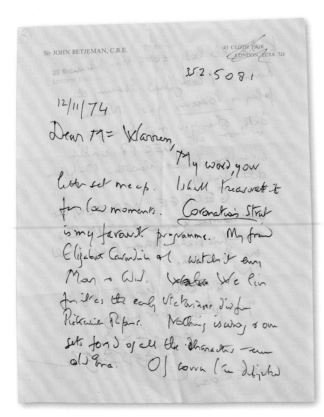
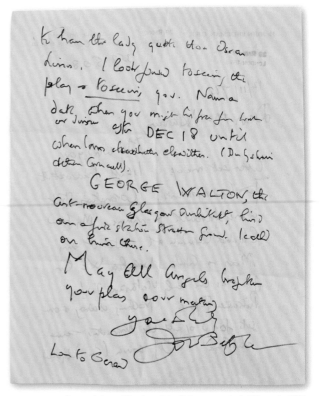

As an admirer of the show, John Betjeman wrote to Warren in 1974

Warren with *Coronation Street* fans, John Betjeman and Lady Elizabeth Cavendish

The Tony Warren Building, opened 20th May 2014

Bringing the vision to life

WHEN Granada TV producer Harry Elton read Tony Warren's first script for *Florizel Street*, which he'd written overnight on his bedroom floor, he immediately asked for a second draft episode. A memo from Tony Warren, which accompanied it, outlined his vision. He said the purpose of the programme was to entertain by examining a community and initiating the viewers into the ways of the people who live there. He described it as 'a fascinating freemasonry, a volume of unwritten rules. These are the driving forces behind life in a working-class street in the

north of England. To the uninitiated outsider, all this would be completely incomprehensible'.

It went on to describe 'seven terraced houses, an outdoor beer licence (which became a grocery), the back wall of a raincoat factory, a pub named the Rover's Return (the apostrophe was later dropped) and the Glad Tidings Mission Hall'. Warren added: 'Geographically, it's four miles from Manchester, or at least it's four miles from what the inhabitants call town and that's Market Street.' The houses were described as having a lobby, a front parlour, a

The original cast of 20 actors, 1960

CORONATION STREET
_____

EPISODE 1

1. THE SHOP: Elsie Lappin tells Florrie Lindley something about the people of Coronation Street and warns her about the Tanners. Linda Cheveski (nee Tanner) enters.

2. THE TANNERS: Elsie asks Dennis when he is going to get a job. She says that she wishes that they were more like the Barlows.

3. THE BARLOWS: Ida is worried that Colin has not returned from school. Frank forbids Kenneth to meet Susan at the Imperial. Colin enters - he has had a bicycle puncture. Frank and Ida leave Colin and Kenneth together. This is an amiable, brotherly relationship. Colin asks Kenneth what he proposes to do. Kenneth just doesn't know.

BREAK

4. THE SHOP: Two girls from the raincoat factory have been working overtime. They are buying shampoos. One hints that another girl has told her that Linda Cheveski is in some sort of trouble. (Linda at one time worked in the raincoat factory and her bosom friend, Norma Pilkington, is still employed by Ellestons).

5. THE TANNERS: Linda tells Elsie that she has left Ivan.

6. THE SHOP: Elsie Lappin settles up - for the last time - with Harry Bailey. Outside, children clamber over his bicycle. Elsie and Harry go out to shoo off the children. Florrie is left to cope with Ena Sharples. Elsie reappears. Ena complains about a bad egg. Elsie Lappin replaces it. Ena exits on a line "I'm not thinkin' o' runnin' away."

7. THE BARLOWS: Frank mends Colin's puncture in the living room. Colin chats with his father and then goes off to the front room to do his homework. Ida enters and asks Frank what sort of fool he's going to look if Kenneth defies him.

8. ALBERT TATLOCK'S: Kenneth tells Albert his problem. At first, Albert is sympathetic but later accuses Kenneth of being a snob. Ida appears and says that Susan has arrived.

9. THE SHOP: Elsie Lappin goes off to her daughter's and leaves Florrie to herself. Florrie glows with the pride of ownership.

10. THE BARLOWS: Kenneth returns to find Susan settled contentedly talking to Colin and Frank. There is a hoot of a horn from outside. The children have clambered into Susan's car. Kenneth looks horrified.

END OF EPISODE ONE

HERE WE GO!

Albert Tatlock and Minnie Caldwell in 1966

The cameras roll on *Coronation Street*'s first scene

living room, scullery and a WC in an outhouse in the back yard. They had three bedrooms although 'a couple of the younger and brighter spirits have converted one of these into a bathroom'. Rent was around 23 shillings a week, 'collected every Friday evening by a woman on a bicycle'. These details informed the original designer Denis Parkin and the descriptions are visible today.

Florizel Street would be bounded at one end by Rosamund Street and a 'Liston Grove' at the other 'but they are no real concern of ours' added Warren, 'because to the people who live there, and to a vast number of people in the north of England, the world begins and ends in their own street'.

One set of residents from Warren's original idea was replaced. Harold and Enid Midgeley were to be a couple in their 20s, with Enid being the daughter of the Barlows at No 3. Lucille Hewitt was originally to be called Janice, and Warren had planned for the Walkers to have a third child, Norman. Albert Tatlock was introduced later.

Granada executives gave Warren's efforts a lukewarm reception and the show might never have been made had Harry Elton not arranged for screenings of the pilots to be shown to Granada staff. Some hated it, most loved it but *everyone* had an opinion and that was important.

Casting Gen.

Harry Latham

—

FRANK BARLOW.

37 48 Late forties - early fifties. He was once a good-looking, muscular, man but has now gone to seed. He usually behaves with an air of gloomy satisfaction and can be quickly roused into violent tempers. Nevertheless he is basically a kindly man.

39 45 **IDA BARLOW.**

Mid to late forties. She still has the remains of what was once a gentle prettiness. She usually wears a faintly troubled expression and is an extremely acute and intuitive woman.

KENNETH BARLOW.

20 Twenty. A Cambridge Undergraduate. His looks which are finely drawn come from his mother. He does not speak, dress or behave like a Northern Working Class boy. Sometimes arrogant he is basically likeable.

CHRISTINE HARDMAN.

39 22 Twenty two, fair and extremely pretty. She is both bright and practical, though faintly inclined to burst into tears in crises.

MAY HARDMAN.

49 Fifties. An extremely gloomy woman suffering from melancholia. She wouldn't dream of wearing make-up so her face is ridiculously pale, and the dark circles round her eyes dominate her sorry outlook.

ENA SHARPLES.

7 Seventies, small, with a crabby walnut of a face and flashing eyes. Doomsday in woman's clothing! One minute she is a poor old woman, the next a screeching fiend. She is wicked, wicked, wicked yet never defeated and somehow one can't help admiring her.

ELSIE TANNER.

48 Late forties with the very battered, and much painted over, remains of good looks. She is easily raised to anger but has the proverbial tart's heart of gold.

DENNIS TANNER.

25 Mid twenties. He is not particularly good looking and rather wiry in build. In conversation his manner verges between the derisive and the defensive.

LINDA CHEVESKI (née TANNER)

26 Twenty-six. She is quite attractive but her figure is better than her face. She dresses accordingly. Her conversation is usually listless but she is capable of shouting and thowing things.

IVAN CHEVESKI.

30 Thirty. Polish but speaks English with a Northern accent. He is good looking, well built and thoroughly likeable.

ESTHER HAYES.

37 Thirties, a spinster, plain. Esther is slightly built and extremely kindly.

HARRY HEWITT.

39 Mid-late thirties, a short wiry bus conductor, rather cocky but quite pleasant.

KENNETH BARLOW.

10 Ten (if we can get someone to look as young as that!) Very small, very plain, bright and likeable.

ALBERT TATLOCK.

70 Seventies. A benign man of Solemn charm. He has an air of authority and a twinkling eye.

FLORRIE ATKINS.

39 Fifties. Large, shortsighted and warm-hearted.

MARTHA LONGHURST.

Fifties. A small bird-like woman with an aggressive manner.

MINNIE CALDWELL.

Seventies. Respectacled and altogether more solemn than Ena. She is inclined to swank about her daughter who has 'got on' and when she does her voice assumes a rather uncertain and rickstty attempt at'refeanment.'

MINNIE CALDWELL.

Seventies, tiny, timid but can sometimes be persuaded to tell fortunes. When she does this she becomes rather knowing and mysterious.

HARRY BAILEY.

Forties and faintly seedy with a glib tongue.

DR. TUSSEY.

Sixties and fiery. He shouts at his patients and yet is capable of enormous kindness.

ANNIE WALKER.

52 Late fifties. A publican's wife and looks it. Brisk, well corsetted, well permed and a bit overdressed.

JACK WALKER.

56 Sixties. A publican. He is large and well meaning and rather slow on the uptake.

Each script, said Forman, should be 'two-thirds misery and one-third normalcy'.

In August 1960 it had been agreed that the twice-weekly, half-hour serial should have a limited run of eight weeks (16 episodes) to be followed by programmes entitled *Old Wives Tale* and *Son of Stag*, although this was amended to 13 episodes.

In October 1960, producer Stuart Latham, known as Harry, detailed the planned production schedule to senior members of staff – two episodes at a time would be rehearsed by a cycle of three directors for live transmission on a Friday, followed by a VTR (video recording) of the next episode for transmission the following Wednesday. He added that the cast list was fairly long and certain characters could emerge as having greater interest or appeal but, initially, no star parts were contemplated. There was pressure at first to include a middle-class figure such as a doctor, but this was resisted and Warren's initial characterisations remained. Now they had to find their cast.

The auditions

Casting director Margaret Morris was in charge of selecting actors for the 23 parts for the first two episodes. She, her assistant Jose Scott and Tony Warren considered all the northern and Midlands actors they could think of, calling many in to audition and using the two dry runs as screen tests for the favourites. The process was complicated by the requirement to cast 'unknown' faces, so these new characters would be more believable to the viewing public.

Pat Phoenix, in her autobiography *All My Burning Bridges*, explained the truculent mood she was in when she turned up for her audition for the part of Elsie Tanner. Her acting career had come to something of a halt and she was sure travelling to Manchester to audition was a waste of time. After she had read for the six-strong panel she took against the 'cheeky young devil' who asked her to remove her coat, presumably to size up her figure for the part. '"No, you'll just have to guess at it, won't you," I said. I'd be damned if I was going to parade for them. I'd been to too many auditions and lost too many parts to take this lot seriously.'

That youth of course was Tony Warren. He loved Pat immediately and she realised she loved the 'glorious, gutsy gift of a part', though she was sure she'd blown the audition with her indifferent attitude.

But, as Harry Kershaw said, when Pat arrived to read Elsie there was no point in seeing anyone else. The casting panel felt the same about Arthur Leslie and Doris Speed, they *were* Jack and Annie Walker. Of course, having worked with Doris in his young acting days, Tony Warren had had her in mind all along.

Ena Sharples, famously, was the hardest to find and virtually the last part to be cast. Scores of actors had been seen and Nan Marriott-Watson, who played Ena in the pilots, was unable to take the part when it was offered. Then Warren suggested Violet Carson, another woman he had worked with several years before. Kershaw recalls that as soon as Violet read, all thoughts of the thin shrew-like woman they had originally envisaged vanished – 'We must have been mad. How could we have possibly thought of anyone else?'

Philip Lowrie, who played Dennis Tanner, went straight into the West End in a play with Margaret Rutherford after he trained at RADA (Royal Academy of Dramatic Art). During that play's run, the Manchester-born actor was called for an audition in his home city. He says: 'Apparently 70 boys were interviewed for Dennis Tanner and it got down to me and an actor called Kenneth Farrington who became my good friend. We did a camera test, I got Dennis and Ken got the character of Billy Walker. I remember getting the first script by Tony Warren. As I read it I thought, my goodness, I've got a good part here.'

Philip says there is a myth that he went for the role of Ken Barlow, but Ken (William Roache) had already been cast. The other person being camera tested on the same day as Philip was Violet Carson as Ena Sharples. Philip recalls: 'A director called Mike Scott was doing my test and at the lunch break he told me to go and put some Brylcreem in my hair. I walked up to Deansgate to the nearest Boots and bought a jar of Brylcreem.

Philip Lowrie in full Brylcreem as Dennis Tanner

'Now, the next thing you've got to do is to get a sign writer in. That thing above the door'll have to be changed.'
– Elsie Lappin, the first words of the first episode

I put the whole lot in my hair for the afternoon, did my hair like a Teddy Boy and did my test.'

Afterwards he went to stay the night with his parents who lived in Ashton-under-Lyne in east Manchester. The following day he returned to London. 'When I got back to my flat the phone was ringing and it was my agent saying "Where have you been? You have to go straight back to Manchester, you've got the part and you start on Monday!"'

Dennis Tanner, Elsie's son, was an ex-borstal boy, although his character quickly developed from criminal tearaway to a cheeky, easily led yet popular type. 'He was a bit tough at first and the script was just so good I thought, this is me,' says Philip. 'It was as if it'd been written with me in mind, but when I met Tony years later he said "Do you realise I wrote that part for myself?" That's why it was such a good part.'

The rehearsals

The full new cast had only a few days to rehearse their lines, but luckily many of the actors had been in rep, and were used to learning scripts very quickly.

Just before the full cast had been decided upon, a message was circulated to senior Granada staff from the director of the first episode, Derek Bennett, inviting them to 'A monster read-through of that fascinating, scintillating, new and exciting series *Florizel Street*. Dress informal, bottles welcome and comments to be kept until afterwards…'

A further confidential memo went out 12 days later, from Granada executive Denis Forman to Harry Elton and Harry Latham, urging them to be 'bold, firm, decisive and radical men and not to be deflected by pleas from directors and writers' because 'a lot needs doing to *Coronation Street* (as it was now titled, ahead of a second option Jubilee Street) before we get it right.'

Just two weeks from transmission of the first episode, it was suggested that it was too miserable. It required some high spirits. Each script, said Forman, should be 'two-thirds misery and one-third normalcy'. It was also regarded as confusing, there should be one strong story as the Tanners, the Barlows ('the nicest people') and Ena Sharples were introduced, everyone else should be incidental. Forman doubted whether the initial shop handover story would be strong enough and found the shop layout 'messy'.

Philip Lowrie says he made lifelong friends in that first week of rehearsals. He remembers: 'On the very first day of rehearsal – 5th December 1960 – the most beautiful girl walked up to me and said: "Are you Philip? I'm Anne (Cunningham), I'm playing your sister Linda." We are still best friends and I am godfather to one of her daughters. She lives down the road from me, so we see a lot of each other.'

It was advised not to do street exteriors in the studio (although that is exactly what happened) and the music 'all part of the sordid, dismal effect of the show' should be a bright piece with a good beat to finish it on the upbeat.

When it came to the actors, Forman wanted to see them act like real people, 'not like music hall and rep actors' (which many of them were). The directors would be asked to bring their performances down 'to vanishing point' and there was a reminder that every viewer needed to be able to understand every line: 'Lancashire is difficult to Scotsmen,' wrote Forman. 'Writers are no judge as to what can be understood and what cannot. If you want an emergency test group, think of an old-age pensioners' home in Aberdeen. Are they going to understand it all?' The missive also confirms that there had been serious talk of 'eliminating' Albert Tatlock, but thankfully the character, played by Jack Howarth, survived.

The first transmission

Work continued furiously ahead of the first transmission of *Coronation Street* on Friday 9th December. Scenes were rewritten, the sets were designed and built, and the executives wondered nervously if their 'experiment' would pay off. Rehearsals and character discussions took place from Monday 5th December and on the Wednesday afternoon, the technical run-through was held. This was the chance for the technical crew to understand the flow of the episodes, and the system of having a 'tech run' on Wednesdays continued for many years.

The sets for transmission were different in some aspects from the sets in the pilots. The latter included flowery wallpaper in the back rooms, but these were dropped for transmission as it was said that the designs got confused with the actors' heads on screen.

Costume fittings took place and characters' makeup and overall appearances were finalised, and on the Thursday the cast rehearsed 'on set' in Granada's Studio 2 for the very first time. Friday was taken up with last-minute rehearsals and at 7pm sharp, as the actors waited to perform and Tony Warren was ill with nerves, the mournful cornet strains of Eric Spear's score sounded in homes across the Granada region and the first scene – children playing on a cobbled street outside a corner shop – began.

Philip Lowrie recalls how nervous he was as he waited for his cue. 'I remember distinctly because I'd never done television before apart from a walk-on part. I was a very young actor and I remember Margot Bryant was very sweet to me. It was going out live and I was in the second scene, where my mother (Elsie) accuses me of taking money from her purse.

'I stood at the top of a staircase quite nervous, but as I'd never done television nobody told me the floor manager would count down. When he started to count down from 10 I started to shake, I was quivering with nerves, terrified thinking how many people were watching.'

Little could he have known, as he stood there shaking, that years later the part of Dennis Tanner would see him included in the *Guinness Book of Records*. Philip left *Coronation Street* after eight years and returned to the show in 2011 after 43 years, beating the 42 years between appearances for colleague Kenneth Cope (Jed Stone) who had reappeared in 2008.

EPISODE 1: THE ORIGINAL LINE-UP

Patricia Phoenix as Elsie Tanner

Philip Lowrie as Dennis Tanner

Anne Cunningham as Linda Cheveski

Frank Pemberton as Frank Barlow

Noel Dyson as Ida Barlow

William Roache as Kenneth Barlow

Alan Rothwell as David Barlow

Maudie Edwards as Elsie Lappin

Betty Alberge as Florrie Lindley

Violet Carson as Ena Sharples

Doris Speed as Annie Walker

Jack Howarth as Albert Tatlock

Patricia Shakesby as Susan Cunningham

The first storylines

Tony Warren's first-ever episode of *Coronation Street* ostensibly set the scene and introduced some of the main characters to the curious viewers. It began with the handover of the Corner Shop from Elsie Lappin to Florrie Lindley, a device that allowed other residents to be discussed between the pair. Florrie was warned not to give credit to the Tanners from No 11. Elsie was then seen for the first time berating son Dennis for not having a job and taking money from her purse. Further down in No 3, Kenneth and his father argued, with student Ken embarrassed to bring his girlfriend to meet his working-class family. We met brother David and then the cameras turned to the interior of The Rovers Return and Annie Walker was introduced to the world, followed shortly afterwards by Ena Sharples nosily questioning Florrie in the Corner Shop. We

learned that Elsie's daughter Linda had left her husband Ivan Cheveski and we met Albert Tatlock.

The following episodes throughout December 1960 introduced more characters – widower Harry Hewitt dealing with daughter Lucille who had run away from care, Christine Hardman looking after her poorly mother May, who died before the year was out, and Glad

Tidings Mission chairman, draper Leonard Swindley, reprimanding caretaker Ena for drinking alcohol. Elsie feared that Dennis was up to no good and Ena, Minnie and Martha settled into their seats in the snug for the first time. Florrie was fined for selling goods past 7pm and Ena was treated in hospital after collapsing. Linda turned out to be pregnant and Concepta Riley arrived back in Weatherfield from Ireland to become the first Rovers barmaid. Viewers immediately took these wonderfully drawn characters to their hearts, and by New Year's Eve it was as if *Coronation Street* had always been there…

The reaction

Coronation Street proved highly popular with viewers, who had never seen anything like it on the small screen. After it was fully networked, it topped the viewing charts – a position it retained for decades, pulling in more than 20 million viewers at times.

Despite its popularity in front rooms nationwide, not everyone was impressed, with the television critics' response mixed. The day after the first episode was transmitted, *Daily Mirror* columnist Ken Irwin wrote: 'The programme is doomed from the outset – with its signature tune and grim scene of a row of terraced houses and smoking chimneys.' However, Mary Crozier in *The Guardian*, predicted it could run forever, and within a few years its stars were mobbed wherever they went and its audiences were international.

60 EST. 1960

CHAPTER 2

Behind the scenes

'The DNA of Corrie is not the people you see on your TV, it's the people who create the characters and give us life.'
— Shelley King, who plays Yasmeen Metcalfe

Ken, Gail, Audrey, Roy… Coronation Street's stars are so famous they are recognisable by their first names alone. But without the hundreds of people behind the scenes, Coronation Street couldn't remain the television phenomenon it has become. From the talented storyliners who plan what is going to happen to our favourite characters to the writers who give them their voice, from the team who decides who is going to join the famous cast to the designers, the prop buyers, the directors and the camera operators, Coronation Street is a huge well-oiled machine that is only as good as the sum of its parts.

Here's a glimpse behind the scenes from some of the people whose names roll in the end credits six times a week.

Iain MacLeod – producing *Coronation Street*

IAIN MACLEOD has *Coronation Street* running through him like Blackpool through a stick of rock. Having spent a great deal of his working life on the programme, he is now in the boss's chair, as producer guiding the show through its milestone 60th year.

Originally a journalist, he became a radio newsreader and from that moved into radio production. 'I was mainly responsible for coming up with interesting stuff for presenters to talk about on radio stations all around the north. It has some crossover with the producer role here as it's all about telling stories. Just as a journalist wants to hook you in and keep you interested, give you all the facts in the most interesting way possible, that's exactly what I do now to a certain degree.'

Iain's first-ever job in television was on *Coronation Street* as a part-time assistant researcher in 2005. He moved around within the soap doing different editorial jobs, including being a storyline writer. He then moved down the M62 to become series editor and producer at *Hollyoaks*. A move across the Pennines saw him take the role of series producer at *Emmerdale*, and by early 2018 he had returned to *Coronation Street* to take over from Kate Oates as producer of the nation's favourite soap.

'Twenty-something me would probably pinch themselves if someone had told me I'd ever be doing this job,' says Iain. 'It's the best job in TV for my money. It's certainly the pinnacle of soap in my opinion.'

Iain describes being producer as like having a box of the best toys in the world. 'You sort of lift the lid every day when you come to work but instead of Action Man and Barbie and Sindy and GI Joe you've got Ken Barlow and Rita and Tyrone and David Platt, and I get to play make believe with them. In conjunction with our very talented writers and storyline writers I get to come up with fantastical, brilliant and exciting, novel and moving make believe.'

So what does the job of producing *Coronation Street* entail? A lot of Iain's time is spent reading – 'I'm lucky I'm an avid, and speedy, reader, which is an essential prerequisite for this job.'

'It's like making the best show on telly with your best mates a lot of the time.'

Iain might read 12 scripts (70 pages long on average) in a morning. He will go through them with their directors and discuss how he wants certain scenes to look, the tone he wants, whether it should be comedic or sad, dramatic or low key. 'We have a very talented bunch of people here, so lots of it could all run without too much input from me, but I do like to involve myself in all aspects such as costume, design, lighting.'

Reading scripts and interacting with directors and writers takes up roughly half the producer's time. The other half is spent reading the storyline documents – the building blocks upon which the eventual scripts will be based.

'So I do a lot of reading and a lot of talent management – we have around 70 actors and 30 writers who all have very strong creative points of view, very clear ideas about the way they want to either write or perform. A fairly large proportion of my time when not reading is spent talking directly to actors about how I want things to play, talking to them about their upcoming storyline so that they know where the scene they're shooting in The Rovers on Monday morning – where they cast a sideways glance at another character – is going. Is that story going to turn into a love story? Or are they secretly plotting their downfall, or do they have a secret they don't want that person to know about?'

Iain's favourite part of the job is the monthly short-term story conference, a two-day meeting with the assistant producer, the storyliners and the scriptwriters. That's where the toybox analogy becomes pertinent – they lift the lid on the toybox, look at all the characters they have to play with and spend two days working out what they are going to do next with them.

The team needs to know what they are doing with those characters for the next month, but often they are planning six months, 12 months or even two or three years in advance.

'Story conference is fun, it's creative, it's a non-judgemental environment for people to put their ideas forward. Sometimes the most ambitious, slightly bonkers stuff catches the imagination of the writers' room. We'll spend an hour or so refining it and before you know it suddenly you've got this incredible two-year story. The best thing is that everybody who works on this show is a massive fan, so being in the privileged position of being able to come up with the next six months of *Coronation Street* is a lot of fun and you do have to pinch yourself sometimes to think that that's what you're allowed to do for a living.' Iain regards *Coronation Street* like a big family. 'It's like making the best show on telly with your best mates a lot of the time.'

Iain follows in the footsteps of talented producers who have helped to retain *Coronation Street*'s position as one of Britain's favourite programmes. He explains: 'My job is like being put in charge of the *Mona Lisa* – I might be able to change the way it's displayed or lit, but ultimately if I go at it with a marker pen and put my own spin on it, it's unforgivable. It's a hugely important cultural thing, *Coronation Street*. My job is not to try to rebrand or rebrief it and make it into something that it's not, but to continue the tradition that Tony Warren established in 1960 and work out what the modern version of that show looks like.'

While *Coronation Street* can't remain frozen in time, it has to have a lineage back to those first shows. Careful custodianship is required. 'Luckily, many of the writers have been on it for decades, so if I were ever to steer the ship into dangerous waters there's a very good system of checks and balances in place. Like everyone who watches and loves *Coronation Street*, you love it for what it is and you don't want to turn it into something else. If you try to make a show that you'd want to watch as a *Corrie* fan, then you can't go too far wrong. Sometimes I come to work and spend all day sitting in a room watching *Coronation Street*. In any other job that would get you sacked, but I actually get paid for the privilege. It's a joy really.'

The biggest challenge, says Iain, is finding stories that have never been done before. 'We try not to be formulaic, things can take surprising twists, and you wind up somewhere totally unexpected.

'You have your big love story/murder mysteries, but sometimes the more poignant heart-breaking stuff is equally memorable and equally brilliant. Jack Duckworth's death really sticks in the memory because it was low key and poignant and gentle.

'People talk about these big stories, but when you ask them what their favourite moment was it's often the smaller comedic stuff. That's what *Corrie*'s always been first and foremost – the soap with the laconic, northern, wry sense of humour.

'We're constantly trying to find that balance between the big drama and the comedy, and I think *Corrie* has historically been better at that than anyone else. It's a continuing challenge and comedy is a very mercurial animal to try to pin down. It's polarising, and what one person might find funny someone else might find utterly infuriating and annoying.

'You have to trust your instincts and sometimes we get it right, sometimes we don't. On balance, *Corrie*'s been going for 60 years because we mostly get it right.'

Casting

ONE of the most important departments at *Coronation Street* is casting: seeking out the right actor to bring the words of the writers to life and to appeal to fans is fundamental to the show's success.

Throughout the decades, actors have burned their characters into the consciousness of the nation – who else could have portrayed imperious Annie Walker but Doris Speed? Patricia Phoenix *was* Elsie Tanner. And William Roache turned out to be perfectly cast as Ken Barlow. Tony Warren's initial feeling that Ena Sharples should be a scrawny shrew of a woman quickly, and fortunately, made way for the idea that she should take the more stockily built, intimidating form of Violet Carson. And as for Hilda Ogden, well, Jean Alexander was a gift. Onwards through the decades, which other actors could have been Rita, Gail, Bet, Reg, Carla or Roy?

It's no accident that these actors have portrayed these iconic characters. There's an art to selecting the right person, so how do the casting director, and the wider team, achieve this?

Coronation Street's casting director Gennie Radcliffe originally wanted to become a theatre director. She studied for a drama degree at Manchester University – 'I never wanted to act' – and then began working at the Library Theatre in Manchester where she was asked to help with the audition process. 'I loved doing that,' she says.

'Starting with a script and going through the whole casting process, then seeing that come alive on stage was such a buzz.'

Gennie wrote to James Bain (former head of casting and recipient, following his death in 2016, of the inaugural Tony Warren award at the British Soap Awards) and casting director Judi Hayfield at ITV, and her letter arrived the day two casting assistants resigned. 'They asked if I could come in for a chat the next day and then said, "right, can you start on Monday?"'

Judi Hayfield was one of *Coronation Street*'s most influential casting directors and she is still involved with the soap. Since the 1960s she has been heavily involved in creating an iconic cast, bringing in actors including Betty Driver, Helen Worth, Sue Nicholls, Johnny Briggs, Lynne Perrie, Sally Dynevor, William Tarmey, Elizabeth Dawn, Amanda Barrie, Kevin Kennedy, Sarah Lancashire, Suranne Jones, Jane Danson, Georgia Taylor and Julie Hesmondhalgh.

Thanks to Judi, Gennie started off booking the extras on *Coronation Street*, then went on to work with casting directors on other ITV shows, including *The Forsyte Saga* and *Blue Murder*. In 2004 she was asked to take over the casting on *Coronation Street* and admits it was something of a baptism of fire. She explains the secret:

In 1960 there were 24 actors...By 2004 there was a regular cast of around 52; now it's 72.

'It's about volume of actors. You have to know a lot of actors, so I would be out at the theatre all the time, three or four nights a week, just soaking up who was out there. And for every small part I cast I'll always have one wildcard, someone I don't know but has come from a trusted agent, and that's how I build up my knowledge of actors.'

In 1960 there were 24 actors in the cast. By 2004 there was a regular cast of around 52; now it's 72 (not counting the under 16s). Agents will know to suggest just two or three people for a role, or they won't suggest anybody if they don't have someone spot on. 'These days, for every part I send out I'll get between 150 and 300 suggestions. I go through all of them. As you develop as a casting director you learn to read the image and the CV really quickly.'

To explain the casting terminology, extras are non-speaking; visiting artists are those actors who come in for a short storyline or the odd episode here and there – perhaps a policeman with three or four lines, a doctor with a couple of scenes or an actor who comes in for several episodes as a love interest for a character. Regular artists are those on a three-month or more contract.

Often, the first meeting a prospective *Coronation Street* actor has with casting takes place in a small comfortable meeting room at the studios' offices at Trafford Wharf. The window looks out over the waters of Salford Quays to the BBC buildings at MediaCity and on one of the office walls are pinned cast cards of all the current actors on the show, complete with picture, name and signature. Rather than being intimidating, this can help an actor as they prepare to read through a scene.

The first main character Gennie, as Assistant Casting Director, cast was Chesney, as a boy in 2003. 'It was a no brainer, Sam Aston was just so adorable and the boy could act! Shortly after that I cast Bill Ward as Charlie Stubbs and some of the more notable ones I cast were Katherine Kelly (Becky Granger) and Michelle Keegan (Tina McIntyre).

'Tina was an interesting one,' remembers Gennie. 'We'd already got a shortlist of six girls when a local casting agent rang and said they had this girl who was something special and could I meet her. I asked her to come in that afternoon. Michelle was really raw,

had barely done anything else before, but there was something mesmeric about her. I had a hunch and put her forward for a screen test. Jack P Shepherd (David Platt), the director and I all said to the producer at the time, we have to go with this girl. She just had it. Everyone asks, what is it that you're looking for? She had it, you couldn't take your eyes off her. You just know, when they bring that character to life, beyond what you ever hope for, that they're right for the role.'

Judi Hayfield says that the secret to finding the perfect actor for a role is knowing the scenes, making regular theatre visits to scout for the show and fighting for the best actor for the part. She recalls casting Julie Hesmondhalgh for the part of Hayley Patterson: 'After meeting Julie we decided there and then in the room that she had the job and were really excited to have found Hayley. I chased her down the corridor to tell her she had got the job!'

For a new regular role, the team nearly always screen test and that test is viewed by several people, including the producer. First, a scene is usually specially written for an audition, perhaps a two-hander with a journey, ups and downs to bring out real emotion from the actors. The actors will have that in advance before they come in. They will read on camera then the team will spend several days meeting the prospective stars and putting them on camcorder. They will be whittled down to eight or ten possibles, then the producer will select five or six to be screen-tested.

Gennie explains: 'If you're casting an older character in their 70s or 80s you might see just 10 actors because you know their work, they're normally pretty established. If I'm casting someone like Emma Brooker (Alexandra Mardell), a teenager, I might see 50 or 60 actors because you don't know who's out there. They're just coming up from drama school and you want to give everybody the chance because you don't want to miss anyone who might be amazing.'

A full on-screen test is usually a scene together with the actor they will mainly be playing opposite – husband and wife, boyfriend and girlfriend, mother and father – and this will be acted out on one of the regular sets with a mini crew. The scene will be edited together and sent round to the producers who will have a conference call with the casting team to decide who will get the part.

'You need to make sure they can cope with being on set. Sometimes you see the nerves and it breaks your heart because we all want everybody to be great, to excel. We always let people read again if they want to. There are so many actors that the amazing casting directors before me have cast that you feel like the caretaker and you've got to do as well as the people who came before you.'

Gennie needn't worry about that, she and her team have been responsible for casting many of our favourite characters – Sophie, Bethany, Michelle, Carla, Tim, Mary, Billy, Beth, Sinead, Alex, Cathy, Gary, Evelyn, Abi, Johnny, Daniel, the Baileys…

'I love it when I audition an actor who makes the hairs on the back of your neck stand up because their performance is so good. I think I've got the best job in the world…'

Assistant casting director Katy Scully, who started working in casting for ITV in 2004 and has worked solely on *Coronation Street* since 2009, adds: 'The main cast is established, but we'll have other people that come in – paramedics, police, boyfriends, etc, so it's going through scripts, talking to directors to find out what they want and then we will narrow the dates down, select people to interview and then we'll cast with the director for a certain block of episodes.'

With the Bailey family, who appeared in June 2019, the team started casting in August 2018. And when they cast some Polish and Bulgarian characters recently, they opened the net wider as agents may not necessarily have such actors on their books. Often they will use Spotlight, an industry talent tool, or agents suggest actors.

'It's really rewarding to find somebody who is not known in the industry or who may have done theatre but is not known to the general public and then giving them the platform to excel and become a household name, as we've done with leading ladies who are now fronting big dramas,' says Katy.

Katy says that one of the challenging aspects of casting is bringing in, rather than individual characters, an entire family. Not only do the characters have to chime with the viewers, the actors have to work well with, and complement, each other. The Bailey family was introduced in 2019 – the first new family to be introduced in one go since the Windasses in 2008 – and made an immediate impact with storylines including gay footballers and absent fathers.

The *Coronation Street* casting team also looks after the actors and deals with any queries they have about contracts or pensions. If new actors are relocating they help them with accommodation and generally settling in to life on the most famous street on TV.

Hair and makeup

IN the bright, clean setting of *Coronation Street*'s busy makeup department, supervisors Jacquelyn Walker and Jane Hatch, and makeup artist Tina Lyons and the team do much more for the actors on *Coronation Street* than transform them into their characters. On duty from 6:45am each day, after the security guards on the gates and Angie on reception, along with costume they are often the first people the actors chat to ahead of a day of filming. And as the actors sit having their makeup applied or their hair blow-dried, it's to the ever-discreet makeup artists that they talk, discuss what's happening on set or even in their home lives. Sometimes actors just need to sit there and read through their lines.

'There's a lot of talking and listening,' says Jacquelyn. 'You could call it therapy really – just like you'd talk to your hairdresser at home.'

Shelley King (Yasmeen Metcalfe) says: 'The backbone of *Corrie* is the people behind the scenes who work there who are so dedicated and caring. In makeup or costume they listen, they counsel, they make you happy. When you go into *Coronation Street* there's a great feeling of love.'

The makeup department at *Coronation Street*'s relatively new home at Trafford Wharf is larger than its previous base at Granada Studios in central Manchester. It is situated next to the costume department on the ground floor of the purpose-built centre, one floor down from the artists' dressing rooms and close to the studios. The team consists of six makeup supervisors, five assistants, two junior assistants and one trainee. There are also regular freelance makeup artists. They are all highly trained professionals, the best in the industry, and often with an art background. Some freelancers have degrees in fine art.

A typical day in makeup has to be incredibly well-planned. With more than 70 actors on roll, plus visiting and background artists, the team's work is planned to the minute. All the actors receive a call sheet detailing what time throughout the day they are required in makeup – makeup does these and they are emailed out on a Friday afternoon. They used to be telephoned through to each actor.

The scripts are read – the team needs to know if a character is to look extra glamorous for a night out or tired and sad if the storyline demands it. There are also sometimes injuries to accommodate – cuts and bruises may be required.

The teams are worked out – how many people are needed on each day of the forthcoming week. The staff are there to await the actors each morning. They make cups of tea for them and wash their hair if required. The earliest the actors are usually needed on set is 8:15am, but although makeup are in early they regularly finish after 7pm, later if there's a night shoot.

The female actors usually need around 45 minutes in makeup; the men much less, around 15 minutes. Occasionally, an actor prefers to do their own makeup. Often actors will go to costume first, but some prefer to have their makeup done early and occasionally the schedule will dictate what happens first.

Hairdressing training is very important, especially today. In the early days there were more wigs involved. If an actor's hair has to be washed and set there is a backwash area and the talented team members are fully trained in hair as well as makeup application. Jacquelyn remembers when Vera Duckworth's peroxide tightly permed style covered Liz Dawn's short hair and similarly Hayley Cropper's short dark wig masked Julie Hesmondhalgh's sleek blonde crop.

As well as making up the actors, the team needs to plan the day so that makeup artists are on set or on the outdoor set ('the lot') to check continuity and touch up actors' makeup. They also need to factor in location shoots, and with four, or sometimes five, units shooting each day, the makeup team needs to cover several areas. There are often changes between scenes – a character may go from a daytime look to an evening scene quickly.

The often inclement Manchester weather means the makeup artists need to be particularly attentive on the lot or on location, keeping a sharp eye out for continuity issues and checking whether makeup needs reapplying between takes.

Each character has their own particular box of makeup and the room, with its four rows of individual makeup stations, is carefully organised with brushes, tissues, towels and cleansers all in their correct places and shooting schedules to hand. Members of the department are responsible for purchasing all the required makeup paraphernalia.

Jane Hatch started in 1977 as a trainee at Granada. '*Coronation Street* was huge then, we still had all the old characters including Annie Walker and Elsie Tanner.' At that time Glenda Wood was the makeup supervisor. 'Glenda used to do Annie Walker all the time. Doris (Speed) was a little deaf, so you had to shout down her ear. She was so funny though. One day I remember she came in, sat down and announced: "Well, there's eyes in there somewhere and you've got to find them."'

Tina Lyons adds: 'Glenda did everything for Doris, even fastening her stockings up for her. She had this old suspender belt and stockings falling down in folds!'

Jack Howarth played crotchety old Albert Tatlock. In real life Jack was clean-shaven and wore a fake grey moustache for the part. On one occasion, his fake moustache was inadvertently popped into the overall pocket of one of the makeup artists who went home and put it in the wash. The following day there was a panic when the moustache was missing ahead of filming, but luckily it was retrieved from the newly laundered overall just in time.

Tina remembers: 'When we were Granada TV trainees they only let us do *Granada Reports* at first – then we did everything, dramas like *Prime Suspect*, or *The Grimleys* or *Stars In Their Eyes*. Then we started working solely on *Coronation Street*.'

Tina's early days saw her work with other original stars of *Coronation Street*. 'Pat Phoenix frightened me at first, she was a massive star. There were only three TV stations at the time, so when one of the *Coronation Street* actors opened a shop or a supermarket thousands of people turned up all jostling to see them. They were like the American stars were. They always used to come in all glammed up on tech run days (the final technical

CORONATION STREET MAKEUP IN NUMBERS

In one month alone, the *Coronation Street* cast goes through…

50 boxes of tissues

20 packs of makeup wipes

10 lipsticks (Rosie Webster would require at least one red lipstick a month)

5 lipliners and lip glosses

6 eyeliners (Michelle Connor needed two kohl eye pencils a month)

5 powders

4 blushers

15 bases

6 eye shadows

15 large cans of hairspray

rehearsal for all the crew; they don't have them these days). They'd be all dolled up with full makeup and jewellery. They really looked the part.'

Tina remembers Jean Alexander (Hilda Ogden) as being 'very nice'. 'She practically did herself. She'd put in her rollers, three of them, and apply her lipstick that used to end up halfway along her lips. And Eileen Derbyshire (Emily Bishop) was one of the loveliest, dearest ladies, very professional, but knew nothing about what makeup we were putting on her.'

Jacquelyn explains the day-to-day demands on the makeup team: 'We'll know if they need their normal look or if we're making them up for a certain scene like a wedding. Or if they need to have a no-makeup look, for instance if they are supposed to look sad we work with that.

'There are a lot of changes – the characters can go from one day to another in the same day, or they come off another "block", so continuity is a big consideration. They quickly might go from day to night scenes. Haircuts are a constant worry as well, especially on the boys who have such short styles.'

When a new character is introduced there is a lot of discussion between the makeup designer and the actor about the particular look. 'You don't want to make somebody up in a way they really don't agree with.'

When Dolly-Rose Campbell began in the role of Gemma Winter, her misapplied makeup – the too-dark foundation, which stopped, unblended, at her jawline – was carefully thought through, as were her too-tight clothes. Dolly says she modelled the character's look on girls she recognised, youngsters trying to emulate the images of famous people they saw on social media, but always getting it slightly wrong.

And Beverley Callard says of Liz McDonald: 'I love the fact that Liz is quite glamorous in one way, with all the makeup, but the makeup is in a timewarp, it's still in the eighties and she would never change it, even when she's 90!'

Tina says one of the best things about working on a programme like *Coronation Street* for such a long time is to work with the young actors as they progress. 'Jack P Shepherd and Brooke Vincent were always adorable; it's lovely to be there as they grow up.'

Barbara Knox has high praise for the team: 'You don't do this on your own, there's the crew and wardrobe, and Jane and Helen (King) who do my makeup. I'd be lost without them.'

Costume

THE costume department at the *Coronation Street* studios is rarely quiet. With dozens of regular cast members to dress, along with extras and visiting artists, this large bright space bustles with activity.

It's a spacious room with offices at one end and laundry facilities at the other where all the clothes are washed, dried and ironed. They have a drying room, but also hang out the clothes at the back of the studios. There is space for repairs and alterations. Rows of clothing rails hold scores of coats, tops, trousers and dresses, with each regular character having a named section. Every item is named too. Rita's smart coats hang close to Ken's suits and Kevin's mechanic's outfits. Carla's sexy tops and Liz's Lycra can be spotted near to Roy's anoraks. According to the costume assistants, there was a shirt belonging to Kirk that was there for 10 years as in real life a young man like Kirk may well keep a shirt that long.

There are also children's warm coats, hospital uniforms, ties and a 'homeless' section. Kids' socks, bags, characters' brollies and school uniforms fight for space with baby clothes, emergency services outfits and a whole section of prison garb – more than one *Coronation Street* character has spent time at Her Majesty's pleasure over the years. Photographs are put up to help with continuity.

Costume is a vital tool to communicate a character's personality. Costume designers work closely with actors and producers to establish the right look for a character from the beginning. Their fictional backstory is discussed and a wardrobe decided upon.

Beverley Callard loves the way her character Liz McDonald's image came about. 'She'd always wear Lycra because she had to pack her house up as an army wife and get ready to move at the drop of a hat and she'd never have had to iron Lycra.

'I love the fact that she tried really hard, but she just failed. Her knickers would always be a size too small, she'd always have a knicker line. I think she never looked at the back of herself. That made her funny without being over the top. She'd always undo one more button than she should, that's Liz.'

The costume staff shop for all the required items and careful consideration is given to where a character would be likely to shop in real life depending on their age and spending ability. Sophie Webster or Emma Brooker would most likely shop in high-street stores while Rita, Audrey and Claudia might favour slightly pricier boutiques. Sinead's 'bo-ho' thrift-shop look was carefully curated, as was Gemma's brash bargain-store dress sense.

As *Coronation Street* portrays an ordinary back street in northern England, the costumes have to support that. Subtle tweaks can make a real difference to a look, and the attention to detail that goes into planning the 'ordinary' appearance of characters is immense.

The costume team is made up of 20 staff and around 20 freelancers. Margaret Kings has been on *Coronation Street* permanently since 2002. She came to ITV in 1993, having worked at the BBC since 1972 as a dresser. Her neighbour was Edna Walker, the show's first costume designer, responsible for buying, among other things, Ena Sharples' famous coat.

Margaret recalls: 'Knowing Edna was how I first got into television. I was at the old Dickinson Road studios where *Top of the Pops* started. When I moved to ITV I did *Prime Suspect 3* and *4*.'

Margaret, who is also responsible for alterations, explains that a small costume archive is kept above the shops on the lot. 'We keep costumes when an actor leaves if there's a chance they might return. If they are not coming back, we keep a couple of key outfits anyway.'

The team is in early as costume is usually organised before actors go into makeup next door. They are often the last out of the building

Costume is a vital tool to communicate a character's personality.

too because most items that have been worn in a day's scenes need to be washed, dried, and ready for the next morning. Margaret explains that dressers don't physically dress the actors. They have master keys to all the dressing rooms, which are situated on the floor above, and take the outfits to each room. The dressing rooms have sinks and wardrobes, a dressing table and comfy chairs. Some are decorated with home comforts the actors bring in and some have a small bed so actors can rest if they're stood down at any point during a long filming day. Dressing rooms are for one, two or even four actors. There is also a visiting artists' dressing room.

'The assistants take the outfits to the dressing rooms and they will lay the clothes over the chair. Sometimes there are three actors sharing a dressing room. You look at your notes and you put out the jewellery they're going to be wearing and the shoes. If it's not established, we tend to let them choose the coat and the jewellery. We do help people if it's a special outfit, but with so many actors these days doing different scenes each day it works better this way.'

Alex Hatzar is head of costume and a costume designer. She trained in textile design. She arrives by 7am each day and sees people before they go on set.

'On a team there's always one supervisor and two assistants,' she explains. 'But if they have more than 15 or 16 cast they'll have an extra assistant. It also depends if they're in the studio, out on the Street, or which actors are involved. In a prep week we will have three supervisors prepping and they will all be prepping four episodes each, so 12 episodes. Then we start filming the week after so we need to make sure we've got everything that they need to start filming.'

In that prep week the supervisors will work out what team they need for what day. The rostering is then completed, but there is flexibility as the schedules can sometimes change.

'In the prep week we're also filming,' says Alex. 'A three-unit day used to be a busy day, now three units is fine! I read the second draft of the script, so that's four weeks ahead of what we film. The assistants in here read the shooting scripts, which are the final scripts, with the supervisors and they update my notes from the second draft. Every week an email goes out called "the week ahead", which is basically points people need to look out for – someone's changed this or that.'

There is a Costume Team WhatsApp group. 'There's a lot of "Has that team finished with that actor?" and the assistants know to go and put out the next costume. You have to check all the units' call sheets because one actor might be with four teams in one day, so we're looking at the cross-overs, seeing who's got that actor in what order. It's logistically difficult. Generally, it's costume first then

makeup, but sometimes to help out with timings we do swap them over. Some of the actors like to go to makeup first.'

The costume team usually finishes around 7pm, but it can be occasionally past midnight if there is a night shoot. In the winter, scenes set in the evening or at night-time can film from half past three, but not in the summer months.

'If we can, we clear dressing rooms as we go, but you could have a scene at the end of the day in The Rovers with 20 cast members,' says Margaret. 'Then you have to clear the dressing rooms, do the washing and sometimes you need it for first thing the next morning. Everyone works together as a team and helps each other out. We used to have a "factory line" where someone would wash, someone would rinse, someone would spin, but the way we work changed when we moved to this site.'

Alex reveals that when the team is working on one of the celebrated 'live' specials, the rehearsals are the hardest part. 'During a live there are few changes, but in rehearsals we're working out the logistics. With the ITV 60th live we prepped and filmed the rest of that block two months before that one episode because that's how far ahead we are. We started buying stuff for the live episode two months before – we had to source period fancy dress for that one.'

There is always someone from the costume department on set, usually the supervisor and her two assistants. Alex explains: 'When we're on set we're looking out mainly for continuity – a) that they have the right costume on from the last time you saw it; and b) things like buttons are right. We write everything down on our continuity notes, and we take photos. Everything is on our iPads nowadays. We used to write everything down and take Polaroids, and in Margaret's early days they had to draw it! There are the occasional mishaps, but we're all human, and we're all quite calm about it too.'

During a prep week the team has a long shopping list for costumes. 'We prioritise what we need for what dates and then I go shopping! We often try to do green/second-hand buying. There's a staffing budget and a costume budget to think about. Every day is different and it's juggling and plate-spinning.'

When a new character is introduced Alex speaks to the actor to get their sizes and ask them what shops they buy from in real life. 'Not that I'd necessarily buy from there, but so I know what they're comfortable with and what style and shape they fit. We're influenced by what age they are, what their jobs are. It's a blank canvas. We love to dress Gemma because she's fun. Rosie Webster was fun too.'

One attribute that's essential for working in costume is tact. Margaret recalls: 'We had one actor who thought she was a size 12 but she was actually a 16 – we had to cut the labels out!'

From page to screen – the journey of a storyline

THE story office at *Coronation Street* is a busy ideas factory. Situated along the floor from the producer's office and next door to the script editors, researchers and archivists, it's where the storylines are planned and fleshed out. The storyline team is generally around eight members strong. It is their job to attend story conferences, pitch ideas, listen to what's decided between the producer and the writers (who work off site) and then detail what is happening in each scene and each episode. The writers are then assigned episodes and they are the ones who turn the storylines into scripts. Many have written for *Coronation Street* for decades and only a *Coronation Street* writer can voice the show's characters.

Senior storyline writer Martin Sterling always loved *Coronation Street* and wanted to be a writer. Despite a school careers adviser telling a young Martin 'people like you don't write' and suggesting he had ideas above his station, Martin became a feature writer.

'I'd done an interview with the then producer of the *Street*, Kieran Roberts, who commented that I knew a lot about *Coronation Street*,' he recalls. 'Out of the blue I got an invitation to go on a writers' workshop. There were 12 of us on the workshop and they selected three of us to come in on a trial, after which the then script editor asked if I'd be interested in any jobs in the future. They were called story associates in those days. About 10 days later I got a phone call asking if I could start in a week. My life was in Norfolk at the time and I just had to drop everything. That was in 2004. It was a bit of a baptism of fire, I must admit.'

Martin's first storyline was bullying Charlie Stubbs ripping the earrings off girlfriend Shelley Unwin (Sally Lindsay). 'At the time there were still a lot of the old guard, the old men in tweed jackets with elbow patches and if a storyliner opened their mouth at conference they were glared at. There was very much a hierarchy and storyliners were not expected to open their mouths, but then I had an idea for Roy and Hayley that I wanted to pitch.

'I was warned I could get a rough ride, but John Stevenson, who was the "guv'nor" of the writers had somehow taken me under his wing and when I nervously pitched the story John was the first to say, I like that story, I think we should play it.'

The story in question saw Hayley getting worried because Roy had a mysterious brown envelope and she was convinced that he was sending away for dodgy magazines, but they were actually holiday brochures and it was a surprise for Hayley that Roy was taking her to Nelson's birthplace in Norfolk for the 200th anniversary of the Battle of Trafalgar. 'It was only a three-episode story but it went down well with the audience and everyone seemed to like it. Once I'd pitched that it became easier and easier.'

...only a Coronation Street *writer can voice the show's characters.*

Latterly, Martin pitched the male rape storyline. 'It was originally going to be another character, not David Platt, but that changed and playing it with David was suggested by one of the writers and it worked really well.'

Martin was also responsible for Nick Tilsley's (Ben Price) brush with death in some quicksand ahead of his exit from the programme for a while in 2017. 'Kate Oates (the producer at the time) said she didn't want another car crash, she wanted something she'd never seen before, which is not easy, and I just heard myself saying "What about quicksand?" and Kate was thoughtful and said "You know, I like quicksand".'

A lot of the storyliners' work is about keeping the characters fresh. The danger of trying to incorporate current issues into the storylines is that other soaps may well have had the same idea, says Martin. Every four weeks there is a story conference with storyliners, writers, casting, the whole production unit, and anybody around that table can pitch a story. There is also a long-term story conference every three months. 'We pick up the stories that we were doing last block and we carry those on, new stories are pitched and basically it's all up for discussion.

'Iain (MacLeod) is brilliant in terms of being democratic. When we get to the end of conference after two days we come back to the storyliners' office and everything goes up on the board. We work in blocks of four and it can be a logistical nightmare, I don't know how scheduling does it.'

The storyliners will talk the stories through. Each is assigned a story and writes the first draft, which Iain then edits. Each episode is written as a five-page document, which the writers are then commissioned to recast as a script.

'Some writers are stronger on comedy, or really big drama,' explains Martin. 'Sometimes it's good to flip it so if someone is a really gifted comedic writer we give them a dramatic episode to see what they'll do with it.'

The scripts go through different colour-coded stages – buffs, pinks and whites. The whites in theory should be the last edit, but it isn't always the case. 'The writers get quite a few edits,' says Martin. 'I've known previous producers who will ask for a rewrite

quite late on, giving them just a matter of days.' The team works six months ahead of transmission. 'We always end up writing Christmas in the hottest month of the year!' says Martin.

'The biggest challenge in this job is that there's just never enough time, but one of the storylines I've been most proud of was the "who pushed Ken" one because it brought Adam and Daniel back and it ran and ran for nearly two years.'

Writer Jan McVerry is a fan of the storywriting process at *Coronation Street*. She started in the story office and script edited before becoming one of the show's writers, as well as writing for other programmes including *Emmerdale*, *Children's Ward* and Liverpool soap *Brookside*. She has worked under 14 *Coronation Street* producers. Like the other 20-odd regular writers, she works mostly from home but meets with the whole writing team, the producers and casting for three days each month, and often gets together with colleagues at other times to discuss pitches and ideas.

'It's very democratic but a very robust atmosphere,' she says. 'If you pitch at story conference you can't be precious, you know it will be challenged, it might be hated or laughed at or embraced or it might be transplanted onto another character. Even the most unlikely ideas that might be pitched will be kicked around the table and someone might take it and turn it into a piece of gold.

'We always have an agenda for the meetings, which takes into account really practical things like if an actor is below their guaranteed time and we have to find stories for them, or a walk-on actor that Twitter went crazy about. There's a lot of housekeeping that goes on behind the scenes. If you're contracted to use an actor you have to fulfil your part of the guarantee.'

There is a particular skill to conjuring up engaging stories for regular characters, especially those who have been with the programme for many years. Jan explains that they know the character inside out but will sometimes enhance a facet of their personality and that can unlock a whole new world for them. That happened with Sally Webster, where her hint of snobbishness was amplified and run with. 'We got loads of great material out of that. It opened up a whole new side to the character, and (actor) Sally Dynevor is so talented she can handle anything we throw at her.'

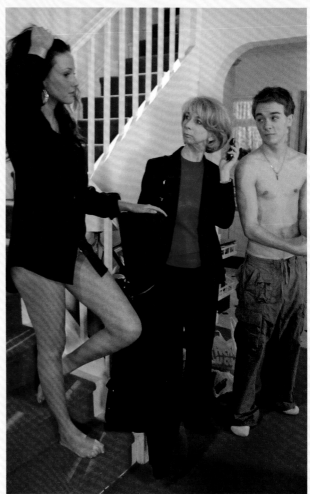

Writing for new characters brings its own set of challenges as it takes time for them to bed in, but Jan says the more stories you write for them the more layers you can add to their personalities. And it helps when the calibre of actors cast is so high.

'Gennie Radcliffe (casting director) has amazing intuition for what will work. When we brought in a girlfriend for David Platt and they found Michelle Keegan, who had done very little acting, it was inspired.'

The inspiration for villain Pat Phelan (Connor McIntyre) came from Jan talking to builders working on an extension on her house. 'We were chatting away and they said there were loads of cowboys in their game, people who would go bankrupt then open up again under another name and not care who it affected. We thought we could use this for the Owen Armstrong (Ian Puleston-Davies) character and wrote Phelan. We originally called him Pete Phelan but there was somebody with that name within a 30-mile radius of Manchester so we changed it to Pat. He was a joy to write.'

Played with such mesmerising charisma and control by McIntyre, once Phelan appeared, the potential in the character was identified and the stories were ratcheted up to create one of soap's ultimate bad guys. The story saw Mikey North's character Gary Windass vow never to be a victim again and go on to develop into a villain himself.

Each script is like a living, breathing organism right up until the time they're in the edit, says Jan, and writers can be called upon to change lines at a moment's notice. Jan remembers being in a car on her way to watch the Grand National, getting the call and having to scribble lines on the back of a paper bag before dictating the scene down the phone from Aintree.

'People can be a bit snobby about soap writing, but actually you need to have a broad palette and a lot of strings to your bow. You have to be able to do the humour as well as the tragedy and the drama. Writing for *Corrie* is about the art of the possible.' And that's a gift for writers, she says, because they can be writing something heart-breaking one moment and farce and hilarity the next. 'We all have our strengths and weaknesses. I tend to get quite a lot of tragedy!'

Jan wrote the 50th anniversary live episode, which she said was like writing a stage play. 'I'm immensely proud of that, we brought about 10 complex storylines together into a glorious hour of drama that had you laughing one minute and crying the next, the very essence of what *Corrie* can do. It was Team *Corrie* at its best.' Jan also wrote the harrowing, and highly praised, episode in 2019 where Sinead received her terminal cancer prognosis.

The writers have backgrounds ranging from theatre, advertising, acting or journalism. 'Damon Rochefort had a number one hit, it's really diverse!'

Notable writers who have contributed scripts over the years include Kay Mellor (*Band of Gold*, *Fat Friends*), Paul Abbott (*Shameless*, *Clocking Off*), Sally Wainwright (*Last Tango in Halifax*, *Happy Valley*, *Gentleman Jack*), Lucy Gannon (*Soldier Soldier*, *Bramwell*), Jim Cartwright (*Little Voice*) and Jimmy McGovern (*Cracker*, *The Street*, *Accused*).

Charles Lawson, who played Jim McDonald adds: 'You can't do anything unless they write for you well and nine times out of 10 the stuff they write for us is very, very good. That's the key to it. Nothing will kill a character quicker than a bad storyline because you can't do anything with it.'

And Barbara Knox sums it up: 'It's lovely to get a marvellous script. It fulfils whatever is inside you that makes you want to be an actress.'

Scheduling

ONCE the storylines are underway, the operation needs scheduling. This is a huge and vital job on a programme using so many actors and producing six episodes every week of the year.

Paul Sparrow is production scheduling manager and he works out of an office whose walls are a moveable mosaic of hundreds of scheduling notes and call sheets. His job entails working with the story team and the writers to make sure their vision, what they write, translates to production. He keeps an eye on budgets, how busy characters are, taking into account holidays, sickness and weather problems, and works with every other department to make sure requirements such as set changes and studio moves are fulfilled. Imagine he is working out a giant metaphorical game of human Jenga and you'd be half way there.

Paul has worked as an assistant director in the past, so knows exactly what a director requires. He also has experience in front of the camera, having worked as a child extra on the *Street*. 'I also did theatre, I originated from the Oldham Theatre Workshop, so straight away when I came in I knew Suranne Jones, Steven Arnold, Alan Halsall. I felt really at home.'

As if his job was not complicated enough, sometimes there is a seventh episode in a week when the network requests it, perhaps an extra episode because of football or schedule changes.

A typical day for the team of three or four means lots of script reading, and reports and schedules to put together. 'Then I'll have a busy week when I'm working on things for story conference, which is typically 24 episodes – budgeting, looking at actors' schedules, making recommendations, looking at what's achievable.'

It only takes one filming unit (usually producing four episodes but occasionally six) to fall behind and that could have an effect on everybody else. 'We need to know things like what has to be shot today, what can be pushed back. We have to consider access to sets for construction, design, lighting.'

Paul and his team work around six months ahead, analysing what will be needed. *Coronation Street* has a 12-hour limit for actors. 'Sometimes we're filming 30 pages of dialogue a day,' explains Paul. 'I have huge respect for the actors. Sometimes they are working in theory with eight or nine directors in a week. Big storylines, such as the Underworld roof fall, can push stuff out because of the design and construction departments having to create that scene.'

Paul's biggest challenge is giving the cast and crew the necessary work/life balance. 'We have to please a lot of different departments at the same time, taking lots of opinions and requests into account. The amount of effort that goes into organising every scene is tremendous. That's the challenge, a lot of plate-spinning!'

Paul has to consider requests from outside *Coronation Street* too. '*Britain's Got Talent* often films on the Street, as does *I'm a Celebrity…* if someone from *Corrie* is on. The press involvement is huge. *Good Morning Britain* is often here. We embrace it all, we understand how important it is to facilitate live broadcasts like that. We've had requests from other networks too – *Antiques Roadshow* was here recently. It's good to do stuff that's different, but it's tricky to schedule it sometimes.'

Ian Bartholomew who has played Geoff Metcalfe since 2018 says: 'What I found most surprising working on *Corrie* was how on earth they schedule it. If you could see the planning office, there's bits of paper in different colours, there's colour coding, things are being moved around all the time to accommodate everybody, how they move people from this scene to that. It's such a huge

operation, it's amazing that it gets made at all and it's as good as it is with three or four units working every day. When you're doing a whole day, every day, on different scenes, with different directors and actors on different storylines completely out of sequence, it absolutely mangles your brain and the fact that people are still walking around vaguely sane is remarkable.'

Paul Sparrow adds: 'It never ceases to amaze me how quickly the writers write or amend episodes and how quickly the cast learn their lines and how well they do it too, it's incredible. Sometimes I stand on set and I'm absolutely blown away, even by a rehearsal. It's just like a theatre performance and we're lucky to see that. There's a really good cast and crew relationship. Everybody is one team and wants it to work.'

On set and on the lot

ONCE the characters are cast and their lines are written, it's time to put the actors to work. The cast and crew often refer to themselves as a big family and their camaraderie is evident to anyone who visits the set. Many members of the crew have been with the show for years and true friendships have built up off camera.

One member of the team who has worked on *Coronation Street* in a number of behind-the-scenes roles is senior location manager John Friend Newman, who has been with the *Street* since 1979.

A former theatre stage manager, he worked as technical director at Manchester's Royal Exchange Theatre before touring Europe with the British Council. He worked on the world premiere of *Chicago*, then

came to Granada for *Brideshead Revisited*. 'After that I became a floor manager,' he says. 'At that time you did *Granada Reports*, which meant you could do live television, and *Coronation Street*, which meant you could work with actors. In those days there was a week's preparation and a week's shoot. We did all the action prop lists and the design lists, marked up the studio floor and briefed the crew for the week ahead. We would always shoot on a Sunday on location, and Monday was usually on the lot (the outside set). Wednesday would be a dress rehearsal and a tech run for the producer. Wednesday night through to Thursday morning we'd put the sets into studio, then we'd work Thursday afternoon

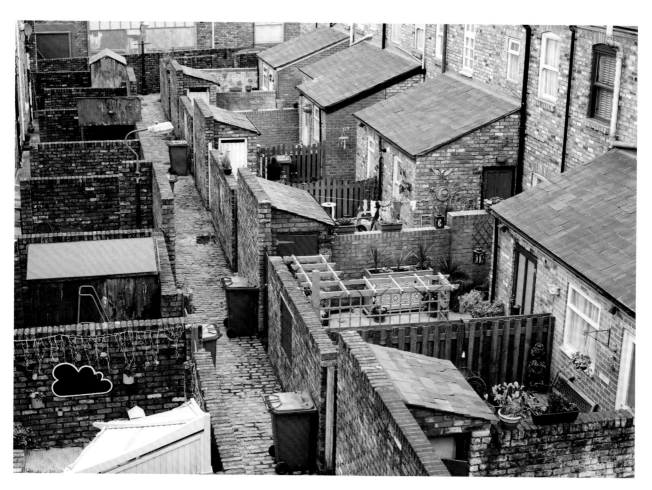

'The crew are the people who know us really, really well and they've made the show just as the actors have. I think they are the interesting ones.'

and all day Friday. On Friday night you didn't overrun because the whole set had to be out, floor scrubbed, as another show would be coming in to use the studio.'

Coronation Street didn't have a static set until Stage 1, which was opened in the early 1990s. 'The difference between the grounding that crews get nowadays to the one we had is you had to work sport, you had to work live, you had to work drama, so I did everything – state funerals, general elections. Now people tend to specialise in one area.'

John didn't work solely on *Coronation Street* but on other Granada programmes as well, and in the mid-90s joined the *Street* full time as location manager. He says the biggest change has been going from the two to six episodes a week. 'It's a much faster turnaround now. It's a much bigger team now than it used to be.'

As senior location manager, John will discuss a script with the director and a designer about what they want and need. 'When we needed the lighthouse used in the Pat Phelan storyline in 2018, I went to look at about 17 lighthouses around the country to find the right one. I need to find out what we're going to do at a location – blow something up, smash a car, break windows? You have to do a risk assessment, organise camera permits, traffic management.

'When the character Joe McIntyre (Reece Dinsdale) drowned up at Windermere in the Lakes, I had to contact Strategic Air Command because we had a 1,000 kilowatt light shining down the lake at night-time.'

John has to ensure crews are not obstructing emergency vehicles. If firearms are involved in a story he has to inform the police, and if they are fired the team has to have both a police officer and an armourer on location with them.

'The lot is considered a location, so I have a unit manager who looks after that, otherwise I'd never get out. It used to be me and a part-time person, now there's four of us.'

One of John's most memorable moments from his years on *Coronation Street* was walking a real leopard down the Street for Julie Goodyear's return as Bet Lynch in 2002. 'Bet's trademark was the leopardskin coat. I was asked in a meeting ahead of her return, "John, can we have a leopard?" We caged the entire street and then we screwed all the doors and windows shut and we put sheets of timber behind all the windows so the leopard couldn't see through the glass because if he could have seen his reflection he would have thought he was another male leopard and he would have attacked it.

'The original idea was Julie saying "I'm back" and morphing into this leopard, but the animal did this walk along the street, got

to the end, looked into the camera and roared, so they morphed it the other way, it was fantastic. He roared, and it turned into Julie saying "I'm back". Wonderful!'

Lot supervisor Andy Ashworth, who has worked on and off on *Coronation Street* for 28 years, regards himself as the 'caretaker of the show'. 'When I started I was making scenery. There were fewer episodes back then with a much smaller crew, a million miles away from how it operates today. Then there was the old crew who had done it all the way through, so if I as a youngster needed to know anything I'd ask Jim and Jimmy, the two main prop men. And they used to tell you the stories of why one of the flight of ducks in Hilda's house hung crooked – on a night-time changeover of the Ogdens' set it was knocked off the wall and broke. They went away and remade it really quickly but they put the pin in the wrong place. The next day they came to film on that set, it was put up and that's the way it stayed after that.'

Dressing props are the people who will dress a set, then the standby props person is in direct conversation with the designer, the first assistant director, the director and the actor. They read the scene, talk to everyone and ask questions about exactly what they want, then go and get the props, making sure that on the day of filming everything that's required is there for the scene. The action prop man stands by the camera and watches what's happening. If someone is playing cards, they make sure the cards are there and that they're the right cards, or if somebody is reading a book, is it the right book? Is it open at the right page? If somebody is holding a mobile and they receive a text message, does it read correctly?

There are assistant scenemasters who can add walls or take them out to get the cameras in the right places. The designer makes sure everything looks right on screen, and they will have had instructions from the head designer.

Andy's job involves a lot of discussion with the designer. 'If they want snow I make sure it snows, if they don't want snow I clear it. I make it rain using rain bars. I make sure the lot is ready for whatever the director wants. There is a lot of cleaning and being on top of all the construction work, so we have to be very keen on health and safety. There's a lot of people working on set at any one time. We always say there's 80 people making a mess and one person cleaning it up.'

Sally Dynevor says the crew is the backbone of the show. 'Some of them that started around the same time as me and are still here; they have grown up with the actors. The crew are the people who know us really, really well and they've made the show just as the actors have. I think they're the interesting ones.'

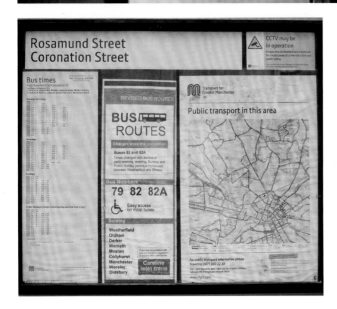

Production

LEE Rayner is *Coronation Street*'s senior production manager. He is responsible for breaking episodes down, budgeting them and advising the producer. 'I facilitate it really, make sure we try to turn what's on the page into reality, and I predict what it's costing.'

Lee has been at *Coronation Street* for eight years. He was a production scheduler and first assistant director, then production manager and senior production manager. He was previously production manager on *The Bill*. His first episode as a first assistant director was the Carla Connor (Alison King) rape and it won a Bafta. He recalls: 'The moment I knew this place was special was recording that scene. I was on the floor and I could hear the gallery in my earphones and the director and the script supervisor were crying in the gallery and I thought, wow, I'm at a place where you can really feel the love. It was such a powerful performance by Alison King, the story was so emotional and violent and shocking and horrible, but the fact everyone was so invested in it was amazing. And it won a Bafta, quite rightly.'

'The volume of work on this show is incredible,' he says. 'I came when there were five episodes a week. Now it's six and it's a massive machine, although we're very lean on production.'

Lee says the biggest challenge is trying to make more ambitious episodes with the same amount of resources. 'We have the world watching us, we're aware there are lenses pointing at us all the time, that adds to the pressure. Everything we do is a story. I do *Death in Paradise* too so that keeps me fresh, but to sit in this story conference room is a privilege – just listening to the pitches is brilliant.'

A normal day for Lee could include editorial meetings, recceing and production meetings. 'I try to leave Fridays free for additional meetings, catching up on emails and reading. And then I might be out on location filming, there could be stunts to oversee. I'm the most comfortable when I walk on set. That's what gives me the currency with the crews because that's where I learned my trade, so I understand the challenges they face. I also understand what can and can't be done. You have to be empathic with the crews because it's long hours and it's physical. If you didn't love working on TV you wouldn't survive, you'd be the most unhappy person.'

Lee adds: 'We have to know where we've come from on *Coronation Street*, know what Tony Warren created and stay true to that while acknowledging that the world is changing and that the issues facing people now are different from those in 1960. They told very brave stories in the 60s and we have to tell brave stories now, not sensational stories, but they have to be true to life. Any story can be told, but as long as it's told with heart and feeling and honesty that's what this amazing team of writers does. It's testament to everyone

who works on the show that *Coronation Street* after 60 years is still as successful as it is.'

The future is uncharted territory he says, 'but as long as we're telling the right stories and people are still gripped by them, then the rest of ITV needs to be working on how we attract viewers. It's going to be exciting times and I believe *Coronation Street* has got a massive future.'

Marc Hough is a first assistant director. He started in 2007 aged 22 as an office boy, became production secretary, then got a staff second assistant director job. 'You were always aware of *Coronation Street* because culturally it's all around. I'm a northerner, it's *Corrie*, you know not to call certain people at 7:30pm when *Corrie*'s on. I remember as a kid looking at the credits – the old ones over the rooftops – and looking down the names and thinking those jobs really exist and I want my name there one day!'

Marc's job as a 'first' is partly to schedule the show. 'It's a bit like 3D chess! We have two weeks of prep, making sure there are no clashes between units, doing recces with the crew so they know what's going on, looking at the details of each scene and working out who is where, and then after the two prep weeks we start to shoot the scenes. It's my job to run the floor, keep everything together, deal with any problems, keep the whole thing running – bring sound, cameras, lighting, actors all together and keep it all running as best we can, as cheap as we can and as quickly as we can.

'I shout "action" and "cut" about 100 times a day. We average about nine or ten scenes a day in the studio, five or six on the Street. It's quicker on the set with lighting and so on. On the Street there's the weather to think about. We work about six to seven weeks ahead. If it's a prep week we work office hours. Shooting weeks it's longer hours, usually a 7am start. I feel the respect people have for the programme. You see what it means to people. There's cast and crew who have been here for 20, 30 years or more.'

Stephen Polack is a second assistant director who has worked on *Coronation Street* for 20 years. He describes the magic of it. '*Corrie* was always something that was up there, it was prestigious and you had to earn your stripes to get on it, you always wanted to do it. I remember my first day, walking through that green room door – there's an aura about that green room and even the cast, and actors that come in now. Because you've grown up with it, because it was on in your home, when you see the reality it's amazing.

'I'd done loads of other shows, but when I saw Eileen Derbyshire walking towards me, it hit me: that's Emily Bishop! And you see it on actors' faces, new people coming in, they're in awe of the place.'

Stephen explains that the third assistant directors work with the

background artists. A second assistant director's main job is to keep the cast as calm as possible. 'Sometimes an actor can go immediately from filming one episode to another that's many episodes before that, it can jump around that much.

'We have a meeting every week where we get all our units together and see how the actor will go from say episode 1 to episode 12 in one day. When we go home on an evening the actors still have to go home and learn lines for different storylines and part of our job is to notice how much pressure they are under. You get to know their personalities and when they might need a tea break. Everyone's under pressure to finish their day and sometimes you have to step in, aware of what the actors are doing.'

Part of Stephen's job is to keep a unit running as smoothly as possible. 'If you see a director is flying through scenes, you start pre-empting what's coming next. Sometimes you're behind so you'll call an actor and say, don't come in yet. Once a scene is finished there's a progress report to fill out and there's a live update that has all of our units on, which has to be kept up to date. They call us "air traffic control". Once they start shooting everything comes through our desk – to the assistant directors, to the directors, to the gallery, everything. The call sheets can change in an instant, and that can be a challenge. But we find a way between us, and swap things around.'

Stephen remembers working on the special live episode for the show's 50th anniversary. He recalls: 'Doing the 2010 live was one of the most scary times of my life, but also one of the most rewarding. One of the best, and the worst things I've ever done!'

In the gallery – the vision mixer

DAYLE Evans-Kar has been on the show since 1985. She has a theatre background, starting as an assistant stage manager straight after drama school, and worked her way up to become a company stage manager in Scotland and York before coming to Manchester.

'My friend happened to work for an agency and she said Granada was looking for people with genuine Scottish accents to be extras for a drama called *Lost Empires*. The director was Alan Grint (who also worked on *Coronation Street*). Then I was asked to do *Corrie*, where I looked after the actors.'

Dayle was also a double, driving for Liz Dawn (Vera) who was only used to driving an automatic and needed to drive a manual. 'So I donned my blonde curly wig and drove down the street as Vera.'

'I loved *Corrie* because my background is rep theatre and this is like a big rep company – you work with different combinations of the same people. It's fun, it never feels like work.'

Dayle started working as an assistant director at the same time as the McDonalds and the Barneses were introduced. 'Then I replaced a first AD, which means you are first assistant to the director. The director provides the artistic content and you facilitate it. You're the director's right-hand man, but you also keep the director to the schedule. You work out with the director how long it might take to do the scenes, take into account what they want and keep them to schedule. You're the one who says "action" and "cut", you're the one who corrals the crew, making sure everybody's ready, and you do the health and safety.'

Dayle worked on the 40th anniversary live as first AD and was the lead first AD on the 50th anniversary live. 'The 40th was the first time in recent times that we'd done a live episode and because of my theatre background I was sent off to schedule it as if it was first night. It's a big deal doing a live episode. It's really hard with the logistics of getting people from the studio to out on the lot and they might be cutting from one location to another.'

Dayle recalls she used visual hand signals from underneath the camera because she couldn't say 'action' and 'cut'. 'You'd hear in your ear "ten minutes to air, five minutes to air… ten seconds to air" and then you'd hear the theme music. If you were in a studio you could see the monitors so you know where you're up to, but out on the Street you wouldn't have that, so you'd be listening in to the director in the gallery and the script supervisor counting out the shots. When your shot was up and coming and you absolutely had to be ready.'

When the show moved to Trafford Wharf in 2014, Dayle changed her job. 'Vision mixing was something I'd always fancied doing. I trained on *Emmerdale* then came back here.' Dayle explains what the vision mixer does as she sits in a gallery facing several monitors in front of a range of buttons and controls. 'A director has three or four cameramen, lighting, a sound guy and me. My muscle memory has to know what buttons to press as I'm looking at the screens. It's very quick, I'm doing essentially a live edit. You might only get one rehearsal to get the feel of who's doing what – but somebody might give a look or reaction you want to hold on. I try to interpret what the director wants. When you're in here everyone – sound, boom guys, all the ADs – can hear what the director is saying. Then we rehearse it again and the director will do a line run, then put them in position, change it if necessary, then we'll go for a take. That's when I feel my adrenaline go.'

There are three vision mixers and three galleries that can be in use at any one time. 'We try to work with one or two directors a day, but sometimes you work with up to four directors a day and that can be challenging in the different ways they work, different personalities. Sometimes they want more input from you, sometimes less. You have to learn how they all like to work.'

The script supervisor will check continuity, time the scenes, note script changes and make sure the actors say what's in the scripts.

The buttons in front of the vision mixer all light up and tell her who's listening in. One screen shows the cut version for the script supervisor. 'The director watches that but I don't, I'm always watching for the incoming shots and looking for the moment to cut.

'Then we'll go for a take. That's when I feel my adrenaline go.'

I might have to fast cut to avoid a boom moving in if someone is sitting down and speaking, for instance. When I started doing this job I thought how on earth am I going to press the buttons, look at the script, look at three cameras, make sure the cameras are in position and the booms are not in shot. It's like when you first drive a car, once your muscle memory has learned it, it makes space to learn something else and it opens up your brain to be able to look and see. I like this job, I get to stay inside these days rather than being out on the Street at 2am in the cold as a first AD!'

Editing

SOPHIE Byrne started as an assistant editor in 1996. 'Six months turned into a year. Then I went off and did other things and then at 24, they offered me the chance to become an editor. At that time there were no female editors at all in Granada, let alone *Coronation Street*. I can remember in 1998 one very experienced director at the time complained to the management to say what were they doing to the standards on *CS*. He then came down, not very friendly, and watched what I'd done. He didn't say anything, went back up to see the manager, said yes, she can do it, and then he was my biggest supporter. It was because I was young, not particularly because I was female, but I'd been quietly training in the background, editing at weekends, which was a brilliant apprenticeship basically.' Since Sophie started 20 years ago, the number of episodes has gone up. 'Then, one editor would "cut" all the episodes, but now we're up to six a week, that's a big change. Now there are three full-time female editors on *Coronation Street*, of which I am one.'

Sophie describes her job as sitting in a small dark room looking at computer screens, not really speaking to anyone. 'With any programme, with anything that's filmed, there'll be a choice of shots,' she explains. 'There may be a wide shot or a medium shot or a close-up, and the editor's job is to say, that shot, that bit there is the best for then. You're taking into account the camerawork, the actor's performance, and you're knitting it together. As a viewer you should watch something and not be irritated; you should see what you want to see. It should tell you the story in a way that just works and you don't know that someone, for example, has decided to cut to a close-up of a book. The editor looks at the shots, checks the script and looks out for mistakes like a boom in shot. It's a day for a day, so if it takes them a day to film it, it will then take at least a day to put it together and watch everything.'

An assistant editor's job is about getting it ready for a person to edit. 'When I was an assistant it was recorded onto tapes and we would play the tapes into the machines in real time, so if it was an hour long it would take an hour to do that. We'd load onto nine-gig drives, they were huge, I could only carry two at a time. I'd carry them around as an assistant and they were massive. Now we film onto drives, and what an assistant does now is move media around.'

Sophie recalls that when she arrived in 1996 there was a bar attached to the studio, the old school bar, and lunch consisted of the editors going to the bar. 'As an assistant your job was to have the number of the bar to get them back if they were a little bit late after lunch! So that's different from now.'

Nowadays the editors work on a block of episodes, varying from four to six episodes. They work a day behind and use notes from the script supervisors. 'They are our communication, and the director for that block will say "best take" and that guides us, and then when they're ready, the director will come in for a couple of days and we go through replacing things with shots they think would be better and getting the episodes to time, because what's filmed is longer than the 22:20 minutes maximum. The editor gets the choice to say, for example, if I had to lose anything I'd lose *that* scene.'

> *'As a viewer you should watch something and not be irritated; you should see what you want to see.'*

The editor then has a meeting with the producer and the editor shows them the 'trims', the scenes or parts of scenes, that they have dropped. 'They might say yes, or no, that's a really important moment. Years ago I once had a Sarah Platt (Tina O'Brien) scene where she's simply scraping food off her plate into the bin. It didn't look like a really vital scene, but it was planting the scene of her thinking she was getting fat and didn't want to eat her food, and actually she was 12 years old and pregnant. We'd dumped this moment and they said no, we need this because it's actually the start of her being pregnant.

'At the end you have what's called picture lock and then it leaves the edit process and goes on to be finished, which means credits being added and dubbing.' Sophie recalls one close call. 'In 1997 we were about to go out, transmitting from London, and the executive producer suddenly appeared at quarter to seven – the episode was due to transmit at 7:30pm. She had reviewed the programme and felt that a child actor in a scene looked too upset, genuinely distressed, and she decided that the scene should not go out. As an assistant editor, I had to get the tape off the engineers who were preparing to transmit and watched awestruck as the editors worked their magic, deleted the scene, and the programme went out on time half an hour later. Last minute panic, but we pulled it together.'

Press and publicity

ONCE an episode is edited and finished, one department's job is to make sure people are watching it. That's one of the main jobs of the *Coronation Street* press office. Alison Sinclair, *Coronation Street's* chief publicity officer, describes it as putting bums on seats. 'If this was a production in a theatre I would be selling tickets, I would be doing publicity that would make people want to go and buy the tickets. When you're publicising a play or film and you want people to come and watch, you tease them, but you don't give away the ending. Our job is to publicise the show, to pull people in, let them know when big things are happening because sometimes you are trying to encourage lapsed viewers to come back, without giving away the ending and get them excited about what's coming up.'

The trick is appealing to the diehard viewers who really want to know what's coming up and are keen to take in everything they can about *Coronation Street*, plus the lapsed viewers or the light viewers, who dip in and out when they know there's something big happening. The press office is also responsible for protecting the brand. 'We have to protect the brand, because it is a hugely important brand to the company (ITV) and an important brand to the country, I believe,' says Alison. 'Anything we spot presswise that might damage the brand we have to nip in the bud.'

The press officers also publicise the actors in the show. 'My job is to get them to talk about their characters and the job they do. Some of them like to publicise themselves as actors, as celebrities and that's absolutely fine. The cast is a mixture of those who like celebrity and those who don't, so my job is to guide either of those down the path they wish to take but also, equally importantly, to protect them because sometimes coming into this show is a real shock.

'One of the things I do when people join the show is to sit them down and do the "welcome to the royal family" chat – so basically you have just married into the royal family (*Corrie* is the royal family of soaps!) and because you are part of this family you are going to have people wanting to know more about you than a) you want them to know; or b) more than you could ever imagine they want to know, and we help them manage that.'

Alison joined *Coronation Street* in 1993 and says it's changed massively. 'When I started there were two TV magazines (*TV Times* and *Radio Times*), two main women's mags (*Woman* and *Woman's Own*) and *Inside Soap* had just started, so that was it. All the newspapers obviously, but no online, so no social media. There is a very voracious group of online publications who have got more pages than a magazine ever had to fill, which they're updating all the time. Now, certainly on a programme night, there's much more

activity and reaction on social media. When I first started it could take weeks before you knew how a new family was bedding in or being received, now it's immediate.' One of the pieces of advice the press office gives the actors is not to Google themselves. 'There's always going to be the trolls and keyboard warriors, so accept this, block and delete.'

The large cast brings its own publicity challenges – the press office wants to make sure that anyone who wants a bite of the publicity cherry gets one. 'To be part of something I remember growing up with and that is still here and really going strong 60 years on and to be part of a team that helps introduce new fans to it, is fantastic.'

The biggest challenge for the press office is keeping the storylines secret. 'It's great when you get the newspapers and the onlines and the magazines to agree not to give away who was responsible for the factory collapse, not to give away who died, to not give away how Pat Phelan was going to leave the show. There are certain moments throughout the year when we speak to the media and we say please keep this secret. And the challenge for us as a team is to make sure, even though there are lots of theories, that people are still coming to the show and are surprised and shocked, but in a good way. And that's a daily challenge.'

Former assistant director and now vision mixer, Dayle Evans-Kar reveals the lengths the crew go to, to keep storylines out of the press when filming off site: 'We don't put exact locations on call sheets in order to prevent the paparazzi finding out where we are. When Rita married Ted Sullivan in 1992 we filmed it at a hotel in central Manchester. We didn't want them to get any pictures so we pretended they were coming out of the front, we set up lights and camera equipment, and then they went out of the back entrance. Then the photographers began chasing after the car!'

Another challenge is keeping older viewers watching, but also attracting younger ones. *Coronation Street's* YouTube and social media channels do a great job of teasing stories and engaging a younger audience. Alison says: 'What I love about *Corrie* is even the young fans that are watching and the young fans that are coming to the show now, they aren't just coming for younger characters that are their age that they can identify with, they love those older, really classic characters, so I think there's something for everyone. I think as long as it always maintains that feel, *Coronation Street* will be fine.'

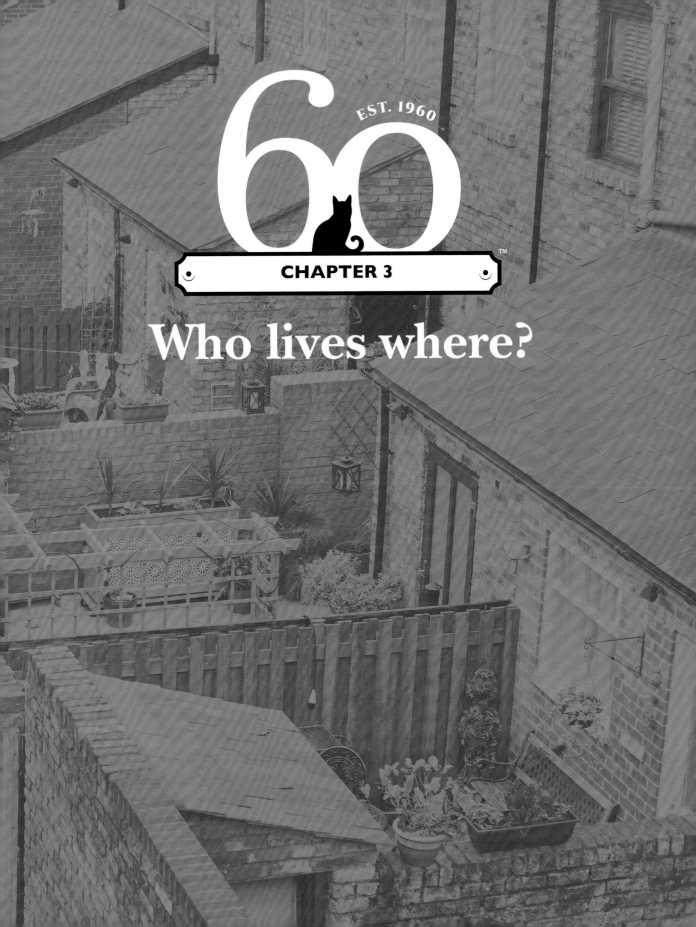

60
EST. 1960

CHAPTER 3

Who lives where?

WHEN *Coronation Street* began, it had to house just a couple of dozen characters. Over 60 years hundreds of characters have graced the cobbles, many living on that cobbled Weatherfield street. There are now more than 70 regular characters, and storylines have dictated that a good deal of them have lived at more than one Coronation Street address. Characters have married, divorced, moved in with lovers or fallen out with flatmates. Several were born on the Street and we have watched them grow up and move into their own Weatherfield homes.

What follows is a guide to who was living where on the Street by 2020, and which famous characters lived in the houses and flats before them. Here, *Coronation Street* actors past and present talk about their time on the Street. A list of the major *Coronation Street* characters from its 60 years can be found in the list of main characters on page 325.

The Rovers

'*Strong and ballsy with a sense of humour.*' Denise Welch, aka Natalie Barnes, on what a Rovers landlady needs to be.

It's been there since the start and is regarded as the very heart of *Coronation Street* – The Rovers Return Inn.

The little 'back street boozer', reminiscent of so many end-of-the-street pubs the land over, has seen more births, deaths and wedding parties than most register offices.

As iconic in soapland as the cobbles that line the street outside its familiar green doors, The Rovers, named after a pub in central Manchester's Withy Grove area, is where our favourite characters have socialised, celebrated, brawled, flirted, sang, laughed and cried.

Every *Coronation Street* fan has a top Rovers moment, whether it's Bet Lynch caught in the 1986 blaze, Martha Longhurst's death in the snug in 1964, baby Tracy's near death when a lorry crashed into the pub in 1979, mortal enemies Ken and Mike's punch-ups in the 1990s, Lucy telling Shelley they were both married to bigamous Peter in 2003 or, indeed, any mention of Betty's famous hotpot.

Located on the corner of Coronation Street and Rosamund Street, The Rovers, like the rest of the original street, was built in 1902. It was part of the Newton and Ridley brewery empire, and although the freehold was sold in 1995 it still sells Newton and Ridley ales.

The pub has seen several licensees and managers over the years – some of the best-loved *Coronation Street* characters have had their name over the door – and dozens of bar staff. The longest-serving employee was popular, level-headed Betty Williams (formerly Turpin) barmaid for 42 years until 2011 and keeper of that famous hotpot recipe. Betty Driver, who played Betty, is sadly missed by cast and crew. Her picture still has pride of place in The Rovers bar.

Denise Welch played Natalie Barnes née Horrocks, landlady of The Rovers from 1998 to 2000. She says: 'Over the four years I played Natalie, they had to soften her. She couldn't remain the bitch for too long, so they put her behind the bar at The Rovers and then made her landlady. It's a pivotal role and I am honoured to this day to be among a handful of women who has been the landlady of The Rovers Return. I'd watched it since the Annie Walker days, it was unbelievable.

'When you're the landlady of The Rovers, for some family members there's no other job you could do that would ever be as good. You are behind the bar an awful lot though, so when you shot a scene in, say, the Corner Shop it was like going on location!'

Amanda Barrie, who played Alma Baldwin, remembers that The Rovers was stressful to do scenes in 'because a lot of people are in there a lot of the time, so if you mess up you all have to go from the start. Plus, I was the only member of the cast who could never remember which way the door opened. Every time I did it I rocked the entire set!'

The original layout of The Rovers comprised the public bar, the select and the snug.

The snug was a small room with access to the bar, and in the pub's earlier days (pre-1960s) it was the only area women were allowed to drink in. This was the domain of harridan Ena Sharples and her pals Minnie Caldwell and Martha Longhurst. Over many a milk stout, the three would gossip to their hearts' content about their neighbours. William Roache refers to them as 'the Gorgons of The Rovers snug'. In 1964, Martha died of a heart attack, sitting alone in the snug while the locals enjoyed a singsong round the piano in the next room.

The select bar was used for functions, performances and wedding parties. Stan and Hilda Ogden celebrated their 25th and their 40th wedding anniversaries there.

The entrance to the pub has remained relatively unchanged, but after a fire destroyed the building in 1986, the pub was modernised by the brewery, with the snug and select being removed and the public bar expanded. New upholstered seating areas were introduced.

A smoking shelter was built in the back yard, as a nod to the law banning smoking in public places that was introduced in Britain in 2007, and after another blaze in 2013 the pub was redecorated.

Before the Grape Street set was built (see page 146), filming occasionally took place on location at The Amalgamated Inn, close to Archie Street, the original inspiration for *Coronation Street*'s very first designer Denis Parkin.

Current Rovers occupants

Johnny, Jenny and Carla Connor and Peter Barlow,
played by Richard Hawley, Sally Ann Matthews, Alison King and Chris Gascoyne

Johnny Connor made his entrance on Coronation Street in 2015. He arrived from Spain to track down son Aidan who had used £100,000 of his father's money to invest in Underworld. Widower Johnny was revealed to be Carla Connor's (née Donovan) father, and although Aidan and sister Kate were horrified to hear of their father's affair, they soon accepted Carla as their sibling.

Johnny married Jenny Bradley in 2017, and in 2018 he was the one to discover Aidan's suicide. Grief drove him briefly into the arms of Liz McDonald, but he and Jenny moved past this and ran The Rovers together successfully, despite his multiple sclerosis diagnosis.

Before joining *Coronation Street*, Richard Hawley was best known for appearing in *Prime Suspect*, *Family Affairs* and movie *Love Actually*.

Sally Ann Matthews first appeared on *Coronation Street* from 1986 to 1991 as troubled teenager Jenny Bradley who was fostered by Rita Fairclough after the death of her mother. She reappeared briefly in 1993 and returned as a regular artist in 2016.

Now married to Johnny Connor, Jenny is a favourite character for many viewers. Her storylines have included the Alan Bradley tram death, the kidnap of Kevin's son, a brush with alcoholism and progression from factory cleaner to landlady of The Rovers.

As a teenager, Sally Ann was a member of the Oldham Theatre Workshop. 'I never really had designs to be an actress,' she says. 'Everyone I knew had proper jobs but did a bit of amateur dramatics too, so I never thought about it as a career for one second…When I came for the role of Jenny I didn't even know what I was auditioning for. When I got the script and saw "Ivy", "Hilda" and "Rita" I thought, oh my God! It was probably good as I wasn't so nervous.'

Sally Ann was seen by casting director Judi Hayfield and secured a recall. 'I had to call my agent from school on the payphone to find out I'd been called back,' she recalls. She met the producer and Mark Eden, who played Alan Bradley. 'And that was it, I got the role.' Initially, given a three-month contract with a three-month option, 'then it just grew and grew and I was here for over five years.'

When Sally Ann first came back in 1993, it was a very deliberate decision because she was 23 and still getting offered rebellious teenager parts. She wanted to show as an actor that she'd grown up. 'I came back for six weeks or so and that worked because after that I was getting offered more age-appropriate things.'

Sally Ann did theatre and toured a lot. In 2010 she was approached to be part of the 50th anniversary celebrations. 'I thought, why not? I realised I was really proud of *Corrie* and anyway, it's never going to leave me, this part. It took another four years though for the right story to come along.'

Sally Ann came back in 2015 for a six-month storyline which saw Jenny grieving for a deceased child and kidnapping Kevin's son Jack, and was asked to stay longer. 'I said yes! I've been lucky, I've had great stories. It's the 60th year and the show has such a wealth of history I think viewers like to hark back to characters they've seen grow up.

'When I joined it was the weekend after the 25th anniversary and I was here for the 30th. Now at the 60th, it's scary! But when I look back at the things I've done, and that I've got married and had two children, of course it's that long. Back in the day we had two episodes a week, rehearsals – it was a very different beast. I think there were only 27 regulars when I was first in it, now there are more than 70. But it has to move with the times and I think that's one of the triumphs of the *Street*, it's kept a lot of its roots. In reality, those cobbles would be unlikely to still be there on such a busy street, but ours are going nowhere!'

Sally Ann took part in a special *Coronation Street's DNA Secrets* in 2018 and was astounded to discover she was related to another *Coronation Street* star, one she had worked with occasionally on the *Street*, Amanda Barrie, who played Alma.

'We rarely had scenes together, but Amanda bought me a beautiful jug for my 21st birthday and it's been on my kitchen shelf in every house I've been in. I always felt a connection with her.'

Working on *Coronation Street*, Sally Ann says she feels like a custodian of this historic television landmark. 'For the show to still be going in this climate and to still be getting the viewing figures it gets when we churn out six episodes a week is fantastic.'

'Peter running a pub is like putting a cat in charge of an aquarium.'
Carla Connor

Carla Connor is current *Coronation Street*'s Elsie Tanner – the temptress with a love life as chequered as a draughtsboard. Always ready with a quip, life has made her a tough cookie and she's careful who she exposes her vulnerable side to.

Arriving in Coronation Street when the Connors were introduced, she inherited shares in Underworld after her husband was killed in a car crash. Traumatic events in her life include a rape, kidney failure and psychosis and have made her one of the *Street*'s most compelling characters. With a toss of her lustrous dark hair and a slug of red wine, the woman with the sharpest cheekbones in soap is a match for anyone. Her on-off relationship with Peter Barlow has been a recurring theme over the years, but it's her friendship with Roy, and previously Hayley, that brought out her softer side.

Alison King has played Carla since 2006, with a break from 2016 to 2017, although she first appeared in the *Street* two years earlier as Mrs Fanshaw, an attractive married woman who seduced Jason Grimshaw.

Alison worked as a dental nurse before landing acting roles. Commenting on why Carla, and indeed the extended Connor family, have proved so popular, Alison says: 'On the whole, *Corrie*'s favourite female characters consist of damaged, strong, feisty, funny women. Carla fits all of these and so the writers can have so much fun with her and are able to throw her into any situation to battle through and survive. However, she has a vulnerability and other layers to keep her real and this lets the public connect with her through moving storylines, such as her rape and psychosis – these are things that people suffer in real life and hopefully they can really connect with the stories we play out.

'It's been wonderful to play Carla and to help create her annoying character, voice, physical traits and to develop her different layers too. It's an honour to work with all the Connors, especially Kym (Marsh, who played Michelle) as we started at roughly the same time.

'As for the storylines, they've all been a challenge and a joy in their own way. They vary so much because they span so many weeks and months with different directors and cast. I love the comedy about *Corrie*; if there's a scene where I can squeeze a bit in, I always make sure I do.

'The best thing about working on *Coronation Street* is that it's like a big family. The diversity of age and experience within the cast makes it a beautiful thing. The crew and production guys have become lifelong friends and, well, my *Corrie* family. If I hadn't joined *Corrie*, I wouldn't have had my beautiful daughter Daisy May. She is my favourite thing about my time on the cobbles.'

When Alison decided to return to *Coronation Street* after time away to work on other projects and spend time with family, she told ITV.com: 'It was like pulling on an old sock or an old pair of stiletto boots! My first two scenes were with Shayne [Ward] on location and the crew who are like family. I got butterflies from excitement about seeing everyone, but not from nerves. It was so lovely, like I had never been away and I was happy I made the decision to return.'

A self-destructive alcoholic bigamist who blames his absent father Ken for a lot of his misfortunes, Peter Barlow has careered from one relationship to another, but it's his love for Carla that brought out the best in him as he nursed her back to health following her psychotic episodes. Peter owned The Rovers for a short time in 2017 when he was in a relationship with Toyah Battersby, while he and Carla were living there with Johnny and Jenny Connor by summer 2020.

Ex-navy man and former bookie Peter Barlow has been married five times, committing bigamy when he married wife Shelley while still married to Lucy (the mother of his son Simon). He has battled with the booze, had a brush with death during the tram crash of 2010 and been arrested for the murder of his mistress Tina McIntyre in 2014.

Chris Gascoyne was the seventh actor to play the role of Peter Barlow and has appeared in the role periodically since 2000. He trained at the Central School of Speech and Drama and has acted in many television shows and on stage, including at the National Theatre and in the West End since he was a teenager. In 2016 Chris Gascoyne took a short break from *Coronation Street* to appear on stage alongside fellow cast member David Neilson in a tour of Samuel Beckett's *Endgame*, with both actors enjoying excellent reviews.

Key previous residents

Jack and Annie Walker, played by Arthur Leslie and Doris Speed

'You can't rehearse majesty, Mr Tatlock. It's something you've either got or you haven't.' Annie Walker

Doris Speed (1899–1994) portrayed snooty Rovers landlady and sometime Mayoress of Weatherfield from 1960 to 1983 so well that more than one fan of the show suspected she may be as snobbish in real life. Nothing could be further from the truth. She was highly respected and popular among the cast and was known for her sense of humour and dedication to her craft. Her fan mail reflected this. During her years on *Coronation Street*, Doris (or Annie) received more fan mail than any other actor. William Roache remembers she was a fanatical bridge player and would take on members of the cast during rest periods.

Tony Warren had written the part of Annie Walker with Doris in mind. He remembered her from the theatre and also worked with her when he was a child actor. Barbara Knox remembers Doris: 'The delightful Doris Speed, what a raconteur, what a clever lady she was. And she'd been in showbusiness all her life, going from digs to digs as a child because her parents had been in the business.'

Doris Speed, who first stepped on a stage at the age of three, never married and looked after her mother Ada for many years, died, aged 95, in a nursing home. She had been smoking a cigarette and reading a copy of *To Sir, With Love* by E R Braithwaite before she quietly passed away in her sleep.

Arthur Leslie (1899–1970) played genial Jack Walker from 1960 until his death in 1970. He worked in theatres in the north-west of England from the age of 17 and after serving in the First World War, was an actor/director at The Hippodrome in Wigan. He was also a playwright. His wife Betty, who he met in rep, and son Tony both had walk-on parts in *Coronation Street* over the years.

Bet and Alec Gilroy, played by Julie Goodyear and Roy Barraclough

'I've got tights older than you.' Bet to a young punter

Julie Goodyear turned Bet Lynch into one of *Coronation Street*'s true icons. With her bleached blonde beehive and love of leopard print she was instantly recognisable, and the archetypal Rovers barmaid. Beneath her wisecracking, give-as-good-as-you-get exterior she could be vulnerable, used to the hard knocks life sent her way, and viewers loved her.

Former factory worker Bet began her 25-year stint in The Rovers as a barmaid in 1970. She had first appeared for several episodes in 1966. After leaving in 1995, she returned twice, in 2002 and 2003.

Bet had given up a son for adoption when she was 16 and this came back to haunt her. Always dressed to kill and ready to flaunt her assets, although sometimes with her dress on backwards, she went from one romantic disaster to another, memorably with flash factory owner Mike Baldwin, until, in 1987, she married former showbiz agent Alec. Ostensibly, they were ill-matched and she did so in order to take over the pub, but even though the marriage did not last, the pair were genuinely fond of each other.

Bet may have been a man-eater who wives in Weatherfield were wary of, but she actually formed some solid and supportive female friendships with barmaids Betty, Liz and Raquel. Even disdainful Annie came to regard her as a hard worker who pulled in the punters as easily as she pulled a pint. From starting out as an under-dressed young barmaid, Bet approached a glamorous middle age wise from all her experience, with a tough outer shell but still a romantic at heart.

Julie Goodyear was born in Bury, Greater Manchester, and was a member of Oldham Repertory Theatre before her longest stint in the *Street*. Beverley Callard as Liz McDonald played opposite Julie for several years. She says: 'To me, Julie was amazing. I loved doing two-handers with her, neither of us suffers fools gladly. I never had a wrong word with her and in The Rovers she taught me everything I knew. She was magic.'

Julie received the Special Recognition Award at the 1995 National Television Awards, and since leaving *Coronation Street* has appeared briefly in soap *Hollyoaks*, and a number of reality TV shows. In 2012 she was the seventh housemate to be evicted from the *Celebrity Big Brother* house.

Theatrical agent Alec Gilroy appeared as Rita Littlewood's agent early on in *Coronation Street*'s history, but it was his full-time return in 1986 as manager of the Graffiti Club on Rosamund Street that saw the character grow into a *Street* favourite. He may have been pompous and always careful with his money, but he was also sharp-witted and provided many comic moments behind The Rovers bar with Bet, Jack and Raquel.

Beverley Callard remembers working with Roy Barraclough (1935–2017) on The Rovers set with great affection. 'I had

amazing comedy with Julie Goodyear and Roy Barraclough, Bill Tarmey and Betty Driver. Those were my favourite days. One of the best times was when Roy Barraclough and I had to work with a real tarantula in The Rovers kitchen. The first spider they got was a Mexican bird-eating spider and it was in this glass case. We couldn't see the spider at first – there was gravel and leaves and a log, but we couldn't see it. Then we realised it was what we thought was the log! It was that big. Its body was the size of two of my fists.

'Roy said: "That's no spider, it's a ****** lobster, and I won't be working with that!" However, we were on set with this spider and we were absolutely terrified. But the spider was so big that on camera and on the monitor it looked rubber, it didn't look real, so they had to change it, get a smaller tarantula replacement. I had to stand with my hands behind me on the work surface and let it run over my fingers. We were terrified but oh, we laughed so much.'

Denise Welch (Natalie) adds: 'Roy used to have me in stitches. Someone gave me a little jug as a present from a holiday and Roy and I would put it in different sets to see how often it would be on the telly without anyone noticing. We'd be watching the monitors and Roy would go: "Eyes left, it's in Gail's front room now."'

Before Roy Barraclough joined *Coronation Street* long term as unscrupulous Alec Gilroy he was famous for partnering with comic Les Dawson in their gossipy bosom-nudging 'Cissie and Ada' sketches. The former engineering draughtsman with a love of amateur dramatics turned professional in 1962. Many theatre and TV appearances followed, including *The War of Darkie Pilbeam* written by Tony Warren in 1968. After 12 years, Roy left *Coronation Street* in 1998 when Alec sold The Rovers to Natalie and left for Brighton.

Licensees

Jack and Annie Walker (1937–70), Annie Walker (1970–84) Billy Walker (1984)
Bet and Alec Gilroy (1985–95)
Jack and Vera Duckworth (1995–98, with Alec Gilroy 1997–98)
Natalie Barnes (1998–2000)
Fred Elliott, Duggie Ferguson and Mike Baldwin (2000–06)
Steve and Liz McDonald (2006–11)
Stella Price and Karl Munro (2011–13)
Steve and Liz McDonald with Michelle Connor (2013–17)
Peter Barlow and Toyah Battersby (2017–18)
Johnny and Jenny Connor (2018–)

Barmen

Ivan Cheveski, Sam Leach, Jacko Ford, Terry Bradshaw, Fred Gee, Eddie Yeats, Wilf Starkey, Frank Mills, Jack Duckworth, Charlie Bracewell, Charlie Whelan, Bill Webster, Andy McDonald, Sandy Hunter, Martin Platt, Gary Mallett, Spider Nugent, Vinny Sorrell, Jim McDonald, Peter Barlow, Timothy Spencer, Harry Flagg, Ciaran McCarthy, Sean Tully, Vernon Tomlin, Lewis Archer, Jason Grimshaw, Tony Stewart, Henry Newton, Ryan Connor.

Cleaners

Martha Longhurst, Hilda Ogden, Clara Midgeley, Amy Burton, Sandra Stubbs, Tricia Armstrong, Joyce Smedley, Vera Duckworth, Edna Miller, Harry Flagg, Anna Windass.

Barwomen

Concepta Riley, Nona Willis, Doreen Lostock, Irma Ogden, Emily Nugent, Lucille Hewitt, Betty Turpin, Bet Lynch, Blanche Hunt, Gail Potter, Dawn Perks, Arlene Jones, Carole Fairbanks, Diane Hawkins, Suzie Birchall, Kath Goodwin, Maureen Barnett, Gloria Todd, Sally Seddon, Alison Dougherty, Margo Richardson, Sandra Stubbs, Vera Duckworth, Tina Fowler, Megan Morgan, Liz McDonald, Angie Freeman, Raquel Wolstenhulme, Tanya Pooley, Jenny Bradley, Carol Starkey, Lorraine Ramsden, Tricia Armstrong, Joyce Smedley, Judy Mallett, Samantha Failsworth, Natalie Horrocks, Lorraine Brownlow, Leanne Tilsley, Amy Goskirke, Toyah Battersby, Geena Gregory, Shelley Unwin, Edna Miller, Eve Elliott, Linda Baldwin, Maria Sutherland, Tracy Barlow, Bev Unwin, Violet Wilson, Michelle Connor, Lauren Wilson, Becky Granger, Kelly Crabtree, Poppy Morales, Tina McIntyre, Eva Price, Sunita Alahan, Gloria Price, Mandy Kamara, Eileen Grimshaw, Sarah Platt, Erica Holroyd, Gemma Winter, Emma Brooker, Charlie Wood, Carla Connor.

Concepta

Emily and Betty

Lewis and Gloria

Natalie

Bev

Leanne

Karl and Sunita

Tina and Matt

Tracy and Liz

No 1 Coronation Street

Tracy and Steve McDonald, and Amy and Ken Barlow, played by Kate Ford, Simon Gregson, Elle Mulvaney and William Roache

No 1 Coronation Street, like its neighbouring terraces, was built in 1902. Albert Tatlock lived there until his death in 1984. After he was widowed in 1959, his niece Valerie moved in to look after him. She became next door neighbour Ken's first wife, and Albert looked upon Ken as a son, selling the house to him in 1983. Ken, his third wife Deirdre and daughter Tracy lived there and when Ken and Deirdre split up for a while, Samir Rachid, Deirdre's third husband, moved in. Ken had mortgaged No 1 to buy the *Weatherfield Recorder* and, when Ken and Deirdre separated, their finances meant that she became No 1's owner (1990). She sold it to Mike Baldwin four years later when she went to live in Morocco and he rented it out to Tricia Armstrong and her son Jamie, before selling it to Ken less than a year later.

'Tracy Barlow, I mean, even her initials are a killer disease!' Eileen Grimshaw

The daughter of Deirdre and Ray Langton, toxic Tracy left a trail of destruction in her wake as she grew up to become *Coronation Street*'s resident sociopath. Spending most of the 1980s 'going to my bedroom to listen to my tapes', Tracy became a troubled teenager – experimenting with drugs left her needing a kidney transplant – and then a very troublesome adult. Utterly ruthless and totally self-absorbed, whenever Tracy is involved in goings-on on the *Street* you can be sure there'll be drama.

She tried to sell her baby, she murdered her boyfriend in cold blood, she spent time in jail and committed perjury in her bid for a reduced sentence, she inadvertently committed arson causing even more deaths. Oh, and she became something of a specialist in wrecking other people's relationships, especially those of her much-married husband Steve and mother-in-law Liz. She'll think nothing of bedding another woman's fella if that will get her what she wants. Sleeping with half-brothers David Platt and Nick Tilsley within days of each other merely meant two more notches on her bedpost. Married four times herself, to Robert Preston, Roy Cropper (after bedding him for a bet, although the marriage itself was never consummated) and twice to Steve McDonald, the father of her daughter Amy, scheming Tracy does not do things by halves.

Disliked and distrusted by many *Street* residents – as Hayley once yelled at Tracy: 'Your mother's ashamed of you. Your daughter barely knows you. Your donor kidney would reject you if it could' – the fearsome florist has been known to strike up real and lasting female friendships, with Beth Sutherland and lately Mary Taylor, who works for her at Preston's Petals.

Patti Clare, who plays Mary, loves the often comic scenes she gets to do with Kate Ford. She says: 'It's been great working with Kate in Preston's Petals – a partnership that we didn't realise would gel. It really softens Tracy and it gives Mary a bit of an edge because she doesn't take any nonsense from Tracy. It's a really nice dynamic.'

And despite making mum Deirdre's life hell, Tracy was distraught when Deirdre died, showing she does have a heart in there somewhere.

Tracy has been played by three actors as well as Salford-born Kate Ford, who took over the role in 2002. Kate, who trained at the Webber Douglas Academy of Dramatic Art in London, picked up the British Soap Award for Best Bitch in 2004 and 2005, and Best Actress in 2007. She left the *Street* in 2007 before returning full-time in 2010.

The McDonald family arrived in Weatherfield in 1989 and tearaway teenage twins Steve and Andy soon made their mark. As a young man Steve's gambling and failed business ventures got him heavily in debt to loan sharks. Eventually, one of his endeavours took off. As co-owner of Street Cars taxi firm and later owner of The Rovers for a while, Steve carved out a living, recently supplemented with an occasional few quid from dressing up mate Tim Metcalfe's horse Tiny as a children's party unicorn.

Steve has walked down the aisle seven times in the 30 years he has lived on Coronation Street, although that includes twice with Karen Phillips and twice with Tracy. He has actually had nine wedding days, with his first attempts to marry Vicky Arden and later Becky Granger, both being halted.

At many points in the 1980s a young Tracy would go up to her room 'to listen to my music'. Characters such as Deirdre often referred to off-screen Tracy being 'upstairs listening to her tapes', and so many fans took to social media to express their delight at Peter's rediscovery of some dusty old boxes of cassettes in December 2016.

Father to Amy and Oliver, both results of one-night stands, with Tracy and Leanne respectively, Steve also grieved for the loss of baby Ruairi with Michelle Connor following a late miscarriage. In 2019 he discovered ditsy Rovers employee Emma Brooker was his daughter from a relationship with hairdresser Fiona Middleton years before and he set about building a relationship with her. No longer the young Jack-the-lad, Steve has settled into affable middle-age, putting up with regular hen-pecking from bossy Tracy and exasperation from permanently embarrassed Amy.

Actor Simon Gregson was still at school in Stockport, Greater Manchester, when he auditioned for *Coronation Street* alongside schoolmate Nicholas Cochrane, who played brother Andy, and despite his lack of experience, went on to become a firm favourite with viewers, being nominated for, or winning, more than a dozen comedy and acting awards.

After her birth, Amy Barlow was briefly named Patience Cropper after her heartless mother Tracy sold her to Roy and Hayley Cropper for £25,000, conning Roy into believing he was her father following a drunken night. After a change of heart, Tracy renamed the baby Amy and used her whenever possible to win Steve, Amy's real father, back.

Amy lived with Steve for three years when Tracy was sent to jail for killing boyfriend Charlie Stubbs, and on Tracy's release she did everything she could to stop her parents' perpetual squabbling. No wonder she was suspicious when they finally reunited.

At 14, Amy became pregnant with 17-year-old Tyler Jefferies' baby and, accompanied by Bethany, had an abortion, despite Tracy and Steve intending to raise the baby as their own.

Elle Mulvaney is the eighth child to play Amy, including the youngsters who played her as a baby and toddler. Elle started acting at the Carol Godby Theatre Workshop in Bury, Greater Manchester, and in 2017 won the Best Young Actor category at the British Soap Awards, having been nominated three times before.

'I'm here in this old life, same old street, having achieved nothing in the past 50 years except a string of embarrassing children who barely know who I am.' Ken Barlow

From the very beginning Ken Barlow has been a part of *Coronation Street* and to many Ken *is* the *Street*. He has mellowed from an idealist young left-leaning university student at odds with his working-class roots to become *Coronation Street's* elder statesman. After a brief relocation to Stillwaters retirement complex in early 2020, Ken quickly found that the change of scene wasn't for him and for now he is back at No 1 with Tracy, Steve and Amy.

Ken has had his fair share of ups and downs on the *Street*. His mother Ida died after she was hit by a bus; his daughter also perished in a road accident. He discovered he had a son he never knew about, Lawrence Cunningham, and another son, Peter, is an alcoholic.

Ken had five children altogether, including adopted daughter Tracy, who arguably has caused him more problems than the others put together. He married four times, to Valerie Tatlock, who died in a fire leaving him with young twins Peter and Susan; to Janet Reid, who killed herself after they separated; and twice to Deirdre Langton. Staid, cerebral Ken, as a younger man, proved quite irresistible to many other women and he had more than his fair share of girlfriends.

His relationship with old Uncle Albert and later his sharp-tongued mother-in-law Blanche Hunt delighted viewers, but it was his ongoing feud with Mike Baldwin, following Deirdre's affair with him, that made the headlines and led to repercussions that continue to impact life on the Street today.

Lately, Ken, as an octogenarian, proved he could still boast an attractive woman on his arm in the form of Claudia Colby (Rula Lenska), Audrey's hairdressing nemesis. 'I get on incredibly well with William Roache, we just hit it off together from the beginning,' says Rula Lenska. 'I like the way the romance with Ken grew, not over the top or gratuitous, it was a subtle affair.'

Claudia managed to put a smile back on widower Ken's face after the death of Deirdre and was there to support him through one of the more recent traumas to befall the Barlows, daughter-in-law Sinead Osbourne's death from cervical cancer and the subsequent suffering of his son Daniel, Sinead's husband.

Ken was at the centre of a 'who attacked Ken?' mystery in 2017 that had notes of *King Lear* when he was pushed down the stairs. His children and grandson Adam were all in the frame, but when Daniel was revealed to be the culprit Ken forgave him, to the anger of his siblings.

Ken has had many different jobs over the years, from teacher and newspaper editor to trolley pusher and taxi driver. He has been an adulterer and an absent father, he has had a chaotic love life and he never achieved what he knew he could do professionally, but for all his flaws he remains the stalwart of the *Street*. And after 60 years, a world record-breaking one at that.

Key previous residents

Albert Tatlock, played by Jack Howarth

Ken's uncle by marriage, Albert Tatlock, a retired town hall clerk, lived at No 1 Coronation Street with his wife Bessie, who died in 1959, and their daughter Beattie. Albert preferred his niece Valerie to his daughter and was happy when she married Ken Barlow. Ken and Albert consoled each other when Valerie died and Ken periodically lodged at No 1. Albert even sold the house to Ken and Deirdre in 1983 rather than leave it to Beattie.

Becoming more crotchety and obstinate the older he got, Albert enjoyed his allotment – and a tot of rum, especially if someone else was paying. To supplement his pension he worked as an occasional caretaker and the gruffest lollipop man in Weatherfield.

The son of a comedian, Jack Howarth (1896–1984) was born in Rochdale, Greater Manchester, and went to school with future songstress and film star Gracie Fields. He was a stage actor, ran a cinema and later a rep company in north Wales. He began in the role of Albert at the age of 64 and died just weeks after his last appearance in 1984.

William Roache remembers meeting Jack when he was a boy boarding at Rydal School. Jack's son was a senior given the job of looking after the new boys. Through him, William met Jack who he described in his autobiography *Ken and Me* as 'this little, round, potato-shaped chap…who ran the theatre repertory company in Colwyn Bay. I remember being very impressed by the ivory-topped cane he carried'. Twenty years later they were founding cast members, becoming two of the longest-serving actors on the show.

Deirdre Hunt was engaged to Billy Walker for a while but broke that off to marry Ray Langton, father of her only child Tracy. Ray had been her boss at Fairclough and Langton Builders, where young Deirdre was a secretary. Ray's affair with Janice Stubbs ended their relationship, and in 1981 Deirdre wed Ken Barlow. Their first marriage was a rollercoaster. Deirdre, bored with Ken, had an explosive affair with Mike Baldwin and, later, Ken's affair with Wendy Crozier ended the marriage.

Deirdre's young Moroccan husband Samir Rachid died when he was attacked on his way to donate a kidney to Tracy, and Deirdre was later jailed for fraud after being duped by handsome 'pilot' Jon Lindsay. The 'Free the Weatherfield One' campaign even reached the House of Commons, when Prime Minister at the time Tony Blair mentioned the travesty of justice.

Ken and Deirdre, of course, were eventually reunited and a highlight of their later years was the often comic dynamic between her, Ken and Deirdre's mother Blanche.

Deirdre worked in the Corner Shop and later in the Medical Centre. She was also a local councillor for a while, but was often annoyed at Ken for loftily treating her work as less important than his own.

Valerie Barlow, played by Anne Reid

Ken's first wife Valerie was Albert Tatlock's niece. The mother of young twins, she died after she was electrocuted, which led to a fire in the maisonettes. Hairdresser Valerie and Ken had married in 1962, and despite Ken's fling with another woman, they rubbed along together fairly happily, planning to emigrate before Val died.

Anne Reid went on to star on stage and screen, most memorably in *Dinnerladies* with Victoria Wood, *The Mother* and *Last Tango in Halifax*. It was while she was working on *Coronation Street* that she met her late husband Peter Eckersley, a former head of drama at Granada and a writer and producer on the *Street*.

Deirdre Barlow, played by Anne Kirkbride

'Ken! DO something...' Deirdre Barlow

With her large glasses and throaty laugh, Anne Kirkbride (1954–2015) played the much-loved Deirdre Barlow from 1972 until 2014.

Oldham-born Anne Kirkbride joined Oldham Repertory Theatre as a stage manager before turning to acting. She posthumously received the Outstanding Achievement award at the 2015 British Soap Awards.

Beverley Callard was great friends with Anne Kirkbride off set. She recalls: 'I used to love the scenes with Liz and Deirdre because usually if Deirdre was in trauma Liz would say the last line of a two-hander, and vice versa, and the line would be "Why's life so flaming complicated!". We must have said that line 30 times! There's a cartoon that Anne Kirkbride's dad (Jack, a cartoonist for the *Oldham Evening Chronicle*) did of Liz and Deirdre, one for each of us, on the cobbles, outside The Rovers, both of us in tears.

'Anne was marvellous to work with, she never got her lines wrong, she was never late. She used to say at the beginning of a scene, as the director would say they were going for a take: "OK, I'll click into Deirdreland then".'

Blanche Hunt, played by Maggie Jones

'Good looks are a curse. You and Ken should count yourselves very lucky.' Blanche to Deirdre

Retired corset-maker Blanche Hunt had raised her only child Deirdre alone following the death of her husband Donald when Deirdre was a young child. Acerbic and often tactlessly honest, her cutting witticisms became the stuff of legend. Even children were shown no mercy. She once asked Simon Barlow: 'Like *Postman Pat*, do you? So long as you remember it's a work of fiction. Early in the morning, when the day is dawning? Your real Postman Pat rolls up around noon wearing a pair of shorts and his breakfast. And, if he's not chucking elastic bands like confetti, he'll be rifling through your birthday cards for ready cash, or leaving your valuables out on the step.'

Blanche left Weatherfield in 1976 and when she returned in 1999, she moved in with Ken and Deirdre, into the front room that had been Uncle Albert's. She liked to fill her time running down Ken with a deadpan delivery, and going to funerals. Blanche died during a trip to Portugal, leaving Deirdre and Tracy upset, and a big Blanche-shaped hole in No 1.

Blanche was originally played in two episodes by Patricia Cutts, who took her own life in 1974. Maggie Jones (1934–2009) played Blanche Hunt from 1974 until 1976 and reappeared occasionally before returning as a regular character in 1999 after featuring in many other TV shows. Thanks to Blanche's often outrageous caustic comments she won Best Comedy Performance in 2005 and 2008 at the British Soap Awards.

No 3 Coronation Street

Ed, Aggie, Michael and James Bailey, played by Trevor Michael Georges, Lorna Laidlaw, Ryan Russell and Nathan Graham

No 3 Coronation Street, originally the Barlows' home and empty between 1964 and 1968, was for many years home to Emily Bishop and her lodgers. One of these, Norris Cole, was given the house by Emily on the agreement she could continue living there. When Emily, and later Norris, left the *Street* the show's newest family, the Baileys, bought the property in 2019. The house had retained its slightly dated look for many years and it was when builder Ed and nurse Aggie Bailey moved in with sons wannabe entrepreneur Michael and footballer James that it was renovated.

In their first few months the Baileys hit the ground running with some talking point activities – Michael's money-making schemes included a Winter Wonderland that was the setting for some festive high drama, while James struggled to tell his father, or his football club that he is gay.

Lorna Laidlaw, who plays Aggie, acted on daytime soap *Doctors* for eight years, occasionally directing the show as well as many plays. 'I was a bit reluctant to jump from soap to soap but did so because

Corrie is an institution in Britain, not just a soap; it's held in such high regard, it's the queen of soaps.

'The Baileys are a family that's rooted on the Street now, they're two doors up from The Rovers and next door to Ken. They've done a restructure of the house, which is interesting, because some of the houses on Coronation Street are like characters, they've generally stayed the same. But this family has turned that house upside down and modernised it. For all of us it has been an amazing experience; the first black family in 60 years to come into the show. The response was global. It created a lot of interest from the black community, and Manchester is a very multi-cultural city so it's a good thing.

'With dad Ed being a builder and getting to connect with lots of people, mum working in the hospital and a son who's an entrepreneur, the family has moulded themselves into other people's stories as well as their own instead of them being a little entity on their own.'

Lorna remembers *Coronation Street* as a child because of the women, she says. 'They were amazing individual characters who drove scenes, who were the matriarchs of the whole programme. The men hovered around them, they were the focus, they were the moon and the stars that everything else floated around.'

Key previous residents

Frank, Ida and David Barlow, played by Frank Pemberton, Noel Dyson and Alan Rothwell

Ken Barlow's father, mother and brother were played respectively by Frank Pemberton, Noel Dyson and Alan Rothwell. Noel Dyson was the first of the original actors to leave *Coronation Street*. In September 1961 her character Ida, a caring and homely woman, was killed by a bus. Frank Pemberton left three years later and Alan Rothwell, whose character married Irma Ogden (Sandra Gough) and died off-screen in a car crash in Australia in 1970, departed in 1968.

Emily Bishop, played by Eileen Derbyshire

'I've always wanted to be stormy, passionate and tempestuous. But you can't be, not when you're born with a tidy mind.' Emily Bishop

Kindly and religious Emily Bishop, played by Eileen Derbyshire from 1961 to 2016 (with two additional guest appearances in 2019) – had her fair share of heartache on the Street. A failed engagement to Leonard Swindley (Arthur Lowe) was followed by the murder of her lay preacher husband Ernest Bishop in a botched robbery (see page 170) and marriage to bigamous Arnold Swain. Emily took in many lodgers over the years, an ideal vehicle to bring new characters to the Street, several of whom became firm *Coronation Street* favourites.

Street stalwart Eileen Derbyshire was born in Urmston, Manchester, in 1931 (her character Emily is two years older than Eileen), she trained at what is now the Royal Northern College of Music in Manchester, and was a speech and drama teacher before acting full time. She worked in repertory theatre and radio before joining *Coronation Street* as 'Miss Nugent' as she was credited at first, in 1961.

Norris Cole, played by Malcolm Hebden

Nosey Norris, bane of Rita's life and object of Mary's affections, lodged with Emily at No 3 from 2000. With money from his brother Ramsay's (Andrew Sachs) will he bought The Kabin, where he worked for Rita. Emily gifted Norris No 3 in 2013. Norris was married three times, firstly to Myrtle, then the fearsome Angela, and, in 2017, to Mary (but only so they could enter a Mr and Mrs competition to try to win a round-the-world trip). Norris moved to Edinburgh in 2018, sold the Kabin and got engaged to Emily's niece, Freda, in 2019, sold his house to the Baileys, then moved back to the north-west to live at Stillwaters' retirement complex with Freda in 2020.

Before taking the role of Norris, Burnley-raised actor Malcolm Hebden had appeared in *Coronation Street* in 1975 as Carlos, a Spanish love interest of Mavis Riley. In 2006, Malcolm and Barbara Knox won Best Onscreen Partnership at the British Soap Awards. Malcolm was an accomplished stage actor before joining *Coronation Street* and was associate director of the Stephen Joseph Theatre in Scarborough, North Yorkshire.

Percy Sugden, played by Bill Waddington

'When you've made gravy under gunfire you can do anything.'
Percy Sugden

When opinionated pensioner Percy Sugden wasn't putting people down he was actively avoiding the attentions of amorous lilac-haired Phyllis Pearce (Jill Summers). Widowed and childless, the former Army Catering Corps cook and Community Centre caretaker lodged along with his budgie Randy with Emily at No 3 from 1988 until 1997. Briefly engaged to Maud Grimes, he moved into a retirement home when the noisy Battersbys moved into the Street.

Bill Waddington (1916–2000) was a music hall performer and comic actor from Oldham, Greater Manchester, who had appeared

in *Family at War* and *Nearest and Dearest*, and featured in the *Royal Variety Performance* of 1955. Before taking the role of Percy Sugden, Bill had previously been cast in four other roles, the last of which was Arnold Swain's best man in 1980.

Spider Nugent, played by Martin Hancock

Geoffrey 'Spider' Nugent was Emily's eco-warrior nephew. He came to stay with Emily following Percy's departure and the pair were very fond of each other. Spider and Toyah Battersby shared a love of green issues and enjoyed an on/off relationship until 2003, when they left Weatherfield together. In 2016 Emily travelled to visit Spider in Peru and help with his charity work.

No 4 Coronation Street

Sally and Tim Metcalfe and Faye Windass, played by Sally Dynevor, Joe Duttine and Ellie Leach

The first owners of newly built No 4 in 1990 were Mavis and Derek Wilton. In 1997 butcher Fred Elliott purchased the property and his son Ashley Peacock lived there. No 4 was the scene of Maxine Peacock's murder at the hands of killer Richard Hillman. In a house swap with Ashley and second wife Claire, the Websters moved from No 13 with daughters Rosie and Sophie. Following Sally and Kevin's divorce, Sally remained in the house, where she now lives with partner Tim and Tim's daughter Faye Windass.

'I am not watching the Queen's speech from a deckchair.' Sally Metcalfe

Sally's first appearance in 1986 saw her splashed with muddy water as young mechanic Kevin drove through a puddle. Since then, Sally has been at the centre of some of the most important events – from her domestic bliss with Kevin being shattered by his affair with Natalie Horrocks, to being diagnosed with breast cancer (a story that preceded actor Sally Dynevor being treated successfully for the same disease) and from the lofty heights of being elected Mayor of Weatherfield to serving time on false fraud charges as her sister tried to seduce Tim. She is now happily settled with Tim

and working as a machinist at Underworld, and life on Coronation Street for the mother of Rosie and Sophie looks a little calmer. For now…

Sally Dynevor went to the Oldham Theatre Workshop at 13 years old and got the acting bug. 'It changed my life and I knew acting was what I wanted to do.' After training at the Mountview Drama School in London, Sally auditioned as one of the Clayton sisters on *Coronation Street* but didn't get the part. Then a few weeks later she auditioned to play the part of Kevin's posh girlfriend, and didn't get that either. 'Then I got a call, came back up and auditioned for Sally, another girlfriend of Kevin's, and got the part. I had two episodes and I was really excited. It went to four, then six, then I got a year's contract and the rest is history.'

On her first day, Sally's first scene was with Michael Le Vell (Kevin) whom she knew from the Oldham Theatre Workshop. 'I hadn't seen him for 10 years but we got on so well. I was thrown in the deep end but I loved it.

'My next day was with Jean Alexander (Hilda Ogden) and I was really nervous. At that time the cast was only about 25 members, it wasn't a big cast but they were all iconic figures. There weren't many young people then, there were these iconic figures you'd grown up with so it was a bit daunting meeting them all. These people hadn't just done drama school and come into *Coronation Street* – they'd had a lot of life before they came in. It was fascinating to work with them, they were all brilliant at what they did.'

Sally's favourite storyline is the affair that split her happy family up (for the first time) in 1997. She recalls: 'Sally was married to Kevin for 10 years without a hitch, nothing rocked the boat and then suddenly Kevin was with Natalie Horrocks. That changed Sally's path on *Coronation Street* because after the affair Sally and Kevin's relationship completely changed and Sally was now having affairs left, right and centre and her world was like a whirlwind. I think Kevin and Sally would still be very happy now if it hadn't been for Denise's (Welch) character coming in.

'As an actor those are the types of things you want to play, playing the happily married couple can be a bit boring, so it changed everything for me, it was brilliant. Also, my breast cancer storyline (2009) was very important to me because it saved my life. I never would have gone for a check-up without it.'

Sally says it's been an honour to play the character of Sally for so long. 'I'm very proud of *Coronation Street*. Whenever I hear the theme tune I feel proud. To me, *Coronation Street* is community, it's love, it's vulnerability. It's knowing these people. It's famous for its strong women but they're vulnerable, they all have chinks in their armour, just like we all have. I love that they still keep the comedy, all those one-liners. No other programme does it like *Corrie* does. We deal with issues but hopefully we don't bang on about them all the time.'

Tim Metcalfe was a suspicious character when he first appeared, an unnamed man who young Faye Windass was contacting online. He turned out to be adopted Faye's father and now the pair have a settled relationship, Tim is happy with Sally and good friends with her ex Kevin. They may be chalk and cheese but laid-back Tim, who runs Street Cars with Steve McDonald, was beside himself when Sally was jailed, and social climbing Sally would be lost without dependable Tim.

A prolific stage and screen actor, Yorkshire-born Joe Duttine previously played a detective in *Coronation Street* before bagging the role of Tim in 2013. His contract was initially short but he was popular with viewers who have loved watching his relationships with Faye, best mate Steve and of course Sally, develop. Joe says: 'Nobody knows how long their character is going to stay. It depends how it develops, how you find your place within the show. Originally Tim

was going to be here for six months and it got extended, and they put me with Sally and that relationship blossomed and we found some chemistry. It sort of works.'

Joe says he thinks Tim is predominantly a comic character. 'If you're going to be in a soap you want to get the funnies. Tim and Sally can be a comic and also tragic couple.' Joe prefers the humorous storylines. 'I like the relationship between him and Steve,' he says. 'I liked the window-cleaning, you can be party to all sorts of storylines with that. And I enjoy the playful storylines with Sally, we have the same sense of humour.'

He hopes Tim and Sally will stay together. 'People in soaps have affairs all the time, but I like to think there are couples who aren't like that, who do really love each other. They might go through difficult, turbulent times but are strong enough to stay together.'

Key previous residents

Mavis and Derek Wilton, played by Thelma Barlow and Peter Baldwin

'Mavis is the only person in the world who looks six times both ways before crossing a one-way street'. Rita Fairclough

Timid Mavis Riley arrived on *Coronation Street* as a clerk at the Mark Brittain Warehouse before working for Rita in The Kabin, a job that would last for 24 years before Mavis decided to leave Weatherfield and run a bed and breakfast in Cumbria following the death from a heart attack (on her birthday) of husband dithering Derek Wilton, played by Peter Baldwin (1933–2015). The pair had made a popular comic couple, but it was for her friendship with Rita that Mavis is best remembered (see page 203).

Mavis, fearing eternal spinsterhood, lived in The Kabin flat for several years with her budgie Harriet, and when she and Derek finally tied the knot they moved into one of the new houses on the Street, next door to young couple Des and Steph Barnes who delighted in pranking their middle-aged neighbours.

Born in Middlesborough, Thelma Barlow worked as a secretary and enjoyed amateur dramatics. Deciding to take up acting full time, she joined the Joan Littlewood Theatre Group and performed in rep throughout the 1950s. She joined the Bristol Old Vic and ran a boarding house for actors in the city.

Following her departure from *Coronation Street*, Thelma found further fame as Dolly Bellfield in the sitcom *Dinnerladies*, with fellow *Coronation Street* stars Anne Reid and Shobna Gulati, followed by many roles on TV including *Doctor Who*, on the stage and in film as well as writing organic gardening books and narrating a documentary marking her former colleague Helen Worth's 40 years on *Coronation Street*.

Fred Elliott, played by John Savident

Fred Elliott, the larger-than-life butcher, revealed to be Ashley Peacock's father, appeared in *Coronation Street* from 1994 to 2006. As well as being a master butcher, he was part-owner of The Rovers for five years. A serial proposer, he died of a stroke as he was due to marry Shelley Unwin's mother Bev.

Ashley Peacock, played by Steven Arnold

Steven Arnold played squeaky-voiced Ashley Peacock from 1995 until 2010, when his character was dramatically killed off in the 50th anniversary tram crash (see page 262). His first wife Maxine was killed by Richard Hillman.

No 5 Coronation Street

Gemma and Bernie Winter, Chesney and Joseph Brown and the quads, played by Dolly-Rose Campbell, Jane Hazlegrove, Sam Aston, and William Flanagan

'I've got more bounce than a pig on a trampoline.' Gemma

Fiz Brown took over the rent of No 5 Coronation Street when the Battersby-Browns moved out in 2007. In 2013 she moved out and younger brother Chesney has lived there ever since. No 5 has an open-plan layout, with the two living areas having been knocked through when Mike Baldwin owned the property in the 1970s.

Originally introduced as a criminally inclined friend of Kylie from her old stomping ground, Gemma has turned her life around, is living with Chesney and is mother to quadruplets.

After a very short stint working in Audrey's salon, Gemma – she of the big mouth and too tight clothes – starting serving in The Rovers alongside her other job at Prima Doner, where she and Chesney became more than workmates.

Gemma's comic moments, such as going into labour in a cable car high above the Welsh seaside town of Llandudno, took a serious turn in 2019 when her twin brother Paul revealed sexual

abuse at the hands of their mother Bernie's ex-partner, while Chesney was mourning the death of his former girlfriend Sinead.

Gemma has a close relationship with Rita, and lived with her in the flat above The Kabin for a while. Their friendship deepened when Rita suffered a brain tumour, and Gemma was by her side in hospital.

Dolly-Rose Campbell acted in radio dramas before landing the role of Gemma. A fan of the show, she was on a public tour of the *Coronation Street* set when she heard she had got the job. She was working in a restaurant between acting jobs and served Barbara Knox, excitedly telling her she was going to be working with her.

Dolly-Rose recalls: 'When I first started I wasn't on the cobbles, everything was on location at Gemma's previous local the Dog and Gun pub, so it was a long time before I actually did get into any of the big regular sets and onto the Street.

'My favourite scenes to work on so far have been the caravan holiday scenes when Gemma and Chesney got lost and Gemma got in the wrong caravan. Then she went to the pub and got drunk with the locals. We had the best crew for that shoot, we never stopped laughing from start to finish.'

Dolly was given six episodes to start with. She proved a popular addition to the cast and quickly became a regular. 'Now they can't get rid of me!' she laughs. 'It's such an iconic TV show in Britain and in other parts of the world. It's a privilege to be part of it.'

A natural comic actor, Dolly picked up the prize for Best Comedy Performance at the British Soap Awards in 2017.

Chesney, brother of Fiz, son of Cilla (played by Wendi Peters) and stepson of Les Battersby, arrived in Coronation Street as a cheeky red-haired lad. In those days, his best pal was a huge Great Dane called Schmeichel (after one of Manchester United's greatest goalkeepers, Peter Schmeichel). A single dad for a while following the death of Katy Armstrong, the mother of his son Joseph, Chesney is now a proud, if tired, father of five. He is manager of Prima Doner and For Your Fries Only.

As a young actor, Sam Aston joined *Coronation Street* in 2003. He had previously been in several TV shows and adverts, making his acting debut at just five years old.

Key previous residents

Esther Hayes, played by Daphne Oxenford

Esther Hayes was one of *Coronation Street*'s original characters, first appearing in the second episode. Well-educated town hall clerk Esther never married and lived in Weatherfield until 1963. She appeared in 65 episodes between 1960 and 1972.

Daphne Oxenford (1919–2012) was well-known as the voice of the BBC radio programme *Listen With Mother*. She originally read for the role of Annie Walker.

Minnie Caldwell, played by Margot Bryant

Introduced in episode two in 1960, mild-mannered widow Minnie was regularly bossed around by friends Ena Sharples and Martha Longhurst. She lived at No 5 from 1962 with lodgers including Jed Stone and Eddie Yeats until her departure in 1976 with her cat Bobby. Minnie enjoyed a spot of gambling and was engaged for a while to Albert Tatlock.

Margot Bryant (1897–1988) had a career in musicals and films before being cast in *Coronation Street*, once appearing alongside Fred Astaire.

Mike Baldwin, played by Johnny Briggs

Flash Mike Baldwin remains one of *Coronation Street*'s most recognised characters. The cockney businessman swaggered into Weatherfield in 1976 to open Baldwin's Casuals. The rag trade was good to Mike and he had plenty of cash, a fact of which he never failed to remind his love rival Ken Barlow. For much of his time in Weatherfield he lived in a flash apartment, but in the 1970s he bought No 5, renovated it and installed his sometime girlfriend Bet Lynch there.

Forever battling with his factory employees, including Vera Duckworth and Ivy Tilsley, he spent much of his time wooing the ladies and downing a scotch in The Rovers.

Married four times and siring three sons with three women, Mike's colourful love life was often the talk of the Street. When he wasn't wooing his next conquest he was fighting with Ken Barlow over Ken's wife Deirdre or his daughter Susan (see page 201).

His longest marriage was to Alma Sedgewick. Amanda Barrie, who played Alma, says: 'We used to get on my train up from London and by the time I'd got to Watford I truly felt married to Johnny Briggs!' And writer Jan McVerry says Mike Baldwin was one of her favourite characters to write for: 'You could just hear his voice in your head.'

Succumbing to the effects of Alzheimer's disease, Mike died in 2006, on rain-soaked cobbles in the arms of enemy Ken.

Johnny Briggs had had minor parts in numerous films before embarking on his 30-year portrayal of Mike Baldwin. When he left the show in 2006 he was presented with a Lifetime Achievement Award at the British Soap Awards.

Ray Langton, played by Neville Buswell

Womanising Ray Langton was a Jack-the-lad who romanced several women in the Street before marrying Deirdre Hunt in 1975. After their daughter Tracy was born, Ray left to live in Holland, but returned in 2005 to try to make amends with her before his death.

Ivy Brennan, played by Lynne Perrie

From 1979 until 1994, 'Poison' Ivy, played by Lynne Perrie (1931–2006), lived at No 5, firstly with son Brian and often out-of-work hubby Bert who died in 1984 (several months after actor Peter Dudley (1935–1983) passed away) and then with second husband, taxi driver Don Brennan (Geoff Hinsliff). The mouthy and staunchly religious factory machinist and shop steward was known for sticking her nose in where it wasn't wanted, usually into Brian and wife Gail's business before Brian was murdered outside a nightclub. Best friends with loudmouth Vera Duckworth, Ivy finished up working at Bettabuy supermarket before leaving her unhappy marriage to Don and spending her final days in a religious retreat.

The Battersbys

Neighbours from hell, the Battersbys were council tenants who moved into No 5 after Don Brennan died. Loudmouth Les (Bruce Jones) and wife Janice (Vicky Entwistle) caused a stir when they arrived with Les's daughter Leanne (Jane Danson) and Janice's daughter Toyah (Georgia Taylor). Lazy Les spent most of the time causing trouble before working as a cabbie for Street Cars. After Janice left him for biker Dennis Stringer, Les married Fiz and Chesney's mother Cilla, a brash barmaid. Rock fan Les left after 10 years in 2007 to go on tour with a tribute band named ZZ Top o'the Morning, while machinist Janice stayed in Weatherfield for a further four years. Both Leanne and Toyah are still walking the cobbles.

No 6 Coronation Street

Yasmeen and Geoff Metcalfe, played by Shelley King and Ian Bartholomew

No 6 Coronation Street was constructed in 1989, with the first residents being the developer's daughter Steph Barnes and new husband Des. They were a new breed on the Street, the 1990s 'yuppies'. No 6 also housed the Harris family (as part of a witness protection scheme), the Mortons and the Windasses. Former librarian Yasmeen is the last of the Nazir family living at No 6. In recent times, she has become the victim of coercive control at the hands of Tim Metcalfe's father Geoff.

Shelley King says Yasmeen is an amalgam of various women she knows. 'The brief outline they gave me of the character was of a Muslim woman who was a librarian who found herself in Coronation Street. Highly educated Muslim women of my age had not really been explored on television and I wanted to show the different aspects of the Muslim community. She married a man, Sharif, who is from a different class and her family don't want to know her.

'Yasmeen has been involved in other people's storylines in the six years I have been here, but the coercive control was the first major

storyline for her. It takes that long to bed in a character, to establish strong characters.'

Shelley grew up watching *Coronation Street*, admiring actors like Violet Carson and Jean Alexander. 'My mum always wanted me to be in *Coronation Street*,' she says. 'I did *Jewel in the Crown* and she was much more interested in *Corrie* than that.'

Known for working on musicals, actor Ian Bartholomew has been nominated for four Olivier awards. 'I came to the end of my contract doing *Half a Sixpence* in the West End and my agent said, what you want now, in an ideal world, is a regular part in a TV series and to be able to live at home, and lo and behold up comes a meeting for *Corrie* and much to my surprise and deep excitement I got cast as Geoff Metcalfe in *Coronation Street*.

'It's like nothing you've ever done before. But having grown up with *Corrie* – it's almost as old as I am – I remember the old black-and-white episodes with just a few characters. It was like nothing that had ever been made before. And the fact that it's still going, when somebody says would you like to be in it, I jumped at the chance.'

The character of Geoff started off being a bit of a bumbling fool, quite good fun and quite jolly, but Ian always knew there was the possibility that they were going to turn him dark, with some troubling scenes. 'I started off quite liking Geoff, then I didn't like him at all. I found a way to understand him. Rather than him just being downright nasty, I don't think he's a well man, he's terribly insecure and has serious issues.'

Ian says it was great fun working with on-screen partner Shelley. 'Everybody brings something to the table and we have a good time, otherwise what's the point?'

Key previous residents

Natalie Barnes, played by Denise Welch

'I'm not pulled as easily as a pint of Newton and Ridley.' Natalie Barnes

Natalie Barnes has gone down in Weatherfield history as one of the show's pivotal characters. Brought in, as Natalie Horrocks, to split up the Websters' happy marriage, she then married Des Barnes and took over The Rovers. Denise Welch, who was an established actress appearing in many TV dramas, played Natalie for four years.

Denise says she always wanted to be in *Coronation Street* and had written to casting director Judi Hayfield asking for a part. Seventeen years later she joined the cast. 'Having been in the industry for a number of years, nothing prepared me for going into *Coronation Street*,' she says. 'We were watched by a third of the nation, it was ridiculous! You're terrified of calling these actors you've grown up with by their real names. And going into The Rovers for the first time, you feel like a fan.

'Nobody thought that [the character] had any lifespan beyond three months because obviously the Websters were going to get back together. But the writing was so good and the public were desperate for someone to love to hate, so that that was it.'

Sally slapping Natalie made front-page news. 'Sally and I became best friends in real life,' says Denise. 'I feel honoured to have played a part in what is considered to be one of the iconic storylines of the last 60 years. Although Natalie had an affair with a married man, the public reaction was really interesting, it was sort of "you are naughty but we like you". The impact of that character was very powerful.'

The Kevin Webster affair and Des Barnes' murder were Denise's favourite storylines – 'my entry and exit ones I guess'. She adds that the relationship she built up behind The Rovers bar with Vera and Jack when she became the landlady and they were her employees had some of the best lines. 'I used to live for those moments because Vera hated Natalie and Jack fancied her. That's *Coronation Street* – the balance between the drama and the absolute hilarity.'

The mother of The 1975 frontman Matt Healy, Denise remembers: 'On the live 40th anniversary episode I was seven months pregnant with my younger son Louis and Matty was an extra. I was so nervous I thought I was going to give birth in The Rovers. It was my last filming day, so I left on the day of the 40th.

Corrie changed all of our lives – I always say it's because of *Corrie* that The 1975 band exists, as I moved to Manchester because of *Corrie* and that's where the band started.

'My dad Vin also came into *Coronation Street* for an episode. When he retired he got an Equity card doing cabaret as a drag artist and then he got cast as Des Barnes' dad at Des's funeral. Nothing to do with me; I didn't know until he'd got it! I remember standing in Des Barnes' house with my dad playing my father-in-law, and Anna Gascoigne, footballer Paul Gascoigne's sister, playing Des's sister-in-law, thinking this is the most surreal thing!'

For Denise, it's the older, stalwart characters that keep the show going. '*Coronation Street* for me is in my DNA. It's part of our life and part of our history. It was my mum's favourite show. No other job I've ever had has beaten the excitement of hearing from my agent that I'd got the part. It's just part of all of our lives.'

The Windasses

The Windass family moved into No 6 in 2008. The family comprised at that time Anna (Debbie Rush), her common-law husband Eddie (Steve Huison) and son Gary (Mikey North). Layabout Eddie, a benefits cheat whose limp changed from leg to leg, always had his eye on the next scam, leaving hard-working café worker Anna in despair. More heartache was to come when Gary was sent to prison for his part in a robbery orchestrated by David Platt and Graeme Proctor. On his release he joined the army, suffered PTSD following a tour of Afghanistan and was discharged for hitting a police officer. He returned to Weatherfield in 2011, when Anna and Eddie began fostering young Faye Butler (Ellie Leach). Eddie and Anna split up that year, with Eddie leaving to work in Germany and Anna formally adopting Faye. After Owen Armstrong bought No 6, he and Anna became an item. Following Faye's hidden pregnancy aged 12, Anna went on to be persecuted by villainous Pat Phelan, leaving in 2018 after traumatic ordeals including blackmail, rape, severe burns and wrongful imprisonment. Anna and Owen had lost No 6 in 2014 and the house was auctioned, with the Nazirs becoming the next inhabitants.

No 7 Coronation Street

Dev, Asha and Aadi Alahan, played by Jimmi Harkishin, Tanisha Gorey and Adam Hussain

No 7 Coronation Street has a unique history; between 1965 and 1982 it didn't exist. After the front of the house collapsed due to a faulty beam, the landlord was too tight-fisted to pay for repairs so asked builder Len Fairclough to knock it down. For several years a wooden bench sat in the space between Nos 5 and 9, but in 1982 Len bought the plot and rebuilt the house. Blanche Hunt and Maria Connor both owned No 7 at one point, and now Devendra 'Dev' Alahan lives there with his twins Aadi and Asha.

Widower Dev has lived at No 7 since 2010, when he and late ex-wife Sunita bought it from Maria Connor. The owner of the Corner Shop, the kebab shop and the chippy used to have a larger business empire, but he sold much of it when facing financial ruin following the 2010 tram crash.

Women have always been Dev's weakness, including Deirdre *and* daughter Tracy. Pregnant wife Sunita left him when she discovered he had fathered other children. When the twins were young, Sunita herself had an affair, which led to her murder, and kind-hearted Mary Taylor moved in for a while to help raise the twins. Recent storylines have seen single father Dev dealing with Asha's attempts at skin lightening and her traumatic sexting ordeal.

Jimmi Harkishin was born in Paris and acted in a number of popular TV programmes as well as the movie *East is East* before landing the role of Dev Alahan, which he has played continuously since 1999.

Key previous residents

The Hewitts

Harry (played by Ivan Beavis,1926–97), married Concepta (played by Doreen Keogh, 1924–2017) after the mother of Lucille (played by Jennifer Moss, 1945–2006) died. When the Hewitts moved to Concepta's home country of Ireland with their son Christopher, Lucille stayed with Jack and Annie Walker to finish her education in Weatherfield.

Len and Rita Fairclough, played by Peter Adamson and Barbara Knox

After Len (played by Peter Adamson, 1930–2002), had rebuilt No 7, he and Rita moved in. The couple had no children and started fostering. Following Len's death in 1983, when he was killed driving home from his secret mistress, Rita fostered Jenny Bradley and became involved with her evil father Alan, who tried to remortgage the property behind Rita's back. Later, she moved into the flat above The Kabin (see page 114) and sold the house to Curly Watts.

Curly and Raquel Watts, played by Kevin Kennedy and Sarah Lancashire

Norman 'Curly' Watts arrived in *Coronation Street* in 1983 as a binman, but the geeky sensitive soul moved on to become an assistant manager at Bettabuy supermarket and was pompous boss Reg Holdsworth's (Ken Morley) sidekick. Permanently lovelorn and desperate to settle down with a nice girl, after living with Emily briefly, Curly famously lodged with the Duckworths for several years immediately prior to buying No 7, where he installed a skylight and telescope in the attic to indulge his hobby of stargazing. Head over heels in love with barmaid Raquel, he was devastated when she left him and fell for love rat Des Barnes. On the rebound, Raquel married Curly after all, but left him to take up a job for an international salon franchise in Kuala Lumpur. Happily, Curly found love with police officer Emma Taylor and they left Weatherfield for Newcastle in 2003 with their son Ben.

Kevin Kennedy was a member of Manchester Youth Theatre as a child. A keen musician, he formed a band with Smiths guitarist Johnny Marr and bassist Andy Rourke before studying drama at Manchester Polytechnic. Following his departure from *Coronation Street* he has appeared on TV and on stage, and also starred in a *Coronation Street* spin-off DVD with Ken Morley, Patti Clare and Malcolm Hebden called *A Knight's Tale*.

'I were always led to believe I were equally good at most things. I were told that when I were at school. They said – "Raquel, you have no particular talents."' Raquel

Ditsy Raquel, the naïve wannabe model with a huge heart, worked behind The Rovers bar for four years, having been taken under Bet Gilroy's wing. A former Miss Bettabuy, endearing Raquel careered from one heartbreak to the next before marrying Curly. In her heart she knew she didn't love him – she was marrying for security – and the marriage lasted less than a year. Famous for her innocent double entendres, Raquel regularly topped the list of viewers' favourite Rovers barmaids.

Sarah Lancashire, the daughter of former *Coronation Street* writer Geoffrey Lancashire, worked in the West End and lectured in drama before joining *Coronation Street* for five years from 1991 to 1996. She reprised the role for a special two-hander episode to mark the millennium in which Raquel returned to inform Curly that he had a daughter, Alice, before asking him for a divorce so she could remarry.

'They're so attentive in the hotel. Do you know I rang him once and the girl from room service was there in the bedroom to answer the phone.' Raquel about her footballer boyfriend Wayne

No 8 Coronation Street

Gail Rodwell, Sarah Barlow, Max Turner, David, Shona, Lily and Harry Platt, played by Helen Worth, Tina O'Brien, Harry McDermott, Jack P Shepherd, Julia Goulding, Brooke Malonie and Freddie and Isaac Rhodes

'Mum, I'm a firm believer in marriage. The more the merrier, I reckon. I wonder where I get that from?' David Platt

The Platt family has been at the centre of *Coronation Street* for decades and no one more so than much-married mum Gail. Gail is an original resident of No 8, having moved in as a newlywed with Martin Platt. Son David now owns the property. No 8 has been the setting for some major life-changing events, from Richard Hillman kidnapping the family in a murder suicide bid to Kylie killing violent ex Callum in order to save her sister-in-law Sarah.

Gail's mother Audrey Roberts is a regular visitor to No 8, always on hand to help out in the latest crisis or to steer Gail into The Rovers for a much needed gin and tonic.

Helen Worth has been on *Coronation Street* since joining in 1974. 'I'd done *The Sound of Music* when I was 12, in the West End for a year,' she says. 'I lived in Morecambe and left there and moved to London to live with a chaperone with my parents' blessing. Then

there was no turning back. I went back to Morecambe to school, but left when I was 15 to go to Corona Theatre School in London. I went into rep and that was where I learned my trade.'

Helen appeared on radio and then TV, notably in *Doctor Who* in 1971. She auditioned three times for *Coronation Street* before landing the role of Gail Potter. 'At the time there were huge audiences. There was a huge love of the *Street*. I'd watched *Coronation Street* with my mum and I was very sorry that she never saw me in it.' (Helen's mother died in a car accident.)

The part of Gail was initially for six episodes. 'Anyway, I never left. I kept coming in and out, which was lovely because I could do other work, but eventually they said, you either come to us and don't do anything else or you leave completely. I chose to stay and I don't think I ever regretted the decision.' Helen believes the character really kicked off when Gail was working with Alma in the café. 'I loved that and then I sort of felt that I was really here.'

Amanda looks back on those days with fondness too: 'My favourite time was when Alma had settled into the café with Gail. It's quite selfish, but I did get fed with bacon sandwiches all the time I was working. And of course you were stationary and people came in and out, so you got to see a lot more of the cast. Normally you're just with the person you're doing the storyline with and that's who you see, but if you're in the café you see everyone. We had the best of both worlds because Helen and I were great friends, it couldn't have been better.'

Helen says she feels incredibly fortunate to have the family she has on the *Street*. 'We do work together well, we're happy to spend a lot of time together, we care about everybody. And we have a kind of shorthand going, I think now, whereby we know what we're going to do with scenes really. We don't have to talk about it too much, it just happens, we've done so many of them. Having said that, I wouldn't be complacent because sometimes the younger ones will throw something into the mix and you think, ooh I wasn't expecting you to do that, so you have to throw something back. It's a ping-pong game and it's so exciting and they are all so wonderful. And each time someone new comes in and you think, the family's going to burst, every time it seems to work.'

After nearly half a century on the *Street* Helen is a true soap icon, but she laughs off the suggestion. 'I can't believe I've been here for 46 years, but the only thing *Corrie* icon status means is that I'm old!' And she adds: 'I'm not Gail. When I leave, Gail stays in the dressing room. I come into work, I do my job and I go home. I love it, I love the people I work with and you can't wish for more than that.'

As Sarah Louise, as she was known then, Gail's daughter struggled in her teenage years, falling pregnant as a schoolgirl in 2000. Life did not get any easier. As her life continued to unfold, she lost another baby, discovered her boyfriend Todd Grimshaw was gay, married then divorced his brother Jason and left to live in Italy. On her return she was involved in Callum Logan's murder, suffered postpartum psychosis and dealt with daughter Bethany's grooming ordeal. Marriage to Adam Barlow and a job running Underworld with brother Nick happily followed for Sarah, although her marriage to Adam did not last long.

Tina O'Brien is the third actress to play Sarah, joining *Coronation Street* in 1999 with a break to do other work from 2008 to 2015. She had previously worked with Jack P Shepherd, playing brother and sister in the factory drama *Clocking Off*. She has appeared in many other TV shows and co-founded a theatre school in Manchester, her home town.

David Platt has emerged from being a tearaway youth to responsible father and one of Coronation Street's most important – and complex – male residents. Always a cheeky young scamp, David became a seriously troubled teenager following the Richard Hillman incident. He tormented his family, vandalised the Street, faked a suicide attempt and pushed poor Gail down the stairs. His former girlfriend Tina McIntyre and his wife Kylie were murdered, his feud with brother Nick who slept with Kylie led to Nick sustaining brain damage, and he was jailed for stealing from grandmother Audrey, not to mention falling for the mother of his wife's murderer! In 2018 David was raped by his friend Josh Tucker, and the repercussions of this harrowing event continue to ripple through David's life today.

In 2000, Jack P Shepherd took over the role of David Platt. Yorkshire-born Jack was just 12 years old and he has grown up on Coronation Street. Like screen sister Tina O'Brien, outside his work on *Coronation Street*, Jack has previously run a drama academy. He

has also worked with screen brother Ben Price on a short film and appeared on stage.

Jack jokes: 'The reason my character is popular with viewers is obviously because he's really good looking. No seriously, I think it's because he's got multiple sides to his personality. He can be nice, loving, funny and loyal or devious, emotional and an absolute nightmare. The storyline when Kylie died was an incredible, very well written episode by Chris Fewtrell. The director, Nickie Lister, did a brilliant job – she was very patient with me. We couldn't have a rehearsal as I needed to save the crying for the real thing.

'Working on *Corrie* is fantastic – it's the people, the whole team. You can mess about and have a laugh but when that red light comes on, we get it done. I socialise with my colleagues, which says a lot. Everyone who leaves *Coronation Street* misses the people.'

Paula Lane, who played David's murdered wife Kylie, says: 'Jack and I had such a great professional relationship, we never took it too seriously but equally we really wanted to deliver. I had so many good storylines with the Platts. I loved the fact Kylie was a bit of a comedy character when she first appeared. She had great wit about her, she loved winding Gail up. I loved those scenes where her and David's relationship was just starting out and they were exploring together and causing havoc. You work with the legends like Helen and Jack who have been there for so many years and you respect them because they've literally honed their craft and they are these wonderful characters.'

No 9 Coronation Street

Tyrone and Ruby Dobbs, Fiz and Hope Stape and Evelyn Plummer, played by Alan Halsall, Macy Alabi, Jennie McAlpine, Isabella Flanagan and Maureen Lipman

'My days of top and tailing ended the night of the first moon landing. I shan't go into detail.' Evelyn Plummer

No 9 Coronation Street is instantly recognisable thanks to the gaudy blue and yellow cladding previous resident Vera Duckworth put up in a bid to 'out-class' the neighbours. She also gave it a name – The Old Rectory.

Tyrone Dobbs became the surrogate son of Jack and Vera, whose own unreliable son Terry (Nigel Pivaro) made their life hell. He bought No 9 from the Duckworths who didn't want to see it go to wastrel Terry, and since they passed away he has continued to live there.

Kind-hearted mechanic Tyrone had a tough childhood, dragged up by his jailbird mum Jackie Dobbs (Margi Clarke). He arrived in *Coronation Street* with Jackie in 1998. A failed engagement to Maria Sutherland followed, and his marriage to baker Diggory Compton's (Eric Potts) daughter Molly (Vicky Binns) saw her cheat on him with his boss Kevin Webster. Molly died in the 2010 tram crash after telling Tyrone baby Jack was really Kevin's son.

Tyrone was physically abused by his next girlfriend, violent Kirsty Soames, and kidnapped their daughter Ruby, fearing for her life. He eventually found happiness with Fiz, but had to cope with her daughter Hope suffering cancer and recently worrying behavioural issues, exacerbated when the daughter of Fiz's killer ex, John Stape, inveigled her way into his family's life.

Tyrone also learned that Jackie was not his real mum when his boorish grandmother Evelyn parked herself and her greyhound Cerberus on Tyrone and Fiz in 2018.

Alan Halsall appeared as an extra in *Coronation Street* before landing the role of Tyrone. In 2013 he won the Outstanding Serial Drama Performance award at the National Television Awards.

'I'm sorry about Evelyn. I should have that printed on a T-shirt.' Fiz

Bubbly Underworld machinist Fiona 'Fiz' Brown was fostered by Roy and Hayley Cropper in 2001 and later took responsibility for younger brother Chesney after their mother Cilla regularly abandoned them. Blindly in love, she married John Stape in 2009 while he was in prison following his kidnapping of Rosie Webster. Fiz was charged with murders that John had committed, but was cleared by his deathbed confession following a car crash. In 2019, the ghost of John Stape returned to haunt Fiz in the form of his conniving daughter Jade, who framed Fiz and Tyrone for physically abusing Fiz and John's daughter Hope.

As well as acting in *Coronation Street*, Bury-born Jennie McAlpine is a restaurateur, opening Annie's in Manchester. Before she joined *Coronation Street*, Jennie performed as a stand-up comedian, having taken up comedy as a teenager, and appeared in rival television soap *Emmerdale*.

Before joining *Coronation Street* as regular character Evelyn Plummer, prolific stage and screen actor Maureen Lipman had appeared once before, as relief Rovers manager Lillian Spencer. Maureen's links with *Coronation Street* go back much further than that – her late husband, respected Manchester-born dramatist Jack Rosenthal, had written more than 130 episodes of *Coronation Street* in the 1960s, and was also the show's producer in 1967.

Maureen has delighted fans and critics of *Coronation Street* with her performance of Evelyn, as the character's withering put-downs and tactless, politically incorrect observations have been as amusing as they are cutting.

'Some people are an open book, some are a closed book and you are more of a colouring book.' Evelyn to grandson Tyrone

Key previous residents

The Cheveskis, played by Ernst Walder and Anne Cunningham

The Cheveskis were Elsie Tanner's daughter, Linda, and son-in-law, Ivan, a Polish immigrant. The couple left Weatherfield for a new life in Canada with baby son Paul in 1961.

Jack and Vera Duckworth, played by William Tarmey and Elizabeth Dawn

Jack and Vera were one of the *Street*'s most loved couples (see page 202), although their love for each other was tested by their infidelities. They lived at No 9 between 1983 and 1995, then again from 2000 to 2009, with a stint running The Rovers in between. Jack would often escape his foghorn-voiced wife's nagging in the back yard where he tended his beloved pigeons. The pair were constantly let down by son Terry and struggled to keep in contact with their grandchildren. Often looked down upon by their Street neighbours, Jack, with his sticky-taped glasses, and Vera, his 'little swamp duck', provided many comic scenes over the years. They may have rowed constantly, but they truly loved each other and theirs was the longest marriage on the *Street*, lasting 50 years.

William Tarmey (1941–2012), real name William Cleworth-Piddington, was a former builder and nightclub singer in Manchester when he became an extra and then popular regular Jack in *Coronation Street*.

Elizabeth Dawn (1935–2017), born Sylvia Butterworth, was also an extra on *Coronation Street* before landing the part of machinist Vera. She was also a publican and, for a time, Mayoress of her home town of Leeds.

No 11 Coronation Street

Eileen Grimshaw, Mary Taylor and Sean Tully, played by Sue Cleaver, Patti Clare and Antony Cotton

No 11 has been the scene of Street Cars' switch operator Eileen Grimshaw's most-talked about life experiences. The mother of Todd and Jason has dealt with cheating blokes, discovered a half-sister in Julie Carp (Katy Cavanagh) and even married a serial killer. And who can forget her feud with Gail, coming to blows on the cobbles?

Sue Cleaver was a well-known face on British TV before she joined *Coronation Street*, starring in Victoria Wood's *Dinnerladies* as brusque delivery driver Glenda. Away from acting, she is a trained mezzo soprano and qualified therapist.

Sean Tully was introduced as the first openly gay major character in 2003. He made an immediate impact and has been Eileen's lodger for several years. Always quick with a witty aside, the knicker-stitcher and part-time barman has faced both homophobia and homelessness over the years.

Actor Antony Cotton joined *Coronation Street* in 2003, having acted on stage and in film. He starred in *Queer As Folk* and has won several awards for his portrayal of Sean. Antony didn't audition to play Sean. 'I always said I would never audition for *Coronation Street*

because I loved it so much that it would have broken my heart if I'd not got it. So whenever roles like "armed robber number two" came up I never went for it because I couldn't bear not getting it.'

Before joining *Coronation Street*, Antony read an interview with the new producer, Tony Wood, and wrote a card to him saying: 'Dear Tony, welcome to Manchester. I hope Weatherfield is treating you well. If you ever need a homosexual on *Coronation Street*, I'm your man. I've got my own house, my own car, I don't do drugs and best of all I'm cheap. C'mon Tony, you know you want it.'

'He discussed having a gay character with Tony Warren who said: "If you cast a gay character there's only one queen in Manchester who can play him and that's Antony Cotton." And he'd just received my card that day!' says Antony. 'I had been offered a 12-month contract for *Family Affairs* but Tony promised to get me in *Corrie* within months so I turned that down. When I joined properly there was no character bio, there'd never been a line written for him, I just appeared. The writers were told, if they were struggling to find Sean's voice to write him as they used to write Raquel – Sean has no enemies, and as far as his love life goes he's like Raquel, always on the shelf but always optimistic that somebody's round the corner.'

Antony adds that he has always loved being part of an ensemble and part of the company, the chorus. 'Big storylines, like the homeless story, are very important but I've loved it when it's been my little storylines like when Sean's dog Shandy died and he sang a song.

'Sean has never been apologetic, he is out there loud and proud. I was accused at first of making him a bit of a stereotype but actually Sean is an archetype – there hadn't been a long-term gay character in a long-running drama until him. I love Sean, he has opened many doors for me. I've been able to use the voice I have because of him for my Armed Forces and other charity work. Sean has one foot in Norris, one foot in Raquel, with Weatherfield in between!'

Mary is a recent addition to Eileen's household, having lived at No 7 for several years, looking after the Alahan twins until the teenagers demanded rooms of their own. Raised by an overbearing mother who Mary often refers to, her comic partnerships with Norris, Roy and Tracy are loved by fans, but the character also had a heartbreaking time when reunited with her dishonest son Jude.

So keen was Patti Clare to appear on *Coronation Street* that she once sent in a script into which she'd written a part for herself. Twelve years ago, the role of Mary came along, Patti's first major television role after 20 years in the theatre. 'I was terrified on my first day on set,' she recalls. 'I think I was in shock! I was in The Rovers with Norris, Rita and Jed Stone. Mary had been Norris's nemesis, he'd been entering all these competitions and coming second, second, second, and this lady called Mary Taylor was coming first, first, first, so he befriended her, they realised they were kindred spirits and that was it. I had about three lines to say – but all I had in my head was, "I'm in The Rovers! That's Rita!"'

Patti was supposed to be there for five episodes. 'I wrote to the producer and the casting director saying, "Thank you so much, I've had a wonderful time, goodbye" and the next day they phoned my agent asking why is Patti saying goodbye? They had more episodes for me, but my agent hadn't told me in case it put me under stress! And that was 12 years ago.'

Patti reckons viewers have got used to Mary and her naïve eccentricities. 'I think people have learned to accept her strange ways. She's genuinely kind-hearted, often trying her best but making the wrong decisions. I think people feel a bit sorry for her. Teenage girls seem to find Mary hilarious, I'm not sure why!' Mary tends to lean more to this comedy. 'The comedy is brilliant because before *Coronation Street* I didn't realise that was an ability I had. Obviously, the writers saw something in Mary and ran with it. The dramatic storylines were really challenging but great to do, and I'm very grateful to have had the chance, and have a little variety.'

Patti loved working with David Neilson as Roy. 'I had great times with David Neilson when Mary had a crush on Roy. There were some beautiful scenes when they both talked about their fathers over a game of chess. I've been really lucky to have had great partnerships over the years, great actors to be paired with.' She adds: 'As an actor, *Coronation Street* is a fantastic learning ground – I still feel I'm learning, even though 12 years is quite a long apprenticeship. Being part of such a huge programme that is really as much a part of British life as the Queen and the weather reports is quite a privilege. I still get a thrill being in The Rovers or looking down the street. It's a lovely feeling.'

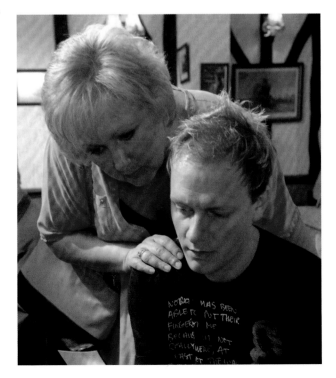

Key previous residents

Elsie and Dennis Tanner, played by Patricia Phoenix and Philip Lowrie

Elsie Tanner's telephone. Since her departure every resident of No 11 has had a red telephone as a tribute to the popular character.

'I've left home so many times me suitcases pack themselves every time I whistle.' Elsie

Elsie Tanner, the *Street* siren, dominated the soap for 23 years. The original 'tart with a heart' with her red lacquered hairdo, pencil skirts and attraction to unreliable, often married, men was compulsive viewing. Her clashes with moralistic battleaxe Ena Sharples enthralled fans, who loved to see them go hammer and tongs at each other on the cobbles.

Elsie worked in clothing store Miami Modes and later as a machinist for Mike Baldwin. She fretted over her wayward son Dennis and enjoyed a long-term friendship with Len Fairclough, whose proposals she turned down twice. The mother-of-two married four times and spent her final years running a bar in Portugal with fourth husband Bill Gregory. It was revealed the pair had died together in 2004 while driving through The Algarve in Bill's sports car.

'Elsie's a sparrow in a dirty street. She wouldn't survive in an aviary with birds of paradise. She tried it once and they nearly pecked her to death.' Len

Patricia Phoenix (1923–86), 'Lancashire's Liz Taylor', had a life almost as colourful as her most famous character. Accepting the role when she feared her acting days were over turned her into a star and she lived the role to the maximum, a true soap icon. Born Patricia Frederika Manfield, she changed her stage name to Phoenix in the 1950s. She was married three times, including to screen husband Alan Browning who played Alan Howard and, on her deathbed, to former Prime Minister Tony Blair's father-in-law, actor Tony Booth. Patricia's own father had married her mother bigamously.

Patricia left *Coronation Street* in 1973, returning three years later before departing for good in 1984, just two years before her death. Barbara Knox remembers working with Pat: 'Pat Phoenix was wonderful. She relished being Elsie Tanner. She came in every day, looking stunning. She really did enjoy it.'

Helen Worth also remembers Patricia fondly: 'I loved Pat Phoenix. She was an extraordinary woman, she lived the part. She'd come in and make breakfast for the crew because in those days we had real stoves, real gas, made real bacon and eggs in the café. Pat loved it, but she knew her status and she used it.'

And Philip Lowrie adds: 'Pat Phoenix was an extremely complicated personality. What Pat wanted, I discovered, was stardom. And she got it, and she was bloody good at it. When we first started she played the character of Elsie Tanner brilliantly, she was overweight, blousy and over the top and I related to her as my mother, but as she got more and more successful she slimmed

Cartoon published after Phoenix's death.

The actress arguably became the country's best-loved soap star, was entertained by the prime minister, and met with huge crowds on a publicity tour of Australia.

Patricia Phoenix

Dear Derek ~ Love

A few humble suggestions that may or may not be usefull. Could go on for ages — But am in fear and trembling of having another apple core thrown at me

Love
Pat

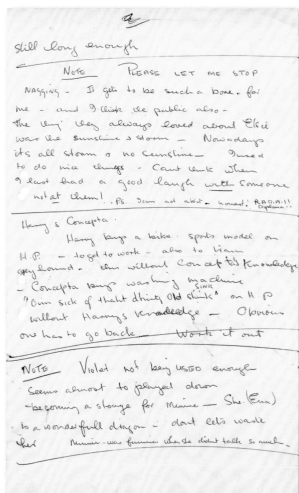

still long enough

NOTE   PLEASE LET ME STOP NAGGING — It gets to be such a bore. for me — and I think the public also — The thing they always loved about Elsie was the sunshine & storm — Nowadays its all storm & no sunshine — I used to do nice things — Cant think when I last had a good laugh with someone not at them! . PS. I am not about — honest! R.A.D.A!! Diploma!!

Harry & Concepta.
Harry buys a bike. sports model on H.P. — to get to work — also to train greyhound. All without Concepta's knowledge — Concepta buys washing machine SINK "I'm sick of thaht dirty Old shink" on H.P without Harrys knowledge — Obvious one has to go back ——— Work it out

NOTE   Violet not being USED enough — Seems almost to played down — becoming a stooge for Minnie — She (Ena) is a wonderfull dragon — dont lets waste her   Minnie — was funnier when she didnt talk so much —

down, she dyed her hair a different colour and she started to play herself.

'She was incredibly successful and everybody loved her, but she was difficult to play with because she never learned her lines! For instance, if the line was something like: "Would you like to have a cup of tea?" and I had a reply to that she would say "How about some tea?" so I'd have to say "Yes, I'd like a cup of tea." You were always having to adapt and compromise because she'd said the wrong line. She used to say she'd be very happy to come in on a Friday afternoon and just record the show rather than do the rehearsals during the week.'

When Philip announced that he was leaving the show, Patricia was 'absolutely furious. "How can you leave me," she'd say. So it was a complicated relationship that I had with Pat. I know she was an iconic character though and good for her. She told me once that she wanted to be like Joan Crawford, and she achieved that!'

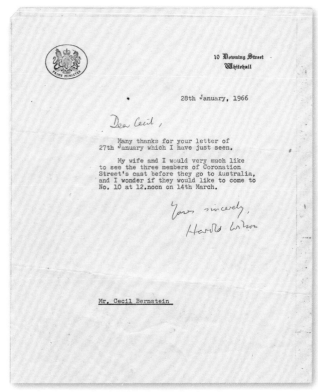

10 Downing Street
Whitehall

28th January, 1966

Dear Cecil,

Many thanks for your letter of 27th January which I have just seen.

My wife and I would very much like to see the three members of Coronation Street's cast before they go to Australia, and I wonder if they would like to come to No. 10 at 12.noon on 14th March.

Yours sincerely,

Harold Wilson

Mr. Cecil Bernstein

Patricia Phoenix provides some pointers to the producers for the development of her own, and other, characters on the *Street*, and is invited to visit Prime Minister, Harold Wilson, in 1966. At the visit, Chancellor Jim Callaghan pronounced her 'the sexiest thing on television'.

Jim and Liz McDonald, played by Charles Lawson and Beverley Callard

The McDonalds moved into No 11 with their teenage twin boys Steve and Andy in 1989. While Liz McDonald has been the mainstay of the family, hot-tempered ex-husband Jim has spent time away from the *Street*. Even then, his return visits have seen him commit manslaughter and armed robbery, spend time in jail, be diagnosed with a muscle-weakening disease and con Liz that her deceased baby girl was really alive.

Charles Lawson started acting in 1980 and was well-known before joining *Coronation Street*, appearing in many TV shows and acting on stage with the Royal Shakespeare Company and at the National Theatre.

He recalls his early days on the *Street*: 'They asked me to join *Coronation Street* first in 1987, but I was tied up at the National Theatre. When they were introducing the McDonalds they asked to see me. It was between becoming a regular on *The Bill* or *Coronation Street*, and I chose *Corrie*. At that time there were only 25 characters, now there are about 160! In those days Bev (Callard) and I would often do five-minute scenes; now they're shorter as the writers have so many characters to fit in. It became apparent very early on that they wanted to write for us and as long as we did it right we weren't going anywhere.'

Charles says he likes Jim very much. 'I'm not like him though. There's always a degree of yourself in the character – neither of us suffers fools gladly – but I'm not violent like Jim can be. I think the viewers like him because, although he's flawed and made mistakes, he's a "real man".'

Jim McDonald had an army past. Charles himself toyed with the idea of joining the marines as a young man and spent time living with three marine pals for a while, which helped to inform the character. Charles has returned to *Coronation Street* periodically over the years. One thing that really makes coming back to Weatherfield is, he says, the cast and crew. 'The crew are absolutely brilliant, they looked after me terribly well. We had tremendous fun, there was a *Coronation Street* cricket team early on and we partied hard as well. I still have a lot of very good friends from the crew who I see regularly.'

No 13 Coronation Street

Kevin and Jack Webster and Abi Franklin, played by Michael Le Vell, Kyran Bowes and Sally Carman

Kevin Webster has been a mainstay of *Coronation Street* since 1983. The mechanic lodged with Hilda Ogden at No 13, which is situated next door to the Corner Shop, and bought the house in 1987, exchanging with the Peacocks of No 4 20 years later. He had met young Sally Seddon the year before, but their happy marriage ended (the first time) when Kevin had an affair with Natalie Horrocks. Tragic relationships with disturbed Alison Wakefield (Naomi Radcliffe) and Tyrone's wife Molly, plus a second failed marriage to Sally followed, and he moved back into No 13 with son Jack in 2014.

He now lives with his garage employee girlfriend Abi, who first appeared in the *Street* in 2017 as the troubled mother of older son Seb (Harry Visinoni) and young twins Charlie and Lexi, who she was unable to look after and agreed to their adoption. The former addict and jailbird has turned her life around and is good friends with Kevin's ex Sally.

Manchester-born Michael Le Vell, born Michael Turner, was a member of the Oldham Theatre Workshop as a child. He appeared in *Coronation Street* as paperboy Neil Grimshaw in 1981, two years before returning as popular young mechanic Kevin.

Key previous residents

Christine Appleby, played by Christine Hargreaves

Christine, played by Christine Hargreaves (1939–84) was one of the original residents from 1960. She looked after her ailing mother May, but as Ena Sharples remarked, No 13 Coronation Street was an unlucky house: 'It has a long, unhappy history, has that house… It was Christine Hardman's mother May, she died on the stairs and nobody heard her calling.'

Hilda and Stan Ogden, played by Jean Alexander and Bernard Youens

Stan: 'What's that lipstick taste of?'
Hilda: 'Woman Stanley, woman.'

The Ogdens lived at No 13 for 23 years. Hilda decorated in a very individual style, with a majestic mural (or 'murial' as *Coronation Street*'s own Mrs Malaprop, Hilda, pronounced it) of the Canadian Rockies, later replaced with one featuring a coastline over which the crooked pot ducks that took pride of place in the back room flew. Hilda took her beloved ducks with her when she moved away to the country. Stan memorably installed a huge serving hatch between the two downstairs rooms at No 13, using canteen measurements by mistake.

Lazy, bumbling Stan and gossipy cleaner Hilda lived permanently on the breadline, and Hilda battled to scrape by while Stan preferred to slope off for a pint in The Rovers. Lodger Eddie Yeats, the jovial binman always on the lookout for the next scam, added a new dimension to their chaotic household.

Rarely seen without her curlers, pinny and headscarf, Hilda fancied she had clairvoyant powers and would offer wildly inaccurate readings to her neighbours.

After Stan died, Hilda took in Kevin and Sally as lodgers before leaving Weatherfield for Derbyshire to keep house for Dr Lowther. The Rovers' regulars were sure to miss her gossip and high-pitched, off-key warbling. Annie Walker once remarked of Stan and Hilda: 'The Ogdens are rather like a crossword. One can enjoy oneself working out what they mean, but it's such a dreadful waste of time.'

Liverpool-born Jean Alexander (1926–2016) worked as a wardrobe and stage mistress in rep before taking up the role of Hilda. She had appeared briefly before as a landlady and went on to create the soap idol Hilda Ogden. Following her record-breaking final appearance on Christmas Day 1987 (watched by 26 million people), Jean appeared for several years in long-running series *Last of the Summer Wine*. In 1988 Jean became the first soap actress to be nominated for a prestigious Bafta, and 16 years later was voted the greatest soap opera star of all time by readers of the *Radio Times*.

'Drop dead, Stan. And then get up and do it again.' Hilda

Born Bernard Popley, Bernard Youens (1914–84) was a stage and screen actor and radio announcer before joining the *Street*. He spent time in rep before serving in North Africa in the Second World War. One of his five children, Michael, worked as a cameraman on *Coronation Street*.

'Never mind yer dinner, look at me murial. Me mountain's turned into a slag heap!' Hilda, after Stan causes soot to fall in the house.

No 15a Coronation Street

Daniel, Bertie and latterly Sinead Osbourne, played by Rob Mallard, Rufus Morgan-Smith and Katie McGlynn

Florrie Lindley took in lodgers in the flat above the Corner Shop in the 1960s and since then notable residents have included Tricia Hopkins, Gail Potter and Sunita Parekh (later Alahan). The flat subsequently became home to Ken's son Daniel and wife Sinead and was the scene of one of the last deaths on *Coronation Street* before its 60th anniversary.

In heartrending scenes, viewers saw young mum Sinead treated for cervical cancer before dying aged just 25. Both Rob Mallard, who joined the show in 2016 as the third actor to play Daniel and had appeared in *Emmerdale* and *Fresh Meat*, and Katie McGlynn, who had worked on *Waterloo Road* before landing the part of kooky Sinead Tinker in 2013, were highly praised by viewers and critics alike for their performances through Sinead's cancer storyline.

Katie McGlynn joined the *Street* when she was 19. She had always watched *Coronation Street* with her grandparents. 'It's quite sad really,' she says. 'My grandad always asked me when I was on *Waterloo Road*, "When are you going to get on *Coronation Street*?" And he passed away right before I got the audition for *Corrie*.'

Katie only expected to be in the show for a couple of episodes. 'It was originally just to annoy the character Katy [Armstrong] who was with Chesney at the time' but, as often happens when the producers and writers spot an actor they think has more potential, those initial two episodes turned into a six-year stint.

'I loved playing Sinead,' says Katie. 'She was so quirky but a nice person, she's like one of those friends you're kind of embarrassed about but you love her to bits. If I could compare her to anyone, she was a bit like Phoebe from *Friends*, a bit weird but with a heart of gold. Over the years they turned her into this quirky hippy type, kind of boho chick, which was brilliant. I loved her, I thought she was a great character.'

Sinead's first scene was in Roy's Rolls with Roy, Roy's mother (Stephanie Cole), Beth Tinker and Kirk Sutherland. 'It was very daunting, it felt surreal and I was really nervous.'

Sinead's cancer storyline was built up over a long time. 'It was my favourite to play,' says Katie. 'The "who pushed Ken down the stairs" storyline was part of it because Sinead had had an abortion, so it all kind of linked in. It was great being part of the Barlows in such a big storyline and then the cancer stuff was amazing.'

Lisa George, who plays Beth Sutherland, Sinead's auntie, says the storyline was the hardest she had ever done. 'It made me cry a lot during filming. It felt so real thanks to working so closely with Katie and Rob. Katie and I are very close and I felt so comfortable with her on set. I loved working with her.'

Katie says she learned a great deal working on *Coronation Street*: 'I've made lifelong friends as well. I couldn't have asked for a better job. I feel lucky to have been part of such a big show. I was sad to leave my friends on *Corrie*, but because I left on such a big story I guess Sinead will always be remembered because of Daniel and Bertie. It feels like I'll never totally be gone from there. The character didn't just leave in a taxi and never come back, there's a part of Sinead still there. And *Coronation Street* will always be a part of me.'

Rob says, 'I found joining the most famous family on *Coronation Street* quite a lot of pressure at first, but it turned into the best way to spend my day. My favourite storyline, without doubt, is being father to baby Bertie and all that involved alongside my fellow actor Katie McGlynn. She's a star!

'I suspect my character is destined to be one of the more tragic characters in *Coronation Street* but, as an actor, working on this show has been so challenging and much more rewarding than I ever expected it would be.'

Sinead originally ran her own business selling homemade soap, and in 2019, she began making beard oil.

No 2a Coronation Street

Emma Brooker, Seb Franklin and Alina Pop,
played by Alexandra Mardell, Harry Visinoni and
Ruxandra Porojnicu

Following drama school Alexandra Mardell, who joined the show
in 2018 as hairdresser Emma, started up Junkbox Theatre company
with friends. Actor Brenda Blethyn saw her perform and asked her
to audition for hit show *Vera*. After that it was back on stage until
the call came from *Coronation Street*. 'I'd been called for other parts,
which didn't quite work out,' says Alexandra, 'but this one did.'

Alexandra was brought in to provide some comic relief amid the
harrowing David Platt rape storyline. 'The better you are at doing
the comedy, the more the writers write for you and that's how it
progresses. I was quite nervous when I got the job and saw that
Emma was quite a comedic role because I'd never done comedy
before. Then I got used to doing the comedy and thought, oh no,
what if I can't do the more serious stuff!'

The 'serious stuff' was discovering Steve McDonald was her real
father, a storyline that brought the character of hairdresser Fiona
Middleton back briefly. 'I used to watch *Corrie* with my mum,'
says Alexandra. 'It was always the show I wanted to be on. So many

actors I aspired to be like had started on this show – Katherine
Kelly, Suranne Jones and Angela Griffin.

'I loved working with Simon (Gregson) on the whole father
storyline, but my favourite storyline was the love triangle between
Emma, Chesney and Gemma, especially as they all became friends.
Some of those scenes I really enjoyed.

'When I first started there was the possibility I could be here for
the 60th anniversary and I was really excited about that.'

Barlow Family Tree

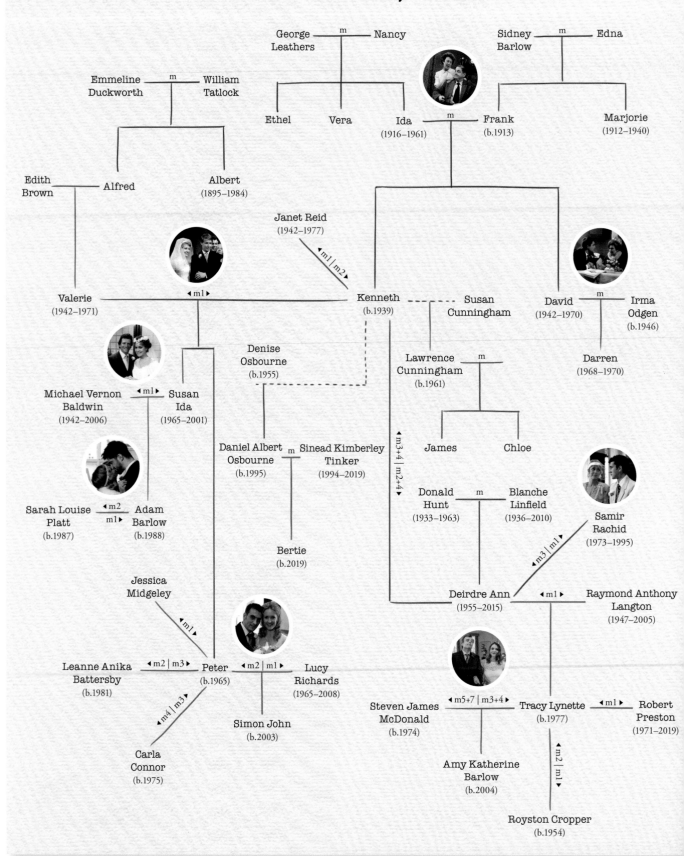

George Leathers — m — Nancy

Sidney Barlow — m — Edna

Emmeline Duckworth — m — William Tatlock

Ethel

Vera

Ida (1916–1961) — m — Frank (b.1913)

Marjorie (1912–1940)

Edith Brown — Alfred

Albert (1895–1984)

Janet Reid (1942–1977) — m1 | m2

Valerie (1942–1971) — m1 — Kenneth (b.1939) --- Susan Cunningham

David (1942–1970) — m — Irma Odgen (b.1946)

Michael Vernon Baldwin (1942–2006) — m1 — Susan Ida (1965–2001)

Denise Osbourne (b.1955)

Lawrence Cunningham (b.1961) — m

Darren (1968–1970)

Sarah Louise Platt (b.1987) — m2 | m1 — Adam Barlow (b.1988)

Daniel Albert Osbourne (b.1995) — m — Sinead Kimberley Tinker (1994–2019)

James

Chloe

m3+4 | m2+4

Donald Hunt (1933–1963) — m — Blanche Linfield (1936–2010)

Samir Rachid (1973–1995)

Bertie (b.2019)

Jessica Midgeley — m1

Leanne Anika Battersby (b.1981) — m2 | m3 — Peter (b.1965) — m2 | m1 — Lucy Richards (1965–2008)

Deirdre Ann (1955–2015) — m3 | m1 — m1 — Raymond Anthony Langton (1947–2005)

m4 | m3 — Carla Connor (b.1975)

Simon John (b.2003)

Steven James McDonald (1974) — m5+7 | m3+4 — Tracy Lynette (b.1977) — m1 — Robert Preston (1971–2019)

Amy Katherine Barlow (b.2004)

m2 | m1

Royston Cropper (b.1954)

Connor Family Tree

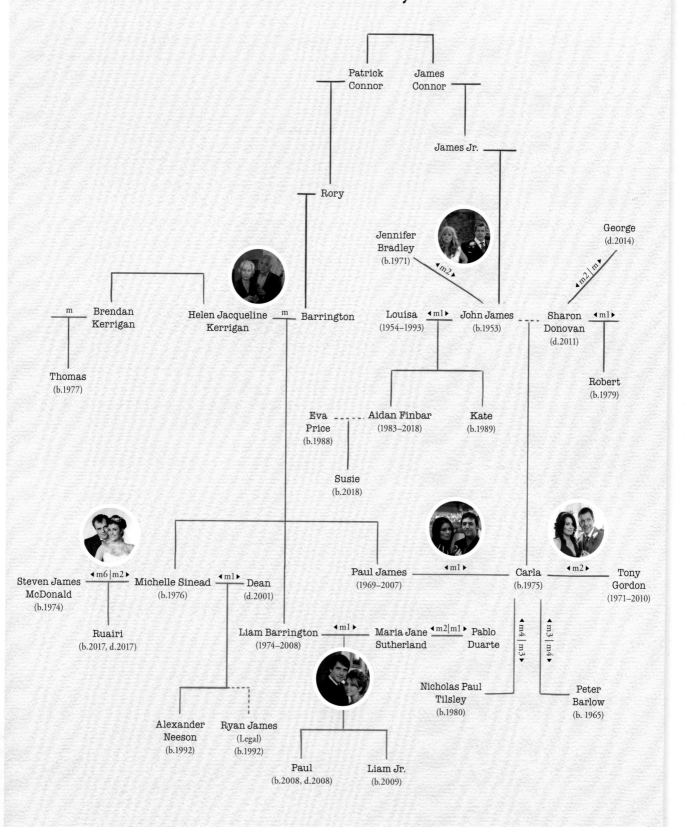

Patrick Connor

James Connor

James Jr.

Rory

Jennifer Bradley
(b.1971)

George
(d.2014)

◀ m2 ▶

◀ m2 | m ▶

m — Brendan Kerrigan

Helen Jacqueline Kerrigan — m — Barrington

Louisa
(1954–1993)

◀ m1 ▶

John James
(b.1953)

Sharon Donovan
(d.2011)

◀ m1 ▶

Thomas
(b.1977)

Robert
(b.1979)

Eva Price
(b.1988)

Aidan Finbar
(1983–2018)

Kate
(b.1989)

Susie
(b.2018)

Steven James McDonald
(b.1974)

◀ m6 | m2 ▶

Michelle Sinead
(b.1976)

◀ m1 ▶

Dean
(d.2001)

Paul James
(1969–2007)

◀ m1 ▶

Carla
(b.1975)

◀ m2 ▶

Tony Gordon
(1971–2010)

Ruairi
(b.2017, d.2017)

Liam Barrington
(1974–2008)

◀ m1 ▶

Maria Jane Sutherland

◀ m2 | m1 ▶

Pablo Duarte

◀ m4 | m3 ▶

◀ m3 | m4 ▶

Nicholas Paul Tilsley
(b.1980)

Peter Barlow
(b. 1965)

Alexander Neeson
(b.1992)

Ryan James
(Legal)
(b.1992)

Paul
(b.2008, d.2008)

Liam Jr.
(b.2009)

1982 The Queen and Prince Philip opened the new set on the Granada lot. Houses were built using reclaimed bricks and tiles from real Salford houses, including some from Archie Street.

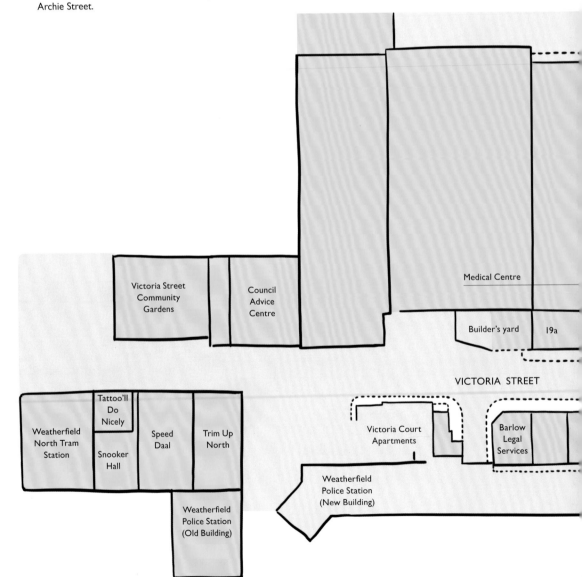

Victoria Street Community Gardens

Council Advice Centre

Medical Centre

Builder's yard

19a

VICTORIA STREET

Weatherfield North Tram Station

Tattoo'll Do Nicely

Snooker Hall

Speed Daal

Trim Up North

Victoria Court Apartments

Barlow Legal Services

Weatherfield Police Station (New Building)

Weatherfield Police Station (Old Building)

1968 In 1968 the set moved outdoors to nearby Grape Street. Initially made of wood, it was rebuilt the following year in brick to withstand the Manchester climate.

1960 The first set was in Studio 2 at Granada. The seven houses, the corner shop and The Rovers were built to ¾ scale.

The set over the years

When Tony Warren drove around the city to find the archetypal Salford street, he could hardly have predicted exactly how famous it would become. He settled on Archie Street – an inconspicuous terraced street in the Ordsall district – for his inspiration. The small street set was built in the Granada studios at a scale that meant the actors had to walk slowly past the backdrop so as not to ruin the 'reality'. Fast forward 60 years and the *Coronation Street* set is a huge lot at MediaCityUK Old Trafford covering 7.7 acres, containing 400,000 facing bricks and 54,000 cobbles reclaimed from the canalside in Eccles.

THE STREET'S

2020

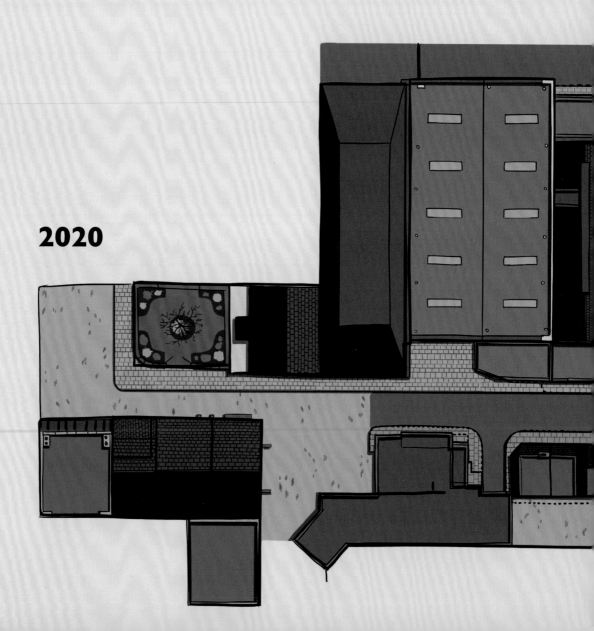

EVOLUTION

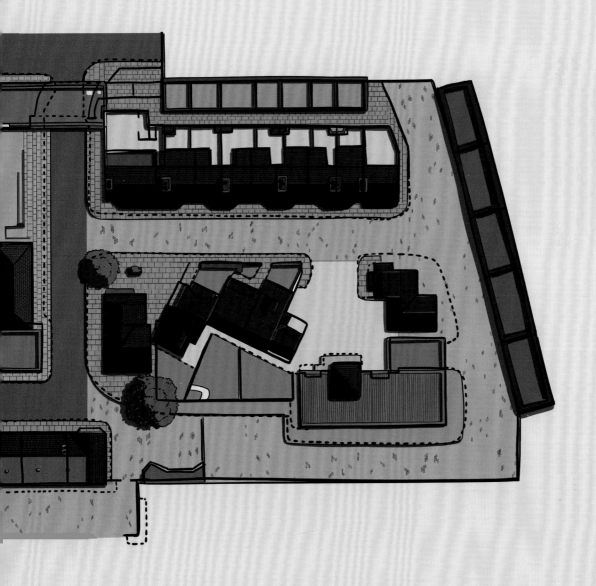

and Community Centre were demolished and, by 1990, three new houses, a garage, salon plus flat and the newly-sited Kabin with its two flats took their place.

1999 The set underwent a revamp, with the addition of Victoria Street, with Roy's Rolls and D&S Hardware.

The set moved location to Trafford Wharf Road. Producers were keen to keep it looking almost identical to its previous incarnation, with the only major changes being an extra window for the Rovers Return, and the road being made wider.

1999 A medical centre and chippy were also added on Rosamund Street, making use of the old derelict Graffiti Club.

1990 When the programme moved to three episodes a week in 1989, the cast had to be expanded and those extra characters needed more houses to live in. The factory unit

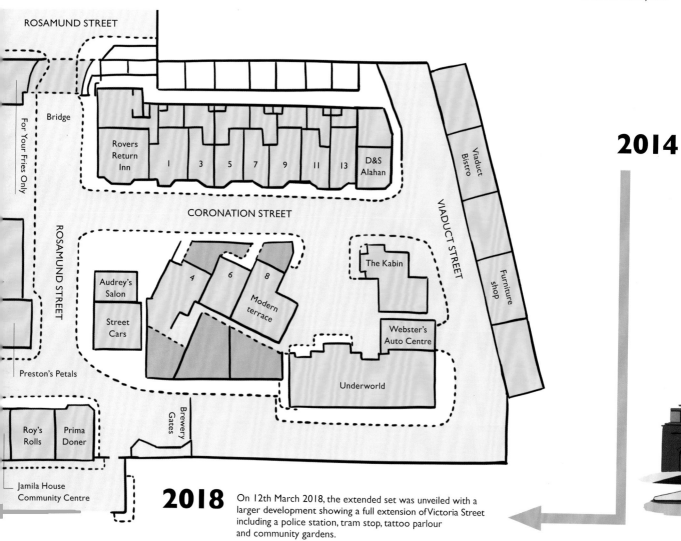

ROSAMUND STREET

Bridge

For Your Fries Only

ROSAMUND STREET

Rovers Return Inn

1 3 5 7 9 11 13

D&S Alahan

Viaduct Bistro

CORONATION STREET

VIADUCT STREET

Audrey's Salon

Street Cars

4 6 8

Modern terrace

The Kabin

Webster's Auto Centre

Furniture shop

Preston's Petals

Underworld

Brewery Gates

Roy's Rolls

Prima Doner

Jamila House Community Centre

2014

2018 On 12th March 2018, the extended set was unveiled with a larger development showing a full extension of Victoria Street including a police station, tram stop, tattoo parlour and community gardens.

Webster Family Tree

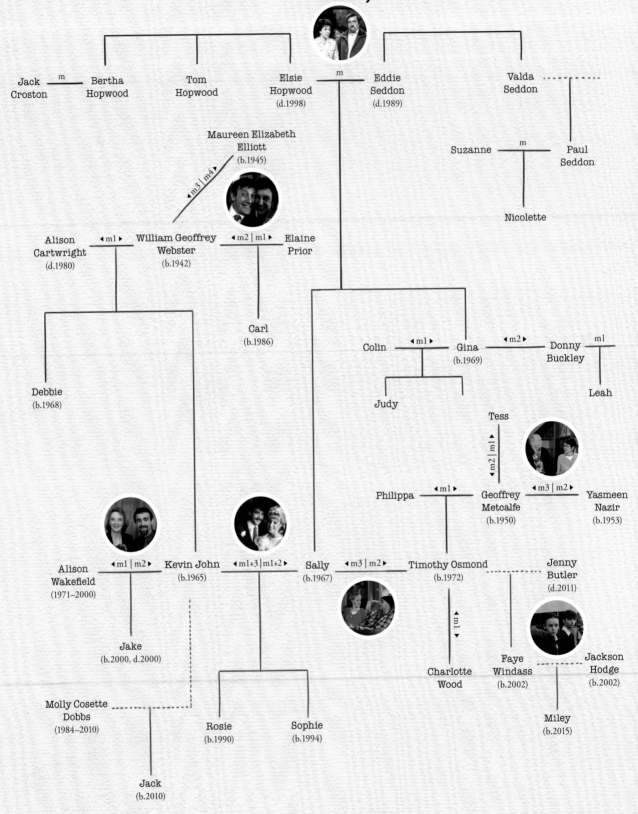

Jack Croston — m — Bertha Hopwood

Tom Hopwood

Elsie Hopwood (d.1998)

m — Eddie Seddon (d.1989)

Valda Seddon

Suzanne — m — Paul Seddon

Nicolette

Maureen Elizabeth Elliott (b.1945)

◄ m3 | m4 ►

Alison Cartwright (d.1980) — ◄ m1 ► — William Geoffrey Webster (b.1942) — ◄ m2 | m1 ► — Elaine Prior

Carl (b.1986)

Debbie (b.1968)

Colin — ◄ m1 ► — Gina (b.1969) — ◄ m2 ► — Donny Buckley — m1

Judy

Leah

Tess

◄ m2 | m1 ►

Philippa — ◄ m1 ► — Geoffrey Metcalfe (b.1950) — ◄ m3 | m2 ► — Yasmeen Nazir (b.1953)

Alison Wakefield (1971–2000) — ◄ m1 | m2 ► — Kevin John (b.1965) — ◄ m1+3 | m1+2 ► — Sally (b.1967) — ◄ m3 | m2 ► — Timothy Osmond (b.1972)

Jenny Butler (d.2011)

Jake (b.2000, d.2000)

◄ m1 ►

Charlotte Wood

Faye Windass (b.2002)

Jackson Hodge (b.2002)

Molly Cosette Dobbs (1984–2010)

Rosie (b.1990)

Sophie (b.1994)

Miley (b.2015)

Jack (b.2010)

Platt Family Tree

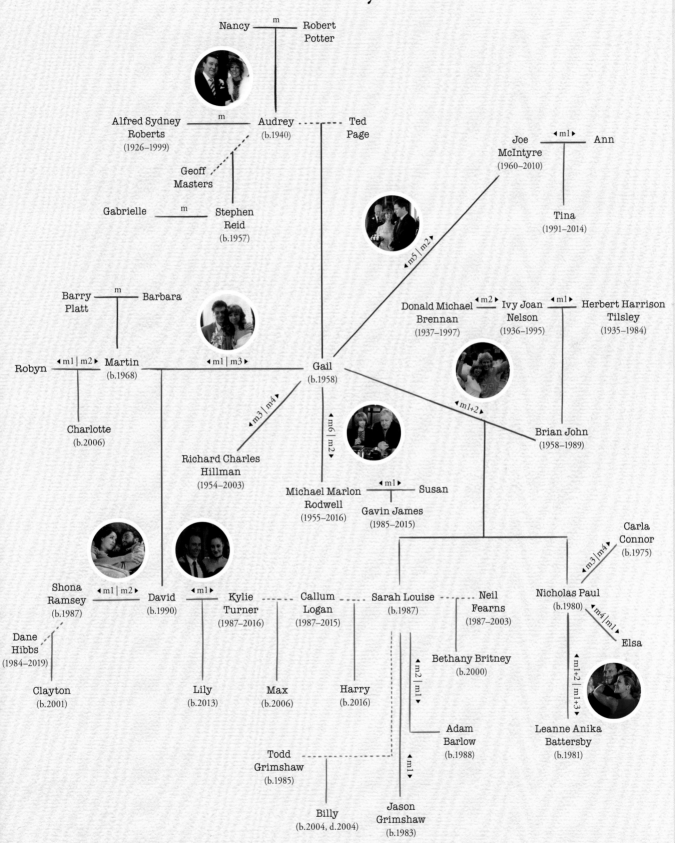

Nancy — m — Robert Potter

Alfred Sydney Roberts (1926–1999) — m — Audrey (b.1940) ----- Ted Page

Geoff Masters

Gabrielle — m — Stephen Reid (b.1957)

Joe McIntyre (1960–2010) ◄ m1 ► Ann

Tina (1991–2014)

m5 | m2 ►

Barry Platt — m — Barbara

Donald Michael Brennan (1937–1997) ◄ m2 ► Ivy Joan Nelson (1936–1995) ◄ m1 ► Herbert Harrison Tilsley (1935–1984)

Robyn ◄ m1 | m2 ► Martin (b.1968) ◄ m1 | m3 ► Gail (b.1958)

Charlotte (b.2006)

◄ m1+2 ►

Brian John (1958–1989)

m3 | m4 ►

◄ m6 | m2 ▼

Richard Charles Hillman (1954–2003)

Michael Marlon Rodwell (1955–2016) ◄ m1 ► Susan

Gavin James (1985–2015)

Carla Connor (b.1975)

m3 | m4 ►

Nicholas Paul (b.1980)

m4 | m1 ►

Elsa

Shona Ramsey (b.1987) ◄ m1 | m2 ► David (b.1990) ◄ m1 ► Kylie Turner (1987–2016) ----- Callum Logan (1987–2015) ----- Sarah Louise (b.1987) ----- Neil Fearns (1987–2003)

Dane Hibbs (1984–2019)

Clayton (b.2001)

Lily (b.2013)

Max (b.2006)

Harry (b.2016)

Bethany Britney (b.2000)

▲ m2 | m1 ▼

Adam Barlow (b.1988)

▲ m1+2 | m1+3 ▼

Leanne Anika Battersby (b.1981)

Todd Grimshaw (b.1985)

▲ m1 ▼

Billy (b.2004, d.2004)

Jason Grimshaw (b.1983)

No 10a Coronation Street

Rita Tanner, played by Barbara Knox

'I've had trifles last longer than some of her marriages.' Vera on Rita's relationships

First appearing briefly in 1964, Rita Tanner has been a permanent character since 1972 and the former nightclub chanteuse is now the Grande Dame of the *Street*. Her storylines have been some of the most popular and best-viewed, including marrying Len Fairclough in 1977. With no children of their own, they fostered, and Rita has looked out for *Coronation Street*'s waifs and strays. Rita moved into the flat above The Kabin newsagent, her workplace for decades, in 1990 when she rented No 7 out.

Barbara Knox had done many years in repertory theatre and radio by the time she became a regular on *Coronation Street*. 'Rep was the finest training in the world,' she says. 'You learned the craft, you worked with an audience, you learned delivery, timing, pauses, you learned to time a laugh. You learned everything about the business and it was a marvellous time. I worked in so many places that had fantastic repertories, first weekly, then fortnightly, then monthly reps.'

Always a disciplined actor, Barbara reveals: 'Even now I go home, get my script and learn it. I don't wait, I try to work on it and do something with it. I worked with some wonderful people over the years. I used to stand in the wings and watch and think, how did she do that?'

Barbara also worked in radio with a number of top comedians, including Ken Dodd and Les Dawson. In 1972 she was 11 weeks into a 13-week contract with Ken Dodd when she got the call from *Coronation Street*. 'I didn't know if he'd release me,' she says, 'but he looked at me and said: "Don't let me down on *Coronation Street*." And that was it.'

The head of casting for Granada at the time was Jose Scott. Similar to today's casting department visiting theatres regularly to spot new talent, Scott and her assistants would go around the repertory companies, seeking promising actors.

'Jose Scott was very good to me,' says Barbara. 'She saw me in a little part and said "I must find something for you," and I didn't have to audition.'

Young Rita had come to work in the Viaduct Sporting Club. She needed somewhere to stay and ended up in Elsie's bed.

Ironically, Rita would go on to marry Dennis when he returned to *Coronation Street* in 2011 after a 43-year absence. He was her third husband.

Philip Lowrie was in two minds about returning to the *Street* but agreed when he knew he would be working with Barbara. 'I didn't want to come back for just a few episodes, but the producer at the time, Phil Collinson, he wanted to offer me a two-year contract, so I was happy to come back. And I was working with Barbara Knox, a tremendous privilege because she is the most wonderful actress and we worked very well together. I had a wonderful time with her. We'd sit in The Rovers Return and rehearse a scene and she'd say, come on Philip, let's do it again, we can get more out of it. Those green eyes would flash and she'd come up with something extraordinary. She's a very, very good actress, one of the best.'

Barbara remembers her return: 'When I came back in 1972 the writers asked me, what do you think Rita does? And I said, she'll work in a club I think. When I got the script it said Rita was a singer. Now I don't sing, but they said don't worry, just come in on Monday.

'In those days we came in on Monday morning just to read through. On Tuesdays we'd rehearse, then Wednesdays we'd rehearse with everyone watching, in the rehearsal room, so props and wardrobe and makeup would know what was going on. Every time it came to the scene where it said Rita is singing they'd give me a beer bottle as a microphone and say, just stand there, we'll sort this out on Wednesday afternoon. On Wednesday afternoon I was told to meet the musical director Derek Hilton. He said, well can you sing? I started to sing and I didn't know but he gave a thumbs up to everyone watching through the glass door. Afterwards I said what would have happened if I couldn't sing and they said, oh we'd have thought of something.'

At first Rita was living with Harry Bates and his two children. It was decided Rita wouldn't have children of her own but that she could foster Sharon Gaskell (Tracie Bennett) and then Jenny Bradley. She also took Sally under her wing, and Sally, Kevin and the girls were like a family for Rita. 'It's nice for Rita to have somebody like Jenny, or lately Gemma, because she has nobody,' says Barbara. 'All the men have gone. I think it's nice for me to be given the privilege these days of working with some of the younger actors, of having a story and helping them along. Rita sort of soldiers on. She also had a lovely relationship with Norris in The Kabin, a fighting one but a funny one.'

Barbara believes she's been fortunate to stay on *Coronation Street* for so long: 'From that first appearance and then coming back it just grew and grew. Apart from my family, *Coronation Street* means everything to me. To have this in my life at 86 is remarkable. To be on this street, this world-famous street, when I came in for a couple of lines, is wonderful. I love it, I hate to think of the day when I don't turn up here.'

No 12 Coronation Street

Brian Packham, Cathy Matthews and Alex Warner,
played by Peter Gunn, Melanie Hill and Liam Bairstow

Brian Packham is the overbearing former headteacher, now owner of The Kabin and living in the flat above with Cathy Matthews, Roy's former girlfriend. Brian previously dated Julie Carp and was subjected to workplace bullying in his former school. Cathy's introduction saw her living as a hoarder who discovered her late husband had been sleeping with her sister. Cathy looked after her nephew Alex Warner who works in Roy's Rolls.

Both Peter Gunn and Melanie Hill had long acting CVs before joining *Coronation Street* in 2010 and 2015 respectively. Melanie appeared in *Auf Wiedersehen Pet* and as Aveline in *Bread*, as well as in *Brassed Off*, in which Peter also appeared (although the two didn't share any scenes). Peter was also a regular in *Born & Bred* and appeared in *Hannah Montana: The Movie*.

Liam Bairstow joined an acting school specialising in working with disabled actors called Mind The Gap in 2009. He came to the attention of *Coronation Street* bosses when he took part in a workshop for disabled talent and his character Alex has become a firm favourite with fans.

No 19a Rosamund Street

Billy Mayhew, Paul Foreman and Summer Spellman, played by Daniel Brocklebank, Peter Ash and Matilda Freeman

Vicar Billy lives in the flat above Preston's Petals with partner Paul, Gemma's twin brother, who he helped through his historical sexual abuse ordeal, and with Summer Spellman, to whom he is guardian. Billy had his own demons to deal with when it emerged, after he had been on the *Street* for several years, that he had been responsible for the road death of Susan Barlow years ago.

Daniel Brocklebank had been acting for 25 years before joining the *Street*, appearing in more than 30 movies. When offered the part, he says it was his mother who pushed him to accept.

'My mum's watched it her whole life and I was with her when I got the call offering me the job. I said thank you, I'll think about it and call you back and my mum said: "What do you mean you'll think about it, you'll phone them back and say you'll take the job. You cannot not do *Coronation Street*." She doesn't miss an episode.

'It's a national institution, it's just part of society in the UK. It was a big move for me, I was in London and I moved to Manchester.'

Billy joined *Coronation Street* as vicar in St Mary's local parish,

and quickly became Sean's new love interest. 'TV vicars tend to be stereotypically a bit insipid,' says Daniel, 'and I wondered why a gay man of his age would join the clergy. So I thought what is he trying to do here? Maybe he used the church to get out of a bad situation; I have known people who have used religion to get themselves away from addiction and it gives them a sense of purpose. That's where the Susan Barlow storyline came from.'

The wonderful thing about *Coronation Street* from an actor's perspective, says Daniel, is that actors have the opportunity to play both drama and comedy. 'Billy, because of his job, is a man of the community so he can slot into various story forms, be they heavy ones like Sinead's death or more comedic ones. It's good to be able to show that range within the character.'

Daniel says Billy is the voice of reason on the *Street*. 'Soaps rely on conflict to propel them forwards and you need a balance. All the characters have a storytelling purpose and I think Billy's is, although he's flawed and he makes mistakes, he's the voice of reason, even though he can't keep his mouth shut, he can't keep a secret! He hasn't led a blame-free life, but he always tries to be the moralistic voice. And he's kind, he has time for people. That's why the audience likes him.'

No 15a Victoria Street

Liz McDonald, played by Beverley Callard

Beverley Callard appeared in *Coronation Street* as June, a friend of Gail and Brian Tilsley, for several episodes before accepting the role of army wife Liz McDonald when *Coronation Street* decided to introduce a new family in 1989. Liz currently lives alone at 15a Victoria Street, above the Street Cars office, after Steve, Tracy and Amy moved to No 1 Coronation Street in 2020.

'I was told Liz had had twins when she was 16, she'd been an army wife ever since, that's all she'd ever known', Beverley recalls about getting the part of Liz. 'So I researched army wives, not officers' wives of course, army wives. I loved doing the research; these women are so feisty and so strong. Now Jim was coming out of the army and they were about to buy their first proper house, which was No 11 Coronation Street. I thought, oh my goodness, I so want to do this.

'Charlie (Lawson) and I read together and I would have chosen him and he said he would have chosen me. If he'd have preferred someone else, he'd have told me!' Beverley and Charlie discussed at length how they were going to play the McDonalds. 'Of course you can't change the lines and the scripts, but there's 50 ways to play each script, so Charlie and I decided that Liz would be the real strength. Soldiers are told what to do and they are used to a regimented way of life. Liz was the one who coped and Jim, although he was a really strong man, did what he was told. We decided that Jim would think much more with his fists and Liz was the strength behind him.'

Beverley was delighted to be able to play out all Liz's storylines over the years, the high drama and the comedy. She says: 'It's a matriarchal show and we must never lose that because that's what Tony Warren created. He was surrounded by these strong women who were like Ena Sharples, Elsie Tanner, Annie Walker, Hilda… they would fight for their families and literally come to blows on the street as they did. Liz was like that.

'I loved my scenes with Simon Gregson, sometimes we couldn't look at each other without laughing.'

Beverley says Liz, with her love of Lycra, short skirts, plunging tops and liberal application of makeup, is not like her at all: 'She's much more confident than I am, much more blasé. I hardly wear any makeup in real life, I wear baggy clothes. I'm not a party animal, we're very different really.'

No 16a Victoria Street

Roy Cropper, played by David Neilson

'You have turned an apology of an existence into a life, fuller and more joyous than I could ever hope.' Roy to Hayley

Royston 'Roy' Cropper, proprietor of Roy's Rolls café since he bought Alma's share of the former Jim's Café, started out in *Coronation Street* as a bit of an oddball loner, and has become one of the show's most loved characters. Highly intelligent, well-read and eager to help anyone, although eccentric and pedantically honest in a childlike way, Roy is happiest settled down in his flat above the café with a book on the history of the steam engine.

'The Stone Roses are not my cup of tea, although the percussion is reminiscent of Wagner.' Roy

His relationship with, and subsequent marriage to, transgender Hayley Patterson (formerly called Harold), a storyline that was well ahead of its time, enchanted viewers, and both David Neilson and Julie Hesmondhalgh won awards for their portrayals. Gentle Hayley's death also brought a controversial subject to the fore – the right to die – and again the show was praised for its handling of the subject.

Hayley and Roy had always been happy to open their doors to any youngster in need – Roy had an unhappy childhood thanks to his domineering mother – and Roy's most recent storyline saw him take in his bereaved niece Nina.

Before joining *Coronation Street* in 1995 David Neilson appeared in numerous roles in TV shows including *Bergerac, Boys From The Blackstuff* and *Heartbeat.* He was also cast in two Mike Leigh films and includes radio and stage appearances on his acting CV.

'My mother made every Christmas hell. She insisted on buying presents for the child she wanted rather than the boy that I was.' Roy

No 18a Victoria Street

Beth and Kirk Sutherland, and Craig Tinker, played by Lisa George, Andrew Whyment and Colson Smith

The flat above Prima Doner was the scene of Aidan Connor's suicide in May 2018. Former residents have included Eva Price, Katy Armstrong and son Joseph, Rob Donovan, Michelle and Ryan Connor, Leanne Battersby, Martin Platt and Katy Harris. Now it's home to Kirk and Beth Sutherland and Beth's son Craig.

Beth was originally an ex of Steve. Her marriage to packer Kirk turned out to be bigamous – Beth was still married to her jailbird ex Darryl at the time – and recent events in the mouthy factory worker's life have included seeing her softer side as the family coped with the death of her niece Sinead.

Soft-hearted Craig has been like a big brother to friends Faye and Bethany and recently achieved his dream of training as a police officer.

Kirk has been a mainstay character on *Coronation Street* for 20 years. The older brother of Maria, Kirk worked in his family's kennels before joining the Underworld staff.

Andrew Whyment starred in award-winning comedy *The Royle Family* before joining *Coronation Street* as Maria Sutherland's brother Kirk in 2000. The dopey but loveable factory packer married Beth Tinker in one of *Coronation Street*'s most memorable weddings – a 1980s-themed party, with Kirk dressed as Adam Ant.

Lisa George has a background in musicals, theatre, TV, radio and film. She supported Chuck Berry and Little Richard on tour and was a backing singer for Joe Longthorne.

Colson Smith joined *Coronation Street* at the age of 13 for what was supposed to be a couple of episodes. Thanks to a positive reaction he stayed.

No 19a Victoria Street

Ryan Connor, Alya Nazir, Imran Habeeb and Toyah Battersby, played by Ryan Prescott, Sair Khan, Charlie de Melo and Georgia Taylor

The flat above the builder's yard has been occupied over the years by characters including Peter Barlow and Shelley Unwin, Charlie Stubbs, Owen Armstrong, Tina McIntyre and Steph Britton. Its current residents are couples Alya and Ryan and Toyah and Imran.

Alya, boss of Speed Daal, became an item with Michelle Connor's switched-at-birth son Ryan. They have recently had their hands full looking out for Alya's grandma Yasmeen during her ordeal at the hands of her sinister husband Geoff Metcalfe, through which Ryan has been a tower of strength for Alya.

Counsellor (and sister of Leanne) Toyah helped solicitor Imran to cope with the loss of his sister Rana in the Underworld roof collapse, and they became an item after Toyah split up with Peter Barlow. Toyah had returned to Weatherfield with Peter in December 2016 following her 14-year break from the Street and for a short while they ran The Rovers. Now Toyah and Imran hope to realise their dream of fostering a child together.

Georgia Taylor originally auditioned for the part of Zoe Tattersall before landing Toyah. As well as *Coronation Street* she is known for acting in many TV series including *Casualty* and *Law and Order UK*. Sair Khan trained in New York and appeared on *Doctors* before joining *Coronation Street*. Ryan Prescott worked in TV, film and on stage after graduating from The Liverpool Institute of Performing Arts. He is the third actor to play Ryan, joining *Coronation Street* in 2018. Charlie de Melo appeared on *EastEnders* among other shows before coming to *Coronation Street* in 2017.

5 Victoria Court

Maria and Liam Connor and Gary Windass, played by Samia Longchambon, Charlie Wrenshall and Mikey North

Hairdresser Maria Connor was widowed when husband Liam was murdered in a hit-and-run. She has raised their son Liam Jnr alone. Never short of male admirers, Maria has been at the centre of many major events since her first appearance in 2000, including suffering a stillbirth, an attempted rape, being stalked and marrying a gay friend for passport purposes, for which she was sent to prison.

Soft-hearted when it comes to her friends and her son, Maria has had a hit-and-miss love life, with many lovers meeting a sticky end. After trying out online dating, with some comedic consequences, she got together with former squaddie and bad boy, loan shark Gary Windass in 2019.

Gary is father to Jake with former partner Izzy Armstrong and Zack with Pat Phelan's daughter Nicola Rubinstein (Nicola Thorp). Surrogate Tina McIntyre carried Jake for Gary and Izzy, who split soon after. Gary moved on with Alya Nazir and then Sarah Platt while Izzy, who lives on Grayling Street in Weatherfield, was jailed for possession of drugs when she was caught using marijuana to deal with the pain of Ehlers-Danlos Syndrome.

Gary suffers from post-traumatic stress disorder as a result of serving in Afghanistan. He was caught up in Pat Phelan's dastardly deeds thanks to working with Owen, his mother Anna's partner at the time, and had gradually edged towards being a bit of a baddie himself by the time he started a relationship with unsuspecting Maria, killing loan shark Rick Neelan (Greg Wood).

Samia Longchambon first appeared as an extra in *Coronation Street* at the age of eight, becoming a popular regular on the show eight years later.

Following a stint in the West End, Mikey North won the British Theatre Guide's Most Promising Newcomer Award. He joined *Coronation Street* as troubled Gary Windass in 2008.

12 Victoria Court

Nick Tilsley, Leanne and Oliver Battersby and Simon Barlow, played by Ben Price, Jane Danson, Emmanuel and Jeremiah Cheetham, and Alex Bain

Nick and Leanne have been married to each other twice, the first time eloping as teenagers. Both have had relationships with other people, but for now they are back together and living with Simon Barlow, Leanne's stepson, and her son Oliver, the result of a one-night stand with Steve McDonald.

Jane Danson first joined *Coronation Street* in 1997, having originally, like her screen step-sister, auditioned for the role of Zoe Tattersall. She has appeared in several TV shows, including the popular Granada drama *Children's Ward*. Her character Leanne was the only remaining Battersby in *Coronation Street* until the return of Toyah in 2016.

Alex Bain was six years old when he joined the cast in 2008, having already made an impact on screen in a cereal commercial. His portrayal of Simon has won him Best Young Actor at the both the Inside Soap and British Soap Awards.

Ben Price is the third actor to play Nick Tilsley, joining in 2009. He trained at the Drama Centre in London and then the Central School of Speech and Drama. He says: 'As time goes on, being in *Coronation Street* means more and more to me. I understand how many people it touches, what you can do with storylines – the brain injury story, cancer stories, losing babies. The more I'm in it, the more I want to take care of it, of "my family".'

Ben's favourite storyline was with David Platt and the brain injury. 'The brain injury flipped Nick, it really fired the character and he became duplicitous, he could nick money off his gran!'

Ben describes Nick as Machiavellian and financially driven. 'He's not had his own family, he's off and on with Leanne, he's not had his own kids or rooted himself and fully had it all, he wants to have it all.'

5 Grasmere Drive

Audrey Roberts, played by Sue Nicholls

'I am woman, I am willing, I am Weatherfield.' Audrey

Audrey Roberts made her entrance 41 years ago at daughter Gail's 21st birthday party. Never the most attentive mother, flighty Audrey flitted in and out of Gail's life for years before marrying Corner Shop owner and widower Alf Roberts (Bryan Mosley) and enjoying life as Weatherfield Mayoress and later local councillor.

She nursed best friend Alma Halliwell as she died of cancer in 2001 and since then Audrey, stalwart of the salon, has become an essential and much-loved *Coronation Street* character. She narrowly avoided being one of Richard Hillman's victims, fell for handsome conman Lewis Archer (although it turned out that he really did love her in the end) and saw her grandsons prosecuted for stealing her inheritance from her undertaker pal Archie Shuttleworth (Roy Hudd).

Before becoming a *Coronation Street* regular, Sue was known to TV audiences from her appearances in soap *Crossroads*, classic comedy *The Fall and Rise of Reginald Perrin* and kids' favourite *Rentaghost*. Sue has won a glut of awards for her portrayal of Audrey, culminating in a Lifetime Achievement Award in 2019 to mark 40 years on the show. Sue's husband Mark Eden played Alan Bradley in the 1980s.

Bryan Mosley (1931–1999) played genial grocer Alf Roberts as a regular cast member from 1971 to 1999. Before *Coronation Street* the former commercial artist had appeared in classic British films *Billy Liar*, *Far From the Madding Crowd* and *Get Carter*, among others. He died just weeks after his character passed away on the programme on New Year's Day 1999.

Glad Tidings Mission Hall

Ena Sharples, played by Violet Carson

The Glad Tidings Mission Hall was a place of worship for nonconformists. Its caretaker Ena Sharples lived in a flat in the Hall's vestry. The main Mission fronted onto Viaduct Street and Ena's entrance to the vestry at the rear was on Coronation Street. The Mission closed in 1968 and the building was demolished to make way for the new maisonettes. Ena later moved into one of the ground floor OAP flats. The Mission was the venue for the residents' 1962 Christmas production of the fictional play *Lady Lawson Loses* and later the Community Centre hosted many parties and classes.

'I don't expect life to be easy. I'd think very little of it if it was.'
Ena Sharples

Violet Carson (1898–1983) was a well-known actor, singer and pianist who had appeared in many film, radio and stage productions and was in her early 60s when Tony Warren suggested her for the character of Ena Sharples, soap's original, and many say best, battleaxe.

In her double-breasted coat and ever-present hairnet, the fearsome moral guardian of the Street was not above a good gossip about the neighbours while indulging in a milk stout with Minnie and Martha in The Rovers snug, and the harmonium-playing harridan was always keen to put 'scarlet woman' Elsie Tanner in her place.

Due to Violet Carson's ill health, her appearances on the programme dwindled after 1974 and she left in 1980 to finally retire in Blackpool.

'They don't need sewers round here, they've got Ena Sharples.'
Elsie Tanner

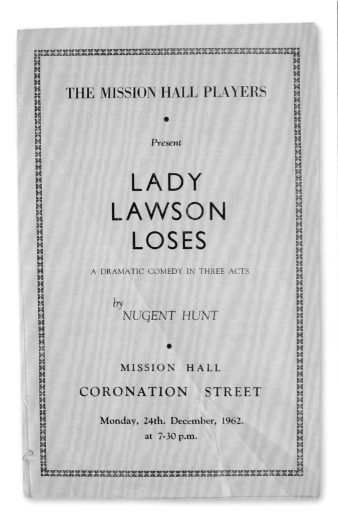

THE MISSION HALL PLAYERS

•

Present

LADY LAWSON LOSES

A DRAMATIC COMEDY IN THREE ACTS

by NUGENT HUNT

•

MISSION HALL
CORONATION STREET

Monday, 24th. December, 1962.
at 7·30 p.m.

EST. 1960

CHAPTER 4

Timeline 1960–2020

THE RESIDENTS SEEK REFUGE IN THE GLAD TIDINGS MISSION HALL WHEN A GAS MAIN EXPLODES IN A NEARBY STREET

As the residents gather in The Rovers to celebrate Billy Walker's return home from National Service, with free drinks courtesy of Annie and Jack, there's the sound of an explosion. A gas main has exploded and is on fire two streets away and the police tell everyone they have to evacuate to the mission. Ena refuses, as she had fibbed to Leonard Swindley that she was visiting a sick friend in order to avoid helping with the mission flowers. She's told in no uncertain terms that she must join the rest of the Street, and so her fib is revealed. There follows a night of companionship, humour and revelation, as the residents bed down in the hall until the danger is over.

DEC 1960

JAN

FEB

MAR

APR

MAY

1961

The first episode is broadcast on 9th December (see page 32).

Ken Barlow holds a student rally in his house. Arnold Tanner returns after 15 years asking Elsie for a divorce.

Episode 13 on 20th January is written by script editor Harry Kershaw, who in 1962 became the show's producer, as writers other than Tony Warren are required.

Davy Jones from *The Monkees* appears as Ena's grandson Colin Lomax.

By March, all ITV regions have picked up the programme.

Jed Stone turns up after release from borstal.

Residents go on a trip to Blackpool.

Billy Walker returns from National Service. This is his first appearance. Emily Nugent (later Bishop) debuts in the same episode. Len Fairclough also debuts this month.

Joan Walker marries Gordon Davies.

Series moves from Wednesdays and Fridays at 7pm to Mondays and Wednesdays at 7:30pm.

Ena moves in with Martha Longhurst.

David Barlow breaks his ankle playing for Weatherfield County FC.

Eric Davies c.c. G.Butler.

CORONATION STREET - P.228/92 & 93.
V.T.R. Fri. 27.10.61.
Sound F/X.   Bill Williams   19.10.61.

    We shall require the following F/X for this production.
Would you please arrange the necessary bookings:-

(1) Fish and chip frying noises (not too violent).   6 Mins.

(2) Street noise - cars etc.,passing at end of
    Coronation Street.   10 Mins. (Or. loop?)

(3) Background office noise - mostly typewriters
    and phone bells. As heard through glass
    partitions.   10 Mins.

(4) Dress Shop noise, i.e. background chatter of
    approx. 5 - 6 people in close carpeted shop.   3 Mins.

(5) Baby cry - (Linda's)   30 Secs.

(6) Car arrive - door slam.   15 Secs.

Bill Williams

Sound effects request for one of the earliest episodes

SEPTEMBER

IDA BARLOW IS KILLED BY A BUS

Frank Barlow is worried when wife Ida is late home from visiting friend Beattie, Albert Tatlock's daughter, who lives in another part of Weatherfield. By 9pm Ken travels to Beattie's to discover his mum hasn't been there all day. He returns to Coronation Street and he and Frank call the police from The Rovers' phone and wait in the pub's back room for news. Officers arrive to deliver the bad news that Ida has been knocked over and killed by a bus. A moving funeral is held for Ida.

PRODUCTION NOTE

Ida Barlow, played by Noel Dyson (1916–95), was the first major character to be killed off. She was responsible for one of the behind-the-scenes legends of *Coronation Street*. Barbara Knox explains: 'When Noel left she bought a plant for everyone to remember her by. Pat Phoenix bought a trellis for it, and she, Eileen Derbyshire, Betty Driver, Jean Alexander and I used to water it. The legend is that if that plant dies, the show dies.

'When we moved from the main studio to Stage 1 in 1990 however, the plant ended up in a skip. It was rescued and I took it home and looked after it. Now it's still here, in the green room. Just a green-leafed plant, a climber, no flowers. Like me, it's still here. I took a cutting home once, which is still healthy, so I have part of it too.'

In 1961 cast members, including Noel Dyson, were invited to turn on the Blackpool Illuminations – one of the highest accolades in those days. Noel Dyson's final contracted episode was scheduled to air right before the switch-on, so the decision was taken to hold over her death until the following episode, meaning that Ida's death would be off-screen and Dyson herself would not feature when her character's death was revealed.

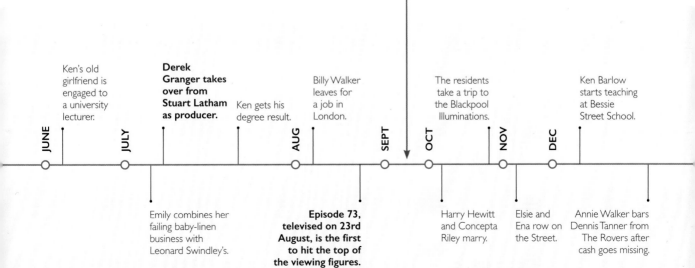

JUNE — Ken's old girlfriend is engaged to a university lecturer.

JULY — **Derek Granger takes over from Stuart Latham as producer.**

Ken gets his degree result.

AUG — Billy Walker leaves for a job in London.

SEPT

OCT — The residents take a trip to the Blackpool Illuminations.

NOV

DEC — Ken Barlow starts teaching at Bessie Street School.

Emily combines her failing baby-linen business with Leonard Swindley's.

Episode 73, televised on 23rd August, is the first to hit the top of the viewing figures.

Harry Hewitt and Concepta Riley marry.

Elsie and Ena row on the Street.

Annie Walker bars Dennis Tanner from The Rovers after cash goes missing.

PRODUCTION NOTE

An inter-departmental memo from 1962 reveals that the two sea lions hired for an episode that March (real names Cherie and Buddy) had travelled from Northamptonshire and enjoyed an overnight stay in animal trainer Arthur Scott's van in the Granada car park. They required a tank measuring 4ft by 6ft, 2ft deep and 'designed to look like a bath' complete with 'steps for them to walk into it'. Their 'rider' requested one-and-a-half stone of fresh herring.

The reason three girls who made up the Rockets were talked about but also failed to appear in the same March episode, was because the storyline occurred during the Equity actors' strike, when guest actors were prevented from appearing.

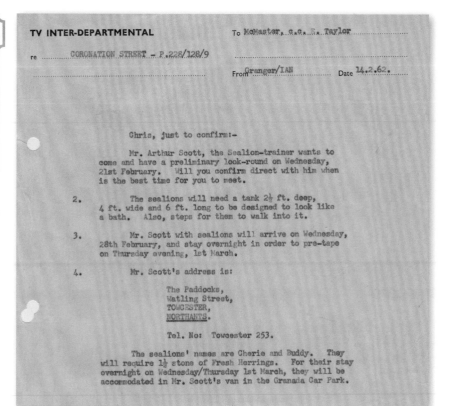

TV INTER-DEPARTMENTAL To McMaster, c.c. E. Taylor

re CORONATION STREET – P.228/128/9

From Granger/IAN Date 14.2.62.

Chris, just to confirm:-

Mr. Arthur Scott, the Sealion-trainer wants to come and have a preliminary look-round on Wednesday, 21st February. Will you confirm direct with him when is the best time for you to meet.

2. The sealions will need a tank 2½ ft. deep, 4 ft. wide and 6 ft. long to be designed to look like a bath. Also, steps for them to walk into it.

3. Mr. Scott with sealions will arrive on Wednesday, 28th February, and stay overnight in order to pre-tape on Thursday evening, 1st March.

4. Mr. Scott's address is:

The Paddocks,
Watling Street,
TOWCESTER,
NORTHANTS.

Tel. No: Towcester 253.

The sealions' names are Cherie and Buddy. They will require 1½ stone of Fresh Herrings. For their stay overnight on Wednesday/Thursday 1st March, they will be accommodated in Mr. Scott's van in the Granada Car Park.

MARCH

DENNIS ORGANISES A CHARITY CONCERT FOR THE OVER 60s

When the Glad Tidings committee decides to arrange a variety concert for the Over 60s Club, Dennis Tanner offers to help out and books variety act Captain Johnson and his Troupe. The Captain is forced to cancel when his van breaks down, but sends over his two performing sea lions Bunny and Sherry. The appearance of the marine mammals results in an amusing twist when Dennis is forced to look after them for the night and leaves them in the Walkers' bathtub, where they are discovered by a horrified Annie when she returns home early from a do in Manchester.

Unfortunately, the only other performers, the Blue Streak Rockets, were ex-strippers whose previous act had been banned in Blackpool, and so the concert for the over 60s is cancelled.

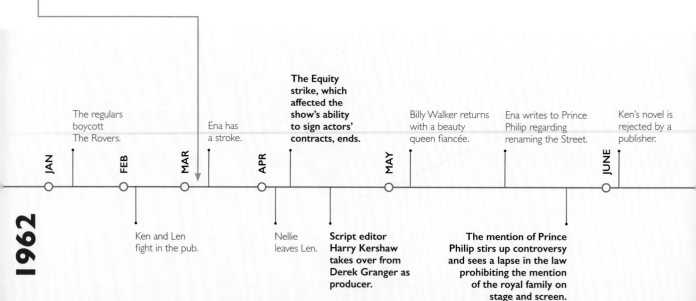

1962

The regulars boycott The Rovers.

Ena has a stroke.

The Equity strike, which affected the show's ability to sign actors' contracts, ends.

Billy Walker returns with a beauty queen fiancée.

Ena writes to Prince Philip regarding renaming the Street.

Ken's novel is rejected by a publisher.

JAN FEB MAR APR MAY JUNE

Ken and Len fight in the pub.

Nellie leaves Len.

Script editor Harry Kershaw takes over from Derek Granger as producer.

The mention of Prince Philip stirs up controversy and sees a lapse in the law prohibiting the mention of the royal family on stage and screen.

PRODUCTION NOTE

Joan Akers' landlady Mrs Webb was played by Jean Alexander, two years before she landed the iconic role of Hilda Ogden. At the time of filming actor Anna Cropper, who played Joan, was married to William Roache.

OCTOBER

BABY CHRISTOPHER IS SNATCHED

When Concepta asks Lucille to take her baby son Christopher on some errands while she prepares for a party, Lucille's friend Brenda Cowan walks off and leaves him outside Gamma Garments in his pram while Lucille is inside the shop. Someone snatches the little boy, leaving Lucille hysterical. The residents search the neighbourhood for the kidnapped baby and his empty pram is discovered nearby. Lucille is under suspicion by police who suggest she may be jealous of Christopher. The residents worry Concepta is on the verge of a breakdown and there are reports that police are planning to drag the canal for Christopher's body.

The baby is found when Elsie visits a young single mother called Joan Akers, to whom she had been recently introduced. She recognises Joan's baby as Christopher and it emerges disturbed Joan had lost a baby who was just three weeks old. The police arrive and Christopher is reunited with his relieved parents.

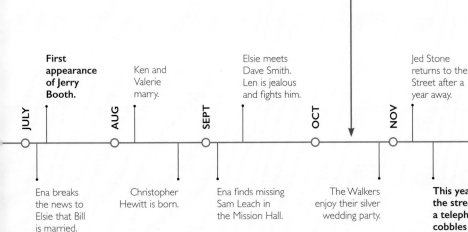

JULY

First appearance of Jerry Booth.

Ena breaks the news to Elsie that Bill is married.

AUG

Ken and Valerie marry.

Christopher Hewitt is born.

SEPT

Elsie meets Dave Smith. Len is jealous and fights him.

Ena finds missing Sam Leach in the Mission Hall.

OCT

The Walkers enjoy their silver wedding party.

NOV

Jed Stone returns to the Street after a year away.

This year sees the first house in the street (No 9) benefit from a telephone, when the famous cobbles are dug up, although The Rovers had a phone from the start of the show.

DEC

Nellie leaves Len.

The Mission Hall Players perform *Lady Lawson Loses*.

PRODUCTION NOTE

Sheila Birtles was the first regular character after the original cast to be introduced to *Coronation Street*. When news of her attempted suicide was leaked to the press and complaints from viewers began to come in to the show, the scenes were cut to lessen the controversial impact of the act and she was shown on screen looking distraught. As times changed, suicide storylines in later years did not shy away from portraying the trauma of characters taking their own lives, notably Janet Barlow, Katy Harris, Hayley Cropper and Aidan Connor.

SEPTEMBER

SHEILA BIRTLES ATTEMPTS SUICIDE

When crooked Neil Crossley takes over as manager of Gamma Garments, Sheila Birtles quickly becomes infatuated with him. Sheila and her best friend and former co-worker at Elliston's raincoat factory, Doreen Lostock, lodged together in the flat above the Corner Shop. Flirty Doreen had moved from job to job, eventually working with Emily at Gamma Garments. Sheila begins seeing Neil secretly, despite also courting Jerry Booth. When their relationship is revealed Jerry and Neil fight, resulting in Sheila plumping for Neil and ending things with Jerry, who quickly takes up with Myra. Neil is a bad 'un though, standing Sheila up and hitting her. She pays Neil's debts for him but is utterly distraught when he tells her he doesn't want to see her any more, leading Sheila to sink into depression, lose her job at the factory and contemplate suicide. Saved by Dennis Tanner, Sheila goes to live with her parents and soon discovers she's pregnant with Neil's child, a son she gives up for adoption.

Three years later Sheila returns to the Street and, despite reuniting with Jerry, she and Neil meet accidentally and again she chooses Neil over Jerry, eventually marrying him and moving to Sheffield.

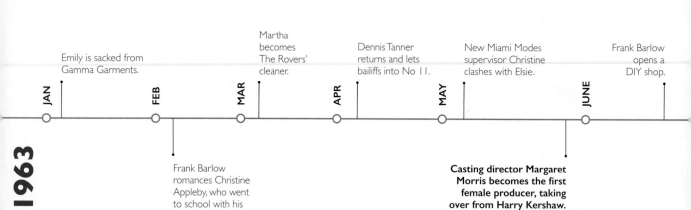

Emily is sacked from Gamma Garments.

Martha becomes The Rovers' cleaner.

Dennis Tanner returns and lets bailiffs into No 11.

New Miami Modes supervisor Christine clashes with Elsie.

Frank Barlow opens a DIY shop.

JAN

FEB

MAR

APR

MAY

JUNE

1963

Frank Barlow romances Christine Appleby, who went to school with his son Ken.

Casting director Margaret Morris becomes the first female producer, taking over from Harry Kershaw.

DECEMBER

ANNIE WALKER'S *THIS IS YOUR LIFE*

On Christmas Day 1963 the residents gather for a party in the Mission Hall. Walter Potts (the singing window cleaner aka Brett Falcon, thanks to Dennis Tanner) had wanted to celebrate his recent commercial success with a bit of a do to say thank you to the Street. The Walkers had planned to be away for Christmas that year, but the brewery could only provide a relief landlord for one day, so their trip had been abandoned. Myra Booth has an idea to make the party really special and the residents are intrigued. Harry and Len decorate the Mission Hall and Emily asks Len if the rumours are true – there's going to be a *This Is Your Life* and one of the residents is the subject. Everyone wonders who it will be and when it emerges that it is Annie Walker the surprise guests delight everyone. With Dennis at the fore with his own version of the Big Red Book, Annie's children Joan and Billy appear, followed by her friend Arthur Forsyth-Jones. The guest list also includes George Stubbins, who led the horse she rode as Lady Godiva at the Pageant of the Ages in 1933. The Annie scowl is out in force when he tells the story!

PRODUCTION NOTE

This Is Your Life was a popular programme on British TV from 1955 to 2003, presented by Eamonn Andrews and then Michael Aspel. Many *Coronation Street* actors have been the subject of the real *This Is Your Life* over the years including Patricia Phoenix, Jack Howarth, Betty Driver, Julie Goodyear, William Roache, Anne Kirkbride and Elizabeth Dawn, as well as screenwriter Tony Warren.

Ena, Martha and Minnie reminisce over the Walkers' early days on the Street and Annie and amateur opera buff Edgar Nuttall duet in a song. Esther Hayes is the final 'surprise' guest and it's an opportunity for Esther to say farewell to the Street for good (she's off to work in Glasgow). The gathered friends join in a chorus of 'For She's a Jolly Good Fellow' to the delight of an over-awed Annie.

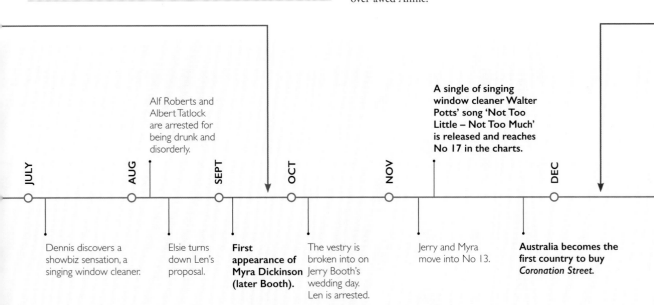

JULY

Dennis discovers a showbiz sensation, a singing window cleaner.

AUG

Alf Roberts and Albert Tatlock are arrested for being drunk and disorderly.

Elsie turns down Len's proposal.

SEPT

First appearance of Myra Dickinson (later Booth).

OCT

The vestry is broken into on Jerry Booth's wedding day. Len is arrested.

NOV

A single of singing window cleaner Walter Potts' song 'Not Too Little – Not Too Much' is released and reaches No 17 in the charts.

Jerry and Myra move into No 13.

DEC

Australia becomes the first country to buy *Coronation Street*.

PRODUCTION NOTE

Martha Longhurst was killed off after Tim Aspinall, a former *TV Times* writer, took over as producer. He produced *Coronation Street* for just five months in 1964, but during his short tenure he sacked several actors and was criticised for his decision to kill off popular Martha. Actor Lynne Carol (born Josephine Caroline Gertrude Mary Faith Harber) did not want to leave the show and the storyline prompted Violet Carson to complain to Granada bosses.

In her autobiography *All My Burning Bridges*, Pat Phoenix, who had briefly lived with Lynne Carol at her home in Blackpool during her rep days, remarked: 'It was thought by some of us that the death of Martha Longhurst was one of the biggest mistakes ever made… We none of us thought Granada would do it and we were confident Martha would get a last-minute reprieve… We knew she (Lynne) did not want to go.'

Phoenix added that Lynne's actor husband Bert Palmer happened to be working in a neighbouring studio at Granada when the scene was filmed. He rescued Martha's hat and glasses from the set and gave them to his tearful wife to keep.

Harry Kershaw observed that killing off Martha may have resulted in 'a few episodes of high drama, which created a talking point […] which boosted our viewing figures,' but 'when the dust settled we were simply left with a *Coronation Street* without Martha Longhurst. The trio had been reduced to a rather sad duet'.

He did, however, add that although Aspinall had dispensed with popular Martha, he was also responsible for introducing Stan and Hilda Ogden, for which he should rightfully be commended.

MAY

MARTHA LONGHURST DIES IN THE ROVERS SNUG

Martha Longhurst has been particularly pleased recently because daughter Lily has asked her to a rented villa in Spain. Martha has to get a passport for her first trip abroad and boasts to an unimpressed Ena who tells her she's only been asked along to babysit.

Martha's thunder is stolen when Frank Barlow has a win on the Premium Bonds and holds a party to celebrate his good luck. Martha heads off to town to collect her precious first passport and returns to The Rovers for the party. While the residents gather round the piano, Martha, feeling unwell, moves to sit alone in the snug. Martha suffers a heart attack. Myra raises the alarm, but it's too late. Ena is distraught as Martha's friends and neighbours solemnly leave the pub.

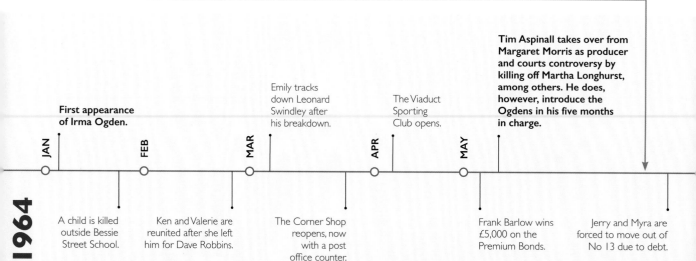

1964

First appearance of Irma Ogden.

Emily tracks down Leonard Swindley after his breakdown.

The Viaduct Sporting Club opens.

Tim Aspinall takes over from Margaret Morris as producer and courts controversy by killing off Martha Longhurst, among others. He does, however, introduce the Ogdens in his five months in charge.

JAN

FEB

MAR

APR

MAY

A child is killed outside Bessie Street School.

Ken and Valerie are reunited after she left him for Dave Robbins.

The Corner Shop reopens, now with a post office counter.

Frank Barlow wins £5,000 on the Premium Bonds.

Jerry and Myra are forced to move out of No 13 due to debt.

EMILY JILTS SWINDLEY AT THE ALTAR

Kindly, religious Emily Nugent worked with pompous lay preacher Leonard Swindley after her baby-linen shop merged with Swindley's Emporium in 1961. They grew closer as she nursed him through a nervous breakdown, and it was she who took advantage of the leap year and proposed to Swindley in 1964. This was never going to be a match made in heaven but Emily at, 34 and fearing spinsterhood, had hoped they would rub along together and at least neither of them would be lonely. The writing should have been on the wall when Swindley fled when she first proposed. Emily admits to Ken ahead of the ceremony that she knows Swindley doesn't love her (he had made it clear their engagement was diverting him from his business). On the day of the wedding, as Jack prepares to give Emily away, she tells him she can't go through with it. Swindley agrees it would be wrong, the wedding is cancelled and Swindley heads off to the honeymoon hotel in Wales alone. Emily would go on to marry Ernest Bishop, with whom she was truly in love and, after his murder, she tied the knot again, albeit unknowingly illegally, to bigamist pet shop owner Arnold Swain.

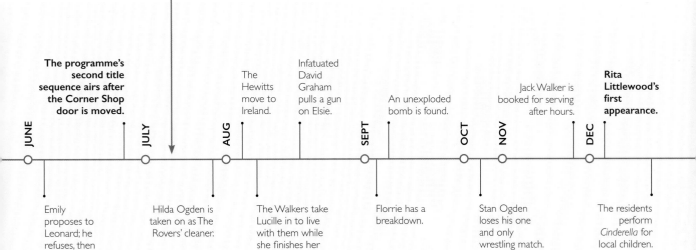

The programme's second title sequence airs after the Corner Shop door is moved.

The Hewitts move to Ireland.

Infatuated David Graham pulls a gun on Elsie.

An unexploded bomb is found.

Jack Walker is booked for serving after hours.

Rita Littlewood's first appearance.

JUNE · JULY · AUG · SEPT · OCT · NOV · DEC

Emily proposes to Leonard; he refuses, then accepts.

Hilda Ogden is taken on as The Rovers' cleaner.

The Walkers take Lucille in to live with them while she finishes her O Levels.

Florrie has a breakdown.

Stan Ogden loses his one and only wrestling match.

The residents perform *Cinderella* for local children.

NO 7 COLLAPSES

By August No 7 had been unoccupied for several months after Concepta and Harry Hewitt left for Ireland. Ken, Len and Jerry are enjoying a pint in The Rovers when they hear a crash and rush outside with Annie and Jack to see that the front of No 7 has collapsed. Len and Lionel Petty from the Corner Shop take charge as the residents worry about the safety of neighbouring homes and Val takes the twins into the The Rovers. The police and landlord Edward Wormold are called and Jack and Annie fret over their charge Lucille Hewitt's whereabouts. The 16-year-old is supposed to be out at a coffee bar with friends celebrating having passed five O-Levels but she is late back. When the attending police officer hears that Lucille sometimes went back inside her former family home, he organises the menfolk into a chain to move the rubble in case she is trapped. Annie becomes increasingly worried before Lucille arrives in the bar through the back of the pub, unaware of what's happened. The following day a surveyor reveals the cause of the collapse was a faulty beam and a weakness in the foundations. When Mr Wormold is told by Len that the repairs will cost £300 he decides to demolish the house.

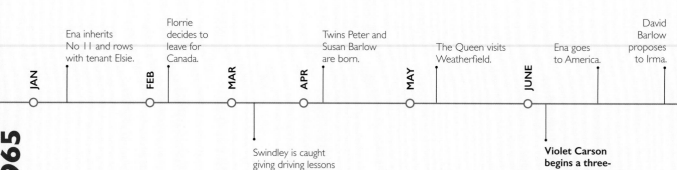

1965

Ena inherits No 11 and rows with tenant Elsie.

Florrie decides to leave for Canada.

Twins Peter and Susan Barlow are born.

The Queen visits Weatherfield.

Ena goes to America.

David Barlow proposes to Irma.

Swindley is caught giving driving lessons to Emily illegally.

Violet Carson begins a three-month sabbatical.

SEPTEMBER

ELSIE TANNER IS INJURED IN A CAR CRASH

When Jack and Annie Walker return from a night at a Cheshire pub and talk about the wealthy businessmen they saw there, Elsie's ears prick up. She makes the trip to Wilmslow herself and meets married accountant Robert Maxwell. As he drives her home, Robert collapses at the wheel and dies as the car crashes. Elsie flees but leaves her gloves in the car, leading the police to track her down and request that she appears at the inquest into Robert's death. This leads to Robert's widow Moira turning up in the Street, accusing Elsie of being 'a back-street tart' and, nearly a year later, making obscene phone calls to her and attacking her with a knife before Len steps in to disarm her.

DECEMBER

JACK WALKER BREAKS DOWN AFTER BEING BLACKMAILED

Opportunist thief Frank Turner spots underage Lucille helping out behind the bar, while Jack and Annie are away attending Irma and David's wedding reception. Turner demands free drinks. Jack knows his licence is at risk and is at the mercy of Frank, who returns to extort more free drinks and cash from him. A worried Jack breaks down in tears and the blackmail ends only when Frank is beaten up in the ginnel by Jack's friend Jerry Booth.

Coronation Street's **first spin-off, sitcom** *Pardon the Expression* **featuring the character of Leonard Swindley, is aired for the first time.**

In a bid to boost business, Emily holds a disastrous fashion show at The Mission.

JULY AUG SEPT OCT NOV DEC

Fellow landlady Nellie Harvey visits Annie Walker.

Ena returns from the US after three months and discovers council plans to demolish Coronation Street and Mawdsley Street in order to build a ring road.

A fire at the Barlows' nearly kills the twins after Ken leaves them alone briefly.

David and Irma marry.

MARCH

JIM HITS ELSIE AND LEN FIGHTS HIM

Elsie Tanner's track record with men has been notoriously unlucky, and Stan and Hilda's lodger Jim Mount is the latest in a long line of wrong 'uns. They began dating in January 1966, but Jim continued to see other women, and by now the cracks are beginning to show. Elsie is hysterical after Jim chats to an old flame in the pub, and when Jim hits her Len fights him. Despite Len warning Elsie that Jim is just out for what he can get, Elsie still believes Jim loves her. She even asks him if he's planning to propose. When he says no, she kicks him out. The Rovers relief landlady – and Jim's ex – Brenda Riley arrives when the Walkers travel to Ireland and the following month Jim and Brenda leave the Street together, to the relief of Elsie, Hilda and Annie.

MAY

BET LYNCH ARRIVES ON THE STREET

When Jocky Elliston takes over the running of Elliston's raincoat factory after the death of his father Jack in 1966, he decides to start manufacturing PVC clothing, in response to its growing popularity in the late 1960s. He recruits extra factory workers to weld the merchandise, one of whom is a young Bet Lynch. Bet and pal Cilla pop into The Rovers to see what their works local is like and pick up something to eat. Landlady Annie can't disguise her distaste as Bet asks for four 'meat and taytor' pies and a large bottle of pale ale. Hilda somewhat ironically agrees with Annie that the factory girls are rather common, but Annie's husband Jack looks forward to the prospect of 30 new potential customers boosting his lunchtime takings. Bet soon makes her mark in the factory over the coming weeks, having an affair with her boss and falling out with Lucille Hewitt. She is jealous of her younger colleague because Lucille is faster on the welding machine and Lucille ends up with a black eye after one altercation.

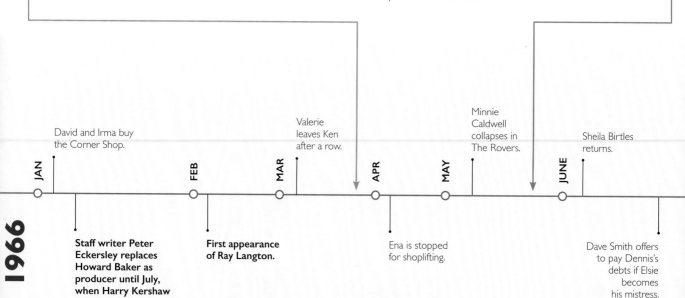

David and Irma buy the Corner Shop.

Valerie leaves Ken after a row.

Minnie Caldwell collapses in The Rovers.

Sheila Birtles returns.

1966

JAN FEB MAR APR MAY JUNE

Staff writer Peter Eckersley replaces Howard Baker as producer until July, when Harry Kershaw resumes the role.

First appearance of Ray Langton.

Ena is stopped for shoplifting.

Dave Smith offers to pay Dennis's debts if Elsie becomes his mistress.

OCTOBER

PAUL CHEVESKI DISAPPEARS

The Cheveskis return from Canada because Linda wants five-year-old Paul to go to a local school. Ivan wants the family to move to Birmingham and Linda and Paul stay with Elsie while Ivan goes to Birmingham to look for somewhere for them to live. Linda admits to Elsie that she had an affair in Canada and that's the real reason they have returned to England. When Elsie goes to pick Paul up from Bessie Street School, she is panic stricken to discover he has disappeared. The residents join the police in searching for the little boy, but he's nowhere to be found. He is rescued from the canal, where he had fallen in while playing, and taken to hospital suffering from pneumonia. When it emerges that Len had blocked the tender for a council fence at the canal, Elsie throws him out, although the pair are later reconciled. When the local paper carries the story of Len blocking the fence, a drunk Ivan attacks him. The following month the Cheveskis move to Birmingham.

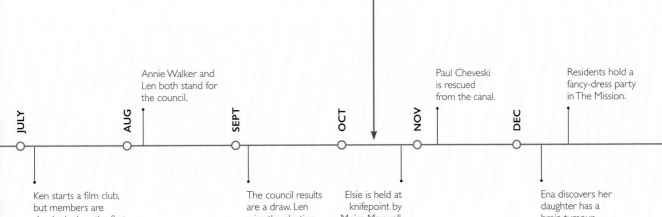

Ken starts a film club, but members are shocked when the first presentation turns out to be a nudist film.

JULY

Annie Walker and Len both stand for the council.

AUG

The council results are a draw. Len wins the election by a coin toss.

SEPT

Elsie is held at knifepoint by Moira Maxwell.

OCT

Paul Cheveski is rescued from the canal.

NOV

Ena discovers her daughter has a brain tumour.

DEC

Residents hold a fancy-dress party in The Mission.

PRODUCTION NOTE

Following the success of *Pardon The Expression* (1965–66), a *Coronation Street* spin-off featuring Leonard Swindley (after Arthur Lowe left the *Street*) and Betty Driver before her 1969 debut in *Coronation Street*, a further spin-off was conceived. *Turn Out The Lights* followed the adventures of Leonard and his boss Wally Hunt (Robert Dorning) after their dismissal from department store Dobson and Hawks. Leonard, having developed an interest in astrology, and Wally, travelled the country solving supernatural mysteries. Produced by former *Coronation Street* producer Derek Granger and designed in part by *Coronation Street*'s original designer Denis Parkin, the series consisted of six 55-minute episodes and featured fellow *Coronation Street* actors Neville Buswell and Noel Dyson. The following year *Dad's Army* was broadcast, seeing Arthur Lowe take on the iconic part of Captain Mainwaring.

ROGUE WORKMEN TARGET TRUSTING MINNIE

Minnie Caldwell's insurance policy has matured and she is worried about keeping the £72 (£1,300 in today's money) in the house. Two men have seen Minnie with the money and one poses as a building inspector, warning Minnie she must get her chimney fixed or he'll report her. The other, pretending to attend to the chimney, steals her money and Minnie breaks down when she discovers it's gone. Ena tells Minnie off for being too trusting, while the residents have a whip-round and collect £5 for her.

MAY

ELSIE IS REUNITED WITH AN OLD FLAME

When Elsie finds out from GI Gregg Flint that her wartime boyfriend and first true love Steve Tanner has been stationed at RAF Burtonwood, 20 miles away, pals Dot Greenhalgh and Val Barlow urge her to get in touch with him. But 22 years have passed and Elsie is worried about Steve seeing the older her. Gregg telephones Dot from Burtonwood and she passes the phone to Elsie. Steve is on the line and the pair agree to meet. They go for a walk and Elsie takes Steve into The Rovers, where she notices the other women checking out her handsome friend. Despite some initial misgivings on Elsie's part – she can't believe Steve could still love her – the pair become engaged the following month, with plans to marry in September.

1967

Vera Lomax dies from a brain tumour.

Elsie gives Emily a makeover.

Turn Out the Lights, the show's second spin-off starring Arthur Lowe as Leonard Swindley, is aired.

Ken is arrested after an illegal student demo. He is charged and spends a week in prison.

A goods train crashes onto the street, burying Ena in rubble (see In the Scene, pages 140–41).

Steve Tanner proposes to Elsie.

JAN | FEB | MAR | APR | MAY | JUNE

SEPTEMBER

ELSIE MARRIES STEVE TANNER, AND HARRY HEWITT IS CRUSHED TO DEATH

In the hours after Elsie and her wartime boyfriend Steve Tanner marry in Warrington, Len and Harry, who had travelled over from Ireland especially for the wedding, decide to pay their old pal Sid Bell a visit. Halfway there Len's van breaks down and mechanic Harry, while attempting to fix it, is crushed when the vehicle falls on him thanks to an unsafe jack. A lorry driver who has stopped to assist them helps Len pull his mate out, but Harry is clearly severely injured. A dazed Len returns to the wedding party and informs Ken that Harry has died in hospital. Then he has to break the awful news to Concepta. She worries how she's going to tell Lucille, but Minnie, believing Lucille is aware of the tragedy, spills the beans before Concepta can inform her stepdaughter that her beloved father is dead. Harry's subsequent inquest records a verdict of accidental death and Lucille decides to return to Ireland with Concepta.

DECEMBER

A CHRISTMAS COMPETITION – BUT WHO'LL BE CELEBRATING?

Albert has organised a tug-of-war competition between The Rovers and rival boozer The Flying Horse. It's to be held on Christmas morning – if Albert can get anyone to join The Rovers' team. He eventually musters enough participants, including two rugby players, and as the big day arrives the menfolk limber up. When the rugby players fail to show up, Albert drafts in Steve and Ivan. Stan's back starts playing up and Albert himself has to take his place. The Flying Horse team wins easily. Unbeknown to anyone, Albert has rashly promised that the winners would receive free beer all day, but when The Flying Horse team members realise Albert would have to foot the bill himself they agree to have just one drink each.

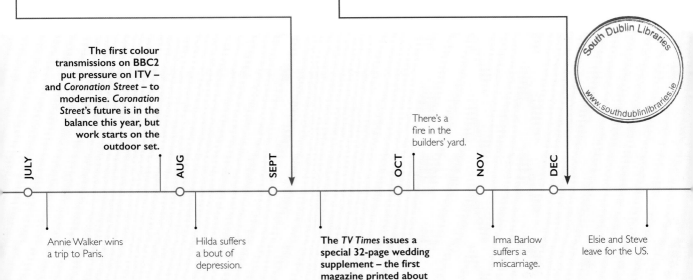

The first colour transmissions on BBC2 put pressure on ITV – and *Coronation Street* – to modernise. *Coronation Street*'s future is in the balance this year, but work starts on the outdoor set.

There's a fire in the builders' yard.

JULY

AUG

SEPT

OCT

NOV

DEC

Annie Walker wins a trip to Paris.

Hilda suffers a bout of depression.

The *TV Times* issues a special 32-page wedding supplement – the first magazine printed about the show.

Irma Barlow suffers a miscarriage.

Elsie and Steve leave for the US.

8TH MAY 1967

SOON after Elsie Tanner meets up with her former wartime beau after 22 years, American Steve Tanner, tragedy hits the Street as a goods train ploughs off the viaduct. The fatal crash would be echoed 43 years later in the *Street's* special live episode marking its 50th anniversary in 2010, when a tram crashes off the same viaduct, killing three characters.

In the scene
The train crash

THE SURROUNDING STORYLINES

Elsie meets her old love – Elsie decides to meet up with Steve Tanner, having been worried about how he would view her after so long, but as they stroll through woodland the years melt away. However, Elsie tells Steve they can't see each other again. She's afraid of getting her heart broken.

Stan's cup-final dilemma – Stan wins a cup-final ticket in a game of darts, but worries about Hilda letting him go to London for the match. Hilda secures her own ticket so they can go together, unaware that Stan has sold his for a tenner.

Elsewhere… – Irma is worried about David coaching a women's football team. She decides to join them but hurts her leg on her first session. Len stands for re-election to the council; he's the only candidate.

THE MAIN EVENT

It's Lucille Hewitt's 18th birthday and she goes out with a friend. Steve calls at No 11 for Elsie, hoping to talk her round. When she doesn't answer he asks in The Rovers if anyone has seen her. Before anyone can answer, there's a loud ominous rumble and Len dashes into the pub shouting that a train has come off the viaduct.

The locals rush outside and are horrified at the devastation. Elsie, along with Jack, who had popped out to buy chips, Ena and Lucille are missing. In the darkness the men work together to pull the rubble away, the train carriage and twisted track metal hovering precariously above them.

The police arrive and it emerges one of their number, PC Jimmie Conway, a regular on the Street, is trapped in his police car. He is rescued, but his fiancée Sonia is still trapped.

Annie, dazed with fear, waits in the pub and weeps with relief when Jack and Lucille walk in unharmed. As Steve helps with the rescue attempts, Elsie appears. Len had known where she was all along and Jerry admonishes him for not telling Steve he knew she was safe.

Sonia's grandmother appears and waits for news with Jimmie and Minnie, but Sonia, an old Bessie Street schoolfriend of Lucille, is declared dead and Jack comforts a shocked Lucille as they look on.

Ena is finally discovered unconscious as the bricks begin to fall again. David Barlow bravely pulls her out as quickly as possible and she is rushed to hospital. Minnie phones

the hospital to find out what is wrong with Ena, but they refuse to divulge anything. Seeing Minnie getting upset, Elsie grabs the phone and, announcing that she's Ena's daughter, forces them to tell her that Ena only has cuts, bruises and a broken arm. As Elsie comments later: 'If that woman fell off Blackpool Tower, she'd bounce.'

THE AFTERMATH

Steve stays at No 11 for the night, sleeping in Dennis's bed. Elsie tells him she is still not sure about starting up their relationship. They do eventually go on to reconcile and marry before immigrating to Steve's native America for a short spell.

Ena returns, striding back into The Rovers, and orders a milk stout claiming she was bored in hospital. Stan secretly burns Hilda's cup-final ticket so they don't have to spend time in London together.

PRODUCTION NOTE

The disaster scenes, spectacular for the time, were all filmed in the studio without the special effects available in subsequent years.

The episode of 10th May 1967, which covered the horror of the crash and the rescue attempts, was directed by Michael Apted, famous for directing movie *Gorillas in the Mist* (1988) and Bond film *The World is Not Enough* (1999), plus the seminal *Seven Up* TV documentary series.

The decision to give Steve and Elsie the same surname coincidentally was made by the programme so Elsie, massively popular at the time, would not have to change her name.

THE TWINS ARE IN DANGER AS BULLDOZERS MOVE INTO THE FACTORY

After Jack Elliston dies, son Jocky takes over the running of Elliston's raincoat factory in Coronation Street. He installs an ineffective manager and when the factory is investigated for producing substandard products, Jocky sells the unit to the council and closes the factory. In early 1968 it is demolished, but as the bulldozers move in, one Street family has a brush with possible death. As news of the demolition reaches the residents, Minnie is more bothered that her cat Bobby has disappeared. Ken and Val's toddler twins, Peter and Susan, follow Bobby into the factory as the demolition work begins. Bobby finds his way out as the Barlows realise the twins are missing. As they search for the children, Minnie guesses they may be in the factory and in danger of losing their lives. The work is halted, and Ken and head demolition worker Miklos bring the children out safely. The incident prompts Val to realise the twins need watching more closely. It puts a strain on her and Ken's relationship.

LES CLEGG FALLS OFF THE WAGON

Les and Maggie Clegg buy the Corner Shop from David and Irma Barlow in early 1968. Les's alcoholism has been a blight on family life, so the move to Weatherfield and the purchase of the Corner Shop is supposed to be a new start, and Les manages to stay off the bottle until June. When Les's bowls team wins a tournament Maggie trusts him to celebrate soberly with his teammates, but Les disappears for two days before returning drunk, where he smashes up the shop and assaults Maggie. Son Gordon steps in and Les is admitted to a psychiatric hospital. It is later revealed that Les dies in the early 1970s.

The Glad Tidings Mission is demolished.

David Barlow puts the Corner Shop up for sale.

First appearance of the Clegg family: Les, Maggie and adopted son Gordon.

Dennis Tanner and Jenny Sutton marry.

JAN FEB MAR APR MAY JUNE

Elsie Tanner returns after the failure of her marriage, ironically on Valentine's Day.

David and Irma leave for Australia.

ESCAPED RAPIST FRANK RILEY HOLDS VALERIE BARLOW HOSTAGE

When Elliston's factory is demolished Ken, Val and the twins move into one of the maisonettes that are built in its place, No 14. By August, Ken is involved in play rehearsals with his students and Val begins to feel neglected. The police warn the residents that an escaped rapist is on the loose and thought to be in the area, as he used to live on Victoria Street. The womenfolk are worried. Ken is running late at rehearsals and the convict, Frank Riley, pushes his way into the maisonette and holds Val hostage. Val is terrified for the safety of her sleeping twins. In a bid to raise the alarm and fearing Riley will rape her, she manages to tap on the sink pipes to try to alert neighbours to her plight. Ena hears her tapping and notices Val's ringing phone is going unanswered – it's Ken trying to get through. She raises the alarm and a stand-off between violent Riley and the police follows. A raging Riley threatens Val with a hammer and plans to use her as a shield before the police force their way in. Following her ordeal, Val has to endure not only Hilda and Annie's gossip speculating that she had been sexually assaulted, but also a grilling from Ken, worried about what happened in the maisonette. They argue, but eventually manage to put the ordeal behind them.

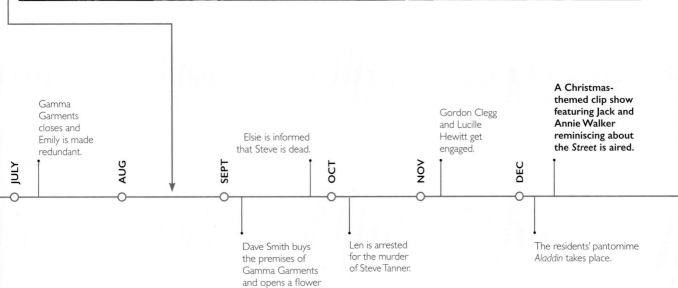

Gamma Garments closes and Emily is made redundant.

JULY

AUG

Elsie is informed that Steve is dead.

SEPT

Dave Smith buys the premises of Gamma Garments and opens a flower shop.

OCT

Len is arrested for the murder of Steve Tanner.

Gordon Clegg and Lucille Hewitt get engaged.

NOV

DEC

The residents' pantomime *Aladdin* takes place.

A Christmas-themed clip show featuring Jack and Annie Walker reminiscing about the *Street* is aired.

ENA IS ARRESTED AT A DEMO

When it's announced that the pensioners' clubhouse is going to be demolished to make way for a car park, the older residents, led by Ena, plan a protest. They march on the Town Hall and deliver a petition to rousing strains of 'We Shall Overcome'. When she is told the petition comes too late, Ena organises a sit-down protest and the two dozen pensioners block the road, prompting the police to intervene. As the police officers carry a stubborn Ena away to be cautioned, Albert Tatlock comments: 'Good luck, chaps have got the Victoria Cross for less than that.' Following a further sit-in at the clubhouse, the OAPs win the day and the council agrees to cancel the demolition.

PRODUCTION NOTE

One of the officers, Constable Wilcox, was played by a young Richard Beckinsale, who later found fame in *The Lovers* (co-written by *Coronation Street* writers Jack Rosenthal and Geoffrey Lancashire), *Rising Damp* and *Porridge*, before his early death at the age of 31.

1969

Jasmine Choong leaves fiancé Billy Walker.

Gordon Clegg calls off his wedding to Lucille.

Audrey Fleming celebrates her 18th birthday.

JAN — FEB — MAR — APR — MAY — JUNE

Minnie Caldwell disappears after her gambling habit is revealed.

Maggie Clegg's sister Betty Turpin arrives on the Street.

OCTOBER

ELSIE IS CHARGED WITH SHOPLIFTING AND THERE'S A FATAL COACH CRASH IN THE LAKES

Elsie and her best and oldest friend Dot Greenhalgh are both working at Miami Modes. Dot, her mind on other things, is sent home from work. She calls Elsie and asks her to bring home some bags she left at work. Elsie is stopped for a random bag check as she leaves and some unpaid-for dresses are discovered. The manager calls Dot into the store but decides on the available evidence to call the police on Elsie and Dot is sent home again.

Elsie is charged and released and Ken later suspects Dot is not telling the truth. He and Ena tell Elsie of their suspicions, but Elsie refuses to believe her friend has set her up. Putting on a brave face, Elsie joins the residents' coach trip to the Lakes. The driver takes the wrong coach, this one has faulty steering, but the trip takes place. On the return journey, as a sing-song is underway on board, the steering goes and the coach smashes into a tree. The injured residents are taken to hospital. They have cuts, bruises and broken bones, but Minnie is the most seriously injured and the driver has died. Ena refuses to leave Minnie's bedside despite requests from the ward sister and spends the night praying for her recovery. Ray Langton is left paralysed by the crash and spends the following months in a wheelchair.

On the eve of the trial, Dot admits her guilt to Elsie but pleads with her not to reveal the truth. The case is dismissed due to contradictory evidence with no verdict given. Elsie and Dot are urged by management to leave the store, and Elsie and Dot's friendship ends.

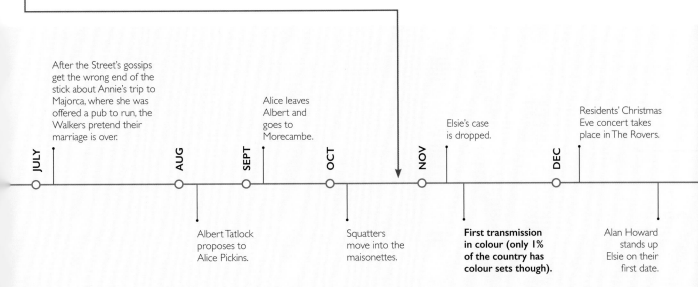

After the Street's gossips get the wrong end of the stick about Annie's trip to Majorca, where she was offered a pub to run, the Walkers pretend their marriage is over.

Alice leaves Albert and goes to Morecambe.

Elsie's case is dropped.

Residents' Christmas Eve concert takes place in The Rovers.

JULY　AUG　SEPT　OCT　NOV　DEC

Albert Tatlock proposes to Alice Pickins.

Squatters move into the maisonettes.

First transmission in colour (only 1% of the country has colour sets though).

Alan Howard stands up Elsie on their first date.

IN FOCUS

THE *Coronation Street* set has gone through several iterations over the years, culminating in its current home in Salford's MediaCity.

The changing face of the Street

According to the show's fictional back story, Coronation Street was built in 1902 and named for the coronation of Edward VII. When *Coronation Street* began in 1960 it was shot, like most television productions at the time, entirely indoors at Granada Television's city centre studios. The cobbles were painted on the floor, and the entire set had to be taken down after filming and re-erected the following week to allow for the filming of other programmes. The set was very small with the houses scaled down to three quarters the size of a normal terraced home, meaning the actors had to walk more slowly than normal to appear in scale with the houses.

After the difficulties of shooting the 1967 train crash in the restricted setting, it was decided to move the wooden studio set and, in 1968, it was rebuilt on some old railway sidings on Grape Street near Granada Studios. The move coincided with a storyline of the demolition of Elliston's raincoat factory and the Glad Tidings Mission Hall, and the building of maisonettes opposite the terrace. (Nowadays the modern houses, home to the Platts, Yasmeen, Sally and Tim, and Audrey's hair salon, stand in their place.)

Camera angles occasionally failed to disguise the fact the houses had no roofs and no backs. Eventually, the wooden set was replaced with bricks, and, in 1982, a brand new set was built on land nearby and included the Rosamund Street end of Coronation Street. Thousands of second-hand bricks and reclaimed slates from demolition areas in nearby Salford were used to lend authenticity to the houses. The old Grape Street plot became the entrance to the original Granada Studios Tours.

Interior/exterior set in 1966

The lot with the masionettes in the 1970s

The Rovers doorway today

Interior set in 1966

IN FOCUS

Outside The Rovers' set

IN 1990, interior filming moved out of the main Granada building and into the Stage 1 building next door. Stage 2, built on the site of Granada's *Sherlock Holmes* set, was used from 2002.

THE MOVE TO MEDIACITYUK

In December 2010, it was announced that production of *Coronation Street* would move from Manchester city centre to a new, purpose-built plot at Salford Quays. Construction began in September 2011 and *Coronation Street* bosses took the opportunity to create a completely new set and to build it to a greater scale than the old Granada set.

The building work took two years and, in 2013, *Coronation Street* moved lock, stock and cobbles to its new production base at Trafford Wharf, part of MediaCityUK. The entire street was painstakingly rebuilt from scratch in a new backlot next to brand new production offices and studios containing the interior sets for many of the famous *Coronation Street* homes.

Andy Ashworth, lot supervisor, explains: 'When the show moved from Quay Street to Salford Quays, I moved 10 weeks before everyone else. We had to recreate everything perfectly, even down to screws in the walls. As the new set was a third bigger than the old one everything had to be photographed and scaled up.

'A special team of artists replicated everything from my photos – even the graffiti on the walls had to be aged just right. They used yoghurt to create moss and sprinkled weeds in places so they would spring up in time.'

The interior sets for Underworld, as well as Preston's Petals, the Prima Doner kebab shop and the community centre around the corner are also filmed within the actual buildings on the backlot. The Rovers Return has a partial interior to allow camera shots looking into the exit to the rear yard and smoking area. All the other interior sets are in the studios. The new lot has around 60,000 cobbles, and some were reclaimed from the disused Quay Street lot in 2018, for use in the Victoria Street expansion.

The lot as it looks today

Aerial view of the lot at Trafford Wharf Road

Cast members celebrate the new lot opening in November 2013

EXPANDING VICTORIA STREET

ON 12th March 2018 the extended Victoria Street set was opened, with filming on the new area commencing the following day. New additions included Weatherfield Police Station, a tram stop, a Costa coffee shop, a Co-op, the curry house Speed Daal, a tattoo parlour, a snooker hall and a community garden complete with a bench commemorating the victims of the Manchester Arena terrorist attack the year before. The inclusion of Costa and Co-op marked an increase in the use of product placement by *Coronation Street*; the first instance of which had been a Nationwide ATM in the Corner Shop in 2011. The new section of Victoria Street is a continuation of the street first added in 1999, which introduced Roy's Rolls, the community centre, Victoria Court flats, the infamous builder's yard and Prima Doner kebab shop. The expansion was required after the show went to six episodes in September 2017; it needed new areas to film in and to accommodate the increasing cast.

Coronation Street and neighbouring Victoria Street now reflect many British high streets

The tram stop

The police station

The builder's yard

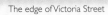

The edge of Victoria Street

The Victoria Court flats were opened in 2008

Prima Doner takeaway

Victoria Street today

NEWS COMES THROUGH OF A FATAL CRASH IN AUSTRALIA

David and Irma Barlow had immigrated to Australia in 1968 when David signed with an Australian football team. Irma was pregnant when they left Weatherfield and their son Darren was born in Oz. In April 1970, a police officer comes to The Rovers looking for the Ogdens; a telex has arrived from Australia saying that David and Irma have been involved in a car crash. Ken and Val break the news to Hilda, and it is arranged that a telephone call will be made from the hospital in Adelaide to the Barlows' flat at 8pm. As the relatives gather they argue about why the young couple left Weatherfield. When the hospital calls, Ken learns that David is dead, Darren is critical and Irma has survived. Ken torments himself with memories of arguing with his brother and Hilda is determined to fly to Australia to be with her daughter. After she leaves, Stan receives a telegram revealing that baby Darren has also died, and Irma later returns to the Street.

BETTY TURPIN IS TERRORISED BY KEITH LUCAS

Keith Lucas was an ex-prisoner who, while stopping off for a drink in The Rovers, realises that Betty Turpin is the wife of the man who put him inside, Cyril. Police officer Cyril is away from the Street on a training course and Keith follows Betty home and threatens her, telling her he wants revenge. Keith terrorises Betty over the next few weeks, demanding free drinks off her in the pub and suggesting Cyril and her sister Maggie were involved. Emily and Maggie realise Betty is acting oddly and, on Cyril's return, Maggie tells him her worries. Betty admits all to Cyril, who tracks Keith down and beats him badly with a piece of lead piping. Cyril is so concerned that he lost control that he decides to leave the police force and finds a job in a solicitor's office.

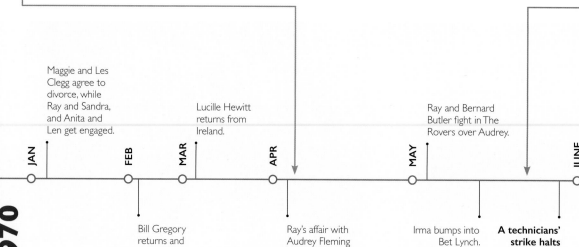

Maggie and Les Clegg agree to divorce, while Ray and Sandra, and Anita and Len get engaged.

Lucille Hewitt returns from Ireland.

Ray and Bernard Butler fight in The Rovers over Audrey.

Jack Walker dies and Annie is distraught.

JAN   FEB   MAR   APR   MAY   JUNE

Bill Gregory returns and woos Elsie, but she turns him down.

Ray's affair with Audrey Fleming intensifies.

Irma bumps into Bet Lynch.

A technicians' strike halts production.

DECEMBER

JOE DONELLI CONFESSES ALL TO IRMA

American GI and pal of murdered Steve Tanner, Joe Donelli arrives back in the Street, telling the locals he is on leave and cosying up to Irma Barlow. His friends, fellow American soldiers Gregg Flint and Gary Strauss, follow him from their base, as Joe has deserted and they have been sent to take him back. Joe is lodging with Minnie and refuses to go back to the barracks. When drunk he confesses to Irma it was he who killed Steve Tanner two years previously over a gambling debt. Len had been suspected of the murder. Irma is now terrified of Joe, but believes the other Americans are in with Joe. They in turn begin to learn that Joe is violent towards women. When the military police arrive to arrest Joe, he escapes and, armed with a gun, holds Minnie hostage. Stan bravely takes her place and a deranged Joe forces Stan to sing 'Silent Night' as he holds a gun to his throat before turning the gun on himself. Afterwards, as the Street recovers from the ordeal, Minnie tells police that she will always remember Joe as a kind young man.

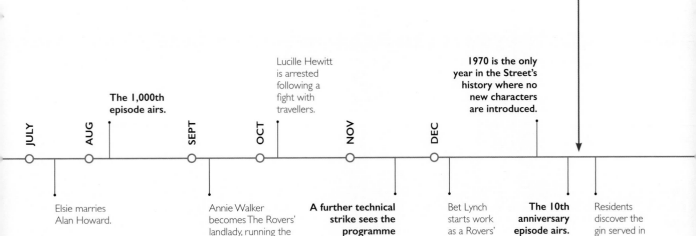

The 1,000th episode airs.

Lucille Hewitt is arrested following a fight with travellers.

1970 is the only year in the Street's history where no new characters are introduced.

JULY AUG SEPT OCT NOV DEC

Elsie marries Alan Howard.

Annie Walker becomes The Rovers' landlady, running the pub alone.

A further technical strike sees the programme transmitted in black and white for three months.

Bet Lynch starts work as a Rovers' barmaid.

The 10th anniversary episode airs.

Residents discover the gin served in The Rovers is watered down.

JANUARY

VALERIE BARLOW IS KILLED IN A BLAZE AT THE MAISONETTES

Ken has accepted a job in Jamaica and he, Val and twins Peter and Susan are preparing to immigrate to a new life in Montego Bay. Ken has sold his car and the couple have packed and are about to say their farewells to the neighbours at a leaving party Annie puts on for them in The Rovers. Ken heads to the party early, leaving Val drying her hair in their maisonette. Her hairdryer is faulty and as Val suffers an electric shock, she pulls an electric fire onto a packing case and starts a blaze. The fire engines arrive and Val is brought out of the burning building as shocked residents look on. She is rushed to hospital but is declared dead. Ken has the difficult task of telling Uncle Albert. Val was just 28 when she died. Following the fire, the maisonettes were deemed unsafe and demolished. Ken spends the following months trying to cope, looking after the twins while holding down a demanding teaching job and running a home, before Val's mother Edith takes over, eventually persuading Ken the twins would be better off with her in Scotland.

PRODUCTION NOTE

The episodes surrounding Valerie's death scored ratings of 18 million, with one, on 8th February 1971, seeing a huge 19 million viewers, one-third of the entire population of the UK at the time, sitting down to watch the show.

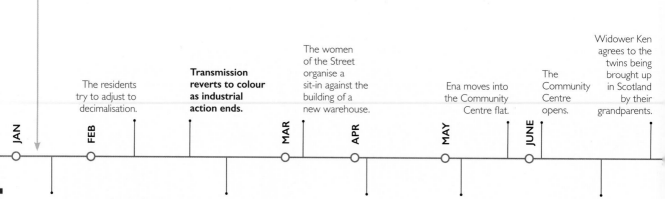

The residents try to adjust to decimalisation.

Transmission reverts to colour as industrial action ends.

The women of the Street organise a sit-in against the building of a new warehouse.

Ena moves into the Community Centre flat.

The Community Centre opens.

Widower Ken agrees to the twins being brought up in Scotland by their grandparents.

JAN FEB MAR APR MAY JUNE

1971

Val's death, which is watched by 18 million viewers and prompted by Anne Reid leaving, allows the writers to demolish the maisonettes as unsafe and better use the other side of the street.

Actor Frank Pemberton returns as Frank Barlow to film Valerie's funeral. He dies seven weeks later.

Lucille recognises the Barlow twins' nanny as the girl who bullied her in the orphanage.

The Mark Brittain Warehouse opens for business.

First appearance of Ivy Tilsley.

SEPTEMBER

ELSIE DISCOVERS JANET IS FLIRTING WITH ALAN

Former town hall clerk Janet Reid is working in the Corner Shop and has taken a shine to Alan Howard, visiting him at the garage and openly flirting with him. Alan is flattered – he's getting nagged at home by Elsie about his debts. They share a kiss but he doesn't want a full-blown affair. Janet follows him on a business trip to Leeds, arriving at his hotel where he turns her down. The Street gossip machine ensures Elsie soon finds out and after confronting Alan, who convinces her he didn't sleep with Janet, she warns Janet off in no uncertain terms. Janet admits she is lonely and just wants what everyone else seems to have – a man who loves her. A couple of years later, Janet went on to become Ken Barlow's second wife.

PRODUCTION NOTE

The ITV colour strike was an industrial dispute that affected independent TV stations from November 1970 to February 1971. ITV had switched to colour transmission in late 1969, but this meant huge investment for each individual TV company, and the main broadcasting union, the ACTT (Association of Cinematograph, Television and Allied Technicians), demanded a pay rise for its members who were expected to use the new equipment. During the strike, programmes continued to be broadcast in black and white, even those recorded in colour. The strike ended on 2nd February 1971 and *Coronation Street*'s final episode to be broadcast in black and white was on 10th February. Apart from several flashbacks, the first moments of the 40th anniversary show and the final scene of the 10,000th episode on 7th February 2020, the programme has been broadcast in colour ever since.

JULY

AUG
Ernest Bishop and Emily Nugent get engaged.

Hilda and Stan get the Street's first colour TV – soon to be repossessed.

First appearance of Mavis Riley.

Lucille is mugged and beaten in the street while carrying betting shop takings to the bank.

SEPT

Alan Howard's flirtation was originally going to be with Irma Barlow, but actress Sandra Gough is absent and later dismissed from the show.

OCT
Innocent Ernie is jailed in Spain for 'offending public morality'.

NOV
A delighted Hilda wins £500 on the Premium Bonds.

Irma's new boyfriend is Weatherfield County FC's star player.

DEC
Alan walks out on Elsie.

Ken returns to teaching at Bessie Street School, as head of English.

ERNEST AND EMILY'S WEDDING

Following a sometimes rocky courtship of three years after they met at his mother's funeral, Ernest and Emily's wedding is set for Easter Monday. When the men on the Street take Ernest out for a few stag-night beers, they kid him about Emily jilting Leonard Swindley virtually at the altar some years earlier. Ernest is horrified and gets drunk, fearing Emily may do the same to him. The following day the guests arrive at Mawdsley Street Chapel for the nuptials. A nervous Ernest keeps driving round the church, convinced Emily won't show and eventually she enters the building before him. He joins her and they are married before a delighted congregation. They honeymoon in the Peak District, Emily no longer the eternal spinster she feared she might become.

PRODUCTION NOTE

Emily Nugent and Ernest Bishop's wedding on 5th April 1972 saw 18.26 million viewers, one-third of the UK population, tune in. The month was the only one that year to see such a spike (average audiences were generally around 14 million). In 1972, fellow ITV soap *Crossroads*, which was fully networked that year, regularly beat *Coronation Street* in the ratings.

1972

Elsie and Alan agree to put their differences behind them and reunite.

JAN

Irma decides to sell up her share of the Corner Shop and move to Wales. Maggie Clegg buys it and becomes sole owner again.

FEB

MAR

Audrey Fleming agrees to sell No 3 to Ernest and Emily.

Some of the residents go for a sail in Jerry Booth's homemade boat, but it capsizes.

APR

MAY

Rita Littlewood moves in on Len Fairclough.

Eric Prytherch takes over from Brian Armstrong as producer, marking the start of two- to three-year producerships rather than six months.

JUNE

First appearance of Alec Gilroy.

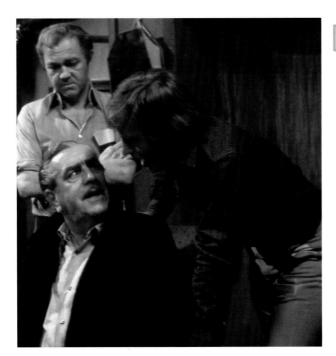

PRODUCTION NOTE

A proposed spin-off featuring Jerry Booth and Ray Langton working away from the Street as insurance salesmen failed to get off the ground. Entitled *Rest Assured*, a pilot programme written by H V Kershaw was recorded but never transmitted.

AUGUST

STAN IS ACCUSED OF VOYEURISM

A worried Lucille spots what she believes is a Peeping Tom looking into The Rovers' living accommodation. Word spreads and soon Hilda believes she has seen him behind No 13. Emily is scared when she thinks someone has been looking into a bedroom window too. Ken takes charge, asking Lucille to accompany him around the Street asking for descriptions of the man. Everyone has something different to say and Ken suspects the culprit is donning a disguise. It's possible that he is someone they may know, he surmises. Hilda purchases some binoculars and takes to surveying the area from her window, while Elsie fears she disturbed the man in her back yard. The residents are worried and decide to patrol the Street. Albert joins them, believing his wartime experience will be of benefit. The vigilantes spot Stan Ogden in the ginnel and suspect he is their man. Hilda angrily supports him as he is accused and insulted. Soon, the police reveal that they have caught the real Peeping Tom on nearby Bessie Street but Billy Walker won't believe it until the man is charged. Hilda and Stan discuss moving away as the rumours continue to swirl and they begin to receive hate mail. When a piece about the arrest of the real culprit is printed in the *Weatherfield Gazette*, Hilda shows it to the regulars in The Rovers and Billy apologises to the Ogdens.

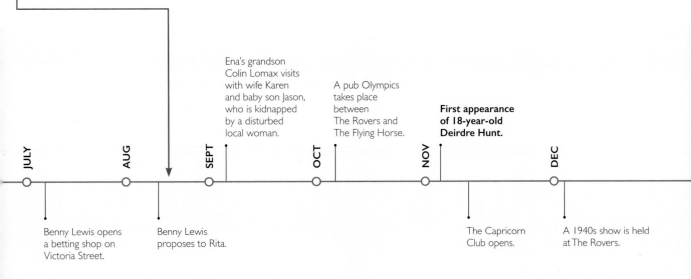

JULY

AUG

SEPT
Ena's grandson Colin Lomax visits with wife Karen and baby son Jason, who is kidnapped by a disturbed local woman.

OCT
A pub Olympics takes place between The Rovers and The Flying Horse.

NOV
First appearance of 18-year-old Deirdre Hunt.

DEC

Benny Lewis opens a betting shop on Victoria Street.

Benny Lewis proposes to Rita.

The Capricorn Club opens.

A 1940s show is held at The Rovers.

BET LYNCH IS BEATEN UP IN THE ALLEY

Following a to-do in The Rovers over a Pools win that Ray was planning on keeping, Bet and the other members of the syndicate settle for £75 each. When Bet leaves the pub with her share in her handbag she is followed by someone. Later, Stan and Hilda find her beaten in the ginnel, her money gone. After being treated in hospital Bet stays at The Rovers to recuperate. The police are interested in the syndicate and Stan, who didn't get a payout, is briefly under suspicion, but Bet suspects petty criminal Norman Leach, who had been blackmailing Alf over a car accident in which Bet was the passenger. Leach has an alibi from his mother and Stan is revealed to have been visiting another woman. Alf goes to the police to tell all about the blackmail as Bet's handbag is discovered. Leach's prints are on the bag and he is eventually jailed for seven years.

MAY

LEN ASKS RITA TO RUN HIS NEW BUSINESS, THE KABIN

Biddulph's newsagent was a run-down shop on Rosamund Street that also offered a café and a lending library. When Len buys it from Walter Biddulph he offers, first Elsie, then Rita the position of manageress, which comes with the added bonus of being able to live in the flat above the shop. Ray also has designs on the premises and promises Deirdre the same position before discovering that Len has beaten him to the sale. Rita accepts the job but has misgivings that Len has a key to the flat. She also wants The Kabin to be called Rita's and she'd like an assistant. Len acquiesces on everything but the name and also hands over the second key. Enter Mavis Riley, who nervously hiccups her way through an interview with Rita before joining her behind the counter. The pair are confused when several male customers call in for their regular copy of *Pig Producers' Monthly* as there's not a piggery for miles around, before discovering that Walter Biddulph had been selling adult magazines disguised within the pages of the farmers' periodical.

1973

Alf Roberts becomes Mayor of Weatherfield.

Annie Walker agrees to become Lady Mayoress.

There is a gas leak and the residents are evacuated.

No 13 (the Ogdens') has to be fumigated.

The Kabin is seen for the first time.

Mavis and Jerry begin dating.

JAN

FEB

MAR

APR

MAY

JUNE

Harry Kershaw steps down as executive producer, but remains as a staff writer until he retires 15 years later.

Hilda holds a Barbara Cartland birthday party.

Albert stops his daughter Beattie blackmailing Jerry Booth.

DECEMBER

STAN AND HILDA'S 30TH WEDDING ANNIVERSARY

Stan and Hilda decide to celebrate their pearl wedding anniversary with a party. Money is tight as always and Stan can't afford to buy Hilda a present, so Maggie gives him a necklace of pearls for her. After a dig from Betty about Hilda's estranged son Trevor, who had left home nine years earlier, Hilda and Stan make efforts to track him down. Despite living rough initially, Trevor had worked his way up to become an estate agent and by 1973 was living in a nice detached house in Chesterfield with his wife Polly and baby son

Damian, a grandchild the Ogdens didn't know they had. When Stan and Hilda arrive on their doorstep, relations are strained between son and parents, with Trevor uncomfortably reminded of his working-class roots. It emerges Trevor had led Polly to believe his parents were dead; Stan is furious and Hilda devastated. They see each other sporadically over the next few years, usually when Trevor wants Hilda to look after his children, as he and Polly went on to have a daughter.

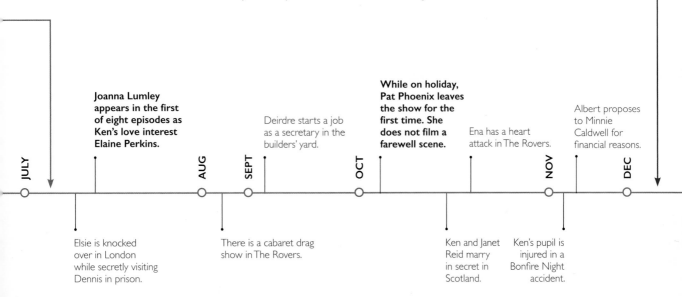

Joanna Lumley appears in the first of eight episodes as Ken's love interest Elaine Perkins.

Deirdre starts a job as a secretary in the builders' yard.

While on holiday, Pat Phoenix leaves the show for the first time. She does not film a farewell scene.

Ena has a heart attack in The Rovers.

Albert proposes to Minnie Caldwell for financial reasons.

JULY AUG SEPT OCT NOV DEC

Elsie is knocked over in London while secretly visiting Dennis in prison.

There is a cabaret drag show in The Rovers.

Ken and Janet Reid marry in secret in Scotland.

Ken's pupil is injured in a Bonfire Night accident.

SOLDIER MARTIN DOWNES DISCOVERS BET LYNCH IS HIS MOTHER

When Bet Lynch was a teenager she found herself pregnant after a fling with an older man who fled Weatherfield when he learned of the pregnancy. Bet gave up the baby, a son, for adoption. Fast forward to 1974 and her son, Martin Downes, now serving with the Royal Transport Corps, arrives in Weatherfield to find his birth mother. He had learned her name was Elizabeth Lynch and she worked as a barmaid in the town. Martin and army pal Steve appear in The Rovers. At first Martin thinks Betty might be his mum, but discovers her maiden name is Preston. He hears that a woman named Lynch will be starting her shift soon, so he waits for Bet. Unfortunately, Bet is dressed to show off a revealing dress she's bought for a wedding and laps up the attention from the pub's male clientele. Martin is horrified at his mother's behaviour and leaves the pub without revealing to Bet who he is. A year later, Steve returns to inform Bet that Martin has been killed in a car accident in Northern Ireland, where the pair had been posted. Despite not raising Martin, Bet was devastated and considered taking her own life before Eddie Yeats stopped her. Bet is reminded of Martin's death when her only photograph of him is stolen in a burglary several years later.

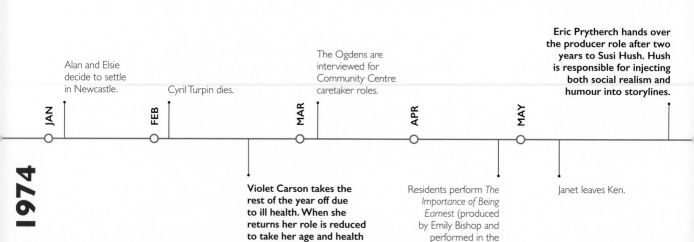

1974

Alan and Elsie decide to settle in Newcastle.

Cyril Turpin dies.

The Ogdens are interviewed for Community Centre caretaker roles.

Eric Prytherch hands over the producer role after two years to Susi Hush. Hush is responsible for injecting both social realism and humour into storylines.

JAN FEB MAR APR MAY

Violet Carson takes the rest of the year off due to ill health. When she returns her role is reduced to take her age and health into consideration.

Residents perform *The Importance of Being Earnest* (produced by Emily Bishop and performed in the Community Centre).

Janet leaves Ken.

OCTOBER

IT'S OFF TO MAJORCA FOR THE STREET'S WOMEN

When Len suggests a woman could never win a spot-the-ball competition, Bet and the girls enter one in *The Gazette* and scoop first prize: a holiday for two to the Bahamas. When the winning group – Bet, Annie, Deirdre, Rita, Mavis, Betty, Emily and Hilda can't decide which two should take the trip, the are told they can swap it for a week's holiday for all of them to Majorca. The girls excitedly jet off for some sun, sand and sangria, and a week of fun and flirting ensues – Mavis surprises everyone by embarking on a romance with a Spaniard called Pedro. Bet meets a property developer and, believing she has a future with him, stays behind when the others return home only to be told in no uncertain terms that their romance was only a holiday fling. The women worry about Bet and her whereabouts, especially when the Spanish police report they can't trace her. Bet eventually returns, pretending she's had a whale of a time. In reality, a lonely holidaying bank clerk had taken pity on her and, learning she was stranded, had paid her air fare home. When he turns up at The Rovers hoping to take her out, Bet lets him down, borrowing cash from Billy Walker to pay him back.

First appearance of Vera Duckworth and Blanche Hunt (originally played for two episodes by Patricia Cutts).

Billy Walker is charged with receiving stolen goods.

First appearance of Eddie Yeats.

JUNE

JULY

AUG

SEPT

OCT

NOV

DEC

Maggie Clegg and Ron Cooke set a date for their wedding.

Gail Potter's first appearance.

Football hooligans run riot in Street.

The female-only trip to Majorca is the first foreign location shoot.

Emily and Ernest have marriage problems.

There is no Christmas Day episode, although it falls on a Wednesday, because of traditionally low viewing numbers for the key festive days.

GORDON CLEGG DISCOVERS HIS MOTHER IS BETTY TURPIN

Unmarried Betty had become pregnant with Gordon in 1949. His father was her wartime boyfriend, a soldier called Ted Farrell, who left the area and never knew of Gordon's existence. Betty's sister Maggie and her husband Les Clegg, who had no children of their own, adopted Betty's child. By January 1975 the Hopkins family are in the process of buying the Corner Shop as Maggie, now married to Ron Cooke, has immigrated to Africa. London-based Gordon is handling the sale. During a row over Maggie's furniture in the shop's living quarters, conniving Megan 'Granny' Hopkins finds Gordon's birth certificate behind a sideboard and discovers that Gordon's real mother is Betty. She attempts to blackmail Gordon but Maggie and Betty had decided the time was right to inform Gordon about who his real mother was and when Granny Hopkins threatens to tell the Street about Gordon's illegitimacy he refuses to sell the shop to the Hopkins, who leave the Street, ashamed of Granny's actions. Betty and Gordon go on to build a loving relationship with Gordon giving Betty away when she married Billy Williams in 1995.

PRODUCTION NOTE

Gordon was played by theatre and film producer Bill Kenwright, apart from appearances in 2002–04, when Geoffrey Leesley played the part. Bill Kenwright, by then very well known both in entertainment and as chairman of Everton football club, reappeared in 2012 for Betty's funeral.

JUNE

BETTY SEES 'MARTHA'S GHOST' IN THE ROVERS SNUG

More than a decade after Martha Longhurst's death in The Rovers snug, she makes a reappearance of sorts. Bet and Betty are looking after The Rovers while Annie Walker is away. One night after all the punters have left, Betty is tidying up and finds a pair of glasses on the bar. She believes she has seen a woman in the snug and hears a voice referring to 'Lily's Wilf'. Lily was Martha's daughter and Wilf her son-in-law. Betty describes her vision to Martha's old pals Ena and Minnie and they decide it must have been Martha's ghost. The eerie occurrence is never fully explained – Ken thinks it's bunkum – and the spectacles are eventually claimed by a customer.

1975

- **JAN**
- **FEB** — Blanche Hunt takes over as manager of the Corner Shop.
- Lynn Johnson is murdered by her husband Roy. Len is implicated, as she was at his house when she was attacked, asking him for help as her local councillor.
- **MAR** — Billy Walker and Deirdre set their wedding date.
- **APR** — Bet Lynch hears her long-lost soldier son has been killed in Northern Ireland and she contemplates suicide.
- **MAY** — Billy and Deirdre break up.
- **JUNE** — Because of a strike by the ACTT union (a technicians' union, which eventually becomes BECTU) three planned episodes are unrecorded.

OCTOBER

A FIRE IN THE WAREHOUSE KILLS EDNA GEE

Mail-order warehouse worker Edna Gee celebrates her 40th birthday. Elsewhere on the Street, Ken has his hands full with some lads he used to teach who are running wild in the area, playing truant, stealing and smashing windows. He persuades Len not to involve the police. The lads spend the night in the Mark Brittain Warehouse storeroom, where one of them discards a lit cigarette. The following morning Edna sneaks off for a cig break in the storeroom, which bursts into flames as she opens the door and the warehouse is engulfed in fire. Eighteen-year-old secretary

Tricia Hopkins, Gail's best pal and flatmate, is caught up in the blaze, as she was in the ladies' loo next door and is overcome by smoke. She escapes and is comforted by Gail. As the residents are evacuated from the Street they gather in a nearby pub where Len learns from the police that a body has been found. It is Edna's and after Ken informs her close friend Ivy, she tries to comfort Edna's husband Fred. Another unidentified body is discovered and the residents are not allowed back on the Street for several days because of potentially dangerous fumes. Scores of workers lose their jobs following the fire, but a year later Mike Baldwin arrives to open up his denim factory on the site.

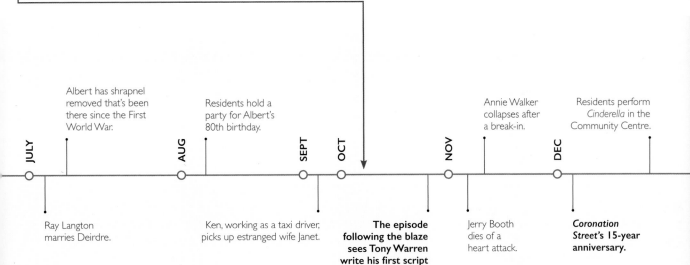

Albert has shrapnel removed that's been there since the First World War.

Residents hold a party for Albert's 80th birthday.

Annie Walker collapses after a break-in.

Residents perform *Cinderella* in the Community Centre.

JULY   AUG   SEPT   OCT   NOV   DEC

Ray Langton marries Deirdre.

Ken, working as a taxi driver, picks up estranged wife Janet.

The episode following the blaze sees Tony Warren write his first script since 1969.

Jerry Booth dies of a heart attack.

Coronation Street's 15-year anniversary.

MARCH

HILDA WINS A TROLLEY DASH

After reading about a man who has tremendous success in competitions, Hilda fancies her chances of scooping some prizes and starts entering anything she can get her hands on, buying dog food (they have no dog) and taking time off work to fill in even more magazine competition entry forms. She and Stan quite fancy the safari or world cruise prize she's sure is just a second-class stamp away. Eventually, her efforts are rewarded – with a two-minute trolley dash in a local food store. Donning Gail's running shoes, Hilda practises in the Corner Shop and, on the day of the dash, manages to grab more than £100 worth of goods with Deirdre's help. Most of it is frozen though and the Ogdens don't have a freezer. Stan doesn't even like most of the produce and the shop owner agrees to buy it back so the Ogdens can pay their TV rental.

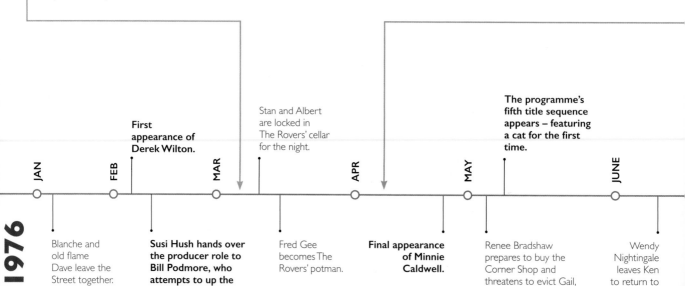

1976

JAN · FEB · MAR · APR · MAY · JUNE

First appearance of Derek Wilton.

Stan and Albert are locked in The Rovers' cellar for the night.

The programme's fifth title sequence appears – featuring a cat for the first time.

Blanche and old flame Dave leave the Street together.

Susi Hush hands over the producer role to Bill Podmore, who attempts to up the comedy quotient on the Street.

Fred Gee becomes The Rovers' potman.

Final appearance of Minnie Caldwell.

Renee Bradshaw prepares to buy the Corner Shop and threatens to evict Gail, Tricia and Elsie from the flat.

Wendy Nightingale leaves Ken to return to her husband.

APRIL

ELSIE RETURNS TO THE STREET

Elsie Tanner makes her return to Coronation Street after nearly three years in Newcastle. Her marriage to Alan Howard has failed and she tells Len they are having a trial separation. The Rovers regulars are surprised to see Len and Elsie drinking together. Rita is highly suspicious of Elsie and Len's friendship and is relieved when she moves into the Corner Shop flat. Ken Barlow, now estranged from wife Janet and renting No 11, refuses to move out when Elsie asks him to, but eventually changes his mind when his married lover Wendy Nightingale reconciles with her husband. After a brief stay in the Corner Shop flat, Elsie returns to her old home, taking in a lodger in the form of Gail Potter, her assistant at Sylvia's Separates. Meanwhile, Ken moves into No 1 for the first time, living with Albert.

OCTOBER

MIKE BALDWIN ARRIVES, OPENING A DENIM FACTORY IN THE WAREHOUSE

Wealthy London businessman Mike Baldwin arrives in Coronation Street when he opens Baldwin's Casuals on the site of the Mark Brittain Warehouse. He interviews Ernest Bishop and gives him the job of wages clerk, telling him he has to interview applicants for the new machinist jobs. Both Bet and Betty apply, but neither is successful. Mike does, however, ask Bet out, admitting he has a wife in London. Bet agrees to go out with him, and Rita is jealous – she'd been flirting furiously with the cockney charmer. The wiley businessman buys No 5, Minnie's former home, from under the nose of the Langtons who are all ready to make an offer. Ray is furious, especially when Mike asks him and Len to renovate the house for him.

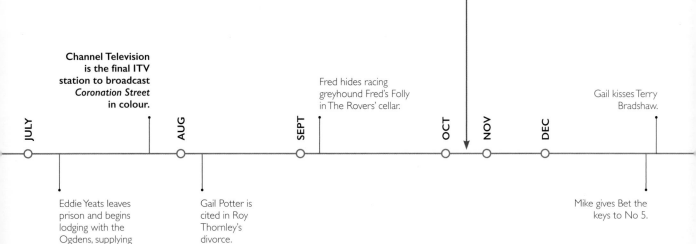

Channel Television is the final ITV station to broadcast *Coronation Street* in colour.

Fred hides racing greyhound Fred's Folly in The Rovers' cellar.

Gail kisses Terry Bradshaw.

JULY   AUG   SEPT   OCT   NOV   DEC

Eddie Yeats leaves prison and begins lodging with the Ogdens, supplying the famous 'muriel' wallpaper.

Gail Potter is cited in Roy Thornley's divorce.

Mike gives Bet the keys to No 5.

FEBRUARY

JANET BARLOW DIES OF A DRUG OVERDOSE

Janet and Ken's marriage had been a brief and unsuccessful union – he had been looking for a wife so his twins could return to Weatherfield from his in-laws in Scotland and grow up with two parents, and Janet was an upwardly mobile woman, remembered as having tried to split Elsie and Alan up.

The couple had split up in 1974 and when Janet returns to the Street three years later, having failed to reunite with her later partner Vince Denton, she begs Ken to take her back. After finding her on his doorstep, Ken tells her they have no future but says she can stay the night, he'll sleep on the sofa. The following morning Ken discovers Janet has taken an overdose. She is dead on arrival at the hospital and Ken is briefly under suspicion. Later, Vince threatens Ken over several thousand pounds in Janet's bank account he claims are his. Ken settles the affair with the help of Janet's sister, but makes his disdain of Vince and his motives clear.

JUNE

THE RESIDENTS CELEBRATE THE SILVER JUBILEE

The Queen's Silver Jubilee in June 1977, marked by street parties across the land, was a chance for the Street's residents to show they can party with the best of them.

Ahead of the big day there is a Bonny Jubilee Baby competition, won by Tracy Langton, and a Glamorous Granny Competition, into which Gail and Suzie mischievously enter Elsie. She is cross with them but at least she reaches the finals, as does Vera, despite not being a granny!

The residents plan to enter a float in the Weatherfield parade. The theme is Britain Through the Ages, with Annie as Elizabeth I; Ena as Queen Victoria; Bet as Britannia; and Ken and Albert as Sir Edmund Hilary and Sherpa Tensing, respectively. However, Stan leaves the lorry lights on overnight, meaning a flat battery that leaves the residents unable to join the parade. They hold a jokey kangaroo court in The Rovers, where Stan is found guilty and ordered to buy drinks for everyone as penance.

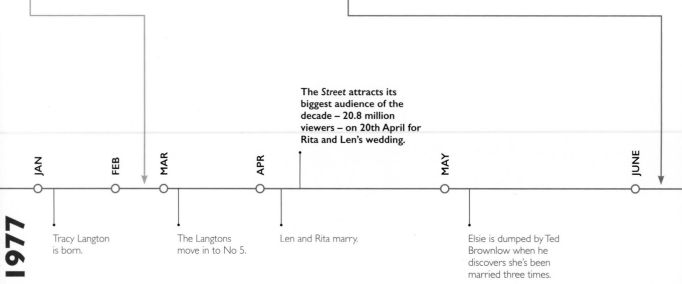

The *Street* attracts its biggest audience of the decade – 20.8 million viewers – on 20th April for Rita and Len's wedding.

1977

JAN | FEB | MAR | APR | MAY | JUNE

Tracy Langton is born.

The Langtons move in to No 5.

Len and Rita marry.

Elsie is dumped by Ted Brownlow when he discovers she's been married three times.

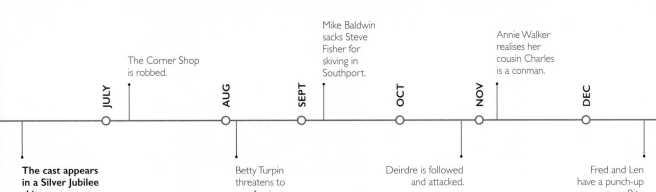

Mike Baldwin
sacks Steve
Fisher for
skiving in
Southport.

The Corner Shop
is robbed.

Annie Walker
realises her
cousin Charles
is a conman.

JULY

AUG

SEPT

OCT

NOV

DEC

**The cast appears
in a Silver Jubilee
skit on stage at
Manchester's
Palace Theatre.**

Betty Turpin
threatens to
sue Annie
Walker for
defamation.

Deirdre is followed
and attacked.

Fred and Len
have a punch-up
over Rita.

ANNIE FEARS SHE'LL LOSE THE ROVERS

When Annie Walker travels to Jersey to see son Billy, Fred organises a 'Lancashire evening' in The Rovers. Suzie and Gail are holding a party down the Street at No 11. A drunken gatecrasher leaves their house and steals Annie's prized Rover. When Fred discovers the car has gone he calls the police, who are interested to see that the pub has been serving after hours. Fred is forced to collect Annie from the airport in Len's van and Annie is furious to hear about the theft of her car. She had also been hoping to impress a new friend by having 'her chauffeur Frederick' collect them. Brewery Newton and Ridley is the subject of a takeover bid at this time and Annie fears the after-hours party will mean the end of her licence. Both Billy and Annie's daughter Joan travel to the Street to support Annie, who is certain she will lose The Rovers. Billy offers to take over the licence but the brewery takeover bid falls through and Annie remains as licensee, to Billy's relief. He didn't really want to swap Jersey for Weatherfield.

THE FACTORY STAFF GO ON STRIKE

When factory cleaner Hilda puts in a bill for new cleaning equipment, Mike refuses to pay it, suspecting she'll use it elsewhere. Hilda threatens to go on strike, but Mike unceremoniously sacks her. The factory workers, led by Ivy, who calls a union meeting, worry Mike could sack any of them at a moment's notice. Ivy accuses Mike of victimising Hilda and the workers vote to go on strike, even though Hilda is not a union member. Vera organises a picket outside the factory and the girls walk out. Mike arranges to bring in non-union workers, leading to violence on the picket line. They refuse to work on the machines. Hilda gets a job cleaning at a local abattoir and leaves her former co-workers to protest in her absence. Mike tells Ivy he'll give Hilda her job back and the strike is called off. Hilda is worried everyone will find out about her abattoir job, so she gives it up.

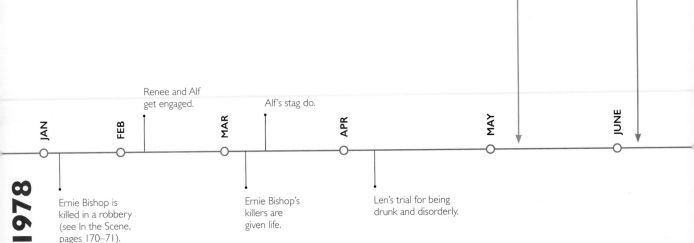

1978

Renee and Alf get engaged.

Alf's stag do.

JAN   FEB   MAR   APR   MAY   JUNE

Ernie Bishop is killed in a robbery (see In the Scene, pages 170–71).

Ernie Bishop's killers are given life.

Len's trial for being drunk and disorderly.

SEPTEMBER

RAY LANGTON PLAYS AWAY

Ray has been chatting up Janice Stubbs for a while and starts lying to Deirdre about doing overtime of an evening. Even though Ray feels guilty at two-timing Deirdre, he continues to see Janice. Soon Elsie, then Len and Emily discover Ray is seeing another woman. Len tells him he's a fool and Emily urges Janice to end the affair. Ray is caught out when he pretends to be playing in a snooker tournament and Deirdre accuses him of lying, while Emily confirms he is cheating on her. Deirdre confronts Janice and dumps Ray, preparing to leave with Tracy, but after much pleading she agrees to stay with him. The Langtons plan a fresh start in Holland but as they are about to depart, Deirdre realises she can no longer trust Ray. He leaves anyway, while Deirdre remains in Weatherfield as a single mother.

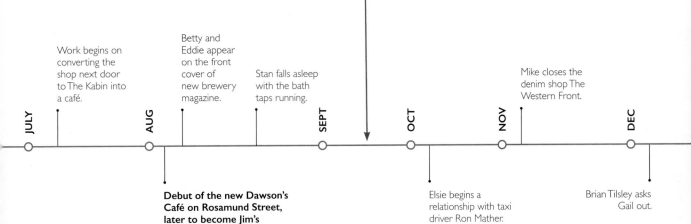

Work begins on converting the shop next door to The Kabin into a café.

Betty and Eddie appear on the front cover of new brewery magazine.

Stan falls asleep with the bath taps running.

Mike closes the denim shop The Western Front.

JULY   AUG   SEPT   OCT   NOV   DEC

Debut of the new Dawson's Café on Rosamund Street, later to become Jim's Café when, in 1980, Jim Sedgewick turns it into a transport caff.

Elsie begins a relationship with taxi driver Ron Mather.

Brian Tilsley asks Gail out.

IN dark and emotional scenes, one of *Coronation Street*'s gentler characters, Ernest Bishop, meets a brutal end. Gun crime has come to the streets of Weatherfield and following this first violent death on *Coronation Street*, the repercussions of Ernie's murder in the factory at the hands of two bungling armed robbers go on to haunt widow Emily decades later.

In the scene
Ernest Bishop's murder

THE SURROUNDING STORYLINES

Ernie and Emily – Ernie and Emily's six-year marriage had been under strain financially after Ernie's photography business closed, so when Mike Baldwin offered him the job of wages clerk at Baldwin's Casuals they were relieved, although by January 1978 lay preacher Ernie is feeling in a bit of a rut. Emily is working at the local hospital and the couple are planning a holiday abroad.

A robbery is planned – Two thugs, Dave Lester and Edward 'Tommo' Jackson, follow Mike and Ernie to the bank. They are armed with a sawn-off shotgun and plan to mug the pair for the cash. The street is too busy and instead they decide to target the factory.

THE MAIN EVENT

Dave and Tommo enter the factory and find Ernie alone in his office, putting the wage packets together. They point the shotgun at him and demand he hands over the cash.

Mike suddenly comes through the office door, surprising them. He bumps into Tommo and the gun goes off, hitting Ernie in the chest. He falls to the floor as the thugs flee through the factory and a panicking Mike calls the police. Ernie is rushed to hospital and undergoes emergency surgery.

Back at the factory, the girls are in shock as they wait to give their statements to the police. Vera is concerned about whether or not they'll get paid, but the other girls are more worried about Emily finding out what has happened – she's not back from her job at the hospital and that's where Ernie is being taken.

Soon, Emily arrives home, and on being told about the shooting, collapses. Betty accompanies her back to the hospital and they wait for news. Ernie dies on the operating table and doctors break the harrowing news to Emily.

Mike is in shock and struggles to answer the investigating officers' questions. With the help of a slug of Scotch he recalls key details as they coax descriptions of the two young men from him.

PRODUCTION NOTE

Actor Stephen Hancock's departure from *Coronation Street* followed his futile demands for a change to the way cast contracts were dealt with to make them, in his eyes, more equitable for other actors. Such was the public reaction to Ernie's death that a Granada documentary – *Death on the Street* – was made. In it, Hancock as well as Noel Dyson (Ida Barlow) and Lynne Carol (Martha Longhurst) discussed the impact of being killed off in the country's most popular show.

Producer at the time Bill Podmore noted in his book *Coronation Street: The Inside Story* that 'when death's winged chariot clatters down Coronation Street, the whole nation mourns'. He explained how Ernie's murder storyline was intended to concentrate, not on the 'usual television drama of cops and robbers… but the utter futility of Ernie's death and the desolation and immense sadness it had caused'.

In 2010, in a TV documentary called *Coronation Street: 50 Years 50 Moments*, Hancock described how he watched the filming of Ernest's burial from behind some trees. 'I remember going as myself to the funeral and watching myself being buried,' he said.

THE AFTERMATH

Mike feels guilty – if he hadn't disturbed the gunmen Ernie might still be alive. He pays for the funeral and offers Emily further financial support.

The robbers are caught and arrested within days. Emily goes to stay with her sister Norah after the funeral. Two months later the thugs stand trial for Ernie's murder with Mike as the key witness and they are both jailed for life.

Emily struggles to adjust to life without Ernie but goes on to marry again – bigamist Arnold Swain. Nearly 30 years later, in 2005, Ernie's killer returns to Coronation Street and seeks out Emily…

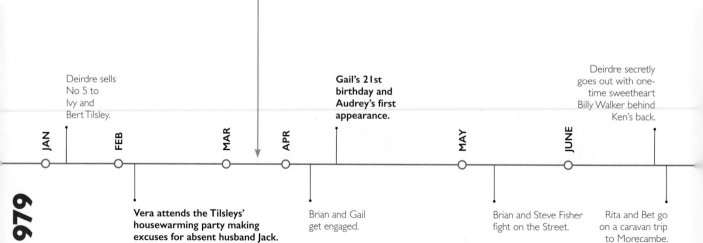

1979

Deirdre sells
No 5 to
Ivy and
Bert Tilsley.

**Gail's 21st
birthday and
Audrey's first
appearance.**

Deirdre secretly
goes out with one-
time sweetheart
Billy Walker behind
Ken's back.

JAN   FEB   MAR   APR   MAY   JUNE

**Vera attends the Tilsleys'
housewarming party making
excuses for absent husband Jack.
William Tarmey appears as an
extra in the party scenes, nine
months before being cast as Jack.**

Brian and Gail
get engaged.

Brian and Steve Fisher
fight on the Street.

Rita and Bet go
on a caravan trip
to Morecambe.

A TIMBER LORRY CRASHES INTO THE ROVERS

Deirdre calls into The Rovers to see Annie, leaving Tracy outside in her buggy. A lorry crashes into the pub, shedding its load of timber. Deirdre is terrified that Tracy is dead. Alf, Len, Mike and Betty are injured, while Emily and Ena try to calm Deirdre. When the lorry driver is discovered to have died, Deirdre fears the worst and runs away. Tracy's doll is found, but there's no sign of Tracy. Detectives search No 3, suspecting Deirdre may have killed her child, when the timber is removed and Tracy still can't be found. Deirdre considers killing herself. Emily remembers seeing Sally Norton, whom she had visited in hospital as a volunteer when Sally suffered psychiatric problems after she was persuaded to give a baby up for adoption. She had been on the labour ward alongside Deirdre when Tracy was born and it was she who had given Tracy her doll. Emily gives a description to the police and they find Sally with Tracy, while Len and Emily find Deirdre. Despite Deirdre believing Sally saved Tracy's life, Sally is charged with child abduction.

GAIL AND BRIAN MARRY

Earlier in the year Ivy Tilsley was horrified when beloved son Brian announced he was engaged to Gail Potter. The pair had been courting for three months, but domineering Ivy believed that, at 20, Brian was too young to settle down. She wasn't too keen on Gail, although no one would have been good enough for her Brian, her only child. Their acrimonious relationship continued until Ivy's death in 1995. She asked Brian to keep the engagement secret for a while until she got used to the idea – in reality to give herself time to split the pair up – but Gail's 21st birthday/engagement party put paid to that. The party saw the arrival of a flirtatious Audrey Potter, Gail's mother. After several ups and downs, and tussles between Ivy and Audrey over the location of the wedding reception, Gail and Brian finally tie the knot, with Mike giving Gail away and Suzie Birchall as bridesmaid. Gail and Brian go on to divorce and marry a second time.

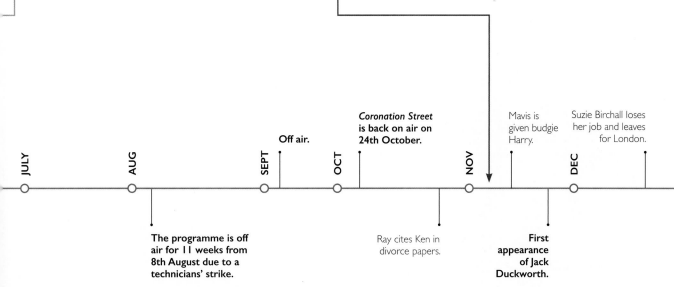

JULY   AUG   SEPT   OCT   NOV   DEC

Off air.

Coronation Street **is back on air on 24th October.**

Mavis is given budgie Harry.

Suzie Birchall loses her job and leaves for London.

The programme is off air for 11 weeks from 8th August due to a technicians' strike.

Ray cites Ken in divorce papers.

First appearance of Jack Duckworth.

IN FOCUS

OCCASIONALLY, the *Coronation Street* story office decides to take the characters away from the cobbles and filming takes place on location. Sometimes they even inject a little foreign fun into their plots.

On location

The show has often left its base to film locally – in Salford and Manchester city centre; at Manchester Airport (and for one episode in 1970 featuring Hilda Ogden, Heathrow); Belle Vue Zoological Gardens; the impressive and historic Midland Hotel in Manchester; Speedwell Cavern in the Peak District; Tatton Park in Knutsford in Cheshire on several occasions, notably for the first episode to be made entirely on location in 1967; Lyme Park in Disley, Cheshire; the Lake District; a caravan park in Poynton (doubling for Abergele, where killer Pat Phelan was hiding out); and, of course, Blackpool, which warrants its own section below.

Cast and crew generally enjoy this break from regular filming in the studio or on the lot (the external Street set). Helen Worth remembers filming the Joe McIntyre storyline in the Lake District with fondness. 'It was a great shoot, we always have fun on location, it's like a holiday really.'

Paris, 2006

Malta 2007

Normandy 1994

Former assistant director Dayle Evans-Kar adds: 'We shot the Joe McIntyre Lake District shoot on a pontoon on Windermere in December, in a blizzard. The scenes were on a boat and we had two stunts a day for six days. That was really tricky. We had to light the lake and the pontoon kept moving as we were right in the middle of the lake and couldn't anchor to anything. Because it was December we couldn't keep the stuntman or the actor in the water for any length of time. It was a very challenging shoot.'

She recalls an amusing occasion filming away from Weatherfield. 'We were doing a Bonfire Night scene in a park. It was a tricky scene to shoot, it was 2am. No mobile phones were allowed, but there was a phone ringing, so we cut. I was shouting, "Who's got a phone! I can hear a phone,

I'm going to sack the person whose phone is ringing." I got closer to the sound and it was Bill Roache. I said, well obviously I can't sack you! He was so apologetic.'

Location shooting adds to the realism of the programme, but it's often been the foreign trips that have stayed in the memories of viewers over the years. The very first foreign trip occurred quite early in the life of *Coronation Street*: in October 1974, when a group of *Coronation Street* women jetted off to Majorca. Bet Lynch won a beach holiday in a competition and decided to take her female pals from the Street along with her. She was joined by Betty, Rita, Mavis, Annie, Hilda, Emily and Deirdre, and all manner of Majorcan merriment ensued. Forty years before Majorca-based *Love Island* became a ratings hit for ITV, the *TV Times*' synopsis of the two *Coronation Street* episodes proclaimed 'Les Girls whoop it up on the Isle of Love…'

Bet was back in Spain in August 1987, when Alec travelled to Torremolinos to search for her after she fled her financial woes. When he found her working in a bar there, Alec proposed. Julie Goodyear had been away from *Coronation Street* for a few months to look after her mother who was seriously ill, and these episodes marked her return.

Seven years later the characters of Percy, Maud and Maureen headed to Normandy, where Percy paid tribute to fallen comrades at the war cemeteries on the 50th anniversary of the D-day landings on 6th June 1994. Maud revealed to Maureen that her real father, an American soldier, was buried there too.

In 1998, Roy travelled to Amsterdam to look for Hayley after she went there to complete her transition to becoming a woman. He found her living on a houseboat and the pair rekindled their relationship.

In 2000, Curly and Emma travelled to ex Raquel's chateau in central France to see his young daughter Alice while Ashley, Maxine, Fred and Audrey headed to the city of love, Paris, before joining them in the Loire Valley. For these episodes, shot entirely on location, the title sequences featured shots of France.

Six years later, *Coronation Street* returned to film in Paris, this time following the Webster family (plus Rosie's boyfriend Craig) as they visited Kevin's dad Bill Webster. Scenes were shot on the banks of the River Seine and the Gare du Nord as well as a hotel in central Paris. Again these episodes included images of Paris in the title sequence.

Shortly afterwards, in 2007, it was Steve's turn to travel abroad – to Malta – with Eileen as friends. Confusion and humorous scenes followed as the pair had to share a bedroom.

ON THE ROAD… TO BLACKPOOL

As Bet Lynch once said: 'You can't beat Blackpool… you can cut the smell of shrimps and best bitter with a knife. It's paradise.'

Until the package holiday took off in the 1970s, for the folk in *Coronation Street*, like many working-class communities in the north of England, Blackpool was, and still is, the very best place for a trip to the seaside, and the Lancashire town has featured many times on the programme.

Just a short drive along the M6, on a good day you can be in Blackpool an hour after leaving Manchester's city centre. With its popular Illuminations and Pleasure Beach, it's been a main tourism centre ever since the 1840s. By the turn of the last century, Blackpool was seen as the archetypal British seaside resort due to its proximity and affordability, popular with visitors from all the nearby mill towns.

No wonder, then, that the first seaside jaunt for *Coronation Street* residents occurred very early in the life of the show, within six months of its launch.

1961: Blackpool is chosen as the destination for the residents' annual picnic trip. Widower Harry Hewitt invites barmaid Concepta Riley to accompany him, and on the coach home she accepts his proposal of marriage.

Leonard Swindley organises a trip to Blackpool's famous Illuminations. Elsie and Bill's affair becomes evident to the group. The coach leaves Ena behind, still having her palm read, and she returns home on a potato lorry, cross that she was abandoned.

1971: When Dave Smith takes Minnie to

Coronation Street's residents set off in the coach.

The first of many Blackpool trips, in 1961

Blackpool for a birthday treat they spot recently widowed Ken with twins Peter and Susan, and a mystery woman. Back on the Street, news spreads about Ken's new love interest, hotel receptionist called Yvonne Chappell.

1980: Len Fairclough tracks estranged wife Rita to Blackpool and finds her working in a launderette. He begs her for a fresh start, but she refuses, saying he'll never change his ways, before returning to Weatherfield a few days later to give their marriage another go.

1985: Rita, Mavis and Bet visit Blackpool, and Bet is on the hunt for a man. The trio meet a group of reps and while the man Bet has set her sights on admits he is married, it is Mavis who meets someone with whom she bonds over a love of literature. Bet is highly put out.

1986: While Brian's away on business, his cousin Ian Latimer takes Gail and Nicky on a trip to Blackpool. When they return home, smitten Gail embarks on a passionate affair.

Blackpool, 1992

1988: Don Brennan organises a trip to Blackpool. Alf Roberts can't attend, as he doesn't want to close the Corner Shop, but is annoyed that Audrey is going with Malcolm Reid, adoptive father of her son Stephen, who is visiting from Canada. Malcolm does make a play for Audrey, but she turns him down. Alf drives to Blackpool and drags Audrey off the return coach, accusing her of having an affair with Malcolm.

1989: Violent Alan Bradley tracks down Rita Fairclough to a hotel in Blackpool. He tries to bundle her into his car but she flees and Alan is struck by a Blackpool tram and killed outright (see In the Scene, pages 198–99).

1992: Deciding to escape the Street for Christmas, Curly Watts and Des Barnes head to Blackpool. Des tracks down Lisa Duckworth, now separated from Terry who is in jail, and spends the day with her and baby Tommy, leaving Curly to eat Christmas dinner alone in the hotel. Lisa eventually moves back to Weatherfield to live with Des. This storyline leads to return visits to Blackpool in the following two years for Des and the Duckworths, after Lisa dies in a car accident and a custody battle for baby Tommy is finally settled between his grandparents the Duckworths and the Hortons.

1994: Rita and the Websters go on holiday to Blackpool, where Rita puts the memory of Alan Bradley to rest. Vera arrives to visit Tommy and meets an old flame Lester Fonteyne. Rita spots Vera kissing Lester in the Tunnel of Love and Vera appeals to her not to tell Jack. He finds a photo of her with Lester after all and they row before eventually putting the fling behind them.

2000: The Duckworths, Norris, Tyrone, Maria and widowed Gary Mallett set off for a week in Blackpool. Tyrone proposes to Maria at the top of Blackpool Tower, Vera and Norris win a ballroom dancing competition, and Gary rescues a boy from drowning, leading to him starting a relationship with the boy's mother and eventually leaving Weatherfield with his twins, to live with her.

2002: Maria and Toyah take off to stay in a caravan in Blackpool. Kirk has also invited Tyrone, Jason and Fiz along. Toyah falls for Croatian student Goran Milanovic, who proposes to her in the hope of staying in the UK, but Toyah turns him down.

2003: Jim McDonald escapes from prison, suspecting Liz of having an affair with her boss in Blackpool. The pair reconcile and plan to flee to Ireland, but Jim is arrested and returned to prison. Bet Lynch attends a brewery function with Liz and gets together with Cecil Newton. They plan to marry, but Cecil dies on the wedding day after suffering a heart attack outside the church.

Blackpool, 1985

Blackpool, 2002

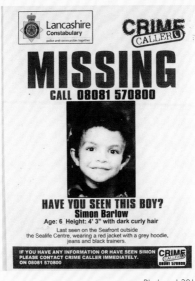

Blackpool, 2010

2010: George and Eve Wilson take grandson Simon Barlow to Blackpool pending a custody hearing. Simon runs away and after a huge police hunt the little boy arrives back in Weatherfield, having made his own way home on public transport.

2011: Tracy and Steve take Amy on a trip to Blackpool, with Steve lying to wife Becky in order to spend time with his daughter. Tracy propositions Steve when they are forced to stay overnight, but he turns her down. Later, Becky finds a family photo from the trip in Amy's bag, planted by Tracy.

2013: Terminally ill Hayley spends the day in Blackpool with Roy, paddling in the sea and dancing together in the Tower Ballroom. The following year, Fiz and Tyrone accompany Roy back to Blackpool to scatter Hayley's ashes, but he can't go through with it. In 2015, Cathy takes Roy on a surprise birthday trip to Blackpool, but the memory of his trip with Hayley proves too much and he travels home alone.

2016: When Sally turns her nose up at Tim's surprise of a trip to Blackpool, Tim takes Kevin and Jack Webster instead. Meanwhile, Johnny Connor encourages Jenny Bradley to visit Blackpool to lay the ghost of her father to rest. In events mirroring the 1989 death of her father, Jack disappears and is rescued by Jenny as he runs in front of an oncoming tram.

Blackpool, 2011

2019: When a private detective traces her son Jude to Blackpool, Mary discovers he is posing as Dr Ken Barlow, a surgeon. Mary gives Jude cash to pay his B&B bill and appeals to him to return to Weatherfield with her. Jude takes the money and disappears. Mary sadly accepts her son will never change and Roy drives her home.

With its fun, glitz and faded glamour, Blackpool has been something of a metaphor for some of the Street's leading ladies over the years, the ones who'd hoped for a little more from life than seeing out their days in a two-up two-down opposite a factory with a back-street boozer for entertainment – Elsie, Annie, Bet and Rita – survivors who always lit up the screen like bright lights on a dark, rainy promenade.

Blackpool, 2013

PRODUCTION NOTE

Actor Violet Carson was ill at this point and, although she was expected to return to the programme, her failing health prevented this. She died on Boxing Day in 1983 at the bungalow she shared with her sister Nellie in Blackpool. The cause of death was heart failure and she passed away in her sleep, aged 85. A memorial service for Carson was held a year later at Manchester Cathedral.

FAREWELL TO ENA SHARPLES

As Street battleaxe Ena grew older she spent more time away from the Street, and in the late 1970s often visited a friend in St Anne's on the Fylde coast, or the Lomaxes in Hartlepool. When the Community Centre and her flat were being renovated in early 1980, Ena moved again to St Anne's despite Elsie offering to put her up. When she returns at the end of March, earlier than expected, her flat is still unfinished and Ena moves in with Albert, who soon gets fed up with her. In April she decides once again to move back to St Anne's. She never returns to Coronation Street.

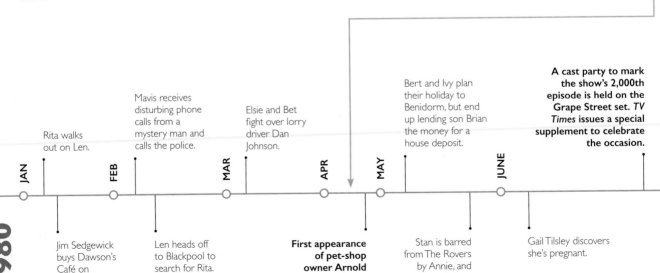

1980

Rita walks out on Len.

Jim Sedgewick buys Dawson's Café on Rosamund St.

Mavis receives disturbing phone calls from a mystery man and calls the police.

Len heads off to Blackpool to search for Rita.

Elsie and Bet fight over lorry driver Dan Johnson.

First appearance of pet-shop owner Arnold Swain.

Bert and Ivy plan their holiday to Benidorm, but end up lending son Brian the money for a house deposit.

Stan is barred from The Rovers by Annie, and Hilda is furious.

A cast party to mark the show's 2,000th episode is held on the Grape Street set. *TV Times* issues a special supplement to celebrate the occasion.

Gail Tilsley discovers she's pregnant.

JAN   FEB   MAR   APR   MAY   JUNE

RENEE ROBERTS IS KILLED IN A CAR CRASH

Renee Roberts, Alf's second wife, wants to move away from Coronation Street. She persuades Alf to sell the Corner Shop and buy a sub-post office in the countryside. As the sale is going through, the pair celebrate at a country pub. Alf has been drinking, so learner driver Renee drives home. As she stalls the car in some roadworks, Alf becomes irritated and gets out of the car to take over the driving. A lorry smashes into the vehicle before Renee can get out. She is rushed to hospital, but dies in the operating theatre from a ruptured spleen and liver. An inquest later rules her death to be accidental but Alf is consumed with guilt, made worse when Renee's mother blames him for her daughter's death.

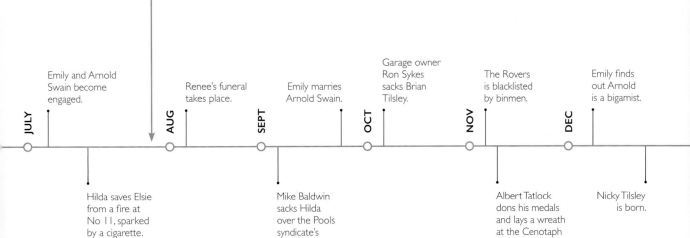

Emily and Arnold Swain become engaged.

Renee's funeral takes place.

Emily marries Arnold Swain.

Garage owner Ron Sykes sacks Brian Tilsley.

The Rovers is blacklisted by binmen.

Emily finds out Arnold is a bigamist.

JULY   AUG   SEPT   OCT   NOV   DEC

Hilda saves Elsie from a fire at No 11, sparked by a cigarette.

Mike Baldwin sacks Hilda over the Pools syndicate's 'big win'.

Albert Tatlock dons his medals and lays a wreath at the Cenotaph in Manchester.

Nicky Tilsley is born.

KEN AND DEIRDRE TIE THE KNOT – FOR THE FIRST TIME

After a brief relationship with factory owner Mike Baldwin, divorcee and mum-of-one Deirdre opts for a safer life with dependable Ken Barlow. They marry in All Saints Church, with Alf Roberts giving away Deirdre, who wears a pale blue dress, and Len acting as Ken's best man. The happy couple honeymoon in Corfu. Just two years later Mike causes havoc in their relationship when he and Deirdre have an affair.

MARCH

EMILY'S ESTRANGED, MENTALLY ILL HUSBAND ARNOLD REAPPEARS

Two years after Ernest Bishop's murder, trusting Emily had started seeing pet-shop owner Arnold Swain. They married in September 1980, but by December it was revealed that Arnold was a bigamist. He'd left his first wife after their honeymoon and told people she had died, but the pair never divorced. In March 1981, angry that Emily had reported him to the police, Arnold reappears on the Street and waits inside No 3 for her. When she returns home he traps her. He is clearly mentally unstable and tells her they should make a suicide pact so they can both be with God. Playing along, Emily escapes and Arnold flees. Later he is arrested when Emily agrees to meet him, accompanied by the police. He is committed to a psychiatric hospital and dies several months later, days after Emily turns down his request to visit him.

PRODUCTION NOTE

Contrary to popular belief, despite Ken and Deirdre's first wedding being the most watched episode of the year with 15.3 million viewers, it did not beat the royal wedding of Prince Charles and Lady Diana Spencer two days later. A higher-rated episode – with 18.45 million viewers (the best of the year two years later) occurred on 23rd February 1983, when Ken and Deirdre reconciled following her affair with Mike.

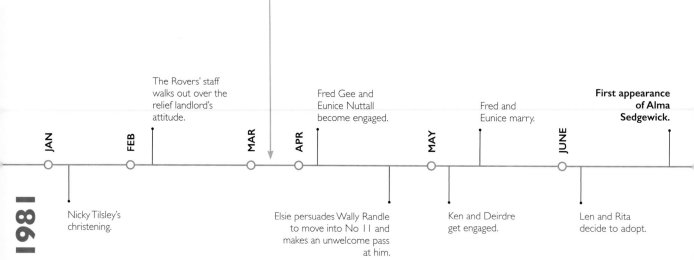

The Rovers' staff walks out over the relief landlord's attitude.

Fred Gee and Eunice Nuttall become engaged.

Fred and Eunice marry.

First appearance of Alma Sedgewick.

JAN   FEB   MAR   APR   MAY   JUNE

Nicky Tilsley's christening.

Elsie persuades Wally Randle to move into No 11 and makes an unwelcome pass at him.

Ken and Deirdre get engaged.

Len and Rita decide to adopt.

SEPTEMBER

MR AND MRS COMPETITION IN THE ROVERS

The brewery announces a Mr and Mrs competition and, determined to win, Hilda tries to coach Stan but soon gives up. Bet, assisted by Len and Rita, comperes the competition in The Rovers and is comically coarse, leading Annie to despair. Bert embarrasses Ivy with his answers about their sex life, the Ogdens get most of their questions wrong and Vera is caught out by claiming Jack has never been unfaithful to her. The winners on the night are young Gail and Brian, who were last-minute entrants, and they celebrate with champagne.

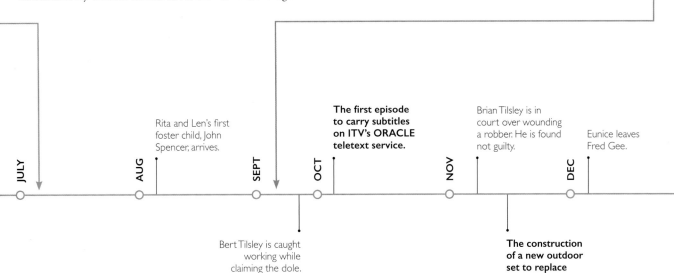

Rita and Len's first foster child, John Spencer, arrives.

The first episode to carry subtitles on ITV's ORACLE teletext service.

Brian Tilsley is in court over wounding a robber. He is found not guilty.

Eunice leaves Fred Gee.

JULY

AUG

SEPT

OCT

NOV

DEC

Bert Tilsley is caught working while claiming the dole.

The construction of a new outdoor set to replace Grape Street commences.

BETTY TURPIN IS MUGGED

There has been a spate of muggings in the local area, and committee member Ken is asked by police to keep an eye on any youngsters flashing cash about. He is not keen on what he sees as spying on the youths, but Deirdre is suspicious of one teenager in particular called Raymond Attwood. When Betty is viciously mugged while walking home one night, Deirdre is cross that Ken won't go to the police about Attwood, whom she's sure is the culprit. Betty is treated in Weatherfield General for a broken arm and cuts and bruises, and after Deirdre visits her she reports Attwood. Ken is furious, but Deirdre calls him idealistic. She is proved right about Attwood and when Ken tries to explain to Betty why he hadn't previously shopped the boy, Betty cannot understand his reasoning.

MARCH

RITA AND LEN FOSTER SHARON GASKELL

Sharon Gaskell is fostered by Rita and Len. The original wild child soon makes her mark on Coronation Street, falling out with Len during her 17th birthday party when she's caught nipping upstairs with her boyfriend. Surprisingly adept at carpentry, she joins Len at the builders' yard and helps him rebuild No 7. Later in the year Sharon falls for Brian Tilsley, causing all manner of upset for Rita and Gail. Although Brian is flattered, her attentions are unrequited and the situation leads to her leaving the Street to work as a kennel maid in Sheffield. A year later, following Len's death, Sharon returns briefly to Weatherfield, courting Curly Watts but dumping him for the more exciting Terry Duckworth before returning to Sheffield.

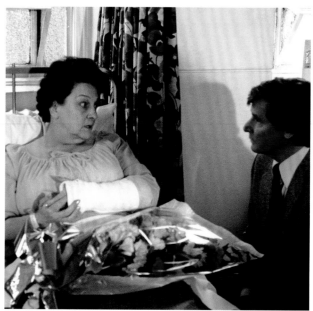

Ken tells Deirdre he doesn't want children.

Eddie Yeats and Marion Willis become engaged.

The new exterior is shown on screen for the first time.

Nicky Tilsley goes missing, but turns up safe.

JAN FEB MAR APR MAY JUNE

1982

Bert Tilsley is in court and pleads guilty to non-declaration of earnings.

The factory girls are put on a three-day week and blame Elsie for losing a big order.

Vera and Bet row over Jack.

The new set is officially opened by Queen Elizabeth II and Prince Philip. The event is shown live on ITV.

Len finishes building the new No 7.

Betty Turpin meets son Gordon's father for the first time in more than 30 years.

BRIAN ACCUSES GAIL OF HAVING AN AFFAIR

Young Gail Potter and Jack-the-lad Brian Tilsley had married in 1979. Despite ongoing interference from Brian's overbearing mother Ivy, the pair ticked along, welcoming baby Nicky in 1980. In 1982, Brian sets off to work in the Middle East for five months. When he returns in July, Ivy is keen to be the first to welcome home her only child and informs him that not only had toddler Nicky disappeared briefly (to return safely) but that Gail was still working in the café. Brian is concerned that Gail has been consorting with the lorry-driving clientele and accuses her of having an affair with café customer Les Charlton. Gail denies being unfaithful but Brian admits he himself had had a fling with a nurse. Brian decides not to return to the job in Qatar and tells Ivy to stop interfering in his marriage. Several years later, Gail has an affair with Brian's cousin Ian Latimer, leading to uncertainty over the father when she becomes pregnant with Sarah Louise.

MAGGIE DUNLOP TELLS MIKE BALDWIN SHE IS PREGNANT

Mike had met Maggie Dunlop at Eddie and Marion's engagement party – Marion was florist Maggie's assistant. The pair hit it off, moved in together and in August Maggie tells Mike she is pregnant. Mike proposes, but Maggie is not sure she loves him and leaves him for Harry Redman, who raises son Mark as his own. A saddened Mike agrees to stay out of Mark's life, arranging for him to benefit from an endowment policy when he reaches 18. Years later Harry Redman passes away when Mark is a schoolboy and Maggie embarks on a relationship with Mark's teacher, Ken Barlow, reigniting the ongoing feud between him and Mike. By 2000, Mark is having an affair with his father's fiancée Linda, although he and his father eventually make up.

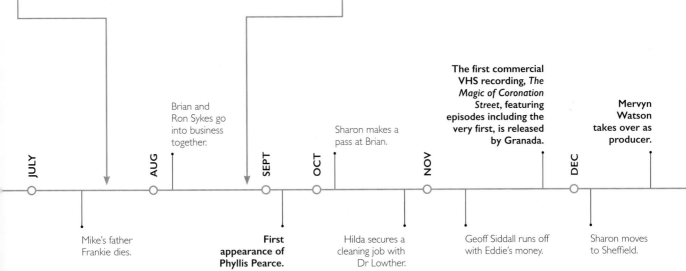

JULY	AUG	SEPT	OCT	NOV	DEC
	Brian and Ron Sykes go into business together.		Sharon makes a pass at Brian.	The first commercial VHS recording, *The Magic of Coronation Street*, featuring episodes including the very first, is released by Granada.	Mervyn Watson takes over as producer.
Mike's father Frankie dies.		**First appearance of Phyllis Pearce.**	Hilda secures a cleaning job with Dr Lowther.	Geoff Siddall runs off with Eddie's money.	Sharon moves to Sheffield.

PRODUCTION NOTE

The episode broadcast on 23rd February secured the programme's highest viewing figure of the year – 18,450,000 viewers tuned in to see Deirdre choose Ken over Mike, and the message 'Ken: 1 Mike: 0' was flashed up on the scoreboard at Manchester United's Old Trafford ground where the Reds were hosting London club Arsenal in a League Cup semi-final. The spectators cheered northerner Ken defeating a Londoner albeit in a love, not football, match.

FEBRUARY

KEN DISCOVERS DEIRDRE'S AFFAIR WITH MIKE BALDWIN

After less then two years of marriage Deirdre, bored with married life to Ken and feeling undervalued, falls victim to the cockney charms of her former squeeze Mike Baldwin. For a few weeks at the start of 1983 she and Mike enjoy a clandestine affair. Emily suspects something is going on and confronts Deirdre, who tells her she feels invisible to Ken. Emily begs Mike to end the affair. In February, during a row over Ken's perceived failures, an exasperated Deirdre informs a horrified Ken that she has found someone else – Mike Baldwin. When Ken catches Deirdre on the phone to Mike, he is furious and, as they argue in the hallway, Mike knocks on the door. Ken warns him off and grabs Deirdre by the throat before telling her she must pack her bags and go. Deirdre finds she can't leave. She begs Ken's forgiveness and they are reconciled before Ken visits Mike at the factory to inform Mike that Deirdre wants to stay with him. Mike only believes Ken when Deirdre tells him herself. Ken and Deirdre leave for a holiday in Malta.

MAY

FRED TAKES BET AND BETTY OUT FOR THE DAY – BUT IT TURNS INTO A DAMP SQUIB

As a May bank holiday treat, potman Fred Gee offers to take Bet, the object of his affections, out to a country park for the day in Annie Walker's Rover 2000. She doesn't want to be alone with Fred, so Betty accompanies them. The Rover had been in Brian's garage having its brakes fixed but, eager at the thought of spending time with Bet, Fred collects it before the job is finished. After a lakeside lunch, Bet and Betty get back in the car, but as Fred puts away the picnic basket and slams the boot, the car rolls into the lake as the women scream in horror. Fred wades into the cold water and carries them to the shore, inadvertently depositing Bet in a cowpat. After the bedraggled trio return to Coronation Street in a taxi, Bet and Betty threaten to sue Fred for the cost of replacing their clothes. Furious Fred demands Brian retrieves the Rover for free even though Annie declares the whole debacle was Fred's fault. Shamefaced, he pays Bet and Betty £7.50 each.

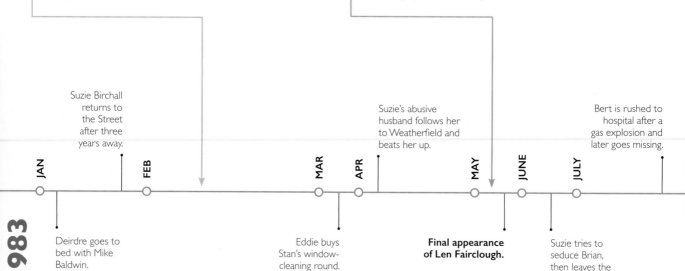

Suzie Birchall returns to the Street after three years away.

Suzie's abusive husband follows her to Weatherfield and beats her up.

Bert is rushed to hospital after a gas explosion and later goes missing.

JAN   FEB   MAR   APR   MAY   JUNE   JULY

1983

Deirdre goes to bed with Mike Baldwin.

Eddie buys Stan's window-cleaning round.

Final appearance of Len Fairclough.

Suzie tries to seduce Brian, then leaves the Street after he rebuffs her.

PRODUCTION NOTE

Much-loved actress Doris Speed made several public appearances after leaving *Coronation Street* in October of this year, and died in a nursing home in 1994, aged 95.

LEN FAIRCLOUGH DIES IN A CAR CRASH

It's the Ogdens' ruby wedding party in The Rovers and Len is late back from a job in Ashton. Rita is wondering where he is when the police arrive to inform her that he has died in a car accident. Friends rally round and Sharon rushes over from Sheffield to help. Amidst her grief Rita realises that the motorway Len died on was nowhere near Ashton. As she sorts out Len's old clothes she finds a beer mat with a Bolton number written on it. When she calls the number a Mrs Proctor answers but cuts the call short when Rita explains who she is. Tracking down Mrs Proctor's address, Rita asks Alf to drive her to Bolton where Mrs Proctor shuts the door in her face. It's only when the woman turns up in Weatherfield that Rita discovers that Len had an affair with the widow. As Mrs Proctor weeps over the loss of her own husband, a tearful Rita hugs and forgives her.

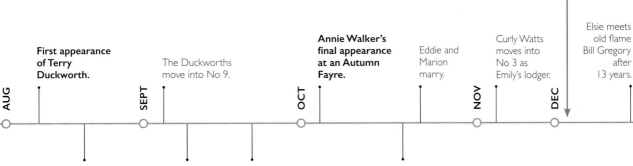

First appearance of Terry Duckworth.

The Duckworths move into No 9.

Annie Walker's final appearance at an Autumn Fayre.

Eddie and Marion marry.

Curly Watts moves into No 3 as Emily's lodger.

Elsie meets old flame Bill Gregory after 13 years.

AUG SEPT OCT NOV DEC

First appearance of Percy Sugden.

Marion tells Eddie she's pregnant.

Ken offers to buy a share of the *Weatherfield Recorder*.

First appearance of Kevin Webster.

ELSIE TANNER LEAVES FOR PORTUGAL WITH BILL GREGORY

Elsie Tanner has had an on-off relationship with Len's former navy mate Bill Gregory that stretches back to 1961 when they had an affair, Elsie unaware that he was married. In 1970, Elsie turned a now-widowed Bill down in favour of Alan Howard and Bill left to run a wine bar in Portugal. Fast forward to the end of 1983 – Len has died in a car accident and Bill returns to pay his respects. Elsie is now divorced from Alan and the pair reunite. Elsie hopes that Bill will stay with her, but he decides to return to Portugal, asking Elsie to go with him. At first she declines, but changes her mind and leaves the Street in January 1984. They go on to marry and live happily in sunny Portugal for 20 years, running their bar. Elsie's daughter Linda Cheveski returns to sell No 11 for her (to Bill Webster), and son Dennis, on his return to Coronation Street in 2011, reveals Bill and his mother have died in a car accident.

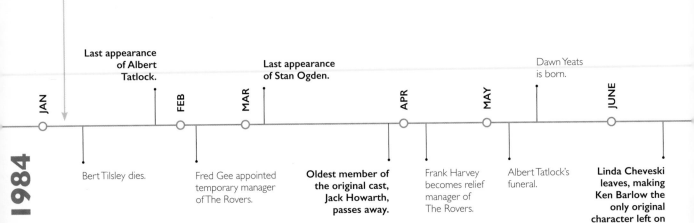

1984

Last appearance of Albert Tatlock.

Last appearance of Stan Ogden.

Dawn Yeats is born.

JAN

FEB

MAR

APR

MAY

JUNE

Bert Tilsley dies.

Fred Gee appointed temporary manager of The Rovers.

Oldest member of the original cast, Jack Howarth, passes away.

Frank Harvey becomes relief manager of The Rovers.

Albert Tatlock's funeral.

Linda Cheveski leaves, making Ken Barlow the only original character left on the Street.

STAN OGDEN DIES

In 1983, ill health had forced Stan to give up his window-cleaning round. By November 1984, Hilda is concerned about his health and runs herself ragged caring for him and fulfilling her cleaning jobs. Stan is taken into Weatherfield General and Hilda fears he'll never return home. In a phone call via Alf Roberts, Hilda learns he has passed away at the age of 65 after suffering a heart attack. Their feckless son Trevor attends the funeral before departing quickly afterwards and Hilda weeps alone at her dining table, clutching Stan's glasses case.

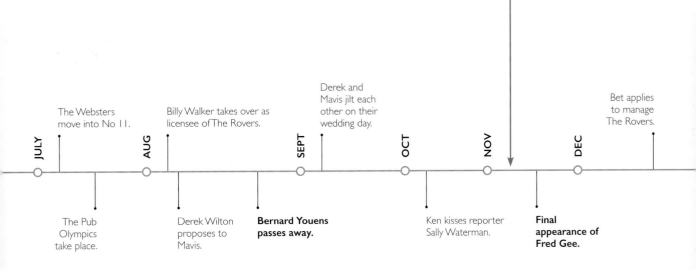

The Websters move into No 11.

The Pub Olympics take place.

Billy Walker takes over as licensee of The Rovers.

Derek Wilton proposes to Mavis.

Bernard Youens **passes away.**

Derek and Mavis jilt each other on their wedding day.

Ken kisses reporter Sally Waterman.

Final appearance of Fred Gee.

Bet applies to manage The Rovers.

JULY   AUG   SEPT   OCT   NOV   DEC

BET BECOMES LANDLADY OF THE ROVERS

In 1984, Annie Walker decided to leave Weatherfield to live with her daughter Joan. She had run The Rovers alone since the death of husband Jack and she wanted to retire. The brewery drafts in Gordon Lewis as manager. Humourless Gordon has stepped in before and is highly unpopular with both staff and customers. He wants to modernise the pub and instructs Bet to dress more soberly. Feisty Bet, spurred on by the regulars, attempts to raise £5,000 to buy the pub outright, but the brewery is looking for a manager, not a sale. Both Gordon and Bet are interviewed for the position by the brewery's Sarah Ridley and Bet reckons she doesn't really have a hope. She's delighted when the brewery boss decides to give Gordon another pub, The Dockers Arms, and makes Bet manager of The Rovers, 14 years after starting there as a barmaid. Two years later Bet marries Alec Gilroy, in part to ensure she can remain in charge of her beloved Rovers.

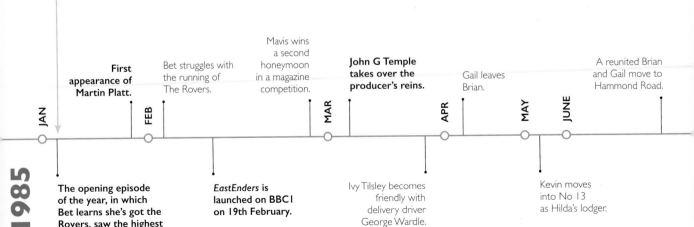

1985

First appearance of Martin Platt.

Bet struggles with the running of The Rovers.

Mavis wins a second honeymoon in a magazine competition.

John G Temple takes over the producer's reins.

Gail leaves Brian.

A reunited Brian and Gail move to Hammond Road.

JAN — FEB — MAR — APR — MAY — JUNE

The opening episode of the year, in which Bet learns she's got the Rovers, saw the highest number of viewers so far – 21.4 million.

EastEnders is launched on BBC1 on 19th February.

Ivy Tilsley becomes friendly with delivery driver George Wardle.

Kevin moves into No 13 as Hilda's lodger.

JULY

ANDREA CLAYTON ANNOUNCES SHE'S PREGNANT WITH TERRY DUCKWORTH'S BABY

The Clayton family moved in to Coronation Street in early 1985. Eldest daughter Andrea was an A level student, for whom her parents Harry and Connie had high hopes. Street romeo Terry Duckworth sets his sights on Andrea and charms her into bed. By July Andrea is pregnant and, undecided what to do about the baby, tells her friend Michelle. Andrea and Michelle had been on double dates with Terry and Kevin and Michelle tells Kevin about the pregnancy. Before long, Kevin spills the beans to Terry who, despite arguments between the Claytons and the Duckworths, promises to support Andrea. Andrea manages to pass her A levels and the family moves away. She has the baby, a boy named Paul, and raises him alone. Fourteen years later she makes contact with the Duckworths again. Paul desperately needs a kidney transplant and none of the Claytons is a match. Vera offers to donate a kidney but Jack, fearing Vera is too old to withstand such a major op, offers Terry money to be the donor instead. Cowardly Terry disappears, leaving Vera to undergo the operation, which proves to be a success.

OCTOBER

TRACY RUNS AWAY

Eight-year-old Tracy Langton has been pestering Deirdre about getting a dog, but Deirdre snaps at her, telling her there's no way she can have one. Young Tracy packs a bag and disappears. When Deirdre discovers she's gone she is distraught, fearing the little girl has been abducted. Ken calls the police. Tracy manages to find her way to Newcastle, where Ken's daughter Susan lives. After a man approaches her she is picked up by the police. Susan calls the Barlows to say Tracy is safe and she brings her home to Coronation Street. She decides to stay in Weatherfield for a while and starts working for Ken at the *Weatherfield Recorder*.

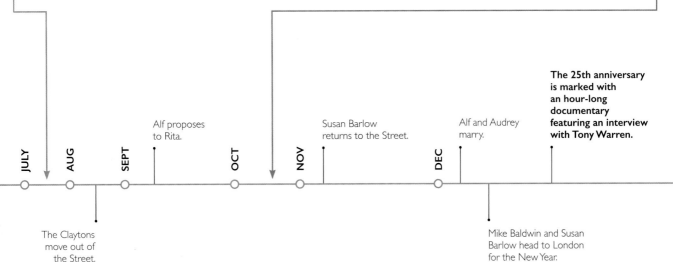

JULY

AUG

SEPT
Alf proposes to Rita.

OCT

NOV
Susan Barlow returns to the Street.

DEC
Alf and Audrey marry.

The 25th anniversary is marked with an hour-long documentary featuring an interview with Tony Warren.

The Claytons move out of the Street.

Mike Baldwin and Susan Barlow head to London for the New Year.

JANUARY

KEN FINDS OUT ABOUT SUSAN AND MIKE

While working with Ken, Susan catches the eye of Curly Watts, who falls head over heels for her. Susan isn't interested and begins seeing her father's nemesis, Mike Baldwin. Ken had seen the pair dancing over Christmas in The Rovers, and when he discovers the flourishing relationship and that Susan has stayed with Mike in his London flat, he is furious and bans her from seeing Mike. Susan, of course, refuses and Mike gives her the keys to his Weatherfield home. Deirdre advises Ken to leave well alone but Ken, still raw over Mike's affair with Deirdre a couple of years earlier, accuses Deirdre of being jealous and tells Susan all about it. This nearly splits Mike and Susan up, but Mike convinces her he loves her. When Ken finds out they are still together he marches over to the factory and floors Mike in front of the factory girls. Mike and Susan are undeterred and Ken is forced to swallow his pride and give Susan away on her wedding day later in the year.

JUNE

THERE IS A FIRE IN THE ROVERS, SPARKED BY JACK'S BOTCHED HANDIWORK

Bet Lynch has a lucky escape after a fire rips through The Rovers. Kevin and girlfriend Sally Seddon return home from a night out in Sheffield and spot smoke billowing from the pub. Kevin raises the alarm, and along with Percy, drags a ladder to the pub and manages to reach an unconscious Bet in her bedroom at the front of the pub before firefighters pull them both out of the burning building. Kevin is checked for smoke inhalation at the scene as the residents praise his bravery. The cause of the fire is unknown initially, but it emerges that it is likely to be down to Jack's botched handiwork on a faulty fuse box in the pub's cellar. The pub is gutted and closes for a major refit.

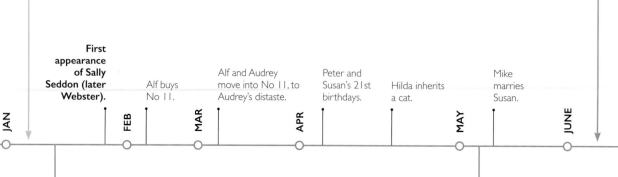

1986

First appearance of Sally Seddon (later Webster).

JAN

First appearances of Jenny and Alan Bradley.

Alf buys No 11.

FEB

Alf and Audrey move into No 11, to Audrey's distaste.

MAR

Peter and Susan's 21st birthdays.

APR

Hilda inherits a cat.

Mike marries Susan.

MAY

Bert's nephew Ian Latimer comes to stay and falls for Gail.

JUNE

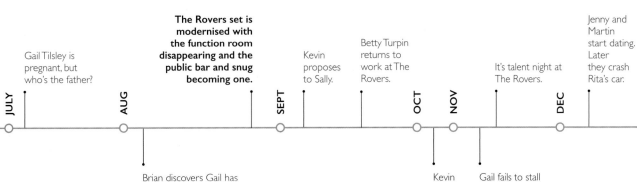

Gail Tilsley is pregnant, but who's the father?

The Rovers set is modernised with the function room disappearing and the public bar and snug becoming one.

Kevin proposes to Sally.

Betty Turpin returns to work at The Rovers.

It's talent night at The Rovers.

Jenny and Martin start dating. Later they crash Rita's car.

JULY

AUG

SEPT

OCT

NOV

DEC

Brian discovers Gail has slept with his cousin Ian Latimer and that the baby she is carrying may be Ian's. He moves back in with his mother Ivy.

Kevin and Sally marry.

Gail fails to stall Brian over the divorce so hires a solicitor.

MAY

DEIRDRE BEATS ALF IN THE LOCAL ELECTIONS, SPARKING ALF'S HEART ATTACK

Alf Roberts had served as an independent local councillor for 20 years when, following a row with Ken over coverage in the *Weatherfield Recorder*, Ken decides to stand against him. When Ken backs out, Deirdre decides to stand instead, and with the help of Susan and Emily who canvass with her, she beats Alf by a handful of votes. The Barlows throw a celebration party to which they invite Alf in order to mend bridges, but Alf suffers a heart attack. Audrey accuses Deirdre of driving Alf off the council and into a hospital bed. Alf slowly recovers and Deirdre takes her place on the council.

OCTOBER

SUSAN DISCOVERS SHE IS PREGNANT

When Susan discovers she is pregnant, Ken is pleased for her and Mike is delighted. He decides his child will grow up in the countryside and takes Susan to see a cottage near Glossop. Susan is horrified at the thought of being isolated with a baby and says she needs some time to herself. She disappears and when she returns to Weatherfield she informs firstly the Barlows and then Mike that she went to London and had an abortion. Mike is appalled and tells her their marriage is over. Susan leaves the Street, but it emerges later that she had the baby in Scotland, a boy named Adam. When Mike finds out about his existence in 2001, Susan attempts to disappear again with her son but dies in a car crash. Adam stays at boarding school and visits Weatherfield sporadically before returning to Coronation Street for good in 2016.

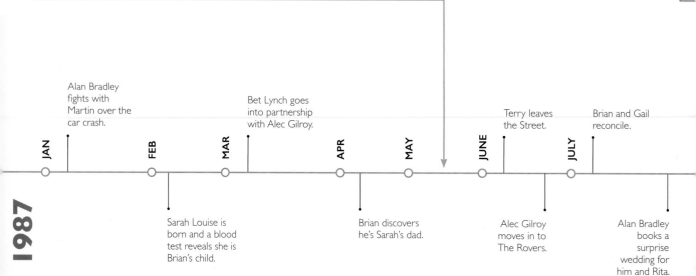

1987

Alan Bradley fights with Martin over the car crash.

Bet Lynch goes into partnership with Alec Gilroy.

Terry leaves the Street.

Brian and Gail reconcile.

JAN | FEB | MAR | APR | MAY | JUNE | JULY

Sarah Louise is born and a blood test reveals she is Brian's child.

Brian discovers he's Sarah's dad.

Alec Gilroy moves in to The Rovers.

Alan Bradley books a surprise wedding for him and Rita.

DECEMBER

HILDA WAVES GOODBYE TO THE STREET

Christmas Day 1987 sees Hilda Ogden leave Weatherfield after 23 years. Hilda's husband Stan had died three years earlier and Hilda, who has been cleaning for Dr Lowther, decides to move with the doctor to the Derbyshire countryside after his wife dies following a robbery in which Hilda was caught up. Hilda feels no one will miss her. She spends Christmas Day with Kevin and Sally, having kindly offered them No 13 for a below-market price. When she calls in at The Rovers she is stunned and delighted that the residents have organised a surprise farewell party for her. In true Hilda style she entertains them all by singing 'Wish Me Luck As You Wave Me Goodbye' in that famous reedy little voice.

PRODUCTION NOTE

Jean Alexander, who won a Best Actress Royal Television Society Award in 1985, would reprise the role of Hilda three times: in a special ITV Telethon performance in 1990, for an audio book in 1996 and finally, in 1998, in a video special, *The Women of Coronation Street*. In 2004 Hilda Ogden was voted the UK's favourite soap character of all time in a *Radio Times* poll.

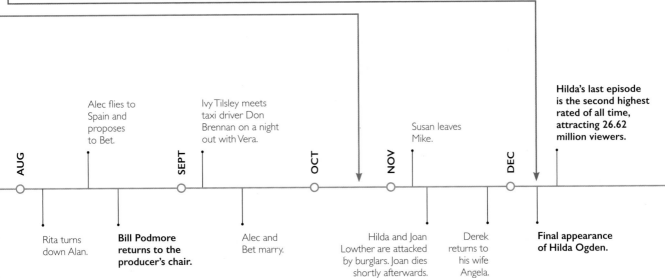

Alec flies to Spain and proposes to Bet.

Ivy Tilsley meets taxi driver Don Brennan on a night out with Vera.

Susan leaves Mike.

Hilda's last episode is the second highest rated of all time, attracting 26.62 million viewers.

AUG SEPT OCT NOV DEC

Rita turns down Alan.

Bill Podmore returns to the producer's chair.

Alec and Bet marry.

Hilda and Joan Lowther are attacked by burglars. Joan dies shortly afterwards.

Derek returns to his wife Angela.

Final appearance of Hilda Ogden.

AUDREY TELLS GAIL ABOUT HER HALF-BROTHER STEPHEN

Audrey reveals to Gail that, when she was 16, she had a baby boy called Stephen, who she was forced by her father to give away to their childless neighbours, the Reids. Stephen, who is a year older than Gail, was raised in Canada. When Stephen's adoptive father Malcolm Reid arrives in Weatherfield in 1988, he attempts to persuade Audrey to marry him. Audrey refuses and stays with Alf. Stephen returns to Weatherfield in 1996 to get to know his sister Gail and goes on to play a part in the lives of Gail's children Nick and Sarah. Nick leaves the Street to work for Stephen in Canada, and later Sarah and her daughter Bethany move to Italy to stay with him after Stephen relocates there.

MARCH

BET LOSES HER BABY

Bet and Alec are astounded to find that Bet is pregnant (she thought she was too old). She'd had a son when she was a teenager, but he had been given up for adoption. Alec doesn't really want children, but starts to come round to the idea. When Bet experiences pains she is taken to hospital where she loses the baby. Putting on a brave face she returns to the pub, but when they are alone she breaks down, admitting to Alec how much she had wanted a child.

Curly Watts and Shirley Armitage move in together.

Ivy marries Don Brennan.

Brian and Gail remarry.

1988

JAN   FEB   MAR   APR   MAY   JUNE   JULY

Baldwin's Casuals moves to make curtains rather than denim.

Bet tells Alec she is pregnant.

Mike is beaten up by love rival Graham Farrell.

Percy Sugden moves in as Emily's lodger.

Ken saves Sandra Stubbs from being beaten by her husband Ronnie.

NOVEMBER

DEREK AND MAVIS ARE MARRIED AT LAST

After a long on-off relationship, the Wiltons marry at their second attempt. In 1984, their first attempt was aborted after neither of them showed up. Salesman Derek went on to marry the fearsome Angela, but always hankered after Mavis and showed up periodically over the years. Derek reappears in August 1988, when Mavis is surprised to meet him at a job interview. After he proposes through The Kabin's letterbox, Mavis surprises her friends by agreeing to the proposal and the pair marry soon after Derek's divorce from domineering Angela is granted. Percy Sugden physically holds on to Derek ahead of the service to prevent him bolting again, the wedding goes ahead and the pair honeymoon in Paris. Eventually, they move into one of the new houses built on Coronation Street and their marriage is full of ups and downs – often involving Angela. Derek dies of a heart attack in 1997 and Mavis is left bereft.

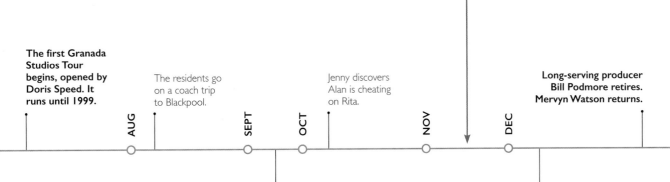

The first Granada Studios Tour begins, opened by Doris Speed. It runs until 1999.

AUG

The residents go on a coach trip to Blackpool.

SEPT

Derek proposes to Mavis.

OCT

Jenny discovers Alan is cheating on Rita.

NOV

DEC

Deirdre escapes from the clutches of Brian Roscoe.

Long-serving producer Bill Podmore retires. Mervyn Watson returns.

BRIAN IS STABBED TO DEATH

Brian and Gail's marriage is on the rocks. Brian hopes for a reconciliation, but Gail tells him she doesn't love him any more and that she knew their second wedding was a huge mistake. They row and furious Brian tells Gail she's a terrible mother and she'll never take son Nicky away from him. Ivy and Don find out about the imminent divorce and staunch Catholic Ivy is distraught. Brian goes out to a nightclub and as he leaves with a girl, some youths hassle her. As Brian steps in to defend her he is stabbed to death. Gail identifies Brian's body and argues with Ivy, who blames Gail for Brian's death and demands her son has a Catholic burial. Gail refuses and arranges a Protestant funeral. It's only when a priest talks Ivy into forgiving Gail that the pair eventually make their peace.

1989

Alan fraudulently secures a loan and opens his own company.

Alan makes a pass at secretary Dawn Prescott who tells Rita about Alan's fraud. He beats Rita up and is remanded in prison.

Nicky Tilsley disappears looking for his dad. He is found at the garage.

Vera finds out Jack has been on a date.

JAN

FEB

MAR

APR

MAY

JUNE

JULY

Alec Gilroy returns from working away on a cruise ship.

First appearance of Wendy Crozier.

THE COMMUNITY CENTRE AND FACTORY ARE KNOCKED DOWN

Standing on the site of the old Glad Tidings Mission Hall, the Community Centre has hosted many parties, dances, competitions and classes since it was built in 1971, along with the Mark Brittain Warehouse, when the maisonettes were replaced following Valerie Barlow's death. It really is at the heart of the Coronation Street community, but after caretaker Percy Sugden's enforced retirement it is selected for demolition by the council. Maurice Jones buys the land and the centre, together with the factory, is replaced with new houses and businesses.

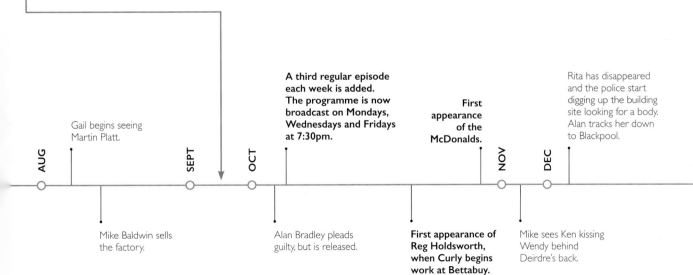

A third regular episode each week is added. The programme is now broadcast on Mondays, Wednesdays and Fridays at 7:30pm.

First appearance of the McDonalds.

Rita has disappeared and the police start digging up the building site looking for a body. Alan tracks her down to Blackpool.

Gail begins seeing Martin Platt.

AUG   SEPT   OCT   NOV   DEC

Mike Baldwin sells the factory.

Alan Bradley pleads guilty, but is released.

First appearance of Reg Holdsworth, when Curly begins work at Bettabuy.

Mike sees Ken kissing Wendy behind Deirdre's back.

8TH DECEMBER 1989

BLACKPOOL has always been a favourite seaside destination for location filming, but in December 1989 it played host to one of the most famous *Coronation Street* scenes ever. The death of evil Alan Bradley was watched by more than 21 million viewers.

In the scene
Alan Bradley's tram death

THE SURROUNDING STORYLINES

Rita, who has suffered a breakdown after a campaign of harassment by her former abusive partner Alan Bradley, has disappeared. The Gilroys receive a call from Cyril, an old friend of Alec who runs a hotel in Blackpool. Rita, who has lost her memory and is regressing to her days as a club singer, is asking for a slot in the hotel's piano bar. Cyril wants to check she's still on former agent Alec's books.

Alec and Bet arrive at The Strand Hotel to find Rita dressed up to the nines and singing in the hotel bar, and asking about Len as if her late husband is still alive. Having been suspected of killing Rita, Alan Bradley hears she's in Blackpool and tracks her down, intent on punishing her.

THE MAIN EVENT
Bet has pretended to be ill to lure Rita to hospital. Alec alerts the police, but Rita disappears again. He also tells Rita's foster daughter Jenny where Rita is and she informs her father Alan. Furious Alan arrives in Blackpool planning to drag Rita home and show the residents that she's alive and he hasn't murdered her.

He rows with Bet in the hotel and leaves in a rage. Rita, unaware, is walking towards him along the pavement. In the hotel, Bet shouts to a hotel employee to call the police.

Alan and Rita struggle on the pavement and Bet watches from the window as Alan tries to bundle Rita into his car.

Rita manages to flee from the vehicle as Alan bellows: 'Come back, you stupid bitch.'

She's nearly hit by a car and Alan gives chase as a Blackpool tram approaches along the front. It narrowly misses Rita but hits Alan, killing him instantly.

Rita stops, dazed, and looks around as Bet rushes to her. Rita falls to the ground and Bet hugs her, telling her the ordeal is over.

Barbara Knox's favourite storyline from the decades she has played Rita is the Alan Bradley story. 'It was beautifully done, so well played out for nearly two years. The letters I got, bin liners full of letters, from women in the same position Rita was in, asking me what should they do. Doctors' wives, a head teacher's wife, even the wife of a judge! You had to respond, tell them to leave if they can, but many had nowhere to go. A terrible problem.

'So I hope through that we might have helped in some way. Mark Eden (Alan Bradley) and I worked very well together. I remember one scene where he had to knock me over a sofa and I said let's do it this way and we just did it. These days we have fight arrangers.'

And Sally Ann Matthews who played Jenny Bradley from 1986 to 1991, then appearing occasionally before returning full-time in 2016, believes the best storyline she has been involved with was the Alan Bradley story. 'The whole lead-up to the Blackpool tram death – him trying to kill Rita – it went on for such a long time,' she

recalls. 'This story was one of the first ones that grew slowly, but they knew two years in advance what the outcome was going to be and I think it was so well done, it gripped the nation.

'I just count myself really lucky that, as a 15-year-old who'd never done any professional acting, any telly, before I came into *Coronation Street*, I was mentored by Barbara Knox, Thelma Barlow and Mark Eden – best grounding ever. I was very, very fortunate that I learned everything from them.'

THE AFTERMATH

Jenny identifies her father's body. She blames Rita and the others for his death. She refuses to allow Bet to help with the funeral at which the only other mourners are Martin, Kevin and Sally.

Twenty-seven years later, Jenny returns to Blackpool in a storyline linked to the 1989 death of Alan. Tim, Kevin and Jack are visiting the seaside town at the same time as Jenny, encouraged by Johnny Connor, to lay the ghost of her father to rest. When

PRODUCTION NOTE

The episode in which Alan Bradley met his death occurred in the week of the soap's 3,000th episode (4th December 1989).

On 8th December 2009, to mark the 20-year anniversary of the famous episode, actor Mark Eden unveiled a blue plaque outside The Strand Hotel in Blackpool, where filming took place.

Sally arrives to try to save her marriage, she and Kevin row, and young Jack runs off in front of an oncoming tram. Jenny spots him and dashes to rescue him, earning forgiveness from the Websters – she had previously kidnapped Jack on her return to the Street, while grief-stricken following the death of her own son.

IN FOCUS

CORONATION Street has always had memorable characters, but the storylines really sing when they are put together as bickering couples or the best of friends. Here are some of the Street's iconic partnerships...

Partnerships

ANNIE AND JACK
(DORIS SPEED AND ARTHUR LESLIE)

To the casual viewer, Annie with her airs and graces, and jovial working man Jack made an unlikely couple. Annie felt she was a cut above many of her Rovers Return clientele and hankered after running a hostelry in the Cheshire countryside rather than in the back streets of Weatherfield. Down-to-earth Jack was responsible for calmly reining in his somewhat snooty wife when she, sometimes inadvertently but often on purpose, insulted the Rovers' regulars. The couple ran The Rovers for many years and brought up their son and daughter on Coronation Street as well as taking in young Lucille Hewitt when her father and stepmother moved to Ireland. And despite their little niggles and marital ups and downs, they loved each other very much, and when Jack passed away in 1970 (following actor Arthur Leslie's death) Annie was distraught.

ENA, MINNIE AND MARTHA
(VIOLET CARSON, MARGOT BRYANT AND LYNNE CAROL)

These three elderly widows were an important co-dependent grouping from the very start of Coronation Street. Arms folded, hats (or hairnet in Ena's case) and coats on, the trio would sit round that small wooden pub table in The Rovers snug, gossiping about their fellow street residents. Sharp-tongued Ena, who could turn milk sour at a glance, was the leader of the pack, but busybody Martha and timid Minnie, of whom she was really very fond despite the occasional falling out, completed the threesome that was so popular with viewers. Who could forget the stricken look on Ena's face when Martha was found to have died of a heart attack in The Rovers snug in 1964 as the locals sang songs around the piano?

STAN AND HILDA
(BERNARD YOUENS AND JEAN ALEXANDER)

Iconic *Coronation Street* couple, workshy window cleaner Stan and busybody cleaner Hilda, first appeared on the Street together in 1964. The pair bickered their way through 20 years of financial strife and proved to be one of the most favourite duos in the history of the show. Despite her nagging of hapless Stan, Hilda's heartrending scenes as firstly, in 1984, she wept over her recently deceased hubby's glasses and, later, sat by his grave telling him why she would never remarry, showed her love for him.

KEN AND DEIRDRE
(WILLIAM ROACHE AND ANNE KIRKBRIDE)

Despite his many relationships over 60 years on the *Street*, it was Deirdre with whom Ken Barlow will be forever linked in the minds of *Coronation Street* fans. Their first nuptials in 1981 coincided with the wedding of the Prince and Princess of Wales and they married again in 2005, just a day before Prince Charles was married for the second time, to Camilla Parker Bowles. Ken adopted Deirdre's daughter Tracy by first husband Ray Langton, but his and Deirdre's relationship was marred by affairs on both sides. Despite this, their love endured and Ken was lost when Deirdre passed away in 2015 following the death at age 60 of actor Anne Kirkbride.

KEN AND MIKE
(WILLIAM ROACHE AND JOHNNY BRIGGS)

In one of the longest-running feuds in TV history, Ken and Mike spent 20 years at each other's throats. Often their fistfights, which both actors say they enjoyed playing out, were over women. In addition to Mike's affair with Ken's wife Deirdre, Ken dated Mike's ex Alma, only for Mike to plot to get Ken out of the way so he could seduce her. Then Ken unwittingly fell for Maggie Redman, not knowing she was the mother of Mike's son Mark, a fact that made him finish with her. Mike also married Ken's daughter Susan, unknowingly fathering her son, Adam, which led to a custody battle over the boy when Susan was killed in a car crash. In truth, Ken and Mike had never got on. When the brash cockney barrow-boy-made-good swanned onto Coronation Street in 1976 to open Baldwin's Casuals, lefty academic Ken's nose was put firmly out of joint. The pair were like chalk and cheese, and Ken disapproved of businessman Baldwin's money-making ways. However, the scriptwriters created as much drama when Ken and Mike were forced to cooperate– one storyline saw them tied to each other during an armed raid on the Freshco supermarket. Their relationship ended poignantly when Mike died in Ken's arms after suffering a heart attack on the cobbles.

IN FOCUS

JACK AND VERA (WILLIAM TARMEY AND ELIZABETH DAWN)

Over more than 30 years, pub cellarman and pigeon fancier Jack Duckworth and his gobby machinist wife Vera became another of *Coronation Street's* iconic couples, known the land over by their first names alone.

Their marriage was one of ups and downs, money worries and extra-marital dalliances. Son Terry was a perpetual and roguish thorn in their side – he stole from them and although he provided them with three grandsons, he even tried to sell one of them. In their later years, Tyrone Dobbs became their surrogate son after he began lodging with them at No 9. They eventually sold the house to him rather than leave it to villainous Terry. Despite their sometimes rocky relationship, Vera's death in 2008 left Jack devastated and, when it was his turn to meet his maker two years later, the touching scene when he fancied himself dancing with his late wife Vera (thanks to a special appearance by Liz Dawn) left many viewers in tears.

BET AND ALEC (JULIE GOODYEAR AND ROY BARRACLOUGH)

Another unlikely Street couple – the quick-tongued barmaid-turned-landlady with a penchant for leopard print and handsome bad boys, and the tight-fisted former talent agent always ready with an acid quip. Despite a short-lived marriage, Bet, always one for whom the road to true love was more than a little bumpy, and Alec were genuinely fond of one another, and with Alec by her side Bet Gilroy achieved a level of respectability on the Street previously denied her. The pair were business partners at first, as Bet battled to increase trade at The Rovers following the fire that nearly killed her. They married but shortly afterwards Bet, at the age of 47, suffered a miscarriage. Following years of entertaining sparring, the couple's parting scene in 1995 was widely praised for its understated poignancy.

STEVE AND TRACY (SIMON GREGSON AND KATE FORD)

For much-married Steve McDonald there was always one constant in his life – his love/hate/love relationship with Street bad girl, the former Tracy Barlow. As the parents of Amy, the result of a one-night stand, the pair's antics have kept fans delighted over the years and they have become a true *Coronation Street* couple. Steve knows all of Machiavellian Tracy's faults, but despite ignoring the teenage crush Tracy had on him when they were younger, there was always something that piqued his interest. As for Tracy, well, she just doesn't like losing, especially to other women. Two weddings – both of which ended in rows during the reception, the second with Tracy punching Steve – a multitude of other relationships between them and a pregnant teenage daughter, their union has never run smoothly. Will they mellow and grow old together quietly? Not likely…

RITA AND MAVIS (BARBARA KNOX AND THELMA BARLOW)

When Rita interviewed a hiccuping Mavis Riley for a job in the newsagent in 1973 it was the start of a friendship that delighted fans for more than 20 years. Straight-talking Rita and dithery Mavis provided many laughs during their time behind The Kabin counter and it wasn't only Rita who had a tear in her eye when Mavis departed the Street in 1997.

Barbara Knox recalls: 'Right from day one Thelma and I hit it off beautifully, I think we laughed from morning to night. Thelma and I had both been in rep and she was as disciplined as I was, she was wonderful. We didn't even have to tell either of us anything, we'd just look and we'd know what to do. I was very sorry when she left.'

LIZ AND JIM (BEVERLEY CALLARD AND CHARLES LAWSON)

The McDonalds, along with teenage twins Steve and Andy, arrived in the Street in 1989. Their stormy relationship saw them lose their baby daughter, divorce, remarry and split again. Former soldier Jim has been jailed three times and Liz has had many other relationships, but there always seems to be something that draws these two back together again. Beverley Callard says: 'I loved working with Charlie. I truly think he's one of the best male actors in the UK. We never had a wrong word, he destroyed me with laughter, but also he could make me cry with his performance because he was so good.

'At first Liz was a bit of a yes woman, and Jim was shouting and bombastic. We spent days, months, years even, bringing out his really vulnerable side, and she appeared to be feminine and maybe a bit feeble, but really she was the strength. We tried to get different dimensions into both characters. As an actor you just do the very best with the script you've got, but we have truly had amazing scripts.'

SALLY AND TIM
(SALLY DYNEVOR AND JOE DUTTINE)

This unlikely couple proved to be one of the most popular pairings on the Street. On paper it shouldn't work – illiterate former window cleaner Tim and occasionally snobby and upwardly mobile Sally – but it does, they truly love each other. Sally's first marriage to Kevin (with whom Tim became friends) was broken up by man-eater Natalie Horrocks and her relationship with Tim nearly suffered the same fate when Sally's jealous sister Gina set her sights on Tim when Sally was in prison serving a sentence for fraud.

Sally Dynevor says: 'It's wonderful now being in the partnership with Joe Duttine as Tim, it's so different from Sally and Kevin. He makes me laugh so much and I think they're great together. The audience thinks that he is the sort of hapless, stupid one where probably he's the sensible one and Sally's the hapless one. I think she really loves him, she's very happy in that relationship. They need each other, Sally and Tim, she really cares about him and I think Sally is happy that she's married and in a safe relationship.'

Joe Duttine adds: 'In terms of the characters' chemistry, they're complete opposites and it sparks an energy. He lets the snobby aspects of Sally go over his head, he doesn't think that deeply about it. He loves the safety she provides him with a house and a family, but also there's a sexual attraction between them. They have that playfulness between them.'

GEMMA AND CHESNEY
(DOLLY-ROSE CAMPBELL AND SAM ASTON)

Couples on *Coronation Street* often have the most challenging storylines thrown at them – affairs, deaths and dodgy relatives all make for compelling viewing. Few couples have had as much to contend with in recent times as Gemma and Chesney. Their partnership started out as a cute, funny friendship, although they both held torches for each other in turn. Chesney's former girlfriend Emma spotted the attraction and stood aside for the sake of true love. That love has been tested to the extreme in the last couple of years with the revelation that Gemma's twin brother Paul had been the subject of childhood abuse, the arrival of Gemma and Paul's morally dubious mother Bernie and the birth of their quads, one of whom, Aled, is deaf. In 2020 Gemma battled with postnatal depression while looking after four babies and Joseph, Chesney's son with the late Katy Armstrong, and the pair struggled to make ends meet financially. Always compelling to watch, this is one partnership that viewers are willing to last.

NORRIS AND MARY
(MALCOLM HEBDEN AND PATTI CLARE)

Norris and Mary tied the knot in 2017 – but only to win a Mr and Mrs competition on Radio Weatherfield. It was their shared love of competitions that brought the odd couple together in 2008 and, although Mary developed feelings for Norris, they were not reciprocated. They were friends and provided many humorous moments for fans ever since Mary parked her motorhome (won in a competition, of course) on Coronation Street. They began divorce proceedings in 2019 when Norris decided he wanted to marry Freda Burgess.

Patti Clare describes her partnership with Norris: 'On my first day on set Malcolm and I started giggling (I think we got told off) and we hit it off straight away. I basically followed Malcolm's lead, to know how to pitch my performance and not belt it out like I'm in a 1,000-seat auditorium and where to position yourself on set. In the theatre you position yourself for the audience, but on telly the audience is down three cameras so that was a bit of a learning curve.

'I've loved all the stuff with Norris, it's been such a joy to work with Malcolm. He's a fun actor to work with and very experienced and good at what he does. I love the fact that they let Mary and Norris become like a double act for quite a long time.'

PERCY AND PHYLLIS
(BILL WADDINGTON AND JILL SUMMERS)

With her purple rinse and husky voice, pensioner Phyllis Pearce made a lasting impression on *Coronation Street* thanks to her amusing infatuation with pompous Percy Sugden. She pursued him relentlessly, but Percy was in turn horrified and annoyed, preferring the company of his budgie Randy. Phyllis worked in Jim's Café before keeping house for Des Barnes and Percy was the Community Centre caretaker until he retired. Percy was often downright rude to poor old lovestruck Phyllis, who once won a poetry competition with an ode to her love for Percy, but they did end up living together in one sense, at the Mayfield Court retirement complex.

ROY AND HAYLEY
(DAVID NEILSON AND JULIE HESMONDHALGH)

One couple who really struck a chord was lonely misfit Roy Cropper and shy Hayley Patterson. As their relationship developed, Roy initially rejected Hayley when she revealed she had been born male but soon supported her through her reassignment surgery and the pair went on to have a pretend wedding and later, when it became legal in real life, an official marriage. Their touching relationship, which saw them foster children, weather malicious attempts by Tracy to convince Roy he had drunkenly made her pregnant and the revelation that Hayley had fathered a son, ended when Hayley took her own life after being diagnosed with terminal pancreatic cancer.

KIRK AND BETH
(ANDREW WHYMENT AND LISA GEORGE)

Dopey Kirk and mouthy Beth have developed into one of the *Coronation Street* couples guaranteed to have the viewers in stitches. Lisa George loved playing Beth and Kirk's 1980s themed wedding scenes. 'It was the best week – I loved the costume and the fact that my character got married!' Although known for the humour, the pair also showed their sensitive side during the harrowing scenes surrounding Beth's niece Sinead's death from cancer in 2019. Lisa George adds: 'It would be amazing for Kirk and Beth to be thought of as one of *Coronation Street*'s great couples. I love our characters' relationship and feel very protective over it.'

DEIRDRE AND KEN SPLIT UP

At Christmas Ken admitted to Deirdre that he had been having an affair with Wendy Crozier and Deirdre spends New Year's Eve alone. When Ken arrives home in the early hours and refuses to give Wendy up she throws him out. Ken spends the night in the *Weatherfield Recorder* office but then moves in with Wendy. He's wracked with guilt over Tracy, who refuses to speak to him when he tells her he's not coming home, especially after she spies him shopping with Wendy. Because No 1 was mortgaged to buy *The Recorder,* Ken must sell the newspaper when Deirdre demands a final settlement. Competitor *The Gazette* buys him out but he remains on the payroll, leaving him working at the paper but with much less control. By March arguments with the new editor lead to Ken leaving *The Recorder* and, unemployed and fretting over his decisions, he becomes depressed. He realises he should never have left Deirdre and Tracy and finally ends things with Wendy.

STEVE MCDONALD RUNS AWAY WITH JOANNE KHAN

The younger sister of Jenny Bradley's student friend Flick Khan, Joanne, arrives in Weatherfield from Canterbury to stay with her sibling after their parents travel to India to look after a poorly relative. At first Andy McDonald catches her eye and he happily shows her around Coronation Street. Soon Joanne transfers her attentions to Andy's twin Steve, after he writes a romantic poem about her. When Flick, worried that her 15-year-old sister will be led astray and into bed by Steve, bans them from seeing each other, carefree Steve steals dad Jim's motorbike and the pair take off for the Lakes. Joanne soon realises it's a huge mistake and hitchhikes her way back to Weatherfield, sleeping rough and avoiding the unwanted attention of two highly unsavoury men on the way. Liz McDonald is worried about Steve's whereabouts and eventually Joanne tells her where he is. She later returns home to Canterbury with her father.

Ken decides to sell the *Weatherfield Recorder* and later in the year returns to teaching

Des and Steph Barnes move into No 6.

The Wiltons move into No 4, but budgie Harriet dies in the move.

Tracy Barlow causes a chip-pan fire.

Sally and Gail both discover they're pregnant. Ivy is horrified.

ITV's charity telethon includes a specially commissioned short episode in which Hilda Ogden returns to the Street.

JAN | FEB | MAR | APR | MAY | JUNE

First appearance of Victoria Arden.

Mike Baldwin is given a job as a salesman.

Rita moves out of No 7 and into 10a, the flat above The Kabin, as The Kabin closes on Rosamund Street and opens on Coronation Street.

Reg Holdsworth moves into the flat above the Corner Shop.

Deirdre agrees to sell No 1 to the brewery to the horror of Bet and Alec Gilroy, but the sale eventually falls through.

DECEMBER

SALLY AND GAIL BOTH GIVE BIRTH

Two key residents of the Street are born within a day of each other. On Christmas Eve, Sally goes into labour alone – mechanic Kevin was called out to repair Alf's car, which had broken down en route to a swanky function – and gives birth to her first daughter, Rosie, in the back of Don Brennan's taxi on Rosamund Street. A day later, Gail gives birth to David, and the two friends tend to their newborns side by side on the maternity ward.

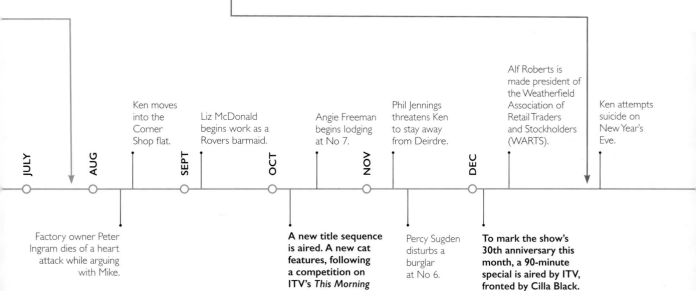

Alf Roberts is made president of the Weatherfield Association of Retail Traders and Stockholders (WARTS).

Ken attempts suicide on New Year's Eve.

Ken moves into the Corner Shop flat.

Liz McDonald begins work as a Rovers barmaid.

Angie Freeman begins lodging at No 7.

Phil Jennings threatens Ken to stay away from Deirdre.

JULY · AUG · SEPT · OCT · NOV · DEC

Factory owner Peter Ingram dies of a heart attack while arguing with Mike.

A new title sequence is aired. A new cat features, following a competition on ITV's *This Morning* programme.

Percy Sugden disturbs a burglar at No 6.

To mark the show's 30th anniversary this month, a 90-minute special is aired by ITV, fronted by Cilla Black.

MIKE AND JACKIE MARRY, BUT IT QUICKLY GOES WRONG

By August 1990 Mike Baldwin had launched Phoenix Fabrics, in direct competition with his boss at the time, Peter Ingram. Peter died shortly afterwards and his wife Jackie began to rely on Mike to help run their factory. Mike was in a relationship with Alma Sedgewick, but embarked on an affair with Jackie who urged him to leave Alma. After Mike and Jackie marry on Jackie's birthday, Jackie informs him she is selling the business and wants them to move to the Caribbean, but Mike talks her out of it, guaranteeing he can turn the struggling business around. When Jackie finds out about Mike's manoeuvring to take control of the business she becomes hysterical, pointing Peter's old rifle at him, before leaving. Their divorce is a drawn-out affair with financial claims and accusations flying. Jackie warns Alma about Mike, yet soon after the divorce is finalised, Alma marries him.

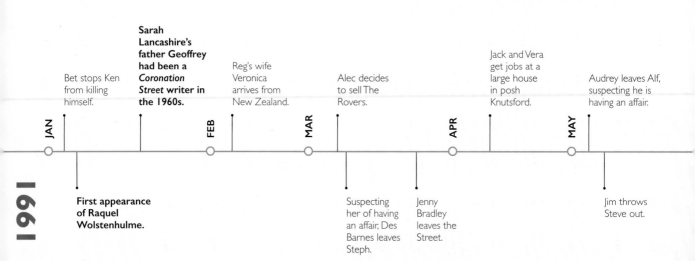

1991

JAN — Bet stops Ken from killing himself.

Sarah Lancashire's father Geoffrey had been a *Coronation Street* writer in the 1960s.

First appearance of Raquel Wolstenhulme.

FEB — Reg's wife Veronica arrives from New Zealand.

MAR — Alec decides to sell The Rovers.

Suspecting her of having an affair, Des Barnes leaves Steph.

Jenny Bradley leaves the Street.

APR — Jack and Vera get jobs at a large house in posh Knutsford.

MAY — Audrey leaves Alf, suspecting he is having an affair.

Jim throws Steve out.

AUGUST

DES BARNES SETS FIRE TO HIS BOAT

Des and Steph Barnes moved into the Street as newlyweds in 1990. Steph's dad Maurice Jones had built the new houses on Coronation Street and sold them No 6 cheaply. They'd only been together a few weeks before they married and soon the cracks began to show. Bookie's assistant Des is obsessed with working on an old boat he'd bought and installed in their garden. Feeling neglected, Steph embarks on an affair and next-door neighbour Mavis tells Des about it. When Des finishes working on the boat he plans a maiden voyage on the canal, but ahead of this he and Steph split up – she wants to be with her lover Simon and blames Des for spending so much time on his boat. Des asks her to meet him at the canal and the boat bursts into flames. Des has set it alight to scare Steph into thinking he's killed himself, but it's to no avail when she sees him sitting on the side of the canal. Des continues trying to fight for his marriage, but Steph leaves and Des is charged with polluting the waterways. Following the split, Des becomes something of a Street romeo, romancing several local women.

Audrey is hiding out at a posh hotel, but Alf cancels her credit card.

Deirdre discovers Phil Jennings is married.

Steph leaves Des for architect Simon Beatty.

Martin adopts Nicky and Sarah.

Mike lures Ken's girlfriend and his ex, Alma, into bed.

Two episodes are shown on Christmas Day, with the first incorporating the broadcast of the Queen's speech in the middle as Alf and Audrey sit down to watch it.

JUNE | JULY | AUG | SEPT | OCT | NOV | DEC

Victoria's parents are killed in a car crash.

The Weatherfield Carnival takes place.

Gail proposes to Martin. They marry later in the month.

Don Brennan begins an affair with Julie Dewhurst and leaves Ivy.

Andy McDonald is beaten up by mistake.

SEPTEMBER

TED SULLIVAN DIES

Rita had known Ted Sullivan for several years as he visited The Kabin as a confectionary salesman. They met up socially at Mavis and Derek's dinner party and began dating. Despite knowing he was dying of a brain tumour, Ted had asked Rita to marry him and retire to Florida and she agreed. It was only on their return to Weatherfield, having visited to look for a home there, that Ted admitted the truth about his prognosis. Rita eventually decided she would marry him but wanted them to stay in Weatherfield, which Ted agreed to. Over the subsequent months, Ted's health deteriorates severely. He has memory lapses and collapses on one occasion. He doesn't want to reveal his illness to neighbours and they are suspicious of his behaviour. In September, Rita finds Ted on a bench at a bowls match. She thinks at first that he's asleep but realises he has died.

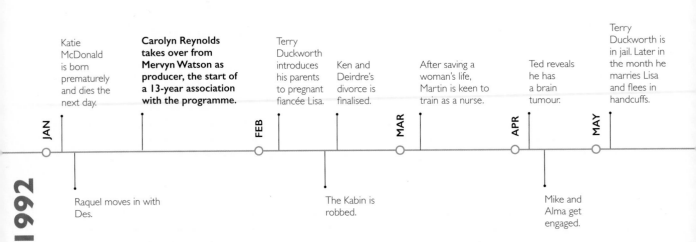

1992

Katie McDonald is born prematurely and dies the next day.

Carolyn Reynolds takes over from Mervyn Watson as producer, the start of a 13-year association with the programme.

Terry Duckworth introduces his parents to pregnant fiancée Lisa.

Ken and Deirdre's divorce is finalised.

After saving a woman's life, Martin is keen to train as a nurse.

Ted reveals he has a brain tumour.

Terry Duckworth is in jail. Later in the month he marries Lisa and flees in handcuffs.

JAN FEB MAR APR MAY

Raquel moves in with Des.

The Kabin is robbed.

Mike and Alma get engaged.

CARMEL ADMITS SHE'S IN LOVE WITH MARTIN

Carmel Finnan was a student nurse with a murky past who inveigled her way into the Platts' home, having become obsessed with fellow student Martin. Gail becomes suspicious of Carmel and when she has to spend the night looking after a poorly Alf, Carmel convinces a drunk Martin that they've spent the night together and declares her love for him. She tells Gail that she and Martin are in love, but Gail throws her out. Carmel later goes on to tell Gail she's pregnant with Martin's baby and when Martin admits he woke to find her in bed, Gail doesn't know who to believe. Martin leaves college and Gail confronts Carmel in her bedsit. They tussle and Carmel falls, breaking her leg. In hospital it's revealed that there is no baby and when her grandfather arrives from Ireland he reveals that Carmel had subjected another man to a similar ordeal. He takes a clearly disturbed Carmel back to Ireland.

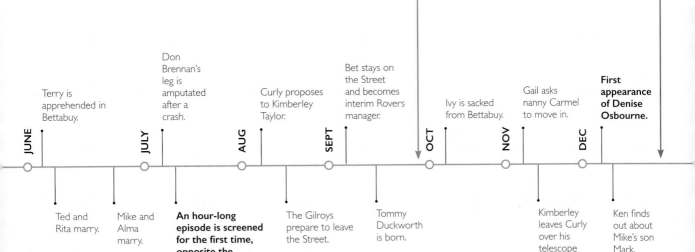

Terry is apprehended in Bettabuy.

Don Brennan's leg is amputated after a crash.

Curly proposes to Kimberley Taylor.

Bet stays on the Street and becomes interim Rovers manager.

Ivy is sacked from Bettabuy.

Gail asks nanny Carmel to move in.

First appearance of Denise Osbourne.

JUNE · JULY · AUG · SEPT · OCT · NOV · DEC

Ted and Rita marry.

Mike and Alma marry.

An hour-long episode is screened for the first time, opposite the launch of the BBC's doomed *Eldorado*.

The Gilroys prepare to leave the Street.

Tommy Duckworth is born.

Kimberley leaves Curly over his telescope obsession.

Ken finds out about Mike's son Mark.

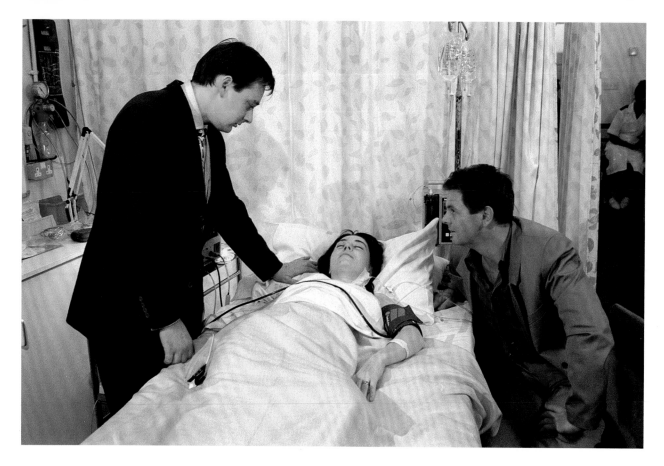

FEBRUARY

LISA DUCKWORTH DIES

Lisa Horton became pregnant with Street bad boy Terry Duckworth's baby and while he was awaiting sentence for GBH he proposed to her. He was jailed and used their wedding day to escape from officers. He was sent back to jail and Lisa gave birth to Tommy in September 1992, having split from Terry. Lisa and

Des Barnes start seeing each other and plan to buy a new house together. When the sale of No 6 is agreed, Lisa pops over to The Rovers to buy some wine to celebrate, but is hit by a car and dies of head injuries. Later, Terry sells the baby to Lisa's parents, the Hortons, to the distress of Vera and Jack who had been looking after Tommy. In 2011, Tommy returns to Coronation Street and embarks on a relationship with Tina McIntyre.

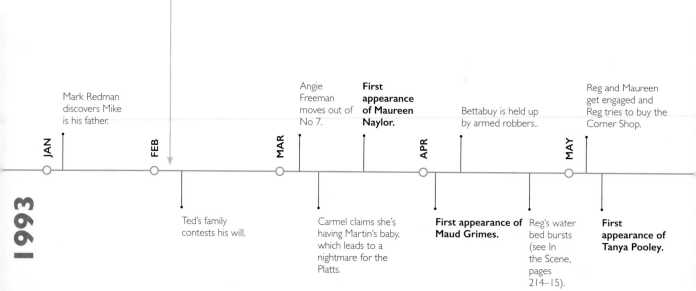

1993

Mark Redman discovers Mike is his father.

Ted's family contests his will.

Angie Freeman moves out of No 7.

Carmel claims she's having Martin's baby, which leads to a nightmare for the Platts.

First appearance of Maureen Naylor.

First appearance of Maud Grimes.

Bettabuy is held up by armed robbers..

Reg's water bed bursts (see In the Scene, pages 214–15).

Reg and Maureen get engaged and Reg tries to buy the Corner Shop.

First appearance of Tanya Pooley.

JAN   FEB   MAR   APR   MAY

AUGUST

KEN GIVES RAQUEL FRENCH LESSONS

Wannabe model and naïve Rovers barmaid Raquel Wolstenhulme has always wanted to better herself. To impress a date she asks Ken Barlow to give her some French lessons. In one of her funniest moments, Raquel reveals a French man in Corfu had once taught her to say 'isn't it a lovely day today'. Ken is somewhat surprised when Raquel innocently goes on to proposition him in French. Ironically, Raquel ended up living in France, married to a Frenchman and raising her and Curly Watts' daughter in a chateau, presumably speaking French perfectly.

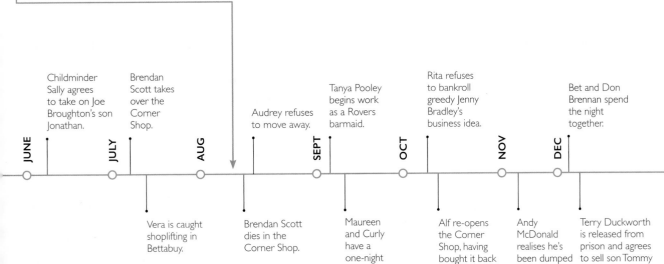

Childminder Sally agrees to take on Joe Broughton's son Jonathan.

Brendan Scott takes over the Corner Shop.

Audrey refuses to move away.

Tanya Pooley begins work as a Rovers barmaid.

Rita refuses to bankroll greedy Jenny Bradley's business idea.

Bet and Don Brennan spend the night together.

JUNE — JULY — AUG — SEPT — OCT — NOV — DEC

Vera is caught shoplifting in Bettabuy.

Brendan Scott dies in the Corner Shop.

Maureen and Curly have a one-night stand.

Alf re-opens the Corner Shop, having bought it back at auction.

Andy McDonald realises he's been dumped by Amy.

Terry Duckworth is released from prison and agrees to sell son Tommy to his in-laws.

30TH APRIL 1993

OF the many comic scenes for which *Coronation Street* is famed, Reg Holdsworth's thwarted attempt to consummate his relationship with first love Maureen regularly appears in the Top 10s of fans' favourite funny scenes from the show. Including, as it does, that other comic partnership Mavis and Derek, the waterbed scene has gone down as a classic *Coronation Street* comedy moment.

In the scene
Reg's passion is dampened

THE SURROUNDING STORYLINES

Pompous Reg Holdsworth fancied himself as a bit of a ladies' man. (but was generally less than successful). He met old flame Maureen Naylor when she started working at Bettabuy and he sought to woo her. As had happened in their youth, Maureen's mother Maud Grimes was determined to split them up – she hated Reg, he was just not good enough for her daughter – and Reg's attempts thus far were always interrupted by a phone call from needy Maud. Will his waterbed help him succeed at last?

THE MAIN EVENT

Reg has finally tempted Maureen up to his flat above The Kabin. He has installed what he believes is something irresistible – a waterbed. Meanwhile, Derek is attending to a faulty light fitting downstairs and sets to work with his drill. When water begins to drip from the ceiling he and Mavis worry that Reg has let his bath overflow. Is he ill? They hurry upstairs and barge into the flat, interrupting a naked Reg and Maureen in bed. As Maureen shrieks in horror, she realises the bed is leaking – Derek's drilling has only gone and punctured it! Mavis and Derek stand in the doorway, embarrassed at what they have disturbed and Maureen, mortified at the situation, scrambles to retrieve her sodden clothes from the flooded flat while attempting to preserve her modesty. Reg is left feeling as deflated his new bed, as his chance to finally sleep with Maureen is washed away.

THE AFTERMATH

Reg and Maureen finally marry the following year, but not before Maureen sleeps with Reg's colleague Curly in revenge for what she believes is Reg seeing another woman. Rita has been on holiday with Bet and when she finds out that her stock is water damaged she finds it hilarious that the cause was Reg's amorous adventures.

PRODUCTION NOTES

More than 15 million viewers watched this episode, which is included in a DVD collection of the best of *Coronation Street* in the 1990s.

RAQUEL DISCOVERS DES'S AFFAIR WITH TANYA

Of all dizzy Raquel's romantic entanglements, it was Des Barnes for whom she fell most heavily. They went out on and off, but Des never respected Raquel. After they got back together in 1994, Des soon slept with Tanya Pooley, who had been having an affair with his married boss. For Des to be cheating on her with her fellow barmaid really added insult to injury for Raquel; Tanya had spitefully sent her on a fake modelling assignment and only took up with Des when she learned how Raquel felt about him. In June 1994, Raquel discovers his affair with Tanya, and on the rebound, gets engaged to Curly Watts. The following year Des seduces Raquel again, but she is heartbroken to realise it was just a one-night stand. Raquel goes on to marry Curly, but she leaves him to go to Kuala Lumpur, pregnant, unbeknown to him, with his child.

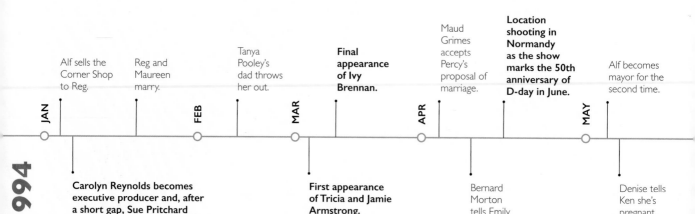

Alf sells the Corner Shop to Reg.

Reg and Maureen marry.

Tanya Pooley's dad throws her out.

Final appearance of Ivy Brennan.

Maud Grimes accepts Percy's proposal of marriage.

Location shooting in Normandy as the show marks the 50th anniversary of D-day in June.

Alf becomes mayor for the second time.

JAN FEB MAR APR MAY

1994

Carolyn Reynolds becomes executive producer and, after a short gap, Sue Pritchard becomes the show's producer. It is the first time the two top posts are occupied by women.

First appearance of Tricia and Jamie Armstrong.

Bernard Morton tells Emily he can't marry her.

Denise tells Ken she's pregnant.

BET'S BOYFRIEND CHARLIE CHEATS ON HER

Charlie Whelan is Bet's lorry driver boyfriend. When Tanya Pooley dumps Des Barnes and her relationship with married Alex ends she sets her sights on Charlie. When Tanya is nasty to Raquel, who has returned from London having been thrown off a modelling course, Bet sacks her. Charlie defends Tanya and goes to see her. Tanya seduces him and they kiss. Charlie feels guilty, but after Tanya delights in telling Bet about the pair of them, Tanya and Charlie leave together for Germany. Bet is left to mend her broken heart, again.

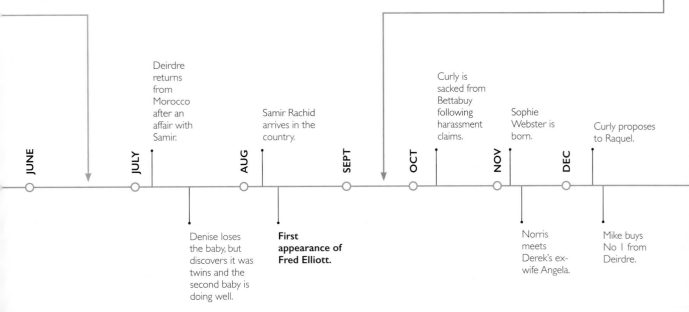

JUNE

JULY — Deirdre returns from Morocco after an affair with Samir.

AUG — Samir Rachid arrives in the country.

Denise loses the baby, but discovers it was twins and the second baby is doing well.

First appearance of Fred Elliott.

SEPT

OCT — Curly is sacked from Bettabuy following harassment claims.

NOV — Sophie Webster is born.

Norris meets Derek's ex-wife Angela.

DEC — Curly proposes to Raquel.

Mike buys No 1 from Deirdre.

SAMIR IS ATTACKED ON THE WAY TO DONATE A KIDNEY TO TRACY

Tracy Barlow hasn't had the easiest childhood and, by 1995, the moody young woman is taking drugs. She suffered kidney failure after taking ecstasy and while in hospital, Martin contacts her family. At this point Deirdre is in Morocco with her new young husband Samir Rachid, a waiter she met on holiday, but she returns to Weatherfield, swiftly followed by Samir. Tracy faces a lifetime on dialysis when both Deirdre and Ken are found not to be suitable kidney donors for her, but Samir offers to be tested too and is found to be a match. He is very much in love with Deirdre and would do anything to make her happy, so he offers to donate a kidney. Before the operation can go ahead, Samir is attacked by a gang and, when a distraught Deirdre is informed that he won't recover, she agrees for the transplant to go ahead and Tracy makes a full recovery.

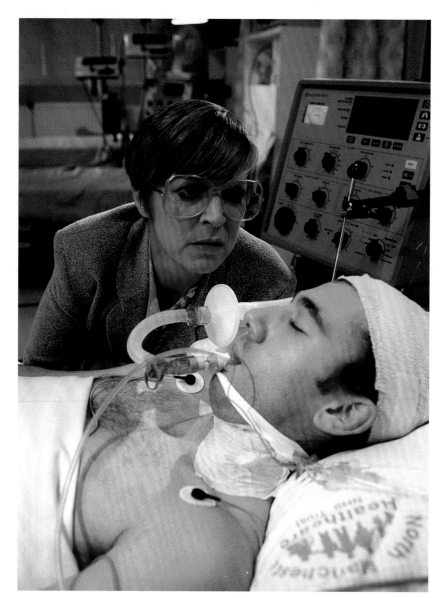

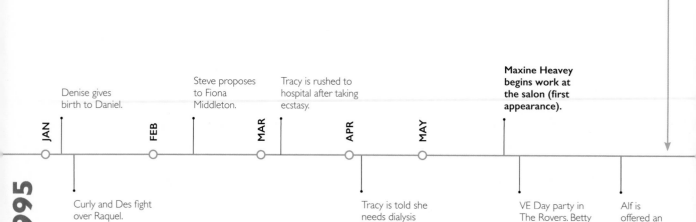

1995

Denise gives birth to Daniel.

Steve proposes to Fiona Middleton.

Tracy is rushed to hospital after taking ecstasy.

Maxine Heavey begins work at the salon (first appearance).

JAN

FEB

MAR

APR

MAY

Curly and Des fight over Raquel.

Tracy is told she needs dialysis because her kidneys are damaged.

VE Day party in The Rovers. Betty meets up with Billy Williams again.

Alf is offered an OBE.

STEVE AND VICKY WED

At 18, Alec Gilroy's granddaughter Vicky Arden has come into a large inheritance following the death of her parents in a car crash. She moves back to Weatherfield and into The Rovers with Bet, investing some of her cash into her ex, Steve McDonald's, fledgling printing business. She loses her money but gets engaged to debt-ridden Steve when Fiona Middleton dumps him. Worried that Steve is only after her money, Bet summons Alec back to the Street three years after he left. Alec tries everything in his power to prevent Vicky from marrying Steve, despite the McDonalds supporting the couple, even offering Steve a £5,000 bribe to leave Vicky alone. Nothing works and Steve and Vicky jet off to St Lucia to wed. Alec leaves again for Southampton, but not before trying to persuade Bet to try again. She wistfully turns him down before asking wealthy Vicky to help her buy her beloved Rovers. When a surprised Vicky declines, Bet too leaves Weatherfield.

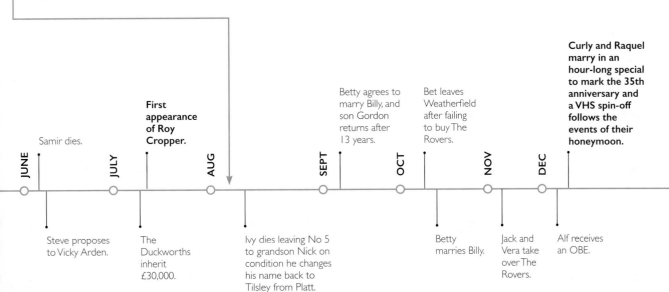

Curly and Raquel marry in an hour-long special to mark the 35th anniversary and a VHS spin-off follows the events of their honeymoon.

Samir dies.

First appearance of Roy Cropper.

Betty agrees to marry Billy, and son Gordon returns after 13 years.

Bet leaves Weatherfield after failing to buy The Rovers.

| JUNE | JULY | AUG | SEPT | OCT | NOV | DEC |

Steve proposes to Vicky Arden.

The Duckworths inherit £30,000.

Ivy dies leaving No 5 to grandson Nick on condition he changes his name back to Tilsley from Platt.

Betty marries Billy.

Jack and Vera take over The Rovers.

Alf receives an OBE.

JIM ATTACKS LIZ OVER AFFAIR

When Liz was a lonely young army wife she had a fling with Jim's forces friend Johnny Johnson and it isn't until 1996 that a suspicious Jim discovers the affair. He had previously accused Liz of being unfaithful and was critical of the way she dressed, believing it was too provocative. A violent man when drunk, he batters Liz after an army reunion and dumps her by the roadside late at night. When he tells sons Steve and Andy what he's done they go searching for their injured mother who eventually files for divorce from Jim. They remarry several years later but split again. Their tempestuous relationship sees them reconciled yet again in 2011 and again in 2018, when he tricks her into believing their deceased daughter Katie is alive.

PRODUCTION NOTE

Actor Beverley Callard recalls: 'The scenes in which Liz was a victim of domestic abuse were ones I loved filming. In one scene, which we shot at 2am on a garage forecourt in winter, I was in a backless Lycra mini dress and I had to lie in the snow. I have never been so cold in my life, but I loved playing that story.'

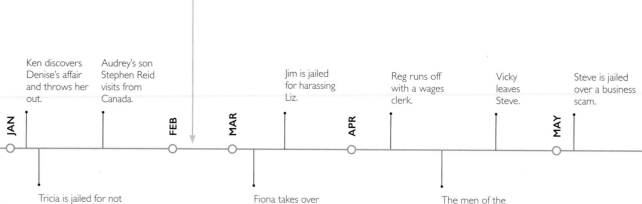

1996

Ken discovers Denise's affair and throws her out.

Audrey's son Stephen Reid visits from Canada.

Jim is jailed for harassing Liz.

Reg runs off with a wages clerk.

Vicky leaves Steve.

Steve is jailed over a business scam.

JAN
FEB
MAR
APR
MAY

Tricia is jailed for not paying her TV licence.

Fiona takes over the salon.

The men of the Street buy a racehorse.

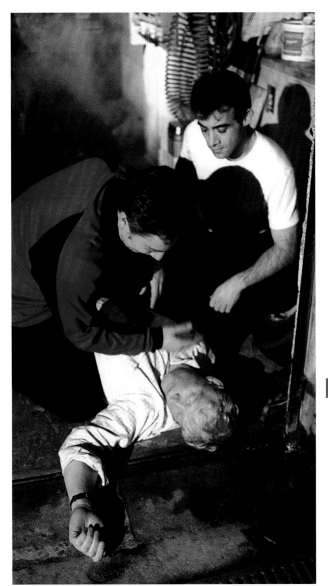

DON BRENNAN ATTEMPTS SUICIDE

Life goes from bad to worse for taxi driver Don Brennan. Having been conned out of thousands by Mike Baldwin in a business deal, his girlfriend Josie then walks out on him. Gail not inviting him over for Christmas proves to be the final straw, and he drinks a bottle of whisky and is breathalysed by the police. He knows he's likely to lose his licence and his job. Gail and Martin relent and invite him after all, but he declines, gets drunk again and heads for the garage where he sits in Martin's car with the engine running. As he breathes in fumes, he collapses with his head on the horn. The sound wakes people up and Martin and Kevin drag him from the vehicle, saving his life.

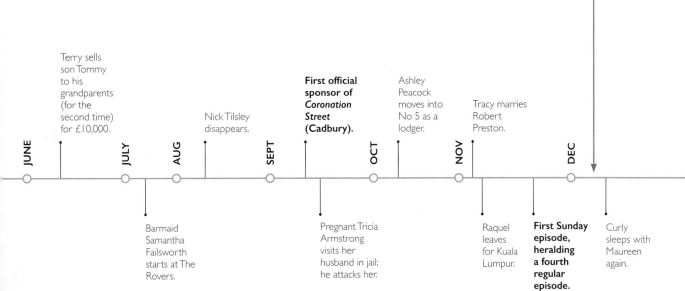

Terry sells son Tommy to his grandparents (for the second time) for £10,000.

Nick Tilsley disappears.

First official sponsor of *Coronation Street* (Cadbury).

Ashley Peacock moves into No 5 as a lodger.

Tracy marries Robert Preston.

JUNE JULY AUG SEPT OCT NOV DEC

Barmaid Samantha Failsworth starts at The Rovers.

Pregnant Tricia Armstrong visits her husband in jail; he attacks her.

Raquel leaves for Kuala Lumpur.

First Sunday episode, heralding a fourth regular episode.

Curly sleeps with Maureen again.

DON KIDNAPS ALMA

After he was conned by Mike Baldwin the previous year, Don blamed Mike for all his problems and vowed to take revenge. He wrote a suicide note to Mike's wife Alma, vandalised a Jaguar he mistakenly thought was Mike's, and finally burned down Mike's sportswear factory to try and frame him for an insurance scam. When that backfires and Mike is able to start afresh by setting up Underworld, Don kidnaps a terrified Alma. His taxi plunges into the canal, but they both survive and Don is charged with attempted murder. He later escapes from police custody, corners Mike in Underworld and attempts to kill him with Alma's car. He smashes into the viaduct wall and dies in the resulting firebomb. Mike survives with hardly a scratch.

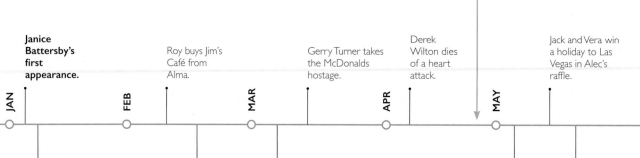

1997

JAN — **Janice Battersby's first appearance.**

Brian Park takes over as producer, with a brief from ITV to target younger viewers. He immediately dismisses 11 actors and the press nickname him 'the smiling axeman'.

FEB — Roy buys Jim's Café from Alma.

Tricia goes into labour in The Rovers.

MAR — Gerry Turner takes the McDonalds hostage.

Don Brennan starts a factory fire.

APR — Derek Wilton dies of a heart attack.

MAY — Jack and Vera win a holiday to Las Vegas in Alec's raffle.

Roy renames the café Roy's Rolls.

Deirdre meets Jon Lindsay for first time.

JUNE

SALLY CONFRONTS KEVIN OVER HIS AFFAIR WITH NATALIE

Natalie Horrocks' son Tony was co-owner of the garage for a while until she took over his stake and became mechanic Kevin's business partner. They began an affair when Sally was away nursing her poorly mother. On her return, Sally begins to be suspicious of Natalie when Rosie tells her Natalie has been at the house a lot. Kevin, undecided about who to be with, is distant with her. Sally arrives at Natalie's house and discovers Kevin and Natalie together, leading to a dramatic showdown. Kevin begs for forgiveness, despite blaming Sally for his straying, but Sally tells him she wants him to leave their home. She discovers Rita knew about the affair and can't believe she wasn't warned. Sally takes the girls to her mother's in Scarborough. Kevin follows them and again begs for forgiveness, but Sally throws him out. Rosie runs away and is found by a coastguard on the beach. The ripples from the affair continue to be felt by the Websters for months to come, with Kevin eventually returning to Sally, but the damage is done and Sally's affair with Greg Kelly the following year leads to their divorce.

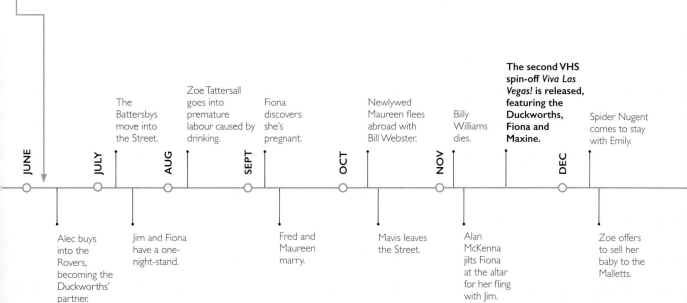

The Battersbys move into the Street.

Zoe Tattersall goes into premature labour caused by drinking.

Fiona discovers she's pregnant.

Newlywed Maureen flees abroad with Bill Webster.

Billy Williams dies.

The second VHS spin-off *Viva Las Vegas!* is released, featuring the **Duckworths, Fiona** and **Maxine**.

Spider Nugent comes to stay with Emily.

JUNE **JULY** **AUG** **SEPT** **OCT** **NOV** **DEC**

Alec buys into the Rovers, becoming the Duckworths' partner.

Jim and Fiona have a one-night-stand.

Fred and Maureen marry.

Mavis leaves the Street.

Alan McKenna jilts Fiona at the altar for her fling with Jim.

Zoe offers to sell her baby to the Malletts.

DEIRDRE IS JAILED FOR FRAUD: FREE THE WEATHERFIELD ONE

Two years after the death of Samir, Deirdre met handsome 'airline pilot' Jon Lindsay at a singles night in 1997. He claimed he had a devious ex-wife and Deirdre quickly fell for him. When Ken spotted Jon serving in the Tie 'n' Fly shop at Manchester Airport he became suspicious, but Jon spun Deirdre a tale, claiming he'd been retired due to failing a medical thanks to an ear infection, but had been too embarrassed to tell her. Deirdre bought the story and they became engaged and moved into a house in another part of Manchester. He spent long spells away, but claimed this was because he was now managing the nationwide franchise of Tie 'n' Fly. In reality, he was also living with his wife and children. When Jon is arrested for mortgage and credit card fraud he makes sure unsuspecting Deirdre takes most of the blame. He receives a suspended sentence, but a horrified Deirdre is jailed for 18 months. The following month it emerges that a former wife of Jon has come forward with new evidence – he had married her bigamously – and the judges order Deirdre's immediate release on bail.

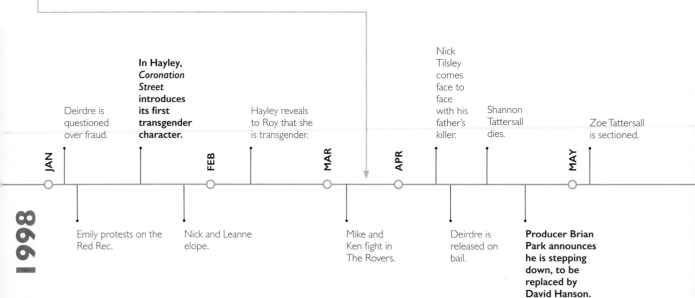

In Hayley, *Coronation Street* introduces **its first transgender character.**

Nick Tilsley comes face to face with his father's killer.

Shannon Tattersall dies.

Deirdre is questioned over fraud.

Hayley reveals to Roy that she is transgender.

Zoe Tattersall is sectioned.

JAN FEB MAR APR MAY

Emily protests on the Red Rec.

Nick and Leanne elope.

Mike and Ken fight in The Rovers.

Deirdre is released on bail.

Producer Brian Park announces he is stepping down, to be replaced by David Hanson.

1998

TOYAH RUNS AWAY TO LONDON AND IS KIDNAPPED

Troubled teenager Toyah falls out with mum and step-dad Janice and Les over Ken giving her private tuition. She runs away, hitching a ride to London, to find her real dad Ronnie Clegg. Ronnie and Janice had split up when Toyah was two, but Janice had always kept a note of his address whenever he moved. Les and Janice discover Toyah has gone and call the police, who say they can't force her to return home as she is over the age of 16. Toyah calls step-sister Leanne and tells her she's going to find Ronnie, so Les and Janice follow her to London. When they arrive at Ronnie's he is surprised, he hasn't seen Toyah. Toyah knocks on the door of what she thinks is her father's house. The man who answers says he is Ronnie, but he is really Ronnie's old cellmate Neil Flynn. Toyah discovers the truth and violent Neil ties her up and drives her to Epping Forest, where she escapes his clutches and runs into the forest. Neil is arrested, distressed Toyah is eventually found and realises Les has been a better father to her than her real dad ever was. They return to Weatherfield and Toyah resumes her tuition with Ken.

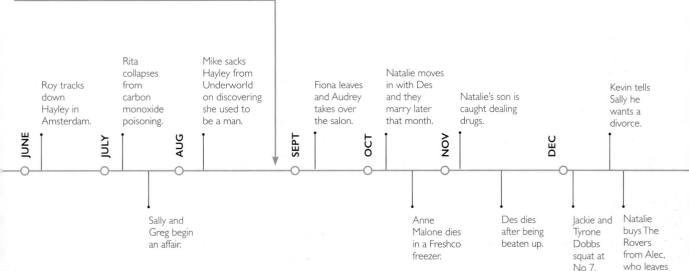

Roy tracks down Hayley in Amsterdam.

Rita collapses from carbon monoxide poisoning.

Mike sacks Hayley from Underworld on discovering she used to be a man.

Fiona leaves and Audrey takes over the salon.

Natalie moves in with Des and they marry later that month.

Natalie's son is caught dealing drugs.

Kevin tells Sally he wants a divorce.

JUNE   JULY   AUG   SEPT   OCT   NOV   DEC

Sally and Greg begin an affair.

Anne Malone dies in a Freshco freezer.

Des dies after being beaten up.

Jackie and Tyrone Dobbs squat at No 7.

Natalie buys The Rovers from Alec, who leaves the Street.

SHARON JILTS FIANCÉ IAN

Sharon Gaskell had been fostered by Rita and Len Fairclough in 1982. In 1999 she returns to Coronation Street ahead of her wedding to Nottingham sales rep Ian Bentley. Rita persuades Sharon to hold her wedding in Weatherfield, where Rita would give her away. Ian starts an affair with recently widowed Natalie Barnes, who knows he has a fiancée but doesn't know it is Sharon. The pair are spotted together and, on the morning of Sharon's wedding, Rita tells her about Natalie. Sharon loves Ian and, making excuses for him, prepares to go ahead with the wedding, but changes her mind at the altar when his vows sound false. She jilts Ian and attacks Natalie while Sally, whose own marriage to Kevin had been ruined by his affair with Natalie, calls Natalie a homewrecker. Later, Sharon and Ian rekindle their relationship and, realising they still love each other, marry and leave the area for good.

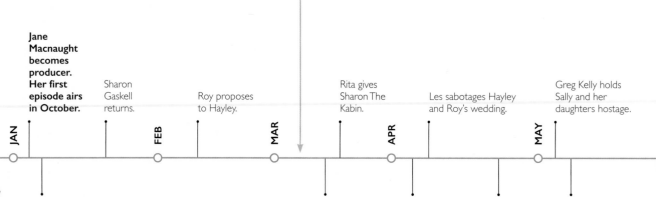

1999

Jane Macnaught becomes producer. **Her first episode airs in October.**

Sharon Gaskell returns.

Roy proposes to Hayley.

Rita gives Sharon The Kabin.

Les sabotages Hayley and Roy's wedding.

Greg Kelly holds Sally and her daughters hostage.

JAN

FEB

MAR

APR

MAY

Alf Roberts dies.

Sharon's aborted wedding achieves the year's highest viewing figures.

Leanne has an abortion.

Julia Stone blackmails Mike.

Fred tells Ashley he is his father.

TRAGEDY FOR THE MALLETTS

Gary and Judy Mallett had moved into Coronation Street in 1995, buying the Duckworths' house when they took over The Rovers. Desperate for a baby, they bought young Zoe Tattersall's daughter, but Zoe subsequently took back the child. Soon afterwards, Judy became pregnant with twins and the couple were delighted when William and Rebecca were born on Christmas Day in 1998. In September 1999, Judy and Vera are involved in a car crash. Terry had sold Vera a car that was actually two vehicles welded together and therefore unsafe. When another car crashes into it, the passenger door buckles, injuring Judy. Days later, on Ashley and Maxine's wedding day, Judy, feeling unwell, goes to hang out some washing in her back yard and collapses. She has suffered an embolism caused by injuries from the car crash and Gary finds his wife dead in the yard.

· PRODUCTION NOTE ·

By 2000, *Coronation Street* was broadcasting four times a week, the fourth episode having been added in 1996. By 2003, a fifth regular episode had been added, following trials the previous year. In September 2017, *Coronation Street* began broadcasting six episodes a week. The increased output, and the corresponding rise in the number of storylines, are reflected in the following pages.

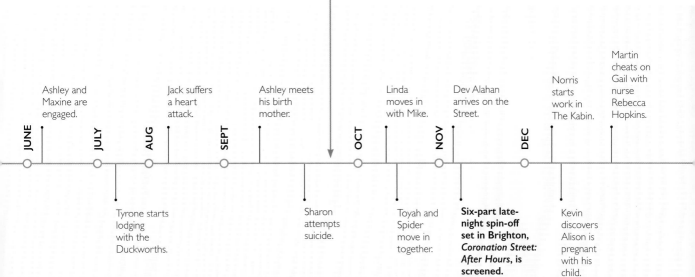

Ashley and Maxine are engaged.

Jack suffers a heart attack.

Ashley meets his birth mother.

Linda moves in with Mike.

Dev Alahan arrives on the Street.

Norris starts work in The Kabin.

Martin cheats on Gail with nurse Rebecca Hopkins.

JUNE | JULY | AUG | SEPT | OCT | NOV | DEC

Tyrone starts lodging with the Duckworths.

Sharon attempts suicide.

Toyah and Spider move in together.

Six-part late-night spin-off set in Brighton, *Coronation Street: After Hours*, is screened.

Kevin discovers Alison is pregnant with his child.

I know that face – famous actors who have graced the cobbles

APPEARING on *Coronation Street* is something of an ambition for many seasoned actors. They may have scaled the heights of Hollywood or trod the boards at the Royal Shakespeare Company, but a slot on the UK's favourite soap is often a welcome addition to their CV.

The following lists the actors who appeared on *Coronation Street*, having either made their name elsewhere or who are so iconic it would be a crime not to mention their early appearance in Weatherfield.

TREVOR BANNISTER

Best known as Mr Lucas in *Are You Being Served?* Bannister appeared in three small roles in *Coronation Street* in 1967, 1972 and most memorably, as a solicitor in 2006.

HONOR BLACKMAN

The Bond girl appeared as Rita's old friend Rula Romanoff for five episodes in 2004.

STEPHANIE COLE

Appeared as Roy Cropper's mother Sylvia Goodwin between 2011 and 2013.

MICHELLE COLLINS

The former *EastEnders* star played the role of Rovers landlady Stella Price from 2011 to 2014.

BERNARD CRIBBINS

The voice of *The Wombles* played Wally Bannister from May to October 2003. Blanche and Tracy were both involved with lecherous liar Wally.

LES DENNIS

The famed comic, gameshow host and actor starred as Michael Rodwell for two years from 2014. His character married Gail and was a victim of killer Pat Phelan. Les was a lifelong *Coronation Street* fan and remembers watching the very first episode as a child. He says: 'I remember those early black-and-white episodes. Then as I got older and got into the business I started to do impressions of the characters, the most famous was Mavis "I don't really know" Riley.

'I visited the set many times and became friends with Thelma Barlow, who played Mavis. It was something that was in my DNA as a fan and always an ambition to one day make it into the *Street*. It was an absolute joy to join. On my first day walking down the corridor with all the dressing rooms and seeing all the famous names, I said to myself, "I'm here!"

'Helen [Worth] and I had a good chemistry straight away and the writers built on that. That's what's lovely about the show – if you give them something they will go away and write for the character.

'Some actors get annoyed when people call them by their character name rather than their real one, but I was delighted when people called me Michael.

'When Gail was going through the e-fits with the police after Michael had burgled her, people said on social media, why doesn't she just say he looks like Les Dennis? That's why I got a kick out of kids going, "Ooh look, it's Michael out of *Coronation Street*."

'The best thing for me was achieving the dream of appearing on *Coronation Street*. When Michael burgled Gail's house and I ran down the cobbles towards The Rovers where my van was, I was so overcome that I jumped into the crew vehicle instead of Michael's battered old van! It's not easy

at my age to run on cobbles, but I didn't mind because I thought, "I'm here, I'm not visiting, I'm here actually playing a character in the *Street*." It was a dream come true.'

DEREK GRIFFITHS
The *Play School* favourite played Freddie Smith from 2016 to 2017.

TIM HEALY
The *Auf Wiedersehen, Pet* star and former husband of Natalie Horrocks actor Denise Welch appeared in a minor role in 1976 and then as Sean Tully's supposed father in 2006.

NODDY HOLDER
The Slade frontman made a one-off appearance on the show's live 40th anniversary as Stan Potter, a friend of Duggie Ferguson.

ROY HUDD
The late comic and music hall expert Roy played undertaker Archie Shuttleworth who left Audrey £80,000 in his will. Roy made 117 appearances in 2002–2003, 2006 and 2010. On his time on the Street, Roy said: 'I thought coming into *Coronation Street* as Archie Shuttleworth was terrific. My first scene was with Blanche Hunt and Debbie, my wife, objected most strongly because they made Archie her boyfriend and Debbie said she was much too old for me!

'David Neilson is a wonderful actor and a lovely bloke to work opposite, I loved doing scenes with him and Malcolm Hebden.' He recalled: 'On my first day filming I was in the green room having a cup of tea when one of the younger actors came over to say hello and asked me how I got into *Corrie*. I said I was asked to read for the part and she said: "Marvellous, it'll be very good experience for you." Bill

Roache was behind me and he said, "Good experience? He's been in the business about 125 years!" The young actor was so apologetic after that, but I thought it was great.

'Being on *Coronation Street* meant a lot to me because I had a marvellous and very different character to play. I'd done comedy parts and Shakespeare and stuff, but I'd never played an undertaker. Daran Little [writer and former archivist] made him a marvellous character for me. He created a lovely running gag for Archie, which was whenever I met anybody as the undertaker I'd look them up and down and say "Five foot eight, I'm not wrong, am I?" He was a fun character!

'I loved every minute of *Coronation Street*. To be part of a team of such good actors was terrific. The *Street* never has a duff actor. They take care of it because they all like it. My wife is the greatest fan and when I got the job you'd have thought I'd been made prime minister! She filled me in with the entire history of the *Street* from day one. She was thrilled when I got it, as were many of my pals in the business, they were jealous!'

PETER KAY
The comic made two appearances in 1997 as a shop fitter and 2004 as drayman Eric Gartside who took a shine to Shelley Unwin.

RULA LENSKA
Established stage and screen actor Rula Lenska, who played Ken Barlow's most recent partner and Audrey's adversary, Claudia Colby, says: 'If anyone had said to me, what's the least likely programme you could imagine yourself being cast in, I would have said *Coronation Street*, because it's all set up in the north and I don't sound right with a northern accent. But I was absolutely thrilled to be asked.

'My first stint was in 2009, which was mostly to do with Audrey and an amazing story about a transvestite who we both befriended and fell out over and I was doubly thrilled to be asked back. With the terribly sad story of Sinead dying, just to be involved in a moving family situation that's beautifully written, is a privilege to be part of the whole set-up, but particularly to be embedded in the Barlow family. I'm incredibly proud of being part of the *Coronation Street* machine and I also had the added plus of sharing a flat with Maureen Lipman (Evelyn Plummer).'

JOANNA LUMLEY
Joanna Lumley is a national treasure – from her role as Purdey in classic 1970s show *The New Avengers* (prompting copycat hairstyles decades before *Friends'* Rachel), to her Bafta TV award-winning turn as Patsy Stone in *Absolutely Fabulous*, her travel programmes and her work as a human rights advocate. But back in 1973, as a relatively unknown young actress, she appeared in *Coronation Street* for eight episodes as Ken Barlow's love interest Elaine Perkins, a performance that is still mentioned by fans today. Elaine was the daughter of headmaster Wilfred Perkins for whom Ken worked at Bessie Street School. Ken fell for posh Elaine, but it was not to be and she spurned him.

Joanna recalls: 'Ken Barlow was the hottest widower on the box at the time. I was quite new and different and no-one knew what was going to happen between them. I loved her being a bit aloof and shy and I hated her having to say that she didn't want to stay in *Coronation Street* but longed to travel the world and not marry Ken. I think the whole country thought "Stuck-up fool" and I must say I agreed with them. I wanted to stay forever! I was thrilled and proud to be chosen for the role. I learned so much from watching the others at work.'

Joanna adds that she was a little in awe when she stepped onto the set for the first time. 'I had seen many episodes and the characters were all larger than real life, so it was a bit scary going to meet this dazzling cast. The set and back lot were enchanting and convincing, and I still treasure a photo of me sitting on the pavement grinning my head off.

'I am quite jealous of anyone new who joins the show. The queue is long, I believe, of those who ache to be in the show for a bit.'

In 2009, a storyline was planned in which Elaine returned and had an affair with Ken, which would lead to him considering moving away from Weatherfield. Joanna was unavailable and the plot was altered with Stephanie Beacham taking the role of actress Martha Fraser. Joanna remembers: 'I screamed "yes please!" But then got another job that put the kibosh on it. What a treat that would have been… me and Ken getting misty-eyed again.'

PADDY MCGUINNESS
Appeared in six episodes in 2015 as camper/wannabe Bear Grylls Dougie Ryan.

IAN MCKELLEN
The renowned actor played Lionel Hipkis, aka Mel Hutchwright, in 10 episodes in 2005 (plus a special video message in 2019 when Sue Nicholls won an Outstanding Achievement Award at the British Soap Awards). Writing on his website, the Manchester-born actor recalled: 'There I was sauntering alongside the familiar façade of Coronation Street, a back lot behind the Granada Studio building. I found myself humming the show's

signature tune, and experienced that sense of familiarity and belonging that Universal Studios and Disneyworld play with when they beckon audiences through the screen into the actual world of *ET* or *Indiana Jones* or *Peter Pan*.'

JIM MOIR, AKA VIC REEVES
The Vic and Bob star played Colin Callen for two months in 2017. Colin was a marketing executive for the sponsors of a Mr & Mrs competition that Norris and Mary Cole entered. He also mistakenly believed that Norris may have been his father.

MAXINE PEAKE
Appeared as abattoir owner's daughter Belinda Peach in 1999.

LINUS ROACHE
The son of William Roache is an established actor in his own right. The former Royal Shakespeare Company actor and star of hit show *Law and Order* appeared as Ken Barlow's son Peter in the 1970s and again 35 years later in 2010 as Lawrence Cunningham, Ken's long-lost son whose mother was Ken's first girlfriend Susan Cunningham.

ANDREW SACHS
The late *Fawlty Towers* actor played Ramsay Clegg, the long-lost half brother of Norris Cole in 2009.

TONY SLATTERY
The star of *Whose Line Is It Anyway?* appeared for five episodes in 2005 as Eric Talford, the owner of Talford Bookies on Rosamund Street.

ROBERT VAUGHN
Veteran Hollywood actor Vaughn – Napoleon Solo in *The Man From U.N.C.L.E.* and star of *The Magnificent*

Seven – appeared as Sylvia Goodwin's love interest Milton Fanshaw in 2012.

MAX WALL
Comedian Max Wall played Harry Payne, an admirer of Elsie Tanner who annoyed Elsie's boyfriend Ron Mather, in 1978.

TIMOTHY WEST
Played Eric Babbage, a wealthy businessman engaged to Gloria Price, who died in The Rovers in 2013. His appearance came 52 years after his real-life wife Prunella Scales' short stint as bus conductress Eileen Hughes in 1961.

JUNE WHITFIELD
In 2010, *Carry On*, *Terry and June* and *Ab Fab* star June Whitfield appeared on *Coronation Street* as May Penn, friend of Blanche Hunt.

NORMAN WISDOM
The slapstick comic and veteran comedy film actor appeared in 2004 as jogger Ernie Crabbe.

IN FOCUS

Regular actors and the parts they've played before

WHEN a programme has been on our screens for as long as *Coronation Street*, the number of actors appearing over the years is bound to be large. So large, in fact, that some of our favourite stars graced the cobbles in other guises, before adopting the characters that made them household names.

JEAN ALEXANDER

Best known, of course, as nosy cleaner Hilda Ogden, Jean first appeared on the *Street* two years before Hilda's 1964 introduction, as landlady Mrs Webb. Mrs Webb lived on Percy Street and let a room to poor Joan Akers, a disturbed young woman who, following the death of her baby, kidnapped little Christopher Hewitt. Mrs Webb appeared twice in October 1962.

PETER ARMITAGE

Peter played Kevin Webster's father Bill throughout the 80s, 90s and 2000s, but previously he appeared as a decorator tasked with refurbishing The Rovers in time for the 1977 Silver Jubilee, a job he neglected in order to do decorating work for Ernie Bishop at No 3.

ROY BARRACLOUGH

Rovers landlord (and previously theatrical agent) Alec Gilroy was a highly popular character, in large part thanks to his partnership and marriage to Bet Lynch, but Roy actually had four parts in *Coronation Street* before landing his most famous role. He first appeared as Alec in 1972 before returning years later in 1986 in the regular role, but before that Roy was cast as a tour guide (June 1965), a guitar salesman (July 1967), a window cleaner (June 1968) and a restaurant customer (June 1970).

ELIZABETH BRADLEY

Before playing battleaxe mother-in-law Maud Grimes from 1993 to 1999, prolific actor Elizabeth made a brief appearance in 1971 as a party guest and another in 1978 as a councillor.

JOHNNY BRIGGS

Cockney businessman Mike Baldwin was the character that made Johnny a household name for 30 years. Former casting director Judi Hayfield recalls how he was one of several actors who came in for a small role and then ended up coming back as a new regular character later down the line. 'Johnny Briggs came in as a lorry driver for an episode originally, but I remembered him and brought him back for Mike Baldwin.'

BEVERLEY CALLARD

Beverley's key character of Liz McDonald arrived on the Street in 1989. Five years earlier she appeared briefly as June, the wife of Gary Dewhurst, a pal of Brian Tilsley.

BRIAN CAPRON

Capron's serial killer character Richard Hillman kept audiences riveted in the early 2000s, but actor Brian Capron had graced the cobbles twice before in 14 appearances between 1981 and 1986 as social worker Don Worthington who brought, first Sharon Gaskell, and then Jenny Bradley to Rita Fairclough's door.

SUE CLEAVER

Ahead of her 2000 debut as Street Cars operator Eileen Grimshaw, and subsequent position as one of the *Street*'s matriarchs, Sue appeared briefly in 1994 as Sister Treece.

JOE DUTTINE

As *Street* favourite Tim Metcalfe since 2013, Joe has certainly made his mark, but eagle-eyed fans will remember him from 2010, when he played a police detective investigating Joe McIntyre's drowning. Joe's uncle, actor John Duttine, also appeared in a bit part in *Coronation Street* in 1977.

MARK EDEN

Mark made the role of Alan Bradley his own when he appeared in the *Street* as the potential love interest of a true *Coronation Street* queen. In 1981 he played trucker Wally Randle, who turned down Elsie Tanner as being too old for him.

FRED FEAST

As Rovers potman Fred Gee, Feast appeared on the *Street* from 1975 to 1984. Prior to that he had appeared as an extra and also a barman.

GEORGIA MAY FOOTE

Georgia played Katy Armstrong from July 2010 to 2015. Previously she appeared in one episode in early 2010 as schoolgirl Jess Burrows.

TRISTAN GEMMILL

Tristan made his mark on the *Street* as Tracy's ex-husband Robert Preston, taking over, in 2015, from actor Julian Kay, who played the role in occasional appearances between 1996 and 2003. During that time, in 2000, Tristan appeared as Leanne's drug counsellor Will Griffiths in two episodes.

LISA GEORGE

As Beth Tinker, Lisa stormed onto the *Street* in 2011 as Steve McDonald's ex. Lisa had trod the cobbles twice before, as a nursing colleague of Martin Platt in 1997 and as a family liaison officer in 2005.

SANDRA GOUGH

Before taking the role of Irma, Stan and Hilda Ogden's daughter and later David Barlow's wife, Sandra appeared in supporting artist roles three times – as an extra from 1961 onwards, and then in two speaking roles in 1963, before starting as Irma in 1964.

STEPHEN HANCOCK

Stephen Hancock's first appearance as Ernest Bishop came in 1967, but the brother of *EastEnders'* Charlie Cotton actor Christopher Hancock had previously appeared in *Coronation Street* twice, as a shop assistant in two episodes in 1961 and as Leonard Swindley's election agent in four episodes late the following year.

GRAEME HAWLEY

Graeme's character John Stape – Fiz's late husband – created repercussions on the Street that are still felt today. His four-year tenure, between 2007 and 2011, was preceded by appearances as a police officer in 1998 and an election candidate in 2001.

MALCOLM HEBDEN

Street favourite Malcolm made Norris Cole a classic *Coronation Street* character, but viewers may remember him from an entirely different role between 1974 and 1975, as Mavis Riley's Spanish love interest Carlos.

GEOFF HINSLIFF

As Don Brennan, Geoff Hinsliff played Ivy Tilsley's second husband from 1987 to 1997. He had appeared in the *Street* in supporting roles in 1963 and 1977.

GEOFFREY HUGHES

Eddie Yeats has to go down in history as one of *Coronation Street*'s favourite characters, but before Geoffrey Hughes made the role his own from 1974 to 1983, he appeared briefly as thug Phil Ferguson in 1967.

SUE JOHNSTON

As Stella Price's mum Gloria, Sue Johnston's time on *Coronation Street* was relatively brief (2012 to 2014), but she made a lasting impression. Sue also appeared in 1982 as a character called Mrs Chadwick.

MAGGIE JONES

As waspish Blanche Hunt in appearances spanning 1974 to 2009, Maggie Jones' key character provided *Coronation Street* with some of the most memorable quotes.

Earlier, in 1961 and 1967, Maggie appeared in two small roles, as a police officer and then a shoplifter named Maggie!

SURANNE JONES

Before Suranne Jones took on the role of Karen McDonald (née Phillips) from 2000 to 2004, she played mechanic Chris Collins' conquest Mandy in 1997.

ALISON KING

Before taking on the – arguably iconic – role of Carla Connor in 2006, Alison appeared in one episode two years earlier as a flirty character called Mrs Fanshaw. Mrs Fanshaw seduced Jason Grimshaw when he and Charlie Stubbs turned up to fit a radiator in her house.

SARAH LANCASHIRE

Sarah's character ditzy Raquel Wolstenhulme is without doubt a *Coronation Street* classic. Her first appearance on *Coronation Street* was in January 1991, but four years previously, in 1987, Sarah had appeared in one episode as nurse Wendy Farmer, a prospective lodger at the Duckworths'.

MICHAEL LE VELL

Michael has played mechanic Kevin Webster since 1983, but he previously appeared as Kabin paperboy Neil Grimshaw in 1981.

MAUREEN LIPMAN

Maureen brought Evelyn Plummer to life in 2018, but in 2002 she was relief Rovers manager Lillian Spencer.

KATHY STAFF

Kathy Staff played Vera Hopkins from 1973 to 1975. She played three small roles before this, as a shop customer, a member of the Mission Hall congregation and an applicant for a caretaker's job at the Community Centre, and was an extra on several occasions in the 1960s.

JILL SUMMERS

Purple-rinsed pensioner Phyllis Pearce was a popular *Street* character from 1982 to 1996. Jill Summers also played cleaner Bessie Proctor in 1972.

WILLIAM TARMEY

Before making the long-running role of Jack Duckworth his own from 1979 to 2010, William had appeared as a Rovers extra many times.

CATHERINE TYLDESLEY

Catherine appeared in one 2006 episode as the midwife who delivered Sunita Alahan's twins. She returned for a seven-year stint as Eva Price in 2011.

BILL WADDINGTON

From 1983 to 1997, Bill Waddington played supercilious pensioner Percy Sugden. The actor had previously appeared in several small parts, including a Rovers customer and a loan shark in the 1970s and, in 1980, as a witness at Emily and Arnold Swain's wedding.

ANDREW WHYMENT

Andrew has delighted *Coronation Street* audiences since 2000 as dopey Kirk Sutherland. He had appeared the previous year as a customer in The Kabin and as an extra on several occasions.

RAQUEL RETURNS

The Street residents mark the millennium with a fancy-dress party. Among the imaginative costumes, Ken dresses as Sherlock Holmes; David is Dracula; Fred is Henry Vlll; Spider and Toyah are Adam and Eve; and Blanche puts in a convincing turn as Carmen Miranda, as Rita relives her singing days with a rendition of 'On the Street Where You Live'. Evil drug dealer Jez Quigley is planning to steal The Rovers' takings and cocaine addict Leanne, dependent on him for her supply, does everything in her power to stop him, even having sex with him. She is injured when the robbery goes ahead after the partygoers leave.

Curly is astounded when Raquel shows up on his doorstep. She tells him about his two-and-a-half-year-old daughter Alice and reveals she is planning to marry her French boyfriend as she is pregnant again. She tells him he can visit Alice whenever he wants and, despite Curly initially hoping to rekindle their relationship, he accepts they can remain friends. Curly grants Raquel's request for a divorce and she leaves the Street for ever.

TEENAGE SARAH HAS A SECRET

Worrying that her daughter is developing an eating disorder, Gail takes 13-year-old Sarah to the GP, who confirms that the schoolgirl is five months pregnant. The father is schoolfriend Neil Fearns. It's too late for an abortion, and Gail and Martin decide Gail should take Sarah to Canada to stay with Gail's brother and then pass the baby off as their own. News of the pregnancy spreads, however, and the family stays in Weatherfield. Martin, who had been having an affair with fellow nurse Rebecca Hopkins, realises he has to stay with Gail and support the family.

Linda gets engaged to Mike but starts an affair with his son Mark.

Kevin Webster and Alison Wakefield get engaged, marrying swiftly later in the month.

A dead body is found in the Victoria Street building site. Natalie Barnes is devastated to discover it belongs to her estranged son Tony Horrocks.

Tony's funeral takes place and Natalie offers a £10,000 reward to bring his killer to justice. Leanne suspects Jez Quigley is responsible.

Street Cars opens, thanks to Steve borrowing £8,000 from Jez Quigley. Eileen Grimshaw is taken on to run the switch.

JAN | FEB | MAR | APR | MAY

2000

The year's second episode is the first-ever two-hander, between Raquel and Curly.

First appearances of biker Dennis Stringer and barmaid Geena Gregory.

Curly meets police sergeant Emma Taylor for the first time.

The Victoria Street set extension is completed, giving the Street three new businesses: Street Cars, Elliott's Butchers and Sally Webster's hardware store.

Steve shops Jez, who is charged by police over Tony's murder.

OCTOBER

RESIDENTS ARE CAUGHT UP IN FRESHCO'S HOLD-UP

Supermarket Freshco (formerly Firman's Freezers) is targeted by two armed robbers, one of whom is Linda's delinquent brother Dean Sykes. They strike at closing time and several Street residents including Ken, Fred, Curly, Ashley, Mike and Alma are trapped in the store during the hold-up. Ken and Mike are locked in the storeroom and all their old rivalries resurface. Dean holds Curly at knifepoint, demanding cash from the safe. Mike suffers his second heart attack and Ken looks after him as the police surround the store. A scared Dean announces he wants £10,000 for the hostages, Curly nearly manages to disarm him but Dean is shot by police officer Emma, Curly's partner. Dean's accomplice Lenny holds Ashley at gunpoint and Fred offers to take his place. Lenny is disarmed and the hostages freed, but Linda is beside herself when Dean dies in the ambulance. The repercussions of the siege affect Linda, Curly and Emma for months to come.

PRODUCTION NOTE

In the first live episode to be broadcast since 1961, *Coronation Street* marked its 40th anniversary with an hour-long special, complete with an appearance from the Prince of Wales and newsreader Sir Trevor McDonald. Slade frontman Noddy Holder also appeared as Duggie's mate Stan, who delivered the fake notice. The programme followed a screening of the first episode, introduced by William Roache, and began in black and white, with Sarah calling David in to get ready for school, in a nod to that very first episode.

DECEMBER

THE RESIDENTS BATTLE TO SAVE THE COBBLES

The council is planning to resurface Coronation Street, but there's no way the residents are going to lose their cobbles. After weeks of campaigning they organise a demonstration and set up a barricade against the council wagons. Audrey is more bothered about meeting Prince Charles when he visits Weatherfield that day to open the council's new planning office.

With the police about to allow the tarmackers to start their work, Ken and Duggie produce a fake preservation order in the nick of time and the Street's cobbles are saved. Ken leads the celebrations with a toast to Coronation Street: 'It wasn't just the cobbles that got us here all together today, it was a feeling of tradition, of community. And I'm proud of where I come from. I've lived here all my life...'

JUNE — Sarah has her baby, a girl she names Bethany.

Alison Webster kills herself after her newborn baby dies.

JULY — Mike Baldwin suffers a heart attack.

Tyrone proposes to Maria on a trip to Blackpool.

AUG — Jez Quigley is found not guilty of murdering Tony Horrocks. He threatens Steve for giving evidence against him.

Leanne leaves Weatherfield for Australia to get away from Jez, who had got her addicted to drugs.

SEPT — Mike discovers Linda's affair with his son on their wedding day.

Jim McDonald delivers a retributory – and eventually fatal – beating to Jez. Jim hands himself in to the police.

OCT — Fred proposes to Audrey. She accepts but quickly turns him down, leaving him heartbroken.

Martin moves out of the family home when Gail asks for a divorce.

NOV — Jack Duckworth wins £59,000 on an accumulator bet.

Liz remarries Jim in prison.

DEC — Curly and Emma are married.

First appearance of Jason Grimshaw and reappearance of Peter Barlow.

TOYAH'S RAPE HORROR

In 2000 Toyah had befriended a neighbour, Phil Simmonds, when they were evicted from their flats in Arnica Street by landlord Duggie Ferguson. Six months later, they meet up again and Phil is disgusted to find Toyah living and working with Duggie at the Rovers. Toyah is attacked and raped in the ginnel but has no idea who her attacker is. Local men are asked to give DNA samples and for a while suspicion falls on Peter, who refuses to give a sample. Eventually, he is cleared. When Phil visits Toyah and calls out to her while she is in the kitchen, she realises it was him who raped her. He attacks her again, but Peter comes to the rescue. Phil is arrested and charged with rape. He denies it for several months before pleading guilty.

FEBRUARY

SUSAN BARLOW DIES IN A CAR CRASH

The existence of Adam had been kept secret from his father Mike since Susan left Weatherfield in 1987. In January 2001, Susan brings Adam to Weatherfield to meet his family. Dev, feeling sorry for Mike, tells him about his son and Mike demands to see Adam. Susan doesn't want Mike involved in her son's life, and in an attempt to get away from him, is involved in a car crash. Susan is killed and Adam suffers minor injuries. In the custody battle that follows between Ken and Mike, Mike is eventually awarded custody of Adam, who returns to his Scottish boarding school, making several visits to the Street as he grows up. Adam returns to the Street full-time in 2016, having qualified as a solicitor while living in Canada.

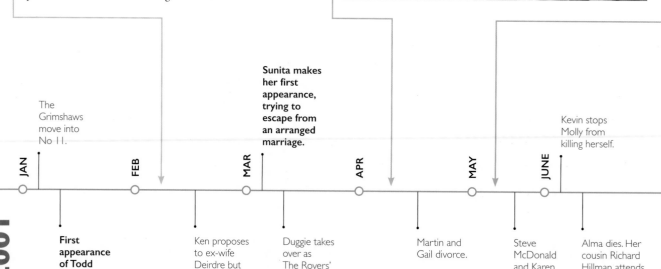

The Grimshaws move into No 11.

Sunita makes her first appearance, trying to escape from an arranged marriage.

Kevin stops Molly from killing herself.

JAN — **FEB** — **MAR** — **APR** — **MAY** — **JUNE**

First appearance of Todd Grimshaw.

Ken proposes to ex-wife Deirdre but she turns him down.

Duggie takes over as The Rovers' landlord.

Martin and Gail divorce.

Steve McDonald and Karen Phillips get married for a bet.

Alma dies. Her cousin Richard Hillman attends her funeral.

MAY

ALMA IS TOLD SHE HAS TERMINAL CERVICAL CANCER

Following a hospital mix-up with smear tests, Alma is told she has a growth that needs further investigation. Soon she is told she has cervical cancer and that it is terminal. She tells close friend Audrey but keeps her diagnosis secret from the rest of the Street. Audrey ends up telling Mike when he comments about Alma's appearance and Mike follows Alma to a hotel in the Lake District. Furious Linda cheats on Mike with one of his clients because he has visited Alma and Mike tells Alma he wants to spend what time she has left together. The cancer affects Alma quickly and she dies in June, with Mike, Audrey and Ken at her bedside.

JULY

ROY AND HAYLEY RUN AWAY WITH WAYNE

After encountering young Wayne Hayes when he tried to steal food from the café, Roy and Hayley took the boy under their wing for a while. They learn that Wayne is being abused by his mother Sheila's partner Alex Swinton, who offers to hand over Wayne for £5000. Roy agrees, but when Alex threatens him for more cash, the Croppers run away with Wayne, sparking a nationwide manhunt. They are captured and Hayley goes to prison after refusing to accept her bail terms. She is released when Sheila finally admits Alex's abuse, confirming the Croppers were trying to protect Wayne. An adult Wayne returns to Coronation Street in 2019, as an accident investigator looking into the factory roof collapse in which Rana Habeeb is killed.

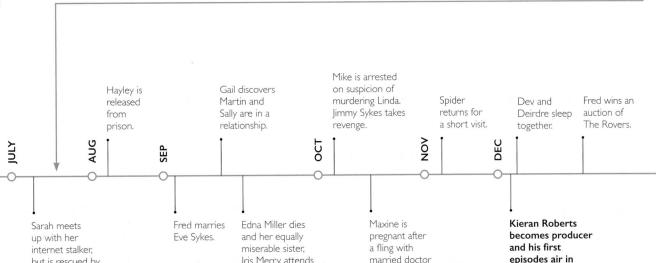

Above the timeline:

Hayley is released from prison.

Gail discovers Martin and Sally are in a relationship.

Mike is arrested on suspicion of murdering Linda. Jimmy Sykes takes revenge.

Spider returns for a short visit.

Dev and Deirdre sleep together.

Fred wins an auction of The Rovers.

Timeline months: JULY · AUG · SEP · OCT · NOV · DEC

Below the timeline:

Sarah meets up with her internet stalker, but is rescued by Dennis Stringer.

Fred marries Eve Sykes.

Edna Miller dies and her equally miserable sister, Iris Merry, attends her funeral.

Maxine is pregnant after a fling with married doctor Matt Ramsden.

Kieran Roberts becomes producer and his first episodes air in March 2002.

RICHARD HILLMAN SHOWS HIS TRUE COLOURS

With business partner Duggie Ferguson out of the way, Richard Hillman can concentrate on turning their construction company around, but he is still severely in debt. Hillman begins to look to the residents of Coronation Street as the answer to his cashflow problems – after all, they've been coming to him for financial advice. He persuades Emily to sign up to an equity-release scheme and cons Jack and Vera's life savings – £20,000 – out of them, claiming he'll invest it wisely for them. Hillman and Gail are planning their wedding, but when Hillman's second wife Patricia turns up asking for her rightful share of the business, Hillman kills her by hitting her over the head with a shovel and she is buried in the foundations at the new flats. Hillman later goes on to identify another body as Patricia's and, convinced he's got away with the murder, goes ahead and marries poor, unsuspecting Gail.

MARCH

CHARLIE RAMSDEN ABORTS HER BABY

Matt and Charlie Ramsden rented No 6 Coronation Street in 2000, when GP Matt began work at the new Rosamund Street Medical Centre. Charlie was a teacher at Weatherfield Comp. Charlie doesn't want children of her own and when, in March 2002, she discovers she is pregnant and has an abortion, Matt is very upset. But Matt has had a drunken one-night stand with Maxine Peacock – ironically he'd been helping Maxine and husband Ashley with their fertility problems – and she becomes pregnant but doesn't know whether the father is Matt or Ashley. Following her abortion, Charlie is sacked for being drunk in the classroom and discovers Matt has slept with Maxine. Matt forces Maxine to tell Ashley the truth and Maxine goes into labour six weeks early. Matt and Charlie leave the area and Ashley has trouble bonding with baby Joshua. He demands a paternity test, but later decides he will raise the child as his own. It's only when Maxine is murdered the following year that he discovers Joshua is not his, but he loves and raises him as his own. Matt returns to the Street in 2006, his marriage to Charlie over for good, but agrees that his son should stay with Ashley and his new wife, former nanny Claire.

Dennis Stringer is killed in a car crash involving Les Battersby.

Duggie Ferguson falls to his death in front of Richard Hillman.

Eve Elliott is exposed as a bigamist.

Roy is arrested for brandishing his replica musket ahead of the Street's historical re-enactment of a Civil War battle on the Red Rec.

JAN

FEB

MAR

APR

MAY

JUNE

Gail gets engaged to Richard Hillman.

First appearance of Archie Shuttleworth, boyfriend of Blanche Hunt.

Rita, Emily, Blanche and Betty are held up on a day out in the country.

Fiz performs a topless protest at losing her Underworld job.

Geena breaks off her engagement to Dev after discovering he slept with Deirdre.

First appearance of Joe Carter.

The programme marks the Queen's Golden Jubilee.

JUNE

BET LYNCH IS BACK

Bet left Weatherfield in 1995, when she quietly looked around an empty Rovers and took a taxi into the night. Seven years later she makes her comeback, at Betty's retirement party. She reveals she has settled in Brighton with Alec's granddaughter Vicky. Celebrating with Betty isn't the only reason The Rovers' best-remembered barmaid has strutted back over the cobbles, however – she's there to testify against former lover Phil Bennett, who stole money from her. Her prickly relationship with Rita continues as they attempt to mend bridges, with both women not shy in telling the other just what she thinks of her. Bet leaves at the end of the month after losing the court case. She meets up with Liz McDonald at a Newton and Ridley function in Blackpool the following year.

DECEMBER

TOXIC TRACY RETURNS TO THE STREET

Tracy left Weatherfield to live in London after marrying Robert Preston, but true to form they split up after she cheated on him. She arrives back in Coronation Street after six years away and seduces Dev almost instantly. Deirdre discovers they are having a relationship when Tracy introduces Dev to her mum in the Corner Shop. Furious Deirdre does her best to split them up, even contacting Robert. When Tracy learns from Sunita that her mother has slept with Dev previously, she forces her to admit all to Ken. Ken forgives Deirdre, but Deirdre throws Tracy out and she moves in with Dev. Tracy is really hoping for a proposal from Dev but when she hears he has described her as 'not marriage material' she takes revenge by cutting up his clothes and maxing out his credit card, before setting her sights on her next conquest, Steve McDonald…

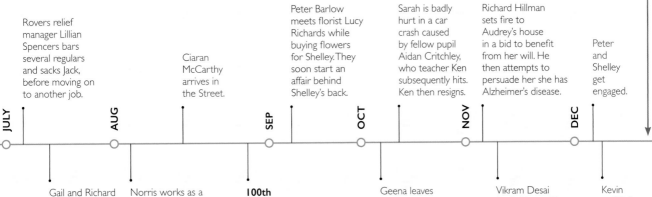

Rovers relief manager Lillian Spencers bars several regulars and sacks Jack, before moving on to another job.

Ciaran McCarthy arrives in the Street.

Peter Barlow meets florist Lucy Richards while buying flowers for Shelley. They soon start an affair behind Shelley's back.

Sarah is badly hurt in a car crash caused by fellow pupil Aidan Critchley, who teacher Ken subsequently hits. Ken then resigns.

Richard Hillman sets fire to Audrey's house in a bid to benefit from her will. He then attempts to persuade her she has Alzheimer's disease.

Peter and Shelley get engaged.

JULY — AUG — SEP — OCT — NOV — DEC

Gail and Richard Hillman marry. Nick Tilsley returns after three years for the wedding.

Norris works as a volunteer for the Commonwealth Games taking place in Manchester.

100th anniversary of The Rovers.

Geena leaves the Street after the end of a relationship with Joe Carter.

Vikram Desai feeds his gambling addiction with Street Cars takings.

Kevin and Sally remarry.

MAXINE DIES AT HILLMAN'S HANDS

Hillman needs money desperately and believes he has no option but to do away with Emily in order to get his hands on the equity she signed over to his dodgy business. He attacks Emily as she's babysitting for Ashley and Maxine, and when Maxine walks in on the scene of the attack, he murders her with a crowbar. Emily survives the attack, but has no memory of who her assailant was. Hillman succeeds in framing young Aidan Critchley and goes on to deliver a moving speech at Maxine's funeral. Audrey and Norris suspect he's guilty and, across Maxine's grave, Audrey emotionally accuses him of killing the young mum. The following month he confesses all to Gail.

JANUARY

MARIA SLEEPS WITH TOYAH'S BOYFRIEND

Toyah started to see her college lecturer in December 2002. When her flatmates Fiz and Maria meet John they are surprised to see that, at 35, he is much older than Toyah. There's a spark between John and Maria and in the New Year they give in to their feelings and sleep together. Maria is guilt-ridden, especially when Fiz works out what has gone on. Maria discovers she is pregnant and John accuses her of sleeping around. Toyah is still blissfully unaware that her boyfriend has cheated on her with her best friend and supports Maria through her subsequent abortion. Toyah can't understand why Fiz is not equally supportive and why she is rude to her boyfriend. An angry Fiz tells Toyah the truth and when Toyah accuses John of forcing himself on her friend, recalling her own rape at the hands of Phil Simmonds, she leaves Weatherfield with her ex Spider, and Maria suffers the wrath of Fiz and Toyah's mum Janice for months to come.

Toyah finds out about John and Maria and confronts him at college. Later she leaves the Street for London with former boyfriend Spider.

Richard Hillman reappears and drives the Platt family into the Weatherfield Canal (see In the Scene pages 242–43).

Ashley interviews Claire Casey as nanny for Joshua.

Vera thinks she's won a dream house – it's a greenhouse. Jack is later arrested on suspicion of growing cannabis in it.

Todd Grimshaw decides to stay at home with Sarah rather than go to university.

JAN   FEB   MAR   APR   MAY   JUNE

2003

Tests show Joshua is not Ashley's son, but Matt Ramsden's.

Peter secretly marries Lucy, while Shelley is burying her sister. Lucy leaves him when she realises he is still with Shelley.

Steve has a fling and Karen kicks him out when she finds a blonde hair in their bed.

***Coronation Street* wins a BAFTA – its third.**

Les is jailed after being framed for assault by Janice's police officer boyfriend Mick.

Martin kisses 16-year-old Katy Harris. She later moves in with him to the anger of her dad Tommy.

JULY

TRACY LURES ROY CROPPER INTO BED – FOR A BET

Stung by Steve's rejection of her following their one-night stand, Tracy tells Shelley's mum Bev Unwin that she can have any man she chooses, and bets with her that she can lure the unlikely Roy Cropper into bed. At brother Peter's wedding to Shelley she drugs Roy and when he wakes up in her bed he believes they slept together and is horrified. The following month Tracy discovers she's pregnant. She plans to have an abortion, but a confrontation with Hayley sees her offer the baby to the Croppers – for £20,000. The Croppers insist she marries Roy, who had attempted suicide in the wake of Tracy's revelations, in order that he has parental rights, and Tracy agrees. Later she tells Steve that he is the father, but he is not interested and insists she goes ahead with her deal with the Croppers. After the baby is born and handed over to the Croppers, who name her Patience, Steve goes on to marry Karen in a ceremony marred by drama as Tracy reveals he is the father of her baby. Tracy decides to raise the child herself, takes her back from the Croppers and changes her name to Amy.

SEPTEMBER

SHELLEY DISCOVERS PETER'S BETRAYAL

Peter Barlow met pretty florist Lucy when he was buying flowers for fiancée Shelley. Peter and Shelley had been going out for a year and were living at The Rovers. Peter kept trying to end things with Shelley but kept losing his nerve, especially when Shelley's sister Sharon died. He was in love with both women and married Lucy on the day of Sharon's funeral. He lives a double life for a while, but when pregnant Lucy discovers Peter is still with Shelley, she kicks him out. Still married to Lucy, Peter bigamously marries Shelley just after Lucy's baby Simon is born and, in September, Lucy announces to Shelley and a packed Rovers that Peter is still married to her and they have just had a baby. A stunned Shelley ends things with Peter for good. Her next relationship is with Charlie Stubbs and life goes from bad to worse for trusting Shelley.

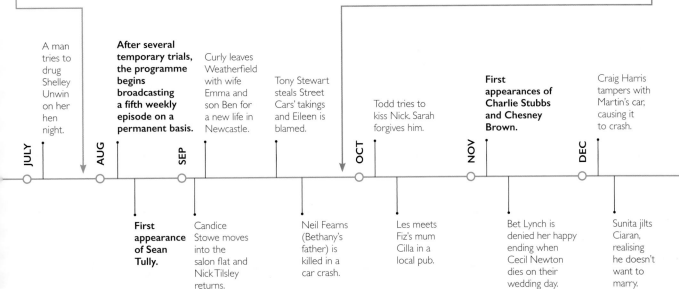

A man tries to drug Shelley Unwin on her hen night.

After several temporary trials, the programme begins broadcasting a fifth weekly episode on a permanent basis.

Curly leaves Weatherfield with wife Emma and son Ben for a new life in Newcastle.

Tony Stewart steals Street Cars' takings and Eileen is blamed.

Todd tries to kiss Nick. Sarah forgives him.

First appearances of Charlie Stubbs and Chesney Brown.

Craig Harris tampers with Martin's car, causing it to crash.

JULY   **AUG**   **SEP**   **OCT**   **NOV**   **DEC**

First appearance of Sean Tully.

Candice Stowe moves into the salon flat and Nick Tilsley returns.

Neil Fearns (Bethany's father) is killed in a car crash.

Les meets Fiz's mum Cilla in a local pub.

Bet Lynch is denied her happy ending when Cecil Newton dies on their wedding day.

Sunita jilts Ciaran, realising he doesn't want to marry.

12TH MARCH 2003

AS the culmination of *Coronation Street*'s long-running storylines become more dramatic, ever more impressive stunts are required. The 2003 scene where psychopath Richard Hillman drives the Platt family into the Weatherfield Canal in a murder suicide attempt has gone down in *Coronation Street* history as one of the best.

In the scene
Richard Hillman kidnaps the Platts

THE SURROUNDING STORYLINE

Gail had become increasingly suspicious of Richard following the death of his ex-wife Patricia and the murder of Maxine. She had confronted him and Richard admitted everything to her, leading shocked Gail to accuse him of being 'Norman Bates with a briefcase'. Richard fled but two weeks later returned with a sick plan to be with Gail forever.

THE MAIN EVENT

Richard lies in wait at the Platts' house and ties up David and then Sarah. When Gail arrives home to find him in her house and no sign of the children, she becomes frantic. Richard announces they are all going to be together and when Gail sees the children bound and gagged in the back of the car, together with baby Bethany, she realises Richard is planning to kill them all.

With the garage doors closed, he forces Gail into the passenger seat and takes the wheel, revving the engine maniacally, in order to gas them all. Audrey hears the noise and alerts Kevin and Martin. Kevin forces open the garage doors and the car speeds out. Richard drives his petrified step-family through the darkened streets of Weatherfield to the soundtrack of The Wannadies' 'You and Me Song' (which adds a grim humour to the terrifying scenes). David and Sarah manage to free themselves from the tape binding their wrists just as Richard, screaming 'I love you' drives the car into the canal. It quickly sinks as Martin, Kevin and Tommy, who have been pursuing the kidnapped family, arrive on the scene.

Tommy bravely dives into the canal and rescues the children before going back for Gail. As Richard clutches at Gail's ankle, Tommy pulls her free and drags her to safety.

As Gail and the children look on, Tommy returns for Richard, but he has vanished. His body is found later, but for a short time the family fear he has escaped.

The shocking crash and the subsequent underwater scenes were praised by fans and critics alike.

Helen Worth remembers having to learn to swim especially for the scene. 'I didn't swim, I still don't, so it was quite hard for me. I had to learn to swim for a few weeks – I've never done it since! I had to learn to breathe underwater.

'It was so exciting filming that scene. We all stood on the sidelines and watched the vehicle go in. It was a rocket that took

it up into the air! And then it cut to us inside.'

The underwater scenes of the family escaping were filmed in a special tank. 'I remember the countdown – three, two, one. I learned to open my eyes underwater, I found that quite easy actually, which surprised me. Even the babies, who were twins, loved it. They went under the water and came up giggling.'

Helen adds that the response to the Richard Hillman storyline was phenomenal. 'Brian (Capron who played Hillman) was absolutely adored. He played the part so brilliantly, with such humour. That part wouldn't have worked half as well if he didn't bring the humour to it. And I think more than 17 million viewers watched the episode where the car plunged into the canal.'

THE AFTERMATH

When Richard's body is retrieved from the canal, Gail, supported by Audrey, confirms it is him, and after the body bag is zipped up Gail throws her wedding ring into the canal. At Richard's cremation at the end of the month, Gail is the only person in attendance – she needs to ensure her villainous husband is gone for good. Aidan Critchley, exonerated of involvement in Maxine's murder after Richard tried to frame him, gives Ken a copy of *Crime and Punishment* to thank him for his support.

PRODUCTION NOTES

Coronation Street's senior location manager John Friend Newman describes how the spectacular scene was brought from the initial idea to the screen: 'The Richard Hillman canal plunge took me three months to plan. I had a big silver Galaxy at that point and [producer] Kieran Roberts got into it and asked if I could make it sink.

'When it came to picking the location for the canal scene, we had to find a section where there were no houses around as we were filming at night and we didn't want to keep people awake. It also had to be a position where you can believe people could drown, but where you can also rescue people from the side of the bank so the gap can't be too big.

'Designer Julian Perkins really helped out – a Ford Galaxy is, I think, 5'3" high and a canal is 4'9" deep, meaning the vehicle couldn't sink, so we cut it in half! The first Galaxy went into the water, then we pulled that one out and dropped a half one in. I believe we bought seven Galaxies and broke five!'

And first assistant director Billie Williams describes how the crew had fun at popular actor Brian Capron's expense during the shoots. 'Brian was renowned for being extremely fussy about his hair and the crew used to take the mick and call for the hairspray tanker to be brought to set before every take. He also never stopped talking, right up until I shouted action. We managed to get our own back when filming the underwater sequences in a tank. For the first time Brian couldn't talk and couldn't fuss about his hair. Revenge was sweet…!'

Brian Capron won Best Actor, Best Exit and Villain of the Year at the British Soap Awards in 2003.

JANUARY

BETHANY IS IN MORTAL DANGER

The father of Sarah's daughter Bethany, schoolboy Neil Fearns, died in a car crash in September 2003. Sarah took Bethany to his funeral where she met Neil's mother Brenda. Brenda is allowed to visit Bethany often, but by January she has become mentally unstable, finding comfort from her grief in religion. She begins taking Bethany to Neil's grave and referring to her as her own daughter. Sarah is worried and bans Brenda from seeing Bethany, but Brenda collects her from nursery and disappears. They are found in the bell tower at St Saviour's Church by Emily, and it's clear Brenda, quoting from the Bible, is planning to jump. She thinks Sarah is evil for getting pregnant again and tells Bethany her mother won't want her when the new baby comes. Emily manages to talk her down, reminding her of the commandment 'Thou shalt not kill', as Sarah screams in anguish below. Bethany is reunited with Sarah and Todd, and Brenda is taken away in an ambulance sobbing. Soon afterwards, Todd asks Sarah to marry him.

MAY

GAIL AND EILEEN FIGHT IN THE STREET

Young couple Todd and Sarah are planning their wedding. Sarah is pregnant with Todd's baby, but Todd begins to question his sexuality. He becomes attracted to a nurse called Karl, who is openly gay. They begin an affair and Karl gives Todd an ultimatum – it's Sarah or him. Todd is torn, but after Audrey offers to pay for the wedding and they visit the church, he admits to Sarah that he can't go through with it because he's gay. Sarah is upset and furious and tells Todd he'll have nothing to do with their baby. When Gail finds out she marches over to No 11 and she and Eileen brawl on the street. Soon Sarah goes into premature labour, but baby Billy dies shortly after he is born. Todd is destroyed and the Grimshaws face the wrath of the Platts. Eileen declares she is proud of her son and eventually Jason, who at first was horrified to learn his brother's secret, accepts Todd's sexuality. Todd moves away to London after finding Sarah and Jason in bed together.

Rita spends a night in jail for contempt of court after being charged with assault for clipping Chesney round the ear in The Kabin.

Nick saves Janice from a fire in Underworld.

Todd tells Eileen he is gay, admitting this to Sarah the following month.

For the first time, three episodes are shown on the same day, due to screenings of Euro 2004.

Sarah and Todd's newborn son Billy dies.

JAN   FEB   MAR   APR   MAY   JUNE

Eric Gartside takes Shelley on a date.

Tracy gives birth to Amy, sells her to the Croppers, then tries to ruin Steve and Karen's wedding.

Kieran Roberts' last episode as producer. He is replaced by Tony Wood.

Penny King turns down Fred Elliott's marriage proposal.

Fred is conned into buying a Thai bride, Orchid Pattaya.

Charlie is annoyed with Shelley and sleeps with her mother Bev.

NOVEMBER

MAYA TAKES HER REVENGE

Solicitor Maya Sharma first appeared on the Street advising Roy and Hayley over their bid to raise baby Amy, but soon became obsessed with Dev. She was an erratic character and displayed signs of becoming increasingly unbalanced. When Dev's ex-girlfriend Sunita was diagnosed with a brain tumour, Dev realised he wanted to be with her and ended his engagement to Maya. Maya started marrying illegal immigrants for money in Sunita's name, and on Dev and Sunita's wedding day, they were both arrested for marrying illegally. Dev confronted Maya who was arrested for bigamy and assisting illegal immigration. She is released on bail and by November has plotted her revenge – she plans to burn down all seven of Dev's shops. She takes Sunita and Dev hostage, tying them up in the Corner Shop flat and sets the shop alight. She watches furiously from her car as they are rescued by Ciaran and Charlie and, maddened, drives straight at them. She misses them, crashing into the viaduct and then, as she starts her car again to have a second attempt, a lorry smashes into it. Maya survives and after leaving intensive care is taken back to jail.

DECEMBER

KAREN LEAVES THE STREET

Karen and Steve had been delighted when Karen became pregnant – Tracy had been calling her 'barren Karen' and using baby Amy to drive a wedge between Steve and Karen. Just before Christmas, however, Karen suffers a miscarriage. She blames herself and is emotionally shattered. Tracy decides she is going to spend Christmas with Peter in Portsmouth, but as she is about to leave, Karen steals her car with baby Amy in the back and drives off erratically. Tracy is horrified and Steve phones Karen, who hadn't realised the baby was in the vehicle. When Steve and Tracy track her down to the Red Rec, Karen has set light to the people carrier and they are convinced Amy is in the burning car. A demented Tracy chases Karen in Steve's car and tries to run her over. Karen escapes into the factory, pursued by Tracy, and the pair fight on the roof. It's only when Steve brings Roy, who has baby Amy, to the factory to show Tracy she's alive that she lets Karen go. She gathers Amy in her arms and returns to No 1. Steve tells Karen it's over and Karen leaves Weatherfield for good.

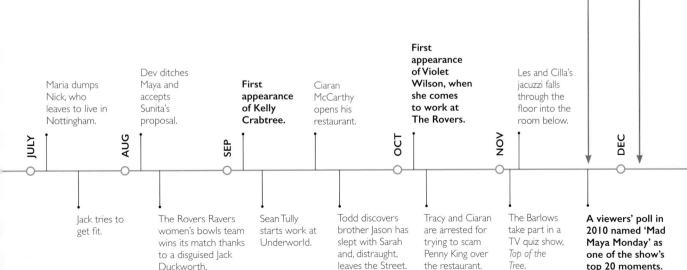

Maria dumps Nick, who leaves to live in Nottingham.

Dev ditches Maya and accepts Sunita's proposal.

First appearance of Kelly Crabtree.

Ciaran McCarthy opens his restaurant.

First appearance of Violet Wilson, when she comes to work at The Rovers.

Les and Cilla's jacuzzi falls through the floor into the room below.

JULY   **AUG**   **SEP**   **OCT**   **NOV**   **DEC**

Jack tries to get fit.

The Rovers Ravers women's bowls team wins its match thanks to a disguised Jack Duckworth.

Sean Tully starts work at Underworld.

Todd discovers brother Jason has slept with Sarah and, distraught, leaves the Street.

Tracy and Ciaran are arrested for trying to scam Penny King over the restaurant.

The Barlows take part in a TV quiz show, *Top of the Tree.*

A viewers' poll in 2010 named 'Mad Maya Monday' as one of the show's top 20 moments.

KATY MURDERS HER FATHER

The Harrises moved into Coronation Street from Sheffield under a witness protection programme after mum Angela witnessed a murder. Tommy got a job in Kevin's garage and Angela found work in the factory. Their daughter Katy discovered she was diabetic, and when nurse Martin helped her to learn how to administer her insulin injections, they fell for each other. Tommy is furious that Martin, 20 years older than Katy, is seeing his daughter. When Katy becomes pregnant Tommy and Angela are unhappy. They mistakenly believe Martin is having an affair with Sally and tell Katy, who as an abortion. When her parents realise their mistake and tell Katy, she confronts Tommy in the garage, having been dumped by Martin, and, as he continues to insult Martin, Katy snaps and hits him across the head with a wrench. Tommy dies and Angela takes the blame to protect her daughter. While she is on remand, her diabetic daughter kills herself by taking a lethal drink of sugar and water. Her suicide note exonerates her mother, but Angela is still jailed for assisting an offender.

JANUARY

SALLY BEGINS AN AFFAIR WITH HER BOSS

The Websters met Ian and Justine Davenport because their daughters Rosie and Gemma were friends at Oakhill School. Ian offers Kevin the chance to run a car dealership, and when Kevin refuses, Ian offers Sally a job as his office manager. Soon Ian declares he is falling for Sally and when she turns him down he tells her she must leave the job. Eventually, Sally succumbs to Ian's charms and they begin an affair after she tells him she only remarried Kevin for the girls' sake. Sally confesses to Gail about the affair and Kevin mistakenly suspects she is seeing Martin. Ian's former assistant tells Sally that both she and another employee had affairs with Ian and warns Sally that he is a sleazebag. When Sally and Kevin go on holiday, Ian sleeps with temp Lisa, and Sally is aghast when Justine tells her Ian has been seeing Lisa and asks her to keep an eye on him for her. Sally leaves the job and tells Kevin it's because she refused to sleep with Ian. When Kevin confronts him he tells Kevin all about the affair, but Kevin chooses to accept Sally's denials in order to preserve their marriage.

Katy tells Martin she is pregnant; she later has an abortion.

Ken proposes to Deirdre, and after turning him down once, she accepts.

Diggory Compton opens a baker's shop on Victoria Street.

Claire starts work as a bus driver, but runs over Chesney's dog Schmeichel.

Sunita finds out she is pregnant.

JAN · FEB · MAR · APR · MAY · JUNE

Tyrone and Maria get engaged.

Ray Langton returns to Coronation Street. He dies of stomach cancer during Ken and Deirdre's nuptials in April.

Mel Hutchwright cons the book club out of hundreds of pounds before leaving the Street in disgrace.

Carolyn Reynolds leaves as executive producer.

First appearance of Lloyd Mullaney. He soon buys Dev's share of Street Cars.

APRIL

KEN AND DEIRDRE REMARRY

Ken and Deirdre attempt to remarry, but the occasion is cut short when they are called to hospital after a man nearly runs Tracy and baby Amy over. Deirdre is astounded to see the man is Ray Langton, her first husband and Tracy's father. Ray has stomach cancer and wants to get to know his daughter before he dies. His reappearance irks Ken, who is jealous Deirdre is spending time with him. Tracy has a tricky time accepting Ray (until it's revealed he has made her the main beneficiary of his will, but she is annoyed that it probably won't be very much). Ray urges Deirdre not to put off remarrying Ken because of him. She moves an increasingly frail Ray into No 1, much to Ken's chagrin, but he later tells Ray he can stay as long as he wants. Ken and Deirdre remarry. At the reception Ray dances with Tracy but, tired, goes to sit down. He clutches his chest and passes away. Blanche sits down and chats away unaware Ray has passed away. Tracy is genuinely upset that the biological father she knew for such a short time has died.

PRODUCTION NOTE

First assistant director Billie Williams remembers one mishap on Shelley and Charlie's wedding shoot: 'We were using a vintage car to take Charlie and Shelley away from the church and the story was Charlie had kidnapped Shelley and driven her to wasteland. We shot this scene first and hadn't shot any of the wedding or outside the church with the car. Day one of the shoot was Charlie driving onto the wasteland, getting out of the car, slamming the door and leaving Shelley terrified in the back. We rehearsed several times and then went for a take. The rehearsals had gone well, but on the take Bill Ward (Charlie) was so in the moment he drove up, got out of the car, slammed the door and the windows shattered with the force of the door slam. Oops!'

SEPTEMBER

SHELLEY DITCHES CHARLIE AT THE ALTAR

Popular Rovers barmaid turned manageress Shelley Unwin had been emotionally scarred by her annulled marriage to bigamous Peter Barlow, so when she began dating hunky builder Charlie Stubbs, he found it easy to manipulate her in a horrifying show of coercive control. Charlie didn't physically abuse Shelley, apart from one occasion where he ripped her earrings out, but he cheated on her with her own mother Bev, humiliated her and isolated her from her friends. He made her overly conscious of her weight, and eventually Shelley retreated into herself, refusing to leave her bedroom. Ironically, Charlie hires a psychologist to help Shelley when they get engaged, but this gives her the confidence to announce at the altar, in front of the entire congregation, that no, she won't marry Charlie – who had slept with a woman he picked up on his stag night – after all. Furious Charlie then kidnaps Shelley and drives her away in the wedding car, but she eventually walks away.

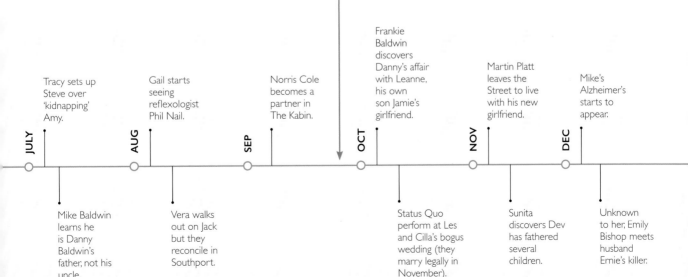

Tracy sets up Steve over 'kidnapping' Amy.

JULY

Mike Baldwin learns he is Danny Baldwin's father, not his uncle.

Gail starts seeing reflexologist Phil Nail.

AUG

Vera walks out on Jack but they reconcile in Southport.

Norris Cole becomes a partner in The Kabin.

SEP

Frankie Baldwin discovers Danny's affair with Leanne, his own son Jamie's girlfriend.

OCT

Status Quo perform at Les and Cilla's bogus wedding (they marry legally in November).

Martin Platt leaves the Street to live with his new girlfriend.

NOV

Sunita discovers Dev has fathered several children.

Mike's Alzheimer's starts to appear.

DEC

Unknown to her, Emily Bishop meets husband Ernie's killer.

MAY

GAIL DISCOVERS DAVID'S DECEIT

It's three years since Gail identified murdering ex-hubby Richard Hillman's body after it was dragged from the canal following his attempt to drown Gail and her children, so when she starts to receive cards signed from Richard, it sends her into a worrying downward spiral. Gail had been in a relationship with reflexologist Phil Nail who was particularly interested in Hillman – he wanted to study the case for his criminology degree. David didn't like Phil and was relieved when Gail stopped seeing him. Gail suspects love rival Eileen of sending the malicious cards and David claims he is worried when Gail starts drinking alone in the daytime. When a card arrives with a smear of blood on it, Gail starts to suspect David, who has a cut finger. She sets a trap for him and David is revealed as the culprit. He says he did it because he misses his dad and he wanted Gail to suspect Phil. The police arrest Phil, and Gail, blaming herself and wanting to protect her emotionally damaged son, says nothing. After a change of heart, she admits to the police that David is to blame, but the police take no action and David and his mum begin to repair their relationship.

APRIL

MIKE BALDWIN DIES IN KEN'S ARMS

Mike Baldwin has been showing signs of dementia for several months and has been diagnosed with Alzheimer's disease. As his illness progresses, son Danny and girlfriend Leanne look after him. Initially, Danny is more concerned about getting his hands on the factory, but as Mike becomes increasingly confused Danny feels guilty. Mike finds his way to Doncaster and turns up at son Mark Redman's home, before spending a rainy night in a nearby park. His family find him and bring him home to Weatherfield, but Mike develops pneumonia and is taken to hospital. Again he wanders off and Ken discovers him standing on Coronation Street in the dark in his dressing gown, staring up at the factory. As Ken puts his jacket around Mike's shoulders and tries to usher him indoors, Mike collapses onto the cobbles. Ken urgently calls an ambulance as Mike's confused mind causes him to ask after Alma, his late wife, and then Deirdre, believing he is still in the midst of their affair of more than 20 years ago. He suffers a heart attack and as Ken clutches his former enemy to him, Mike passes away. As old friends Rita and Emily look on, Danny dashes from his car and hugs his father's body.

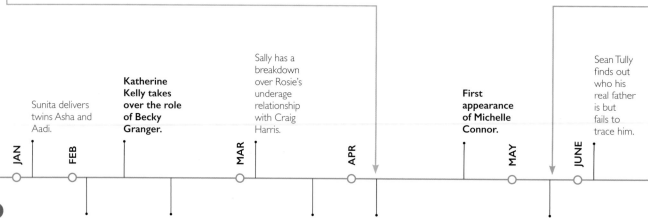

Sunita delivers twins Asha and Aadi.

Katherine Kelly takes over the role of Becky Granger.

Sally has a breakdown over Rosie's underage relationship with Craig Harris.

First appearance of Michelle Connor.

Sean Tully finds out who his real father is but fails to trace him.

JAN | FEB | MAR | APR | MAY | JUNE

Sunita leaves the Street with the twins, ending her marriage to Dev.

Producer Tony Wood's final episode airs. Steve Frost moves from *Emmerdale* to take over, and Kieran Roberts returns as executive producer.

Matt Ramsden demands access to son Joshua Peacock.

The Alzheimer's Society broadcast its first television advert to coincide with Mike Baldwin's diagnosis. *Coronation Street* researchers had worked with the charity on the storyline.

Kelly Crabtree is arrested over thefts committed by friend Becky Granger.

JULY

LEANNE BLACKMAILS DANNY BALDWIN AND LEAVES THE STREET

Leanne's relations with the Baldwin family were complicated – she was seeing Jamie Baldwin but had an affair with Jamie's father Danny. Danny's wife Frankie discovered the affair and Leanne left the Street for a short while. On her return, she and Danny reignited their relationship, which coincided with Mike Baldwin's dementia. Leanne unhappily helped to look after Mike in his final days, but both she and Danny had an eye on Mike's estate. Danny manipulated Mike into leaving everything to him rather than his half brothers Mark and Adam. When Mike dies, Leanne discovers Mike had updated his will and left Adam his fair share. When Danny dumps Leanne, realising he is still in love with Frankie, Leanne exacts her revenge, demanding £100,000 for the will. Despite him eventually bowing to her demands, Leanne gives Adam a copy of the will and disappears off to Spain, leaving the Baldwin boys to fight it out. To add insult to injury, later in the year Frankie and Jamie begin a relationship.

AUGUST

JASON FLEES FROM HIS WEDDING

As if Eileen and Gail's relationship was not tested enough when Todd broke Sarah's heart by admitting he was gay while she was pregnant with his child, the news that Sarah is now seeing Todd's brother Jason shocks both their mothers. Jason had been seeing Violet but ended up proposing to Sarah. Sarah buys a second-hand wedding dress that's too big and Audrey and the factory girls alter the dress for her. Sarah arrives at the register office to discover that cowardly Jason, unable to go ahead with the wedding after all, has disappeared through a toilet window. Sarah is heartbroken but eventually the pair reconcile and marry at Hallowe'en the following year, despite David's attempts to stop the marriage. David and Sarah's relationship goes from bad to worse and she plants drugs on him in order to bag a job in Italy earmarked for him by their uncle Stephen. When Jason finds out, he refuses to go to Milan and Sarah and Bethany leave without him. It is eight years before mother and daughter return to Weatherfield.

JULY — Ashley and Claire Peacock welcome baby Freddie.

Shelley Unwin leaves the Street and Liz McDonald takes over as Rovers manageress.

AUG

SEP — Claire Peacock attacks Hayley while suffering from post-natal depression.

OCT — Fred Elliott dies of a heart attack on the day of his wedding to Bev Unwin.

Maria and Tracy fight over Charlie Stubbs.

Craig Harris leaves the Street.

The Street films on location in Paris for the second time as the Webster family's trip ends in heartache for Rosie.

NOV — Frankie Baldwin has an affair with Danny's son Jamie.

DEC — **First appearance of Carla Connor.**

Frankie and Danny Baldwin separately leave the Street.

JANUARY

TRACY BLUDGEONS CHARLIE STUBBS

Tracy Barlow and Charlie Stubbs had trouble written all over their relationship from the beginning. Both as manipulative as each other, it was never going to end well. Tracy faked a pregnancy, spending the money Charlie gave her for an abortion on shoes. Charlie cheated on Tracy, once with ex Shelley, who became pregnant as a result and vowed as she left the Street that Charlie would never see his child. When Tracy discovered he was seeing Maria they split but Tracy soon exacts her revenge. Persuading Charlie to give things another go, she begins to paint Charlie as an abuser, burning herself with an iron and pretending to her family and neighbours that Charlie is victimising her. Charlie is charged with assault – he attacked Peter, assuming Tracy had picked him up – and he orders Tracy out of his house once and for all. Tracy hits him over the head with an ornament and, cutting herself with a kitchen knife, places it in Charlie's hand. She claims self defence, but when Charlie dies in hospital Tracy is charged with murder to the horror of Deirdre and Ken. She receives a life sentence.

MARCH

CARLA DISCOVERS HUSBAND PAUL'S SECRET

Michelle Connor arrived in Weatherfield with son Ryan in 2006, five years after the death of her partner Dean in a road accident. Michelle was childhood friends with Carla and they became sisters-in-law when Carla married Michelle's brother Paul. Carla and Paul arrived on the Street a few months after Michelle, with Paul buying shares in the factory from a departing Danny Baldwin. Paul is Carla's first husband of four (to date). Paul and Michelle's brother Liam admits to Carla when drunk that he and Paul were responsible for Dean's death. He, Paul and Dean had been out drinking and crashed on the way home. Paul had been driving but had dragged Dean's dead body into the driver's seat to avoid prosecution. Carla is horrified and, when Michelle finds out, she disowns both her brothers. Paul dies later in the year in a car crash after kidnapping Leanne, who has been working as a prostitute he visited and was now seeing his brother Liam.

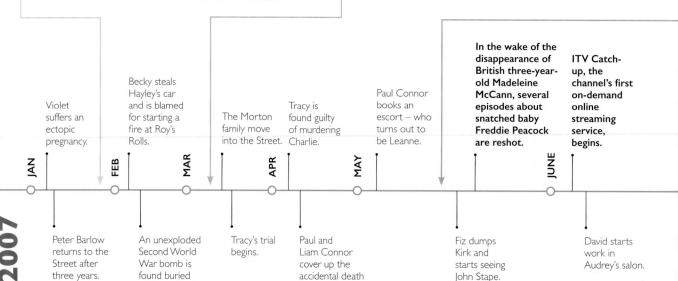

In the wake of the disappearance of British three-year-old Madeleine McCann, several episodes about snatched baby Freddie Peacock are reshot.

ITV Catch-up, the channel's first on-demand online streaming service, begins.

Violet suffers an ectopic pregnancy.

Becky steals Hayley's car and is blamed for starting a fire at Roy's Rolls.

The Morton family move into the Street.

Tracy is found guilty of murdering Charlie.

Paul Connor books an escort – who turns out to be Leanne.

JAN

FEB

MAR

APR

MAY

JUNE

2007

Peter Barlow returns to the Street after three years.

An unexploded Second World War bomb is found buried behind No 4.

Tracy's trial begins.

Paul and Liam Connor cover up the accidental death of a worker in Underworld.

Fiz dumps Kirk and starts seeing John Stape.

David starts work in Audrey's salon.

JACK AND VERA CELEBRATE THEIR GOLDEN WEDDING ANNIVERSARY

Jack and Vera Duckworth have the longest marriage on *Coronation Street* to date. In 2007 they celebrate their golden wedding anniversary with a party in The Rovers, where a tipsy Jack makes a touching speech in which he remembers first seeing Vera when he worked on the fairground waltzers. She was the prettiest girl at the fair, he declares, and sings Frankie Laine's 'I Believe'. Unbeknown to the couple, grandson Paul Clayton commits identity fraud with some of Jack's documents to secure £30k in loans, putting up No 9 as security. When the Duckworths put the house up for sale, Paul is forced to come clean to Jack, who doesn't tell Vera the truth, knowing it would break her heart to hear what her beloved grandson has done. However, the couple can no longer afford their much hoped-for dream retirement home.

LIZ CHEATS ON VERNON AHEAD OF EX JIM'S RETURN

Musician Vernon Tomlin caught Liz's eye in 2005 and he became The Rovers' cellarman the following year, when Liz took over as landlady. By May 2007 Liz, sick of fiancé Vernon's laziness, is enjoying a fling with married drayman Derek. Guilt-ridden Liz admits all to Derek's wife and Derek informs Vernon that Liz cheated on him. Vernon plans to leave, but relents and a wedding is planned for New Year's Eve. By this time, though, Jim McDonald returns to the Street having been released from prison after serving time for manslaughter. He still loves Liz, who has doubts about her feelings for Vernon, and he nearly manages to derail the wedding, beating Vernon up in The Rovers' yard. Liz and Vernon do marry, but it lasts less than a year.

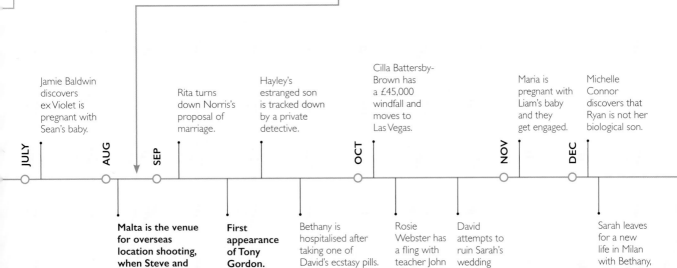

Jamie Baldwin discovers ex Violet is pregnant with Sean's baby.

Rita turns down Norris's proposal of marriage.

Hayley's estranged son is tracked down by a private detective.

Cilla Battersby-Brown has a £45,000 windfall and moves to Las Vegas.

Maria is pregnant with Liam's baby and they get engaged.

Michelle Connor discovers that Ryan is not her biological son.

JULY | AUG | SEP | OCT | NOV | DEC

Malta is the venue for overseas location shooting, when Steve and Eileen enjoy a holiday there.

First appearance of Tony Gordon.

Bethany is hospitalised after taking one of David's ecstasy pills. He is arrested, and thrown out by Gail.

Rosie Webster has a fling with teacher John Stape.

David attempts to ruin Sarah's wedding to Jason.

Sarah leaves for a new life in Milan with Bethany, but without Jason.

MARCH

TINA HAS AN ABORTION AND FURIOUS DAVID TAKES HIS ANGER OUT ON GAIL

When David's first girlfriend Tina discovers she's pregnant she confides in Gail, who thinks David is too immature to deal with it. Gail offers to pay for an abortion and Tina agrees not to tell David. After the abortion, unsuspecting David is cross when Tina says she can't go to a gig with him and he soon finds out what's happened, forcing Gail to come clean. He packs his bags, angrily pushing Gail away, and she falls down the stairs. David flees, but when he sees his mother unconscious in hospital he is guilt-ridden. He forgives Tina and is relieved when Gail regains consciousness and can't remember what happened. After Audrey becomes suspicious, her boyfriend Bill reports David to the police, but Tina lies and gives him an alibi. They soon split up again and Gail confronts David when she regains her memory. He goes on a rampage in the Street, leading him to be sent to a young offenders' institute for four months. On his release, the on-off couple start seeing each other again and David begins working for Tina's father, kitchen fitter Joe McIntyre.

JANUARY

VERA DIES

Vera and Jack's plans to retire to Blackpool are coming to fruition at last and the couple travel to the seaside to see their new house. When they return to Coronation Street, Vera who hasn't been in the best of health, is feeling weary and stays at home while Jack pops to The Rovers. When he comes home he finds Vera asleep in her chair. When he can't wake her up he realises his wife of 50 years has quietly passed away. He can't quite believe it and sits next to Vera singing to her. Later, after Vera's body is taken away by paramedics, Jack steps into his back yard and breaks down. When Terry returns for the funeral he doesn't recognise his own son Paul.

Sunday episodes are dropped in favour of a second Friday instalment.

Liam and Maria marry, despite Liam's feelings for Carla.

David loses it and goes on a rampage before being sent to a young offenders' institute.

The Websters and the Peacocks swap houses.

Michelle's boyfriend Steve and Becky have a one-night stand.

Liz tells Vernon their marriage is over.

JAN　FEB　MAR　APR　MAY　JUNE

Liam has an accident chasing dog Ozzy on a trip to the Lakes with Maria.

A DNA test confirms that Alex Neeson is Michelle's real son.

Violet gives birth to Dylan in The Rovers. Later, Violet and Jamie leave the Street, to Sean's distress.

Maria's baby is stillborn, but she doesn't tell Liam.

Gail meets her father Ted Page for the first time, and learns that Ted is gay.

Carla blackmails Liam over their affair.

SEPTEMBER

JOHN STAPE KIDNAPS ROSIE WEBSTER

Previously a furious Fiz had finished with John Stape when it was
revealed that he was cheating on her with 16-year-old Rosie Webster,
and John left the Street with his tail between his legs. He returns to
Weatherfield in July 2008, still obsessed with Rosie, but now blaming
her irrationally for his troubles. In September he kidnaps Rosie and
keeps her in the attic of his late grandmother's house, cooking up a
story about having to feed his grandma's cat to explain his regular
absences to Fiz with whom he reunited. At first, Kevin and Sally
suspect Rosie is with a boyfriend – especially after Janice and Leanne
pinch the factory workers' Lottery win and blame Rosie – but they
soon become very worried about her. Sophie, feeling neglected, adds
to their ordeal by sending them a postcard saying 'Sophie's next'.
Rosie implores John to free her and only escapes after several weeks
when Fiz, seeing John has forgotten his keys, arrives at the house and
discovers Rosie. John admits everything to his horrified girlfriend and
is arrested and later jailed for two years.

OCTOBER

LIAM CONNOR IS KILLED

Liam's passionate affair with Carla is carrying on, and it is only
a matter of time before Carla's fiancé Tony Gordon takes his
revenge. On his stag night he organises a hit-and-run and Liam, his
best man, is knocked over. As he lies dying on the cobbles, Tony
whispers in his ear that the best man lost and calls him roadkill.

Tony's efforts to get rid of Liam would turn out to be
unnecessary, as he is unaware that Carla had earlier broken Liam's
heart and ended their affair, resolving to marry Tony after learning
Liam's wife Maria is expecting a baby. At the moment of his death,
Maria was on her way to inform Liam of her pregnancy, and in a
grotesque twist, it is Tony who delivers Liam's son the following
year, a boy that grieving Maria names Liam.

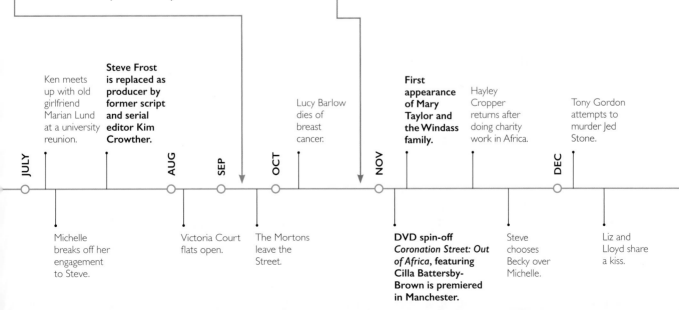

Ken meets
up with old
girlfriend
Marian Lund
at a university
reunion.

**Steve Frost
is replaced as
producer by
former script
and serial
editor Kim
Crowther.**

Lucy Barlow
dies of
breast
cancer.

**First
appearance
of Mary
Taylor and
the Windass
family.**

Hayley
Cropper
returns after
doing charity
work in Africa.

Tony Gordon
attempts to
murder Jed
Stone.

JULY · AUG · SEP · OCT · NOV · DEC

Michelle
breaks off her
engagement
to Steve.

Victoria Court
flats open.

The Mortons
leave the
Street.

**DVD spin-off
*Coronation Street: Out
of Africa*, featuring
Cilla Battersby-
Brown is premiered
in Manchester.**

Steve
chooses
Becky over
Michelle.

Liz and
Lloyd share
a kiss.

MICHELLE DISCOVERS STEVE HAS BEEN CHEATING

Much-married Steve McDonald has always had a problem sticking with one woman, and in 2009 he finds himself going out with Michelle but falling for Becky, with whom he'd previously had a one-night stand. When mum Liz finds out about Steve's dilemma, she urges him to come clean to Michelle. Instead he tells Michelle what she wants to hear, that they'll be together for ever, and then lies to Becky that he's finished with Michelle. He hasn't got the guts to face the wrath of either woman and he really doesn't want to hurt Michelle. When Becky discovers, in The Rovers, that Steve has lied to her she ends it, furious at him. Fed up, Steve suggests to Michelle they should go to Ireland for a break but when Michelle is asked to go on a short tour with a band, Steve urges her to accept. Steve encourages fellow musician JD to make a play for Michelle, hoping to offload her, but she finds out and Lloyd then confirms Steve's infidelity. Michelle and Steve split acrimoniously. Now that Steve's free to be with Becky, he discovers her in bed with Jason and, to add insult to injury, Ryan punches him for his treatment of Michelle.

TONY GORDON ADMITS TO CARLA THAT HE HAD LIAM KILLED

When Tony Gordon arranged the hit-and-run that killed Liam following his discovery of Carla and Liam's affair, he called upon his henchman Jimmy Dockerson to commit the act. Jimmy returns to scare off Jed Stone on Tony's behalf after Jed caused Carla to become suspicious of Tony. She tells him that Liam was everything that Tony is not and that he was the love of her life. Tony admits his part in Liam's death and veers between anger and then pleading with Carla to understand that he did it for her. He tells Carla to kill him because he can't live without her, but a weeping and scared Carla flees Weatherfield and Tony is left alone in the flat. Tony then moves on to romancing Liam's pregnant widow Maria, delivering her baby son and even getting engaged to her. Hearing of these developments, a concerned Carla returns to the Street in a bid to stop Maria marrying her husband's murderer. Tony orders Jimmy to kill Carla, but Carla escapes and flees again. Tony eventually confesses to the police, naming Jimmy as Liam's hitman, and they are finally arrested.

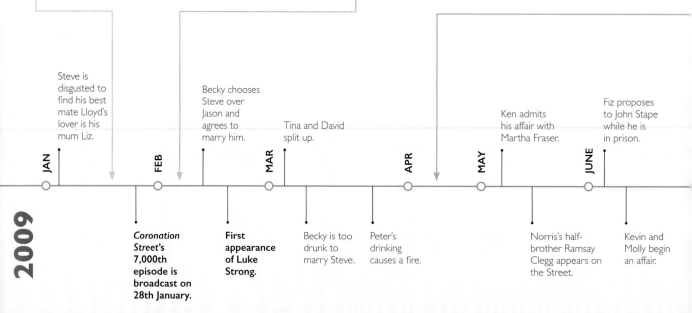

Steve is disgusted to find his best mate Lloyd's lover is his mum Liz.

Becky chooses Steve over Jason and agrees to marry him.

Tina and David split up.

Ken admits his affair with Martha Fraser.

Fiz proposes to John Stape while he is in prison.

JAN FEB MAR APR MAY JUNE

2009

Coronation Street's **7,000th episode is broadcast on 28th January.**

First appearance of Luke Strong.

Becky is too drunk to marry Steve.

Peter's drinking causes a fire.

Norris's half-brother Ramsay Clegg appears on the Street.

Kevin and Molly begin an affair.

EILEEN AND JULIE CARP DISCOVER THEY'RE SISTERS

Eileen's father Colin Grimshaw, with whom she had a distant relationship, has a brief romance with Rita, which results in him proposing to her on his 70th birthday. During the party Julie Carp's mother Paula, Eileen's childhood friend, arrives worried that Julie has slept with Jason. She announces that they are related – because Colin had slept with her when she was 14 and she became pregnant with Julie. Colin's shameful secret is exposed and Rita and his family turn their back on him. When Colin suffers a stroke Eileen refuses to visit him in hospital but reluctantly relents when he is discharged and allows Julie and Jason to nurse him at No 11. Julie is desperate to get to know her father, but when the police arrive, tipped off by an angry Paula, to question Colin over the abuse, he collapses and dies. Eileen and Julie would go on to develop a close sisterly bond.

KEVIN AND MOLLY PREPARE TO LEAVE THEIR SPOUSES

Baker's daughter Molly Compton married Tyrone in January 2009, but her friendship with Tyrone's boss Kevin, forged on the fun runs they took part in, soon turned into a full-blown affair. Although she feels guilty, Molly has grown bored with Tyrone and urges Kevin to leave Sally so they can be together. At Christmas, they plan to tell Tyrone and Sally, but Sally informs Kevin that she has been diagnosed with breast cancer and Kevin knows he cannot leave her now. Molly declares it's unfair and Kevin, astounded at her selfishness, ends the affair. The repercussions last for a long time, though, as Molly goes on to discover she is pregnant and it's not until Kevin organises a secret DNA test the following year that he discovers baby Jack is his.

David is furious when he discovers his ex Tina is seeing Jason.

Becky is arrested on drugs charges on her rescheduled wedding day.

Jack Duckworth moves out of No 9 to live with Connie Rathbone.

Fiz and John Stape marry while he is still in prison.

The final DVD spin-off to date, *Romanian Holiday*, is released. In it Roy, Hayley and Becky visit Bran Castle, colloquially known as Dracula's Castle.

Sally tells Kevin she has breast cancer, scuppering his plans to leave her for Molly.

JULY   AUG   SEP   OCT   NOV   DEC

Maria gives birth to Liam junior. Tony Gordon delivers the baby.

The programme moves from Wednesdays to Thursdays.

Luke finishes with Rosie.

Tony Gordon proposes to Maria.

Joe McIntyre proposes to Gail.

Final appearance of Blanche Hunt (due to the death of actor Maggie Jones).

Becky is pregnant.

IN FOCUS

THE viewers of *Coronation Street,* on whose cobbles evil has regularly stalked, really love their baddies. However, soap law means the bad guy (or girl) always gets their comeuppance in the end.

Villains we love to hate

Remember when evil Alan Bradley tried to suffocate Rita after impersonating her late husband Len in a bid to remortgage her house, before driving her to a breakdown and dying under a Blackpool tram in 1989?

And how murdering psychopath in a suit, Richard Hillman, who killed his ex-wife with a shovel, murdered poor Maxine and attempted to see off Emily and Audrey, drowned when he tried to kill the Platts by driving them into a canal?

Continuing this ignoble tradition, *Coronation Street*'s most recent arch villain has been, without doubt, killer builder Patrick Phelan. Phelan first appeared as a crooked property developer in 2013 and was brought back in 2016 by producer Stuart Blackburn. He blackmailed business partner Owen Armstrong, terrorised Owen's partner Anna, forcing her to sleep with him, and ripped off his neighbours.

'I am the darkness and the light. I'm a creator and a destroyer. I'm the accuser. I'm the prosecutor. I'm the Lord of Hosts. I'm the layer-in-wait. I'm the worst thing you can imagine.' Pat Phelan

After marrying unsuspecting Eileen, sinister Phelan stood smiling over love rival Michael Rodwell as he died of a heart attack. In a shock twist, he held Michael's surrogate son Andy Carver in a cellar for nine months, then forced him to shoot dead his former business partner Vinny. He killed Andy and mechanic Luke Britton.

His dastardly reign of terror ended during a siege in the bistro, when Phelan shot daughter Nicola Rubinstein and Michelle Connor, and he was killed by a vengeful Anna on her return to the Street from prison.

Connor McIntyre, the unassuming actor who played Phelan, says the complicated character was a gift to play. 'I think we got quite close to understanding the complexity of that character,' he says. 'He was a dangerous, psychopathic narcissist. To be given a character like Pat Phelan, a three-dimensional villain, was fantastic.

'The one-dimensional bully thing only lasts for so long, but the writers, once they became intrigued by the character, gave him another side. You'd see him with the kids, with Eileen. He was definitely a wrong 'un – and nuts! – but he made one bad decision after another.'

Connor started acting when he joined the Barbican Theatre in Plymouth, having worked in a variety of jobs and undertaken a degree in fine art as a mature student. He was invited in to watch a rehearsal, and having never been in a theatre before, says it was an epiphany for him. He appeared in several TV roles and was invited back

to *Coronation Street* to resurrect Phelan for one of the most talked-about storylines in recent years. He adds that the first time he had a scene at No 1 with William Roache as Ken, he gave Uncle Albert's sideboard a little rub, for luck.

'The actors we had and the writing and the sets that they built for Phelan and the lighting, which was like a movie for some scenes, were just great. I asked myself, "How can we make this believable?" Because it did stretch credibility.

'I was given such opportunities with this role. It's an absolute privilege for Phelan to be mentioned alongside Richard Hillman and Alan Bradley, because they really are iconic television villains.'

Connor adds that his mum and dad would have been proud he was in *Coronation Street.* 'No matter what else I go on to do they would have said, "*Coronation Street,* yeah, that's it." Although my mum would have added, "Couldn't they have given you someone nicer to play!"'

Connor was reunited with Les Dennis, who played Michael Rodwell, when they performed in pantomime together after they left *Coronation Street.* They were voted Best Ugly Sisters at the British Pantomime Awards 2018 – the same year Connor was named Villain of the Year – which Connor says they were delighted with.

'Villain and ugly sister of the year,' he laughs. 'What could be better than that?'

WEATHERFIELD'S WORST RESIDENTS

LEWIS ARCHER (Nigel Havers) *Charming conman who ripped off Gail.*

NATHAN CURTIS (Christopher Harper) *Pervert who groomed Bethany.*

JOE DONELLI (Shane Rimmer) *Former GI who killed Steve Tanner and later held Minnie and Stan hostage.*

ROB DONOVAN (Marc Baylis) *Murdered Tina and framed Peter.*

TERRY DUCKWORTH (Nigel Pivaro) *A wrong 'un from childhood who stole from his parents and sold his baby.*

CARMEL FINNAN (Catherine Cusack) *'Nanny from hell' obsessed with Martin.*

FRANK FOSTER (Andrew Lancel) *Assaulted Maria and raped Carla.*

TONY GORDON (Gray O'Brien) *Murdered Liam Connor and tried to drown Roy.*

CAZ HAMMOND (Rhea Bailey) *Stalked and tried to frame Maria for her own murder.*

CLAYTON HIBBS (Callum Harrison) *Murdered Kylie and attempted to kill his mother, Shona.*

JON LINDSAY (Owen Aaronovitch) *Fraudulent 'pilot' who let Deirdre take the rap for his crimes.*

CALLUM LOGAN (Sean Ward) *Violent drug dealer killed by ex Kylie.*

GEOFF METCALFE (Ian Bartholomew) *Yasmeen's abusive husband*

KARL MUNRO (John Michie) *Philandering arsonist who murdered Sunita.*

JEZ QUIGLEY (Lee Boardman) *Drug dealer who killed Tony Horrocks and had Steve beaten up. Died after Jim's revenge attack.*

JADE ROWAN (Lottie Henshall) *Made Fiz and Tyrone's life hell.*

MAYA SHARMA (Sasha Behar) *Lawyer who held ex Dev and wife Sunita hostage and burned down Dev's businesses.*

KIRSTY SOAMES (Natalie Gumede) *Subjected Tyrone to domestic abuse.*

JOHN STAPE (Graeme Hawley) *Killer who kidnapped Rosie Webster.*

CHARLIE STUBBS (Bill Ward) *Mentally abused Shelley Unwin.*

JOSH TUCKER (Ryan Clayton) *Raped David Platt.*

JOE MCINTYRE DIES IN THE LAKE DISTRICT WHILE FAKING HIS OWN DEATH

Joe McIntyre was Gail's fourth husband. They met after the kitchen fitter's daughter Tina began dating Gail's son David. Joe became addicted to painkillers following a back injury and soon found himself spiralling into debt and at the mercy of heartless loan shark Rick Neelan.

Joe bought a boat with the aim of doing it up and selling it for a profit. He named the boat *Gail Force* before proposing to Gail. The couple honeymooned in the Lake District, but Joe was preoccupied with his debt problems and the threats he was receiving from Neelan. He researched life insurance and planned to return to Windermere to fake his own death.

After taking the boat to the Lakes, Joe reveals his plans to Gail. The couple argue on the banks of the lake and Joe sails off on choppy waters, leaving a terrified Gail alone. A strong wind causes

the mast to knock Joe into the water and he is unable to clamber back onto the boat. He perishes in the icy waters and on the day of his wake Gail is arrested and charged with her husband's murder – a couple had heard Gail and Joe arguing in the Lakes on the night of Joe's disappearance and Tina had informed the police that Gail had asked her to lie to them. She is remanded in custody and after a traumatic trial four months later, Gail is found not guilty and returns to the Street.

Sally undergoes successful surgery to treat her breast cancer.

Jason proposes to Tina. She later leaves him after confessing to kissing Nick.

Joe McIntyre and Gail marry.

Gail is arrested for Joe's murder.

JAN

FEB

MAR

2010

Return of Mary Taylor.

Becky tells Steve she's pregnant. She suffers a miscarriage two months later.

Joe's plot was inspired by the real-life case of John Darwin, who faked his own death canoeing off the coast of Hartlepool in 2002.

Kelly Crabtree leaves the Street.

John Stape's criminal record is revealed and he loses his teaching job. He assumes the identity of Colin Fishwick, to acquire another position.

JUNE

TONY GORDON HOLDS CARLA AND HAYLEY HOSTAGE

Psychopath Tony Gordon is serving a prison term for arranging the murder of Liam Connor after discovering Liam and wife Carla's affair. He begins to plan his escape – and plot his revenge on Carla and Roy, who he blames for his downfall.

He pays his ex-cellmate Robbie to hold up an ambulance he is travelling in after faking a heart attack, and heads back to Coronation Street. Robbie takes Carla and Hayley hostage at Underworld but is shot dead by Tony as his support for him wavers. Tony douses the factory in petrol and frees Hayley so he and Carla can die together. As Tony lights a match and the fire begins to take hold, Carla manages to escape. Tony chases her but, deciding he wants to die, turns around and walks back into the burning building, perishing in the subsequent explosion.

APRIL

CORONATION STREET AIRS ITS FIRST LESBIAN KISS

Sian Powers quickly became Sophie's best friend when she started attending Weatherfield High School aged 15. She dates Ryan Connor, but the teens' relationship is up and down and when Ryan makes a clumsy pass at Sophie it ends for good. At first Sian thinks Sophie made a move on Ryan, but when she discovers the truth she apologises to Sophie and the pair kiss. Sian is unsure about her feelings for Sophie at first, but eventually the pair begin secretly dating.

APR

Rita and Audrey fight over Lewis Archer.

Peter and Leanne get engaged.

MAY

Blanche Hunt passes away while in Portugal. Tracy is allowed out of jail to attend the funeral.

The programme is shown daily at 9pm in between *Britain's Got Talent* for the first time.

JUNE

The programme is broadcast in high definition for the first time.

Gail's trial begins.

AUGUST

ROY AND HAYLEY MARRY

Roy and transgender Hayley had been married by a progressive vicar in 1999, but their union was not recognised by UK law at that time. After the law changes and two months from when Roy feared Hayley was going to die at the hands of Tony Gordon, Hayley legally becomes Mrs Cropper. Steam train enthusiast Roy is delighted that his transport to the wedding is a classic locomotive – and he's allowed to drive it. The wedding party boards the train with the bride and her bridesmaids, Fiz and Becky, in the final carriage. Mary, highly put out because she wasn't allowed to be the wedding planner and didn't receive an invitation to the service, uncouples the carriage and as the rest of the train heads off into the distance, the bridesmaids resort to using a manual pump wagon to get Hayley to the venue. They end up a little bedraggled but happily the service goes ahead.

Phil Collinson takes over from Kim Crowther as producer. Collinson had actually appeared in the programme in one episode in 1997.

Fraudster Lewis Archer leaves the Street with illicit winnings from Barlow's Bookies.

Nick dumps Natasha, then relents when she reveals she's pregnant. She has had an abortion but doesn't tell Nick.

Sophie and Sian's relationship is revealed.

Molly Dobbs gives birth to son Jack.

JULY

AUG

SEP

2010

Tina moves in with Rita after Jason throws her out, annoyed at her relationship with Graeme Proctor.

The real Colin Fishwick is killed.

Owen Armstrong buys the builder's yard from Bill Webster.

First appearance of Kylie Turner.

A letter from Ken's first girlfriend is discovered, which reveals he has another son, Lawrence.

Gail tells Nick the truth about girlfriend Natasha's abortion.

TRACY RETURNS TO THE STREET

Tracy was jailed for life in 2007 for the murder of Charlie Stubbs. In December 2010 a forensics expert involved in her trial is exposed as a fraud and Tracy is released pending a retrial. She returns to the Street on Christmas Eve, blackmails Steve and Becky over the buying of young Max, gains custody of Amy, and sleeps with both David and his half-brother Nick within days of each other in order to humiliate Gail. She taunts Becky over her inability to have a baby and also falls out with Claire after mocking tram crash victim Ashley. Tracy is badly beaten and taken to hospital where she informs detectives that Becky was her assailant. The real attacker was Claire who, aided by friends, leaves the country with her sons to escape the law. When Tracy leaves hospital, her conviction for Charlie's murder is officially quashed.

NOVEMBER

JACK DUCKWORTH DIES

Two years after the death of his wife of 50 years, Vera, Jack returns to Weatherfield from Middleton where he had enjoyed a short companionship with a fellow pigeon fancier named Connie. He informs Tyrone that he has non-Hodgkin's lymphoma and not long left to live. Jack spends his last few weeks carrying out anonymous acts of kindness for his neighbours and advises Molly on her relationship with Tyrone following her affair with Kevin. Knowing it will be his last, Tyrone organises a birthday party for Jack in The Rovers. As Ken raises a glass to him, Jack slips off back to the house and falls asleep, dreaming of dancing with his beloved Vera. Tyrone and Molly return later to find he has passed away in his chair.

OCT

Jack Duckworth reveals to Tyrone that he has only weeks to live.

David blacks out at the wheel and runs over Graeme. He is diagnosed with a form of epilepsy.

Kylie offers to sell son Max to sister Becky for £20,000.

NOV

Kevin finds out he is Jack's dad.

The Joinery bar opens. Nick and Leanne sleep together.

Elizabeth Dawn, who played Vera, had retired from the show in 2008, however, she was happy to return to film the touching dance scene in 2010.

DEC

50th anniversary tram crash and live episode (see In the Scene, pages 262–63).

Tyrone hands over baby Jack to Kevin.

9TH DECEMBER 2010

AS part of a full week of episodes to mark *Coronation Street*'s milestone 50th anniversary, a special hour-long live episode was broadcast on 9th December, exactly 50 years after the first-ever episode, which was also shown that night. The storyline mirrored the train crash of 1967 and contained spectacular CGI and special effects. The episode was subtitled *Four Funerals and a Wedding*, leading to fevered speculation in the press and online ahead of transmission, over which characters would lose their lives.

In the scene
50th anniversary tram crash

Becky and Steve row with hard-faced Kylie. She demands a further £5,000 from them or she will keep Max.

Meanwhile, the explosion causes Gary, suffering from post-traumatic stress disorder, to suffer flashbacks to his time in the army in Afghanistan. He hides out in No 6 where mum Anna finds him.

Baby Jack is rescued and rushed to hospital, where he needs a blood transfusion. Kevin tells the medics that he is Jack's real father but Tyrone is still unaware. Sally comforts trapped Molly as her life ebbs away and with her dying breath Molly tells her Kevin is Jack's real dad. She pleads with Sally not to hate them.

THE MAIN EVENT
The explosion has damaged the rail tracks overhead and a tram dramatically derails, crashing into the Corner Shop and injuring Sunita, Molly and baby Jack. After a moment of suspense, a rear tram carriage smashes down onto The Kabin opposite and Rita is crushed beneath falling shelving.

No 13, next to the Corner Shop, sets alight and, with the emergency services held up in a nearby traffic accident, Lloyd manages to rescue Claire and sons Freddie and Joshua and their friend Russ, and Simon Barlow is saved by Jason.

Pregnant Fiz goes into early labour and is rushed to hospital, fearing her baby will die. John is forced to go with her, leaving Charlotte inside No 5.

Ashley helps Nick to pull unconscious Peter out of danger, but falling masonry kills him and Claire is beside herself with grief when Audrey breaks the awful news to her.

THE SURROUNDING STORYLINES

Peter's stag do Nick has been having an affair with Peter's fiancée Leanne and intends to tell Peter about it during his stag do at The Joinery, the bar under the viaduct. Over at The Rovers, Leanne's hen party is underway. Just as Nick is about to spill the beans to Peter, a gas leak causes an explosion to rip through The Joinery, and Peter and Nick, together with Ashley, are trapped in the office.

Molly leaves Tyrone Molly told Tyrone she was leaving him and taking baby Jack with her. When he refused to allow her to take Jack away she told him that he wasn't Jack's real dad but refused to reveal who the biological father was. She walked out on devastated Tyrone and headed to the Corner Shop to say her goodbyes.

Max is missing Becky discovered Max had vanished from his bedroom. Becky and Steve had paid Becky's delinquent sister Kylie £20,000 for the boy after failing to conceive.

Charlotte Hoyle's death Charlotte had turned up at No 5 demanding John Stape leave Fiz for her. When he refused she threatened to tell Fiz and tried to attack him with a hammer. John wrestled the hammer from her and hit her as the explosion in The Joinery occurred.

PRODUCTION NOTES

Lot supervisor Andy Ashworth remembers the work that went into filming before and after the live episode. In 2010 he had just been made prop master, so physically everything seen on screen he made sure was correct.

He explains: 'With the tram crash episode, we did that twice because we were filming the aftermath before the live episode.' The actual crash and most of the immediate aftermath was pre-recorded. Then scenes of the Street getting back to normal also had to be filmed prior to the live episode, for which the devastation had to be recreated weeks later.

'I had six skips with various props in them and I had everything planned to go where I needed it. I had hundreds of photos of the crashed tram and The Kabin that I'd taken for continuity purposes,' recalls Andy. 'The day before we were due to film I discovered that skips 2 and 3 were missing. They'd been got rid of because they were thought to be in the way. So within a day I had to buy a new telegraph pole and chop it down because a telegraph pole had come down as the tram came off and track down a load of rubble to use! Then again for continuity purposes, we had to melt snow that had fallen (in the week of the live broadcast). The team effort on that was fantastic because we knew it was going to be such a big thing.'

Actor Paula Lane, who had joined *Coronation Street* to play Kylie shortly before the 2010 live episode agrees. She describes the live instalments she worked on in 2010 and 2015 as 'an adrenaline rush like no other'.

At the British Soap Awards 2011 *Coronation Street*'s anniversary live episode swept the board with gongs for Best Storyline, Spectacular Scene of the Year and Best Single Episode, as well as Lifetime Achievement for Bill Tarmey and five other awards.

John returns to the Street and pulls Charlotte's body from the house, planting her in the rubble to look like a victim of the disaster. He's mortified when a police officer says she's still alive. She later passes away in hospital to John's relief.

An unseen taxi driver is reported to have been killed, bringing the death toll to four. As for the wedding, Leanne is warned that Peter may not pull through and the pair are quickly married in hospital.

Becky uses the chaos caused by the crash to steal cash from the Corner Shop safe, in the hope of paying off her sister.

THE AFTERMATH

Rita is rescued from The Kabin. Premature baby Hope Stape pulls through. Gary feels guilty for not helping in the rescue attempts. Sally struggles to forgive Kevin for his affair with Molly and the pair divorce. Peter recovers slowly and is confined to a wheelchair for several months. He lapses back into alcoholism. Claire eventually leaves for France with Freddie and Joshua.

DENNIS TANNER MAKES A RETURN TO THE STREET

After a 43-year absence, original cheeky bad boy Dennis Tanner returns to Weatherfield. The son of siren Elsie Tanner, Dennis is down on his luck and sleeping rough. When Sophie and Sian volunteer at a local soup kitchen they befriend Dennis and take him for a bite to eat at Roy's Rolls. When Dennis realises it's so close to his childhood home on Coronation Street, he returns that night and is tackled by Rita who, a few days later offers him her sofa to sleep on. It emerges that Dennis is distantly related to Eileen Grimshaw and her half-sister Julie Carp (Elsie's maiden name was Grimshaw). Dennis and Rita grow close once again, much to Norris's chagrin, and go on to marry. The union, however, does not last.

Tracy names Becky as her attacker, before Claire Peacock confesses and flees to France with her sons to escape prosecution.

Eileen takes £10,000 from the builder's yard account. She is arrested the following month, but let off with a caution.

The spin-off, *Ken and Deirdre's Bedtime Stories*, is released online between February and April, and *Just Rosie* is released online in September.

Frank Foster tries to rape Maria.

With Tina's agreement, her boyfriend Graeme Proctor agrees to marry Xin Chiang to help her get a visa. He later falls for her properly.

JAN

FEB

MAR

2011

John Stape suffocates Colin Fishwick's mother, Joy.

First appearance of Faye Butler, the Windasses' foster child.

Tracy's murder conviction is overturned. She tells Peter about Leanne and Nick's affair. Peter demands a divorce at his and Leanne's marriage blessing. They later reconcile.

Planning permission for the new *Coronation Street* site in Trafford is granted.

David's cage dancing holiday fiancée is revealed to be Kylie.

Janice Battersby leaves the Street.

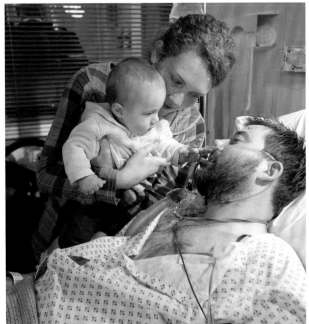

JULY

FIZ IS ARRESTED FOR MURDER

John Stape's third victim was Colin Fishwick's mother Joy, who he befriended through guilt but accidentally killed. After John admitted to stealing Colin's identity and revealed Colin was dead, Joy had an angina attack and, when a nosy neighbour called round, John put his hand over Joy's mouth to prevent her from calling out, accidentally smothering her. Her death was initially treated as natural, but a desperate John then held a suspicious Chesney and Charlotte Hoyle's parents captive and Fiz, who had given birth to their baby Hope, overhears his confession. He tries to snatch Hope then disappears, and Fiz is charged firstly with fraudulently claiming Colin's inheritance by posing as Mrs Fishwick junior (which she did in order to protect John) then, while on bail, is

further charged with the murders of Colin, Charlotte Hoyle and Joy Fishwick. She had helped John move Colin's body when he had to retrieve it from the spot he'd buried it at Underworld and she admits this to police. She is convicted of one murder, that of Colin, and sentenced to life in prison, despite a deathbed confession from John. This is soon is overturned and she is released, having served enough time on remand for the crimes of which she was guilty. The residents are delighted to see her back home in Weatherfield, apart from Sally who blames Fiz for everything John put daughter Rosie through. The name John Stape would return to haunt Fiz when his daughter Jade Rowan appears in 2019, determined to avenge her father's death.

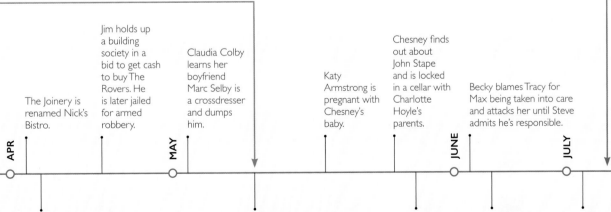

The Joinery is renamed Nick's Bistro.

Audrey signs the salon over to David, and Gail tries to pay Kylie off ahead of her wedding to David.

APR

Jim holds up a building society in a bid to get cash to buy The Rovers. He is later jailed for armed robbery.

Claudia Colby learns her boyfriend Marc Selby is a crossdresser and dumps him.

MAY

Philip Lowrie's return is marked in *Guinness World Records* as the longest break away from a serial.

Katy Armstrong is pregnant with Chesney's baby.

Chesney finds out about John Stape and is locked in a cellar with Charlotte Hoyle's parents.

JUNE

Betty Williams' final scenes are broadcast.

Becky blames Tracy for Max being taken into care and attacks her until Steve admits he's responsible.

Stella Price starts managing The Rovers (her first appearance).

JULY

Stella reveals she is Leanne's mother.

SEPTEMBER

FRANK FOSTER RAPES CARLA

Despite Maria's claim that businessman Frank Foster had sexually assaulted her when she went to his house to discuss an Underworld order, Carla later becomes involved with Frank after he bought into the factory. They quickly become engaged, but on the eve of the wedding, Carla calls it off – she's really in love with Peter Barlow. When she confesses this to Frank he rapes her, leaving Carla suicidal. The police are called and Frank is arrested but released on bail. In the run-up to his trial he removes equipment from the factory, setting up a rival business to Underworld, and takes several staff members with him, including Sally with whom he embarks on a relationship. Peter supports Carla through her ordeal and they start a secret affair behind his wife Leanne's back.

DECEMBER

SIAN LEAVES THE STREET

Sophie and Sian decide to get married, but the wedding is ruined when Sophie gets cold feet at the altar. She had kissed Dev's daughter Amber, her bridesmaid, on a drunken night out several months before and developed feelings for her, which were unrequited. Dev's ex-wife Sunita informs Kevin of his daughter's dilemma ahead of the wedding and he dramatically halts the service. Sian is devastated to hear of Sophie's betrayal and flees the church. The couple split shortly afterwards and Sian leaves the Street for good.

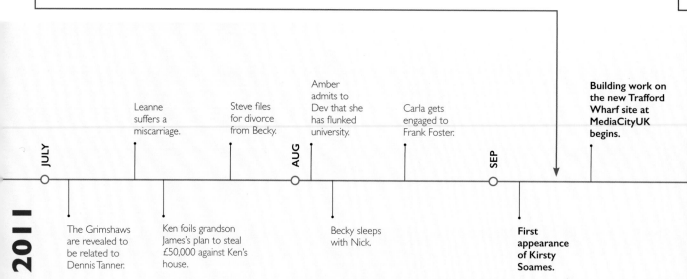

2011

Leanne suffers a miscarriage.

Steve files for divorce from Becky.

Amber admits to Dev that she has flunked university.

Carla gets engaged to Frank Foster.

Building work on the new Trafford Wharf site at MediaCityUK begins.

JULY

AUG

SEP

The Grimshaws are revealed to be related to Dennis Tanner.

Ken foils grandson James's plan to steal £50,000 against Ken's house.

Becky sleeps with Nick.

First appearance of Kirsty Soames.

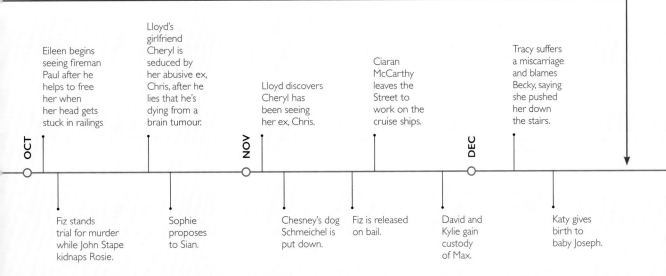

Eileen begins
seeing fireman
Paul after he
helps to free
her when
her head gets
stuck in railings

Lloyd's
girlfriend
Cheryl is
seduced by
her abusive ex,
Chris, after he
lies that he's
dying from a
brain tumour.

Lloyd discovers
Cheryl has
been seeing
her ex, Chris.

Ciaran
McCarthy
leaves the
Street to
work on the
cruise ships.

Tracy suffers
a miscarriage
and blames
Becky, saying
she pushed
her down
the stairs.

OCT

NOV

DEC

Fiz stands
trial for murder
while John Stape
kidnaps Rosie.

Sophie
proposes
to Sian.

Chesney's dog
Schmeichel is
put down.

Fiz is released
on bail.

David and
Kylie gain
custody
of Max.

Katy gives
birth to
baby Joseph.

FRANK IS KILLED IN UNDERWORLD

Frank has dumped Sally and when Carla confronts him in Underworld to demand answers from him following his acquittal on the rape charge, he admits everything to her and taunts her. He has tricked her into signing her share of the factory over to him and he gloats, laughing at her alcohol issues and threatening to rape her again. Later that night, Sally, who by now believes Carla's accusations, finds Frank's body on the factory floor. Both Peter, who had previously beaten up Frank, and Carla are prime suspects until, on the day of the funeral, Frank's mother Anne confesses to Sally that she overheard her son's showdown with Carla. She admits she rowed with him upon realising his guilt, blaming him for his father's fatal heart attack and, lashing out with a glass bottle, had killed him.

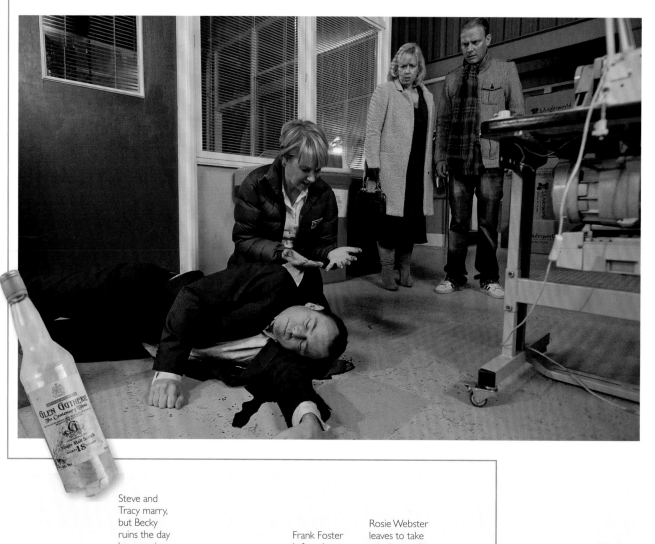

Kirsty discovers she's pregnant.

Steve and Tracy marry, but Becky ruins the day by exposing Tracy's lies about her miscarriage

Frank Foster is found not guilty of rape. He returns to Underworld.

Rosie Webster leaves to take part in a reality TV show. She doesn't return until 2017.

Gail discovers Audrey is seeing Lewis again.

JAN

FEB

MAR

Becky and Kylie cook up a ruse to get hold of Tracy's medical records.

Becky leaves for Barbados with hotel manager Danny Stratton.

Leanne finds out about Carla's affair with Peter.

Leanne leaves to stay with sister Toyah in London.

Lewis Archer returns to Coronation Street, vowing to win Audrey back.

Rita and Dennis hold an engagement party.

Dev's daughter Amber Kalir leaves the Street.

MAY

KIRSTY SOAMES HITS PARTNER TYRONE

Tyrone met police officer Kirsty in late 2011 and the pair began a relationship. By mid-2012 things take a darker turn when pregnant Kirsty's abusive behaviour begins to emerge. When Kirsty, who had suffered abuse as a child at the hands of her father, fears she might lose her job, Tyrone says he may be able to get her a position at the

PRODUCTION NOTE

English Heritage denies ITV the listed status it had applied for to protect the old set ahead of the move to MediaCityUK.

factory. Furious Kirsty lashes out, hitting a stunned Tyrone across the face. Kirsty is full of self-loathing, realising that she can't control her temper but the physical abuse escalates. When their daughter Ruby is born later in the year, Kirsty fails to name Tyrone on the birth certificate and starts to claim she is the victim of his abuse. Tyrone, who has begun a relationship with a sympathetic Fiz, is charged with assault and it's only during his trial that Kirsty realises she is a danger to her daughter and admits what she has done. Tyrone's charges are dropped and Kirsty is jailed.

Stella throws Karl out after finding out he is up to his eyes in debt. Karl starts seeing Sunita.

Betty Williams dies.

APR

Tina and Tommy Duckworth begin a relationship. Terry Duckworth returns to the Street.

Lesley Kershaw dies after being electrocuted.

MAY

Nick finishes with Eva when she wrongly accuses him of sleeping with Kylie.

Loan shark Rick Neelan tells Tommy he has inherited his dad Terry's debt, after Terry disappears.

JUNE

Feeling used by Karl, Sunita proposes to Dev.

Dennis and Rita marry.

Marcus and Sean split up as Leanne and Nick get back together.

SEPTEMBER

TINA OFFERS TO BE A SURROGATE FOR IZZY

Tina's boyfriend Tommy Duckworth is heavily in debt to loan shark Rick Neelan thanks to an ill-fated bid to set up a lap-dancing club with his unreliable father Terry. Tina agrees to become a surrogate for Gary and Izzy after Izzy suffers a miscarriage, and Owen pays her to undertake the pregnancy. Tommy disagrees with the whole thing and he and Tina split. Tina gives birth to a baby boy the following year and initially decides to keep the child and name him Joe after her late father. Eventually, she agrees to hand him over to Gary and Izzy and they rename him Jake. Following the birth, Tina and Tommy are reunited.

SEPTEMBER

KEN MEETS WENDY CROZIER AGAIN

In 1989 Ken had an affair with colleague Wendy Crozier and left Deirdre for a short while. Ken and Wendy's paths cross again 22 years later when they both became governors at Bessie Street School. Now Wendy Papadopolous, her husband has passed away and she wants to reignite her relationship with Ken but he rejects her. Regardless, Wendy lies to Deirdre that they slept together. Deirdre believes Ken and Wendy leaves his life for good.

2012

JULY

Steve discovers Lloyd has set up a rival cab firm, Fare Ladies.

Carla and Peter leave Weatherfield to sail around the world.

Rob Donovan's first appearance as Carla's younger brother. He is released from jail after serving time for armed robbery.

Stella catches Karl and Sunita together.

AUG

Izzy has a miscarriage.

Tina finds out about Kirsty's abuse of Tyrone.

Katy offers to be a surrogate for Izzy and Gary but they decide against it.

SEP

Ruby Soames is born.

First appearance of Gloria Price.

Lloyd finds out Jenna is his daughter.

OCTOBER

GAY MARCUS FALLS FOR MARIA

Throughout 2011 widowed single mother Maria had a torrid time of it. She was dumped by boyfriend Chris Gray, who went back to his former partner Cheryl when he was diagnosed with a brain tumour, and she fell out with Carla following Frank Foster's attack on her, only to come to Carla's aid after Carla herself was raped. By 2012 a vulnerable Maria begins to develop feelings for her gay friend Marcus, who, desperately wanting to be a father after witnessing Sean's relationship with son Dylan, has been supporting Maria and helping to look after her son Liam. When Maria discovers a lump in her breast is benign, she kisses Marcus in relief despite having recently started seeing Jason Grimshaw. They eventually sleep together and begin a relationship, to the amazement of Marcus's ex Sean. The following year sees Todd Grimshaw return to Weatherfield and attempt to split Marcus and Maria up purely for the challenge. He orchestrates a situation where Maria walks in on him and Marcus in a compromising situation and Maria finishes with Marcus, kicking him out of their flat. They eventually make their peace as Marcus leaves the Street for good.

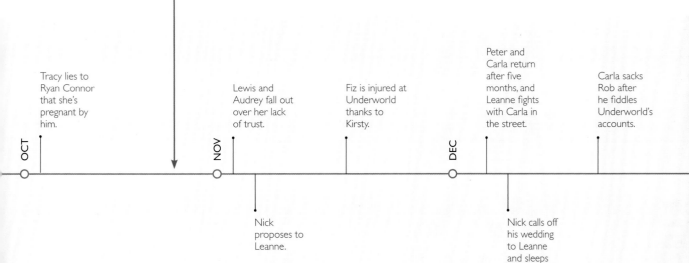

Tracy lies to Ryan Connor that she's pregnant by him.

Lewis and Audrey fall out over her lack of trust.

Fiz is injured at Underworld thanks to Kirsty.

Peter and Carla return after five months, and Leanne fights with Carla in the street.

Carla sacks Rob after he fiddles Underworld's accounts.

OCT

NOV

DEC

Nick proposes to Leanne.

Nick calls off his wedding to Leanne and sleeps with sister-in-law Kylie.

TWO COUPLES GET ENGAGED

Firefighter Paul Kershaw first appeared on the Street during the 2010 tram crash when he battled unsuccessfully to save trapped Molly Dobbs. He returned when he was called to help free Eileen's head after she got it stuck in railings during her 50th birthday celebrations. They began dating, but it was clear Paul was hiding something – he was a married man. It emerged that Paul's wife Lesley had early onset Alzheimer's disease. Eileen told Paul his wife needed him and they could not remain friends. When Lesley died Paul returned to Eileen and in March 2013 they get engaged. The relationship would flounder, however, when Paul suffers survivor's guilt after colleague Toni dies in a blaze at The Rovers and is then accused of racism by Lloyd Mullaney.

Chesney and Katy started going out together as teenagers and soon the young lovers decided to try for a baby. Joseph arrived at Christmas in 2011 – while Katy was playing Mary in a nativity play at Weatherfield Community Hall. Life as a young mum became stifling for Katy who felt she was getting old before her time and she responded eagerly to Ryan Connor's attentions. Chesney's marriage proposal surprises her and she accepts, but Gary has rumbled her and Ryan's illicit relationship, fights with Ryan and Chesney discovers the truth. He ends things with Katy and the couple share custody of baby Joseph until Katy leaves to live in Portugal with her mother. Joseph would return to live with Chesney on Coronation Street when Katy dies in a car crash in 2017.

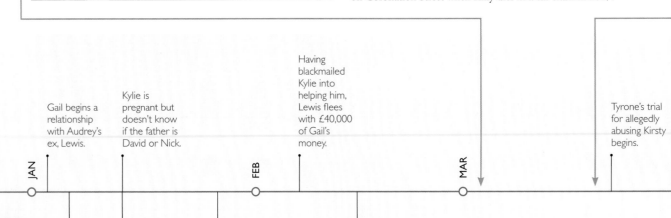

Gail begins a relationship with Audrey's ex, Lewis.

Kylie is pregnant but doesn't know if the father is David or Nick.

Having blackmailed Kylie into helping him, Lewis flees with £40,000 of Gail's money.

Tyrone's trial for allegedly abusing Kirsty begins.

JAN

FEB

MAR

2013

Karl leaves Sunita.

Nick and Leanne remarry on their second attempt.

Kirsty halts her wedding to Tyrone, citing his affair with Fiz, and later accuses him of abusing her.

Gloria Price's new fiancé Eric Babbage dies in The Rovers.

MARCH

KARL SETS FIRE TO THE ROVERS

Karl Munro can't contain his jealousy at his ex Stella's relationship with builder Jason and by March 2013 has cooked up a revenge plan that proves fatal. Stella had kicked him out after discovering his affair with Sunita and his previous plans to win her back have failed. As the Street's residents party in the Bistro and enjoy a charity Full Monty performance by some of the men, Karl sneaks into The Rovers' cellar and sets a fire, hoping Jason's handiwork will be blamed. Sunita has followed him and as they argue, she falls and hits her head. Norris and Emily raise the alarm when they spot the pub is ablaze and Karl, realising Stella is inside, rushes into the flames to rescue her. Firefighter Toni Griffiths dies in the fire, but Stella and Sunita are brought out alive and taken to hospital.

Fearful that Sunita will tell police that he was to blame, Karl removes her breathing tube, killing his former lover. He is reunited with Stella who believes he saved her life, but suspicions are raised on the Street and Karl eventually admits his guilt and is jailed for life.

Karl murders Sunita in hospital.

Stuart Blackburn takes over from Phil Collinson as producer.

Tina gives birth to Izzy and Gary's baby two months prematurely.

David finds out about Nick and Kylie sleeping together.

APR

MAY

JUNE

Stella breaks up with Jason and reconciles with Karl.

First appearance of Sinead Tinker when her aunt Beth sets her up with Chesney.

AUGUST

LILY PLATT IS BORN AFTER DAVID'S FEUD WITH HIS BROTHER

Throughout her pregnancy Kylie has been unsure whether the father is David or Nick. After relations between her and David sank to an all-time low, Kylie slept with Nick when his Christmas wedding to Leanne fell through. When she discovered she was pregnant, she planned to abort but was stopped when David found her positive pregnancy test – one of their many falling-outs had been over her desire to put work before another baby. Crooked Lewis Archer had discovered her secret after hearing her discuss the pregnancy with

Nick and forced her to help him con £40,000 out of unsuspecting Gail. Penniless Gail became a lodger when David and Kylie bought No 8. Kylie's tryst with Nick led to David's secret vendetta against his brother. Eventually, while David and Nick were fighting in the Bistro van, a truck collided with it and Nick was left brain-damaged. When Kylie gives birth to baby Lily at No 8, with Gail and David delivering the baby, David secretly organises a DNA test, which reveals he is indeed Lily's father. Kylie works out that David was responsible for Nick's brain damage and reveals all to the family. David is ostracised for a while and Kylie turns to drink before David worms his way back into his family's – and Kylie's – affections.

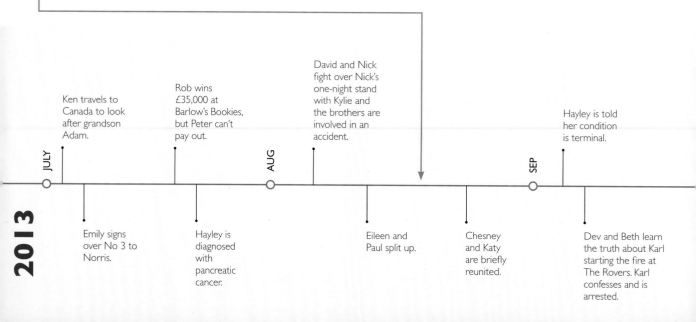

2013

JULY

Ken travels to Canada to look after grandson Adam.

Emily signs over No 3 to Norris.

Rob wins £35,000 at Barlow's Bookies, but Peter can't pay out.

Hayley is diagnosed with pancreatic cancer.

AUG

David and Nick fight over Nick's one-night stand with Kylie and the brothers are involved in an accident.

Eileen and Paul split up.

Chesney and Katy are briefly reunited.

SEP

Hayley is told her condition is terminal.

Dev and Beth learn the truth about Karl starting the fire at The Rovers. Karl confesses and is arrested.

BRIAN AND JULIE'S RELATIONSHIP BREAKS DOWN

Brian Packham and Julie Carp began dating after Brian and his wife Margaret separated. Julie wanted children and was devastated when a suspected pregnancy turned out to be a growth, which meant she could never have a baby of her own. Determined to begin fostering, Julie is heartbroken when Brian, fed up of dealing with children thanks to his teaching career, secretly tells the foster agency that he doesn't want to be involved. When a devastated Julie discovers his lies, Brian leaves the Street. He would return two years later to try to win Julie back.

PETER MARRIES CARLA… THEN KISSES TINA

Following the departure of her boyfriend Tommy, Tina grows closer to Peter while acting as nanny for his son Simon. She is friendly with his fiancée Carla, but when Carla retires drunk on their wedding day, Peter and Tina kiss, and they begin a torrid affair.

OCT

DNA results reveal David is Lily's father.

At Lily's christening, the truth about David, and Nick's brain injury, comes out.

NOV

Leanne agrees to take Nick back.

Karl is jailed for life for murdering Sunita and causing the death of a firefighter.

DEC

Nick becomes violent due to his brain injury, and he and Leanne split again.

Liz McDonald returns as co-owner of The Rovers with Steve.

Hayley tells Roy she wants to take her own life.

Tommy, now abroad, breaks up with Tina.

Final scenes are filmed at Coronation Street's Quay Street studios.

HAYLEY TAKES HER OWN LIFE

In 2013 Hayley had been diagnosed with pancreatic cancer, and following an operation to remove the tumour was informed that her condition was terminal. During her final months she reconnects with her son Christian and vows to live life to the full while she can. Roy surprises her with a trip to Blackpool where the pair dance at the Tower Ballroom. When her cancer advances quickly, Hayley makes the decision to take her own life. She fears morphine-induced delirium could make her regress mentally back to Harold, who she was before her transition, but she wants to die as Hayley. Roy disagrees vehemently but eventually acquiesces and after Hayley has said her private goodbyes to friends and neighbours, she prepares a cocktail of drugs and dies in Roy's arms in their bedroom to the strains of Vaughan Williams' 'The Lark Ascending'.

First appearance of **Michael Rodwell who starts a relationship with Gail after breaking into her house and undergoing restorative justice with her.**

Tracy discovers Rob kissed Tina and she temporarily splits from him.

Lloyd starts seeing Andrea Beckett, Steve's friend from night school.

Marcus cheats on Maria with a manipulative Todd.

JAN

FEB

MAR

Kylie and David are reconciled.

Gloria and Dennis Tanner leave Weatherfield together.

Both Carla and Tina tell Peter they think they're pregnant, but only Carla is correct.

APRIL

ANNA IS BLACKMAILED INTO SLEEPING WITH PAT PHELAN

Dodgy builder Pat Phelan was a client and then business partner of Anna's boyfriend Owen Armstrong, but the pair fell out over money. When Anna's son, Gary ,discovers Phelan has made inappropriate advances to his mother he attacks Phelan, who then blackmails Owen and Gary into working for him for minimum wage. He claims he has CCTV of the attack and Owen is worried that Gary will be sent to prison if Phelan turns the tapes over to the police. Phelan gets Owen blacklisted and also makes him forfeit the £80,000 Phelan owed him. In a bid to persuade Phelan to stop destroying her family, Anna agrees to sleep with him. Her sense of revulsion and guilt makes her reveal everything to Owen and their relationship is pushed to breaking point, but survives. He leaves Weatherfield but is destined to return two years later to become one of its most evil villains…

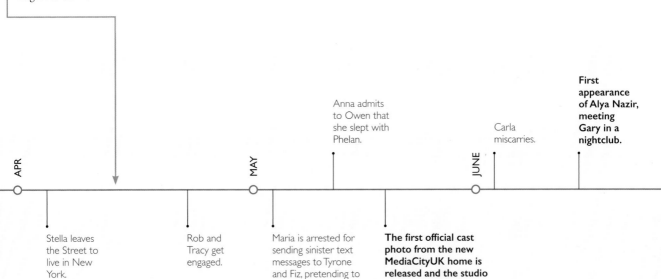

APR

Stella leaves the Street to live in New York.

Rob and Tracy get engaged.

MAY

Maria is arrested for sending sinister text messages to Tyrone and Fiz, pretending to be Kirsty.

Anna admits to Owen that she slept with Phelan.

The first official cast photo from the new MediaCityUK home is released and the studio is named The Tony Warren Building.

JUNE

Carla miscarries.

First appearance of Alya Nazir, meeting Gary in a nightclub.

MAY

ROB MURDERS TINA

Former jailbird Rob Donovan is engaged to Tracy Barlow and running Barlow's Buys. He took over Peter's bookies when Peter was unable to honour a £35,000 win and warned his sister Carla that Peter was not good enough for her. Peter and Tina started their affair at Peter and Carla's wedding, and Tina wanted Peter to run away with her. Rob discovers the affair and when Carla announces her pregnancy in The Rovers, Rob follows an upset Tina back to her flat. He tries to persuade her that Peter really is no good for her but Tina lashes out, saying she'll tell Carla all about the affair and while she's at it, report Rob and Tracy for dealing in dodgy goods at Barlow's Buys. Rob can't bear the prospect of going back to prison and, as they argue, Tina falls from a balcony. She survives the fall but maintains she'll tell Carla everything. Rob grabs an iron bar and batters her to shut her up. Tina dies a few days later in hospital and first Carla and then Peter are suspected of her murder, with Peter

eventually being wrongly convicted. It is only later that Carla works out that Rob was really to blame and, as he prepares to marry Tracy, Carla calls the police. Rob goes on the run but is apprehended weeks later when Tracy turns him in.

2014

PRODUCTION NOTE

In September 2014 it was announced that much-loved actor Anne Kirkbride would be taking a three-month break from the show. She was expected to return to filming in the spring of 2015, but she passed away on 19th January after a short illness. Just two days later her screen husband William Roache paid a touching tribute to Anne at the National Television Awards.

OCTOBER

DEIRDRE LEAVES THE STREET FOR THE LAST TIME

The stress of Peter's impending trial is getting to Deirdre and, when she tearfully flings a trifle at the wall, Ken suggests she takes some time away from Weatherfield to visit her old pal Bev Unwin in the Peak District. Deirdre extends her stay when Bev's brother dies.

The following year, a welcome home party is planned in Weatherfield for Deirdre's 60th birthday on 8th July 2015. The sad news that Deirdre has died suddenly from an aneurysm is broken to Ken and Tracy by Bev and later to the residents by Liz McDonald.

OCT

Kylie meets up with ex Callum Logan, Max's father.

Peter is found guilty of murdering Tina. Rob admits everything to Carla and does a runner from the police on his and Tracy's wedding day.

Rob is arrested for Tina's murder. Peter is released from prison and leaves Weatherfield.

David throws Kylie out over her drug-taking.

NOV

DEC

First appearance of Gemma Winter.

Steve is told by a GP that he may be suffering from depression.

Michelle and a depressed Steve split up.

Michael meets who he believes to be his estranged son Gavin.

Roy is arrested for attacking a burglar, who turns out to be Gary.

JANUARY

KIRK AND BETH MARRY

Kirk and Beth, a former squeeze of Steve McDonald, worked together at Underworld. When Beth began online dating, Kirk offered to drive her to meet a date. The evening was a disaster and resulted in Kirk getting punched. Kirk and Beth grew close and in January 2015 their 1980s-themed fancy-dress marriage, with Beth dressed as Madonna and Kirk as Adam Ant, was one of the Street's most memorable. It would later emerge that Beth was still legally married to Darryl Parkins, the father of her son Craig.

JANUARY

STEVE CRASHES A MINIBUS CARRYING THE UNDERWORLD WORKERS

In late 2014 Steve McDonald was diagnosed with depression but he didn't share his diagnosis with anyone. He and Michelle split when Michelle discovered he knew about Tina and Peter's affair. In January the staff of Underworld are getting all glammed up to attend a business awards night. Carla is up for one of the gongs and the team plan to make a night of it. Steve is drafted in at the last minute to drive, but he is distracted by an overtaking driver and the minibus veers off the road, turning over and landing on its roof, hanging over the edge of a quarry. As the occupants struggle to free themselves in the dark, the bus teeters and it's Tracy who rescues Carla. Tracy's foot gets stuck in a seatbelt, but she manages to wriggle free as the bus plunges down the side of the cliff. Most of the passengers suffer broken bones, cuts and bruises, but Sinead is left paralysed. The trauma of causing the crash prompts Steve to tell Michelle about his depression. They reconcile and marry later in the year.

Michael collapses with heart problems shortly after he and Gail are engaged. Andy Carver reveals his real identity to Steph Britton.

Anne Kirkbride passes away. Production is halted the following day and William Roache pays tribute to his screen wife at the National Television Awards.

Kevin meets up with Jenny Bradley via an online dating site, heralding Jenny's return to Weatherfield after 21 years.

Gail learns that Andy's an imposter when she meets the real Gavin Rodwell, who dies in a car crash shortly afterwards.

JAN

FEB

MAR

Sean and Billy the vicar start a relationship.

Eva and Jason split up.

APRIL

FAYE WINDASS GIVES BIRTH, AGED 13

Faye Windass is Anna's adopted daughter whose real father Tim Metcalfe reappeared in her life in 2013. In 2015 Faye is teased by schoolmates after putting on weight and, after doing a pregnancy test, realises she is pregnant. She had slept with a boy from school the previous year 'so that he would like her'. She confides in friend Craig and plans to have the baby in secret, then leave it at the local hospital. When she goes into labour, Craig fetches her mum and

Faye gives birth to a baby girl whom she names Miley. After Craig is initially accused of being the father, Faye owns up to Anna and the real father, Jackson Hodge, and his parents are introduced to the newborn baby. Young Faye can't cope with life as a mother and eventually the Hodges ask to raise Miley themselves. Faye readily agrees, much to Anna's disappointment, and later the Hodges immigrate to Canada with their son and Miley.

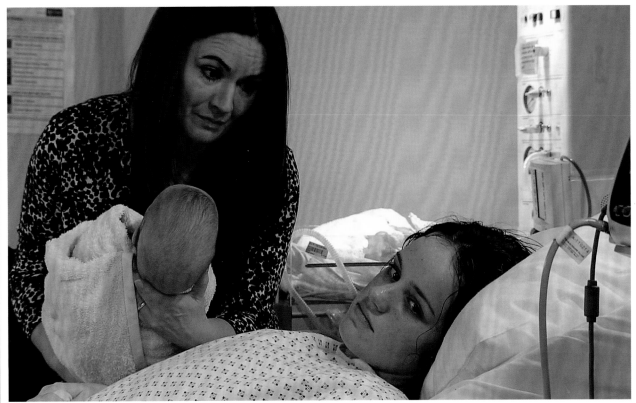

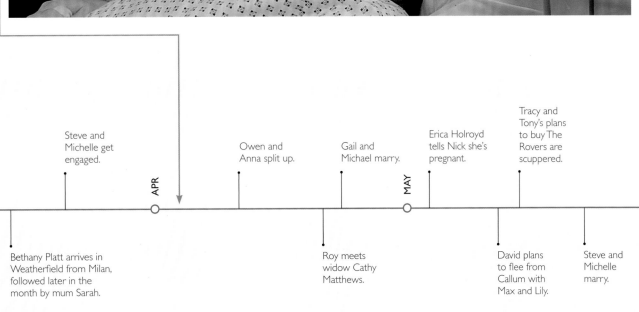

Bethany Platt arrives in Weatherfield from Milan, followed later in the month by mum Sarah.

Steve and Michelle get engaged.

APR

Owen and Anna split up.

Roy meets widow Cathy Matthews.

Gail and Michael marry.

MAY

Erica Holroyd tells Nick she's pregnant.

David plans to flee from Callum with Max and Lily.

Tracy and Tony's plans to buy The Rovers are scuppered.

Steve and Michelle marry.

TRACY SETS FIRE TO THE VICTORIA STREET FLATS

When Carla ruins Tracy's chances of taking over The Rovers, Tracy takes revenge by creeping into Carla's flat in Victoria Court intending to kill the sleeping Carla. She flees when she hears a loo flush and leaves a candle too close to a lamp. A blaze starts and Tracy is secretly satisfied, until she is informed that her daughter Amy is inside the building. Kal Nazir is killed in the fire when he and partner Leanne try to rescue Amy. Sophie's partner Maddie Heath also dies as a result of the fire, after getting caught in an explosion at the nearby builder's yard caused by the fire. Amy survives and Tracy spreads the rumour that a drunk Carla must have started the fire by accidentally leaving the candle burning.

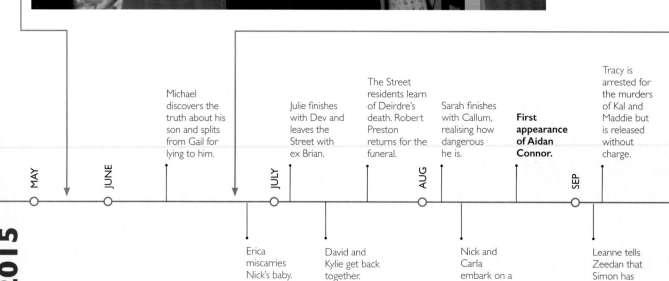

Michael discovers the truth about his son and splits from Gail for lying to him.

Julie finishes with Dev and leaves the Street with ex Brian.

The Street residents learn of Deirdre's death. Robert Preston returns for the funeral.

Sarah finishes with Callum, realising how dangerous he is.

First appearance of Aidan Connor.

Tracy is arrested for the murders of Kal and Maddie but is released without charge.

MAY

JUNE

JULY

AUG

SEP

Erica miscarries Nick's baby.

David and Kylie get back together.

Nick and Carla embark on a relationship.

Leanne tells Zeedan that Simon has been hitting her.

2015

JUNE

TROUBLED JENNY KIDNAPS KEVIN'S SON JACK

Jenny Bradley returned to Weatherfield, 21 years after her last visit. Now Jenny is grieving the loss of her young son Tom, who drowned in a paddling pool, but she keeps this secret. After matching with old pal Kevin on a dating website, she begins dating him and makes up with Rita, who assumes she is still money-grabbing and untrustworthy. Jenny becomes obsessed with Kevin's four-year-old son Jack, and Sophie and Maddie are increasingly suspicious of her mental state. Maddie is killed before she can tell

Kevin she believes Jenny is planning to kidnap Jack and, during Maddie's funeral, Jenny makes her move, running away with the child to Hull. Realising she is losing her mind and reliving her grief over Tom, she calls Rita for help and Rita, Kevin and Sophie arrive in Hull to talk her down from a high-rise balcony. With Jack safe in Kevin's arms, Jenny is arrested and sectioned, before returning to the Street the following year with many bridges to build.

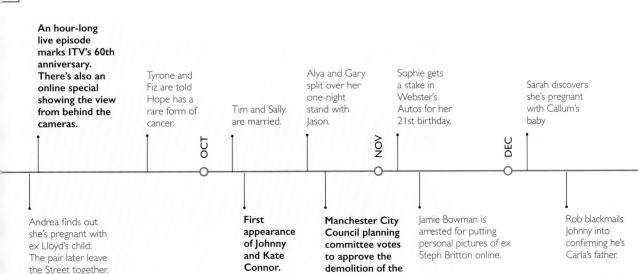

An hour-long live episode marks ITV's 60th anniversary. There's also an online special showing the view from behind the cameras.

Tyrone and Fiz are told Hope has a rare form of cancer.

Tim and Sally are married.

Alya and Gary split over her one-night stand with Jason.

Sophie gets a stake in Webster's Autos for her 21st birthday.

Sarah discovers she's pregnant with Callum's baby

OCT • NOV • DEC

Andrea finds out she's pregnant with ex Lloyd's child. The pair later leave the Street together.

First appearance of Johnny and Kate Connor.

Manchester City Council planning committee votes to approve the demolition of the Quay Street set.

Jamie Bowman is arrested for putting personal pictures of ex Steph Britton online.

Rob blackmails Johnny into confirming he's Carla's father.

23RD SEPTEMBER 2015

FIVE years after the spectacular tram crash live episode marking *Coronation Street*'s 50th birthday, cast and crew were involved in another acclaimed live special – this time the hour-long episode marked network ITV's 60th anniversary.

In the scene
Kylie kills violent Callum

THE SURROUNDING STORYLINES

Violent drug dealer Callum Logan – the father of Kylie's son Max – was harassing the Platts. He owed money and was demanding thousands from Kylie and David in return for relinquishing his parental rights over young Max. Sarah, with whom he had had a brief relationship, attempted to record him talking about his illegal activities, but he attacked her inside No 8.

Elsewhere, Roy was back in Blackpool where Cathy had taken him as a surprise birthday treat and where she had intended to tell him how she felt about him.

THE MAIN EVENT
A nervous Sarah attempts to record Callum confessing to his crimes, but when Michelle calls her he discovers the hidden phone and attacks her. He pins her to the floor. Sarah is terrified for her life. Callum suddenly slumps on top of her – Kylie has hit him across the head with builder Tony's heavy wrench.

Roy arrives home from Blackpool alone and, ignoring the surprise party organised for him in the café, takes himself straight up to the flat. Cathy realises it was a mistake to take Roy to Blackpool, where he last went with Hayley when she was dying.

Realising Callum is dead, Kylie and Sarah desperately try to hide his body before Bethany arrives home. David returns and, taking charge, wraps Callum in a duvet cover and, planning to move it when they can, he and Kylie place the body down the manhole in the garage that's being converted into Gail's annexe.

Callum's mother Marion tries to call her son, causing Kylie to panic and when Gemma texts his phone David texts back, pretending to be Callum and saying he has left No 8. David comforts Kylie and promises everything will be fine.

Unaware of the horror unfolding across the road, the residents wave Lloyd and Andrea off as they leave the Street.

THE AFTERMATH

The events of that night would have significant repercussions for the Platt family for several months. Sarah suffered psychotic episodes after giving birth to the late Callum's son, whom she named Harry, and keeping the grisly secret nearly broke Kylie and David.

Callum's remains were discovered the following year when Tyrone crashed a pick-up truck into the annexe at No 8, cracking open the newly laid concrete covering the manhole in which Callum's body had been hidden. Still wrapped in the child's pirate-patterned duvet cover David and Kylie had grabbed in their panic, the corpse was identified thanks to a credit card and Jason's late father Tony was blamed for the killing.

PRODUCTION NOTES

This was the first live episode filmed on the new, larger, Trafford Wharf set. Vision mixer Dayle Evans-Kar was then an assistant director in charge of organising the 2015 live episode. She explains the intricate logistics of filming when everything has to run to time and no mistakes can be made: 'With the Callum story things were happening on the Platt set, which is in the studio, but then the kitchen and the back garden parts of it were on the lot, so the actors would have to really run between scenes.

'I had eleven first ADs (assistant directors) on it, five of us on the street, two of us took one half of the street and the others took the other half and then we had first ADs in each studio with second ADs to each area and a third AD for the supporting artists, and then runners who would escort the actors from one place to another, so I had to work out the logistics of all of that.

'We had about 500 people working on the live and a lot of those people had never done live TV before. You go on adrenaline and during the four-minute commercial breaks you're working out where you're going next for the following 12 minutes. It's like a ballet.'

A stand-by scene was planned in case something went wrong during the live transmission. Tyrone was potentially going to take a phone call. Dayle reveals: 'Alan [Halsall] did that because he wasn't available to rehearse for the live but was there on stand-by on the night. It wasn't used but it was there in case we needed it.'

NB: An online-only programme was also made showing the view from behind the cameras throughout the live broadcast.

PRODUCTION NOTE

When Sally sought election to the local council, *Coronation Street* even produced a hilarious online 'campaign video' with the message 'Don't be silly, vote Sally!' in which Sally uses daughter Sophie's lesbianism and even her divorce from Kevin as proof that she is the woman for the job.

SALLY JOINS THE RULING CLASSES

Carla is injured as raiders speed away from the Bistro. Sally declares the Street needs speed bumps and decides to get herself elected to the local council. She prepares to stand as an independent, leading to several weeks of hilarity as, adopting a sartorial style reminiscent of Margaret Thatcher, she takes on opponent Norris Cole in local hustings. Standing on a ticket of law and order, the wheels nearly come off her campaign with the revelation that husband Tim had been arrested during the poll tax riots of 1990, but defiant Sally turns this to her advantage and, after delivering a barnstorming speech in The Rovers, she is duly elected. Of course, elevation to the political class brings out Sally's snobby, social-climbing side to amusing effect.

MAY

CALLUM'S BODY IS DISCOVERED

On the day of of their wedding, Carla confesses to Nick that she slept with Robert Preston. Nick, although furious, decides that he will marry her anyway, but publicly announces during the reception in the Bistro that he is leaving her after all. A distressed Carla flees the reception, jumps in a car and in an uncontrollable rage, drives at her nemesis Tracy, but mows down Cathy by mistake. Tyrone is manoeuvring the garage tow truck and swerves in the rain to avoid Carla's car, skidding into the Platts' conversion – where evil Callum Logan's body was hidden after Kylie killed him.

Following Tyrone's tow truck collision, the gruesome discovery of Callum's remains is made and Gail, Sarah, David and Kylie are hauled in for questioning. Thanks to David, innocent builder's mate Jason Grimshaw is implicated but his brother Todd, believing he is protecting his former partner Sarah, lies to detectives that builder Tony Stewart had, before he died, confessed to killing Callum. A dead man taking the blame is the get-out-of-jail card the Platts need.

Emily heads off to Peru to volunteer with her environmental activist nephew Spider Nugent.

Cathy finds some love letters from her sister Nessa to her late husband and burns them, accidentally setting fire to her house. Roy rescues her.

Leanne reports stepson Simon to the police for assaulting her.

Eileen refuses to heed Anna's warning against dating Phelan.

JAN

FEB

MAR

Hope has a successful operation to treat her cancer.

Kevin and Anna begin a relationship.

The Bistro is raided and Carla is badly injured when she tries to tackle the robbers.

Tracy tells Carla she knows that she slept with Robert.

Gemma arrives for work experience in Audrey's salon and reveals her real name is Gemini.

Sarah gives birth to Callum's son Harry five weeks early.

JUNE

LEE MAYHEW HOLDS SARAH PLATT HOSTAGE

The impact of Callum's death, when pregnant Sarah was attacked by him in No 8, and the family collusion in hiding Callum's body beneath their home's half-built extension, had preyed on Sarah's mind throughout her pregnancy. Her mental instability was exacerbated further with the knowledge that an innocent man – Tony Stewart – albeit dead, was being blamed for the killing.

When baby Harry is born, Sarah begins to exhibit delusional signs of post-partum psychosis. She fears that Callum isn't truly dead, that he is coming back to kill them. It is in this delicate state that she encounters vicar Billy's heroin addict, ex-jailbird brother Lee. Lee had been asking Billy for money and, when he finally refuses, Lee cons Sarah into accompanying him to a flat and, holding her hostage, demands Billy, who is close to Sarah, hands over £1,000. David arrives to rescue his distressed sister and Billy tells Lee he never wants to see him again.

Gary Windass is arrested for possession of cannabis after he buys the drugs for ex Izzy's pain management.

Tony Stewart is found dead in his flat following a heart attack.

Carla's hen party ends with the girls getting arrested in a nightclub.

Billy's troubled brother Lee is found unconscious.

Izzy is found guilty of cannabis possession and also assaulting a police officer.

Jason leaves for Thailand. Jason Grimshaw's final appearance.

APR

MAY

JUNE

Michelle resists an affair with her childhood ex Will on her 40th birthday.

Jenny saves Kevin's young son Jack's life after a Blackpool tram nearly runs him down in an echo of the death of her father Alan Bradley in the town in 1989.

Billy realises his feelings for Todd and ends his relationship with a gutted Sean.

Callum's funeral takes place.

JULY

KYLIE IS STABBED TO DEATH

Kylie and David think they have finally shaken off the shadow of her dead ex, Callum, and are planning a new life on Barbados with her sister Becky. Callum's dodgy friend Macca and Macca's stepbrother Clayton Hibbs have been demanding free kebabs off Gemma, their old mate from the estate, and trying to pass off fake £20 notes in the kebab shop. When Gemma refuses to give them cash Clayton attacks her. Panic-stricken, Craig looks on immobile with fear and Kylie rushes to Gemma's aid. Clayton stabs her and, in heartbreaking scenes, a bleeding Kylie dies in husband David's arms on the cobbles outside The Rovers as Clayton escapes. David breaks the news of Kylie's death to Max and Lily and later argues with a scared Gemma about her refusal to help the police. He plans to hunt Clayton down. Gemma relents and Clayton is finally arrested and charged, while David is left to raise Max and Lily alone.

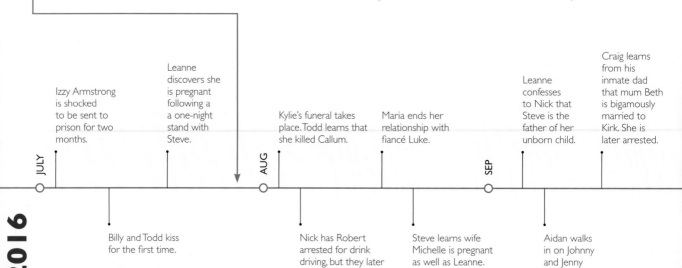

Izzy Armstrong is shocked to be sent to prison for two months.

Leanne discovers she is pregnant following a a one-night stand with Steve.

Kylie's funeral takes place. Todd learns that she killed Callum.

Maria ends her relationship with fiancé Luke.

Leanne confesses to Nick that Steve is the father of her unborn child.

Craig learns from his inmate dad that mum Beth is bigamously married to Kirk. She is later arrested.

JULY

AUG

SEP

Billy and Todd kiss for the first time.

Nick has Robert arrested for drink driving, but they later settle their differences and go into partnership running the Bistro.

Steve learns wife Michelle is pregnant as well as Leanne.

Aidan walks in on Johnny and Jenny kissing.

2016

NOVEMBER

MICHAEL DIES DURING A ROW WITH PAT PHELAN

Michael Rodwell burgled Gail McIntyre's home in 2014, but she later ended up marrying him. Michael's feud with Phelan started when Phelan began a relationship with Eileen Grimshaw, whom Michael had been courting after he and Gail split because she lied to him about the true identity of his son. Despite reconciling with Gail, Michael has the measure of Phelan and sets out to expose him, eventually securing proof of Phelan's crimes ripping off residents with his bogus Calcutta Street flats project. When Phelan confronts him, Michael suffers a heart attack. Psychopathic Phelan coldly watches him as he breathes his last, makes the sign of the cross and walks away. Micheal's death means that Phelan can continue his cover-up and Eileen remains oblivious.

DECEMBER

TOYAH BATTERSBY RETURNS TO THE STREET

It's Christmas Day and Toyah Battersby returns to Coronation Street after 14 years, following the collapse of her marriage to Toby Chapman, and is plunged immediately into a web of relationship lies, infertility and blackmail. Nick, believing partner Leanne is having an affair with Peter Barlow, fights with him, not knowing that Peter is actually in a secret relationship with Toyah. Leanne is furious to discover that Toyah is seeing her ex, and disowns her, but they make up when Leanne goes into labour and Toyah is on hand to deliver the baby. Toyah and Peter make a go of things, buying The Rovers together and attempting to have a baby via IVF.

Troubled David outs Clayton online as Kylie's killer.

David crashes his car en route to kill Clayton, and Anna is severely burned in the resulting explosion.

Adam Barlow and Daniel Osbourne return to the street after nine years.

Mary reveals to Norris that she was raped as a teenager and had a baby boy, Jude Appleton, who turns up on her doorstep later this month.

Anna falls down the stairs and knocks herself unconscious while looking after young Jack.

OCT

NOV

DEC

Ken suffers a stroke during a row with Peter.

Yasmeen is distraught to discover that Sharif has been having an affair for seven years.

Cathy calls off her wedding to Roy when she realises he doesn't really want to get married.

MICHELLE SUFFERS A MISCARRIAGE

Michelle became pregnant in 2016, but the following January she suffers a miscarriage at 23 weeks. Baby Ruairi dies moments after he is delivered, leaving both Michelle and Steve devastated. Michelle struggles to cope and directs her anger at Steve. The day before Ruairi's funeral Michelle contemplates suicide but is saved by Robert Preston who talks her out of jumping from a bridge. After the funeral Steve and Michelle scatter their son's ashes on a beach. There is further heartbreak to come for Michelle as during a brief separation the previous year, Steve had slept with Leanne, who goes on to give birth to another son, Oliver. When Michelle learns the truth, she punches Leanne and tells Steve their marriage is dead.

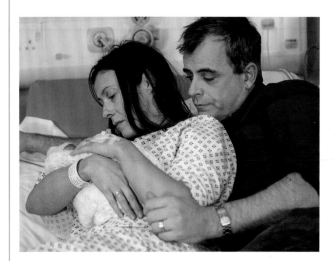

KEN IS ATTACKED, BUT WHO IS THE ASSAILANT?

When Ken discovers that Sinead is pregnant with his son Daniel's baby, he believes she is holding him back from taking up an MA course at Oxford University. Stung by his criticism, Sinead has an abortion. Shortly afterwards Ken is attacked in his home and is discovered at the foot of his stairs. At first it's thought he has had a stroke, but the family is told it is likely he was pushed. The finger of blame points in several directions with Ken's children, grandchildren and even Pat Phelan in the frame. When the assailant is revealed to be Daniel, Ken forgives him to the disbelief of the rest of the Barlow clan. As he recovers, Ken explains how guilty he feels over missing Daniel's upbringing, and reminds his children that he had reason to suspect any one of them.

Leanne gives birth to Oliver, and Steve announces he's the father, ending his marriage to Michelle.

Sinead is pregnant. She has an abortion after Ken challenges her but tells Daniel she had a miscarriage. He soon discovers the truth.

Johnny proposes to Jenny Bradley.

Rosie Webster returns to the Street after five years.

JAN

FEB

MAR

Phelan brutally attacks Andy before marrying Eileen.

Sinister Nathan Curtis begins a relationship with Bethany.

Sally receives malicious prank calls.

PRODUCTION NOTE

Kate Oates took over from Stuart Blackburn as producer in 2016. Her appointment heralded darker storylines such as Bethany's grooming and David's rape, which attracted praise and criticism in equal measure. Oates also oversees two major changes to *Coronation Street* – the addition of a sixth episode, taking the weekly output to three hours, and plans to extend the Victoria Street section of the exterior set, introducing new venues such as Speed Daal, the Weatherfield tram station, a larger police station and the community garden, plus sponsorship opportunities with the Co-op and Costa Coffee.

JUNE

BETHANY'S GROOMING NIGHTMARE CONTINUES

In 2016 Bethany suffered bullying at the hands of schoolmate Lauren. Combined with her mother's fragile mental health in the wake of Callum's murder and Harry's birth, this led to Bethany suffering self-esteem issues, and when the 16-year-old met handsome 35-year-old Nathan Curtis, manager of a tanning salon, she fell for his charming patter. Sarah was opposed to the relationship because of Nathan's age and this drove Bethany away. By June 2017 she is living with Nathan and being coerced to sleep with his friends. Still convinced that Nathan loves her, Bethany is unaware she has been groomed, that there have been other victims, including Shona Ramsey, or that Nathan is planning to sell her into prostitution abroad. Nathan shows his true colours when Bethany fails to steal her passport from Sarah and she escapes from him, reporting him to the police and bravely testifying in court. Evil Nathan and his friends would finally be convicted of rape.

APR

Tracy meets up with Rob after he escapes from jail and she and Amy go into hiding with him.

Nathan coerces Bethany to sleep with police officer Neil Clifton then proposes to her.

Sally's stalker is revealed to be the stepdaughter of her sister Gina.

Daniel has a breakdown after admitting to attacking Ken.

Shona admits to David that she is Kylie's killer Clayton's mother.

Eva finds out about Aidan and Maria.

MAY

JUNE

Michelle gets together with Robert.

Adam is arrested over the attack on Ken.

Terminally ill Drew Spellman asks Billy to look after daughter Summer.

Aidan starts seeing Maria behind girlfriend Eva's back.

Nick is trapped in quicksand and is rescued by nemesis Peter.

Johnny is diagnosed with MS.

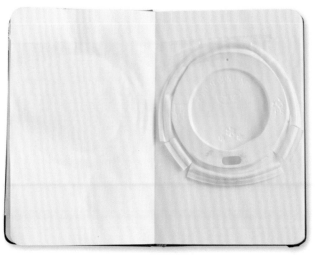

AUGUST

MICHELLE IS KIDNAPPED BY INFATUATED EX WILL

Will Chatterton had been a teenage boyfriend of Michelle and had always held a torch for her. When they met by accident in 2016, when Michelle was acting as wedding planner for Will and his fiancée Saskia, they came close to having an affair. A year later, Will makes contact with Michelle again. Michelle and Steve have split for good and she is seeing Robert Preston, but agrees to go for a drink with Will. Michelle fears she is being stalked by Robert's former colleague, drug dealer Rich Collis and Will promises to protect her. The stalker is, in fact, Will and when Michelle is kidnapped and locked in the boot of her car by an unknown assailant, Will is shown to be the culprit. Michelle and Robert believe Rich is to blame and Will tips the police off to catch Robert beating up Rich so that he is sent to prison. Eventually Michelle realises obsessed Will is behind her ordeal after finding pictures of herself in his belongings. She recruits Leanne to help her find evidence in Will's house, but he discovers them. Leanne is injured in the ensuing fight and it's Steve who comes to the rescue, punching Will and rescuing the women.

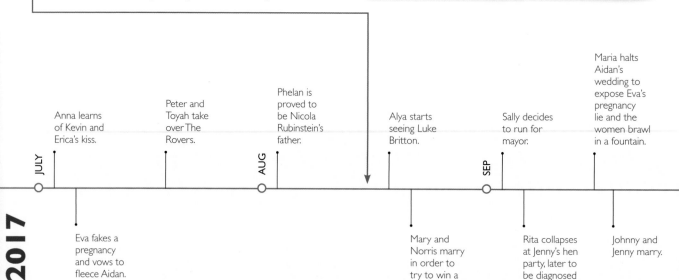

2017

JULY

Anna learns of Kevin and Erica's kiss.

Eva fakes a pregnancy and vows to fleece Aidan.

Peter and Toyah take over The Rovers.

Phelan is proved to be Nicola Rubinstein's father.

AUG

Alya starts seeing Luke Britton.

Mary and Norris marry in order to try to win a competition.

SEP

Sally decides to run for mayor.

Rita collapses at Jenny's hen party, later to be diagnosed with a brain tumour.

Maria halts Aidan's wedding to expose Eva's pregnancy lie and the women brawl in a fountain.

Johnny and Jenny marry.

PRODUCTION NOTE

Classic *Coronation Street* episodes begin airing on ITV3 in October as the channel begins replaying episodes consecutively, starting from Alan Bradley's arrival in 1986. By 2020 ITV3 was up to the mid-1990s. When production was halted early in 2020 due to the COVID-19 pandemic and screenings were reduced, fans flocked to ITV3 to get their *Coronation Street* fix!

DECEMBER

BILLY CONFESSES ALL TO PETER

Vicar Billy Mayhew had a chequered past before landing on Coronation Street and, in December 2017, believing he is going to die after sustaining an injury, he unburdens himself to Peter. He confesses that in 2001 he left Peter's sister, and Adam's mother, Susan for dead after causing her car to crash while making a getaway from an armed robbery. Peter locks Billy in his car boot, having forced alcohol down his throat, then threatens to throw Billy from a cliff in revenge. He only means to scare him but Billy falls and a fearful Peter flees the scene. Billy survives but his injuries lead him to become dependent on painkillers and his life unravels over the subsequent months as Adam feeds him stronger drugs to make him pay for what he did to his mother, before abruptly cutting off his supply. In desperation, Billy contacts his dealer brother Lee who gets him hooked on heroin.

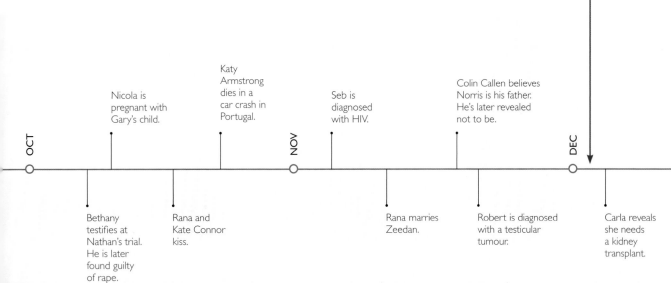

Nicola is pregnant with Gary's child.

Katy Armstrong dies in a car crash in Portugal.

Seb is diagnosed with HIV.

Colin Callen believes Norris is his father. He's later revealed not to be.

OCT NOV DEC

Bethany testifies at Nathan's trial. He is later found guilty of rape.

Rana and Kate Connor kiss.

Rana marries Zeedan.

Robert is diagnosed with a testicular tumour.

Carla reveals she needs a kidney transplant.

NO street in Britain is complete without pets. The Brits love their animals, and the residents of Coronation Street are no different. Whether it's dogs and cats or racehorses and rats, furry friends have always appeared on the Street, and many have been central to some hilarious storylines.

The pets of *Coronation Street*

Who can forget Mavis's budgies, Jack's pigeons or Craig's rat? Or, in more recent times, Sally's racing syndicate being saddled with a nag rather than the thoroughbred they had paid for? There have been many pets over the years, some have featured for longer than others, and of course there's been a cat on the opening titles of *Coronation Street* since the 1970s. In 1990 the programme held a competition to find a new cat for the credits and the winner featured for more than 10 years.

Fergie and Jack

Monica and Tyrone

Harriet and Mavis

Cerberus and Evelyn

One of the Nazirs' six chickens and Kal

Tiger and Natalie

Ozzy and Maria

Tiny arrives unexpectedly at Sally's

HERE'S AN A–Z OF *CORONATION STREET*'S CUTIES...

ALBERT – Stray dog adopted by Suzie Birchall

ARCHIE – Budgie, given to Ena but taken in by Martha

BARNEY – David's rabbit

BEAUTY – Mavis's third budgie

BELLA – Maxine's cat

BETTY'S HOTSHOT – The Rovers' racehorse

BEYONCÉ – stray pigeon found by Tyrone

BOBBY – Minnie's first and second cats

BOO – Eva and Aidan's cat

BOOMER – Vera's dog

CERBERUS – Evelyn Plummer's greyhound

CHARLOTTE BRONTË – Yasmeen's chicken, killed by Geoff

CLEO – Factory cat, brought in by Vera to catch mice

CONKY – Tracy Langton's hamster

DARRYL – Craig Tinker's rat

DAVID – David Platt's dog, inherited from a salon client

DINAH – Lillian Spencer's mynah bird

DOLLY AND MOLLY – Jack's pigeons, killed by a fox

DOLORES – Tommy Deakin's donkey

DOUGAL – Sam Tindall's dog

ECCLES – Ken's dog, originally named Lady Freckles and inherited by Blanche

FERGIE – One of Jack's pigeons

FLASH – Mandy Kamara's tortoise

FRED'S FOLLY – Alf and Fred's greyhound

FURY – Eddie Yeats' guard dog

GILBERT – Albert Tatlock's pigeon

HARRY/HARRIET – Mavis's first budgie, renamed after it laid an egg

HARRY – Mavis's second budgie, originally a stray called Boris

HARRY'S LUCK – Don Brennan's greyhound

JARVIS – Becky Palmer's budgie

JOHN – Jesse Chadwick's parrot

KITCHENER – Alice Pickins' mynah bird

LEANNE – Simon Barlow's rabbit

LITTLE HILDA – Eddie's favourite chicken

LITTLE TITCH – Charlie Moffitt's greyhound

LUCKY LOLITA – Harry Hewitt's greyhound

MARMADUKE – Betty's cat

MITZI – Jenny Bradley's dog

MONICA – Tyrone's dog

MONTY (turned out to be Phoebe) – Stray cat befriended by Norris

MR WOO (and its replacement Mr Woo 2) – Rita's dog

OZZY – Dog given to Liam Connor by Maria

PEANUT – Beth and Kirk's dog

PORKY AND BESS – Pigs owned by Keith Appleyard

RANDY – Percy Sugden's budgie

RAT FEATURES – Sophie's guinea pig

ROMMEL – Cat inherited by Hilda

ROVER – Abandoned dog taken in at The Rovers

SARACEN – Vicky's horse

SCAMPER – Joyce Smedley's dog

SCHMEICHEL – Chesney's dog

SUNNY JIM – Jed Stone's cat

TIGER – Natalie's cat

TINY – Tim and Sally's horse

TUCKER AND ZAMMO – Kittens taken in by Trevor Dean (also known as Purno and Black)

DAVID IS RAPED BY JOSH TUCKER

Josh Tucker began work as a mechanic at Webster's Autos after the murder by Pat Phelan of Luke Britton. He set about gaining popularity on the Street by organising a charity boxing match in Luke's memory and paid particular attention to helping David train. They became friends and enjoyed the occasional drink together. After a row with girlfriend Shona, David joins Josh on a night out, but Josh spikes his drink then takes him back to his flat where he gives him more alcohol before raping him. The next morning David realises what has happened and is horrified but keeps his ordeal secret. He and Shona split for a while and David takes up with young Emma Brooker. Aidan's suicide two months later prompts him to reveal his secret to Shona, who persuades him to report the rape to the police. Josh is released without charge but another potential victim beats him, leaving him temporarily blind. Billy takes pity on him and tries to rehabilitate him, leaving David furious. A year later, Josh is accused of raping another man and remanded in Highfield Prison at the same time David is serving time after being convicted of conning Audrey out of thousands of pounds. During a riot, Josh accuses David of stabbing him but retracts his accusation under pressure from Paul Foreman. He is eventually convicted of raping David and another man and jailed for 15 years.

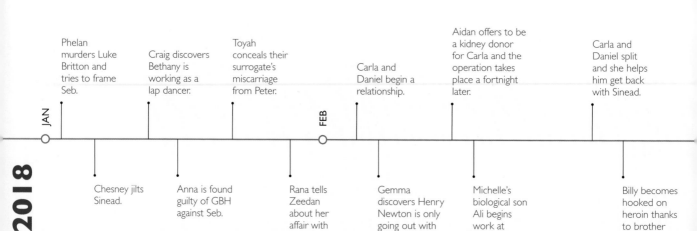

2018

JAN

Phelan murders Luke Britton and tries to frame Seb.

Chesney jilts Sinead.

Craig discovers Bethany is working as a lap dancer.

Anna is found guilty of GBH against Seb.

Toyah conceals their surrogate's miscarriage from Peter.

Rana tells Zeedan about her affair with Kate.

FEB

Carla and Daniel begin a relationship.

Gemma discovers Henry Newton is only going out with her for a bet.

Aidan offers to be a kidney donor for Carla and the operation takes place a fortnight later.

Michelle's biological son Ali begins work at the medical centre.

Carla and Daniel split and she helps him get back with Sinead.

Billy becomes hooked on heroin thanks to brother Lee Mayhew.

MAY

AIDAN ENDS HIS OWN LIFE

When Eva Price found out that her fiancé Aidan Connor was cheating on her with hairdresser Maria, she set about exacting a harsh revenge in which she pretended to be pregnant, before Maria revealed all at their country house wedding. Although Eva and Aidan reconciled, Aidan finished things when he discovered Eva had played a part in the closure of the factory. In early 2018 Aidan donated a kidney to his half-sister Carla, who helped him to relaunch the business. Eva then discovered she was pregnant for real and arranged to give the baby to Toyah who had struggled to get pregnant. Aidan had been suffering from suicidal thoughts although no one had an inkling about his state of mind. As his father Johnny was preparing to leave Weatherfield for Spain, Aidan visited Eva for one last time and then took his own life, and it was Johnny who discovered his son's body in the flat he had previously shared with Eva. To the surprise of his family, Aidan left Underworld to Alya Nazir.

PRODUCTION NOTE

A bench paying tribute to the victims of the Manchester Arena bombing is unveiled as part of the new Victoria Street set. It is seen on screen the following month.

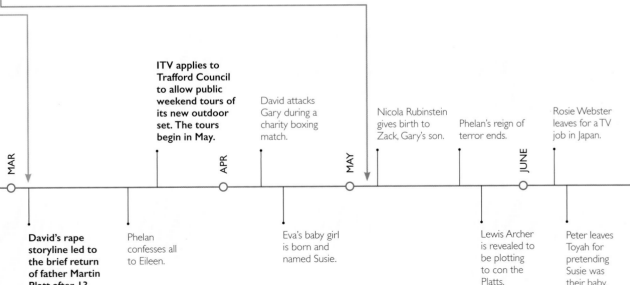

MAR

David's rape storyline led to the brief return of father Martin Platt after 13 years.

ITV applies to Trafford Council to allow public weekend tours of its new outdoor set. The tours begin in May.

Phelan confesses all to Eileen.

APR

David attacks Gary during a charity boxing match.

Eva's baby girl is born and named Susie.

MAY

Nicola Rubinstein gives birth to Zack, Gary's son.

Phelan's reign of terror ends.

Lewis Archer is revealed to be plotting to con the Platts.

JUNE

Rosie Webster leaves for a TV job in Japan.

Peter leaves Toyah for pretending Susie was their baby.

JUNE

PHELAN'S REIGN OF TERROR ENDS

After terrorising Anna Windass and her family, evil Pat Phelan returned to Weatherfield and took up with Eileen Grimshaw, who ignored all warnings about violent Phelan and married him. Phelan was instrumental in the deaths of Michael Rodwell and Vinny Ashord, he caused Anna to be locked up for GBH and kept Andy Carver prisoner in a cellar for nearly a year before killing him and Luke Britton. After admitting everything to a horrified Eileen, he disappeared, feared drowned but survived and hid out in a guest house and then a caravan park, before being tracked down by Gary Windass, intent on making Phelan suffer for what he did to his family. Phelan escapes from Gary and accidentally shoots his daughter Nicola Rubinstein. During a siege in the Bistro, as residents prepare for Robert and Michelle's wedding, Phelan threatens and injures Michelle before being stabbed to death by none other than Anna Windass, who has been released from jail.

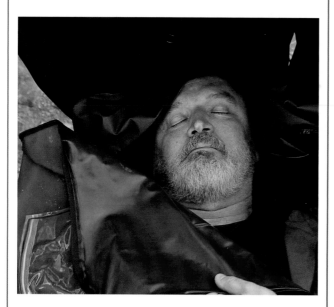

AUGUST

SALLY IS ARRESTED FOR FRAUD

Sally was very proud to be elected Mayor of Weatherfield and it brought out even more of her snobbiness, but pride comes before a fall and, during a circus-themed fundraising event, Sally is arrested then charged with fraud after being taken in by handsome conman Duncan Radfield. He had swindled £40,000 out of the Mayor's Charity Fund by persuading Sally to transfer the funds without going through the proper channels. He even claims in court that he and Sally were having an affair and when Sally is found guilty and sent to jail, her sister Gina makes a move on hubby Tim, who begins to doubt Sally.

JULY — Jack Webster contracts sepsis and has to have a leg amputated.

Rapist Josh is beaten up.

AUG

Johnny Connor kidnaps baby Susie and after she is returned, Eva leaves Weatherfield with her.

SEP — Jim McDonald returns to the Street and lies to Liz that his girlfriend Hannah is actually their daughter Katie.

Tyrone meets his grandmother Evelyn Plummer, after learning he was snatched at birth.

OCT — Steve and Tracy marry, while Liz discovers Jim and Hannah's scam to rip her off.

Daniel and Sinead have a pagan wedding.

OCTOBER

PREGNANT SINEAD IS DIAGNOSED WITH CERVICAL CANCER

Following Sinead's abortion and Daniel being revealed as Ken's attacker, the pair get back together. Sinead and Chesney's relationship is at an end and she realizes she is still in love with Daniel. Daniel is delighted when Sinead becomes pregnant again and the couple get married when Daniel surprises Sinead with a pagan ceremony in the community garden. The couple's joy is short-lived, however, as Sinead, who had secretly been undergoing tests, is diagnosed with cervical cancer and must decide whether to abort the baby and have treatment immediately or delay treatment and give her baby a chance. She chooses to delay treatment, but baby Bertie is born prematurely by caesarean, three months after the ceremony, as Sinead's condition has quickly advanced and she needs more aggressive treatment to save her life.

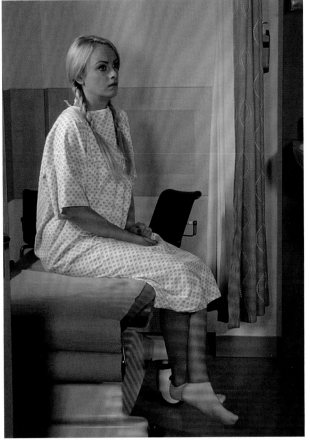

Sally's fraud trial – she's jailed for four years.

Audrey inherits £80,000 in friend Archie Shuttleworth's will.

A drunk Jenny knocks down Liz, and Johnny takes the blame.

NOV

DEC

Leanne is injured when Ronan Truman tries to kill the Connors, prompting Nick to return to her side.

Kate and Rana get engaged after each proposes to the other.

Jenny begins to spy on Liz after finding out she slept with Johnny.

Kate Oates' last episode as producer. She leaves to go to *EastEnders*, and former story editor Iain MacLeod takes over.

Tim is horrified when he wakes up in bed with sister-in-law Gina.

JANUARY

LEWIS ARCHER DIES

Charming male escort and conman Lewis Archer had had an on-off relationship with Audrey since 2010. Gail was suspicious of Lewis but was not immune to his charms herself when he took revenge on her splitting him and Audrey up by pretending to be in love with her and stealing £40,000 from her. She discovered his betrayal when he left her a humiliating confession tape admitting to stringing her along. In 2018 Lewis returned to Weatherfield intent on scamming more money out of Gail, teaming up with a dodgy medium along the way. He reconciled with Audrey and repaid Gail. In January 2019, Audrey finds Lewis dead in her bedroom, 20 years to the day after Alf died. He had been about to propose to Audrey. Thanks to Gail loudly voicing her suspicions, Audrey believes he is responsible when £80,000 – money she inherited from her friend Archie Shuttleworth – vanishes from her account. Later in the year, it emerges that the real culprits are her grandsons Nick and David.

MARCH

THE UNDERWORLD ROOF COLLAPSES, KILLING RANA

When Sally is released from jail following the trumped-up fraud conviction she argues with sister Gina on the roof of Underworld. Suddenly, the roof collapses and Sally falls to the factory floor below. The factory staff are dazed and injured and although Sally survives, Rana, who had been in to the factory collecting her bag containing her wedding vows ahead of her marriage to Kate, is trapped. A weeping Kate insists on being let into the dangerous area and when the firefighters agree, she is able to exchange wedding vows with her beloved Rana and hold her in her arms as she passes away.

JAN

Mary realises her son Jude is a hopeless fantasist and lets him disappear with £800 of her money.

Sally is released from jail.

Gina traces Duncan's wife who forces him to confess to framing Sally.

Amy discovers she's pregnant.

FEB

Peter rescues Simon from his boat after a grieving Roy accidentally sets it alight.

Clayton takes Shona hostage at knifepoint. She escapes by stabbing him but he survives.

MAR

David and Nick open Trim Up North barber's shop using Audrey's money.

Michelle and Robert break up over Michelle's admission she no longer wants a baby.

APR

Billy and Paul embark on a relationship.

Gemma discovers she is pregnant by Chesney after they split up.

Gina leaves the Street.

PRODUCTION NOTE

Aidan Connor's suicide storyline wins three British Soap Awards, including one for Gail's poignant monologue upon hearing the news – a scene that was also shortlisted for a BAFTA Award for 2018's 'Must-See Moment'.

MAY

Norris Cole returns to the Street engaged to Freda Burgess.

Kirk Sutherland goes on a comedy singing trip.

Steve loses his taxi licence after chasing Weatherfield County FC footballer James Bailey, over a fare dodge. James is knocked over.

David admits to Audrey that he and Nick stole her money, not Lewis.

JUNE

David and Nick are charged over the theft of Audrey's money.

Gemma and Chesney learn they are expecting quadruplets.

Norris leaves for Edinburgh.

Gary kills loan shark Rick Neelan.

The Bailey family moves into No 3.

Geoff's control over Yasmeen increases as she becomes more dependent on him after being mugged.

Robert proposes to Michelle, despite making Tyler's mum Vicky pregnant.

MAY

GUILT-RIDDEN CARLA IS SECTIONED

The factory roof collapse leads to one of Carla's darkest times. She believes the accident was her fault because she hadn't listened to Gary when he warned her Pat Phelan had botched an earlier roof job. She had instructed Gary to repair some fire damage and put the roof issue on the back burner. When she discovers Rana has been killed, a tearful Carla insists she should tell the police what she knows, but Peter persuades her to lie and blackmails Gary into keeping quiet. What they don't know is that Gary is responsible for the accident – he had been desperate to earn money to pay back loan shark Rick Neelan. A guilt-ridden Carla admits at Rana's memorial that she knew the roof was unsafe. Roy asks her to move out of the flat, shocked at her behaviour, and Alya starts sending her messages purporting to be from Rana. Suffering from psychosis Carla runs away, living in a squat before returning to Roy's. Her psychosis worsens, she believes she can see Rana and as she attempts suicide by jumping from a fire escape she is saved by Peter, before being sectioned. Peter and Carla get back together after he supports her recovery. Gary goes on to kill Neelan in self-defence, burying his body in woodland and pretending to everyone, including Neelan's teenage daughter Kelly, that the loan shark has moved abroad.

JULY

Geoff blames Alya's friends for robbing a vulnerable Yasmeen, when he is the real culprit.

Maria joins a dating site.

Nick blames his brain injury for his actions. David tells Imran that his brother is to blame for the factory roof collapse.

Gail heads off to Bangkok.

David is sent to jail and Nick given a suspended sentence.

Gemma and Paul's wayward mother Bernie turns up and makes a pass at Chesney.

AUG

Steve learns that he's Emma's father after discovering her mother is his ex Fiona.

First appearance (on a video) of Emma's mum and Steve's ex Fiona Middleton since 1998.

SEP

Ray Crosby makes an unwanted pass at Michelle.

Eileen's boyfriend Jan Lozinski is shot for exposing a human trafficking ring.

Jade Rowan arrives to help with Hope, after she starts a fire at the factory.

Bernie's ex Kel appears and Paul is unhappy to see him.

SEPTEMBER

JAMES REVEALS HIS SECRET TO BETHANY

James Bailey arrived in Weatherfield with his family in May 2019. He is a talented footballer with Weatherfield County FC but is hiding a secret – he is gay and doesn't want his father Ed or the County fans to find out. He confides in Bethany and she agrees to pretend to be his girlfriend to get his father off his back. Older brother Michael overhears and is taken aback to discover that their mother Aggie has known for years about James's sexuality and fully supports him. Aggie urges a reticent James to come out to his father, now that Michael knows the truth.

DECEMBER

MICHELLE CONNOR LEAVES THE STREET

After the death of her baby and subsequent split from Steve, Michelle thought she had found happiness with Robert Preston. They overcame his testicular cancer and gambling problem, but when Robert's double life – in which he was engaged to his pregnant lover Vicky Jefferies as well as Michelle – was uncovered, it was the end of the line. Vicky is the mother of teenaged Tyler, the boy who had got Amy pregnant, and she was thankful to Robert for giving Tyler a job in the Bistro. When Robert found out that Vicky was pregnant he couldn't leave her because he was desperate for a child of his own and Michelle couldn't face another pregnancy after losing Ruairi. Michelle pretends to forgive Robert and they go ahead with their wedding as planned. During the service, instead of saying her vows, Michelle stuns the congregation by reading out Vicky's text messages instead. Vicky and Michelle then work together to get revenge on Robert, leading to him being arrested over the disappearance of his pregnant lover. Michelle helps Vicky give birth to baby Sonny, before relenting and admitting everything to Robert, who days later is accidentally shot dead outside The Rovers by a crazed Derek Milligan. Michelle had already persuaded Robert to sign the Bistro over to her and sells it unwittingly to her lecherous former employer, Ray Crosby. Craving a fresh start, she leaves for a new life in Ireland.

Debbie Webster returns after a 34-year absence from the Street. She wants to give a large inheritance to brother Kevin.

Ken celebrates his 80th birthday.

Gemma goes into labour in a cable car over Llandudno.

Emma suffers a ruptured appendix.

Daniel kisses Bethany in a moment of weakness, and Sinead passes away just days later.

Roy's long-lost half-brother Richard dies, leaving daughter Nina orphaned.

Shona is shot by disturbed Derek Milligan and slips into a coma.

OCT

NOV

DEC

Asha Alahan's use of skin-lightening cream is discovered by her father Dev.

Sinead is told her cancer is terminal and she has just weeks to live.

David is released from prison and he and Shona marry in the Bistro.

Maria reveals she's pregnant with Gary's baby.

Vicky gives birth to baby Sonny.

PRODUCTION NOTE

Coronation Street's 10,000th episode is broadcast on 7th February. The hour-long episode sees Rita learn that former husband Dennis Tanner has died. Accompanied by a selection of Street friends she heads to Blackpool to scatter his ashes. True to form, the trip is highly eventful and the episode contains plenty of nods to bygone characters.

MARCH

GEMMA STRUGGLES WITH THE QUADRUPLETS

Happy-go-lucky Gemma's previous cheeky demeanour has all but disappeared as she battles with looking after four babies and Chesney's son Joseph. She is still reeling from the revelations that twin Paul was groomed and abused by her mother's former partner. The quadruplets – Aled, Carys, Bryn, Llio – were named after the medics who attended to Gemma when she went into labour on a trip to Llandudno in late October 2019. And if the lack of sleep, a disastrous sponsorship deal with local supermarket Freshco, worries over money and snide comments from a couple of mums at a baby group are not enough to cope with, Gemma and Chesney are informed that Aled has profound hearing loss. Gemma begins to have disturbing dreams and when her worried mum Bernie, suspecting post-natal depression, marches her off to see Dr Gaddas, Gemma claims she is just tired. Even the fitting of Aled's specialist baby hearing aids doesn't boost her mood and she eventually tells Rita that she can't cope. Chesney and Bernie rally round as Gemma seeks medical help and launches a vlog to help fellow struggling mums.

APRIL

YASMEEN FINALLY SNAPS AND ATTACKS ABUSIVE GEOFF

Over many months the slow-burn menace of the once jovial Geoff Metcalfe grew and grew. By early 2020 Geoff's control over Yasmeen is almost complete – he's alienated her from her family and friends, installed a hidden camera in her house, pushed for them to marry on a trip to Las Vegas, persuaded her and others that she has a drinking problem, inveigled his way into owning part of Speed Daal and made her highly dependent on him. Yasmeen's granddaughter Alya isn't fooled by Geoff and, together with boyfriend Ryan, she sets about exposing him, going to the police to ask, under Clare's Law, whether he has a record of this kind of behaviour. In February Geoff, having taken up his magic act again, humiliates helper Yasmeen and locks her in a box. Then he kills and cooks his wife's favourite chicken, Charlotte Brontë, serving the bird up for an unwitting Yasmeen to eat. It's only when Yasmeen contracts chlamydia after Geoff frequents an escort service, that she finds the strength to tackle her husband, ultimately lashing out at him during one of his terrifying tirades. Yasmeen faces a legal battle to clear her name, while Geoff's past threatens to unmask his true colours.

JAN

Tracy wakes up in Paula Martin's bed, horrified that she has drunkenly cheated on Steve.

Jade reveals she is John Stape's daughter and frames Fiz for abusing Hope.

Shona comes out of her coma but can't remember who David is.

FEB

Bertie and Maria catch measles, and Maria miscarries.

Maria sleeps with ex Ali before accepting Gary's marriage proposal.

Footballer James comes out as gay to his dad Ed.

Abi torches Ray's car so he blackmails Kevin into selling him the garage.

Gemma and Chesney learn that one of their quads, Aled, has hearing loss.

MAR

Sarah and Adam marry in a Charles Rennie Mackintosh-inspired wedding.

Tracy wants to buy No 1 when Ken announces that he and Claudia are moving.

A drunk Daniel proposes to Bethany, but calls her Sinead. Bethany leaves for London.

APR

The Barlows arrange for grieving Daniel to visit a retreat.

On 18th March ITV announced *Coronation Street* would be broadcast three times a week.

1960

SEP 1961 Ida Barlow is knocked over and killed by a bus.

OCT 1962 Concepta Riley's baby Christopher is snatched, but later found by Elsie.

SEP 1963 Sheila Birtles contemplates suicide after her violent lover Neil ditches her. She is saved by Dennis Tanner.

MAY 1964 Martha Longhurst suffers a heart attack and dies in The Rovers snug.

Dramatic beginnings

As the residents gather in The Rovers to celebrate Billy Walker's return home from National Service, with free drinks courtesy of Annie and Jack, there's the sound of an explosion. A gas main has exploded and is on fire two streets away and the police tell everyone they have to evacuate to the Mission.

AUG 1965 No 7 Coronation Street collapses. The plot remains vacant until 1982, when Len Fairclough builds a home for him and Rita.

SEP 1965 Elsie Tanner is injured in a car crash with a married man she met earlier that night. He dies and she flees the scene.

MAY 1966 Bet Lynch makes her first appearance, as a new factory girl, due to Elliston's raincoat factory expanding its operations.

MAR 1966 Elsie Tanner is hit by lover Jim and Len fights him in the pub.

SEP 1967 Elsie marries Steve Tanner, and Harry Hewitt, who had travelled from Ireland for the occasion, is crushed by Len's broken-down van.

FEB 1968 Twins Peter and Susan are in danger as bulldozers demolish the raincoat factory. They are brought out safely.

AUG 1968 Escaped rapist Frank Riley holds Valerie Barlow hostage, but Ena raises the alarm and Frank is apprehended.

OCT 1969 Elsie is wrongly charged with shoplifting, set up by her friend Dot, but is later cleared.

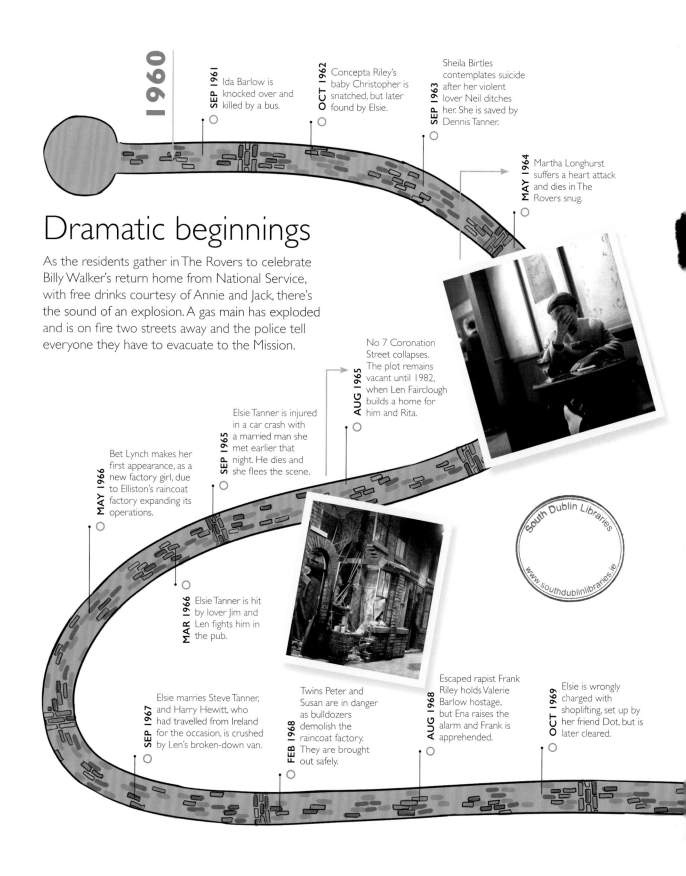

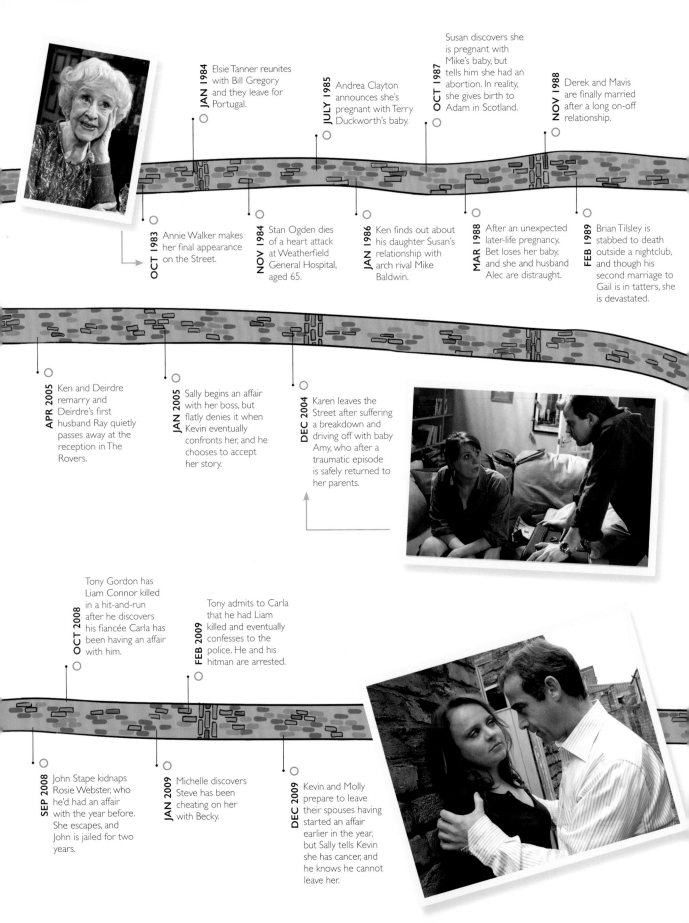

JAN 1984 — Elsie Tanner reunites with Bill Gregory and they leave for Portugal.

JULY 1985 — Andrea Clayton announces she's pregnant with Terry Duckworth's baby.

OCT 1987 — Susan discovers she is pregnant with Mike's baby, but tells him she had an abortion. In reality, she gives birth to Adam in Scotland.

NOV 1988 — Derek and Mavis are finally married after a long on-off relationship.

OCT 1983 — Annie Walker makes her final appearance on the Street.

NOV 1984 — Stan Ogden dies of a heart attack at Weatherfield General Hospital, aged 65.

JAN 1986 — Ken finds out about his daughter Susan's relationship with arch rival Mike Baldwin.

MAR 1988 — After an unexpected later-life pregnancy, Bet loses her baby, and she and husband Alec are distraught.

FEB 1989 — Brian Tilsley is stabbed to death outside a nightclub, and though his second marriage to Gail is in tatters, she is devastated.

APR 2005 — Ken and Deirdre remarry and Deirdre's first husband Ray quietly passes away at the reception in The Rovers.

JAN 2005 — Sally begins an affair with her boss, but flatly denies it when Kevin eventually confronts her, and he chooses to accept her story.

DEC 2004 — Karen leaves the Street after suffering a breakdown and driving off with baby Amy, who after a traumatic episode is safely returned to her parents.

OCT 2008 — Tony Gordon has Liam Connor killed in a hit-and-run after he discovers his fiancée Carla has been having an affair with him.

FEB 2009 — Tony admits to Carla that he had Liam killed and eventually confesses to the police. He and his hitman are arrested.

SEP 2008 — John Stape kidnaps Rosie Webster, who he'd had an affair with the year before. She escapes, and John is jailed for two years.

JAN 2009 — Michelle discovers Steve has been cheating on her with Becky.

DEC 2009 — Kevin and Molly prepare to leave their spouses having started an affair earlier in the year, but Sally tells Kevin she has cancer, and he knows he cannot leave her.

1980

APR 1980 Ena Sharples moves to St Annes and never returns to the Street.

MAR 1981 Emily's estranged, mentally ill, bigamist husband Arnold reappears. He traps her in her home, but is later arrested by the police.

AUG 1982 Maggie Dunlop tells Mike Baldwin she is pregnant, but leaves him for Harry Redman, who raises Mike's son, Mark, as his own.

JUL 1980 Renee Roberts, Alf's second wife, is killed in a car crash.

MAY 1982 Betty Turpin is mugged by teenager Raymond Attwood, whom idealistic leftie Ken is reluctant to report.

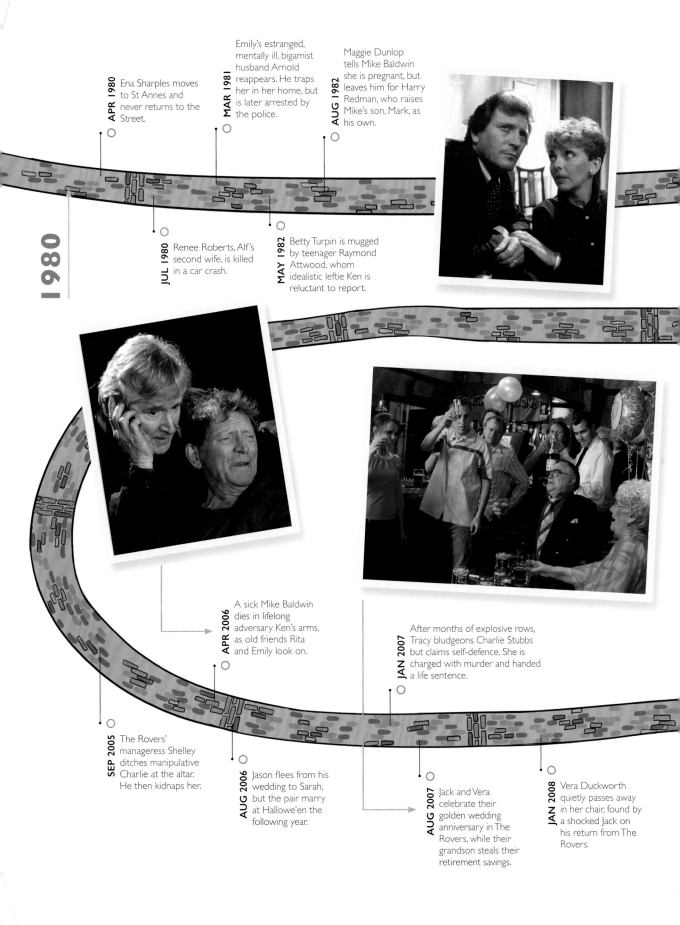

APR 2006 A sick Mike Baldwin dies in lifelong adversary Ken's arms, as old friends Rita and Emily look on.

JAN 2007 After months of explosive rows, Tracy bludgeons Charlie Stubbs but claims self-defence. She is charged with murder and handed a life sentence.

SEP 2005 The Rovers' manageress Shelley ditches manipulative Charlie at the altar. He then kidnaps her.

AUG 2006 Jason flees from his wedding to Sarah, but the pair marry at Hallowe'en the following year.

AUG 2007 Jack and Vera celebrate their golden wedding anniversary in The Rovers, while their grandson steals their retirement savings.

JAN 2008 Vera Duckworth quietly passes away in her chair, found by a shocked Jack on his return from The Rovers.

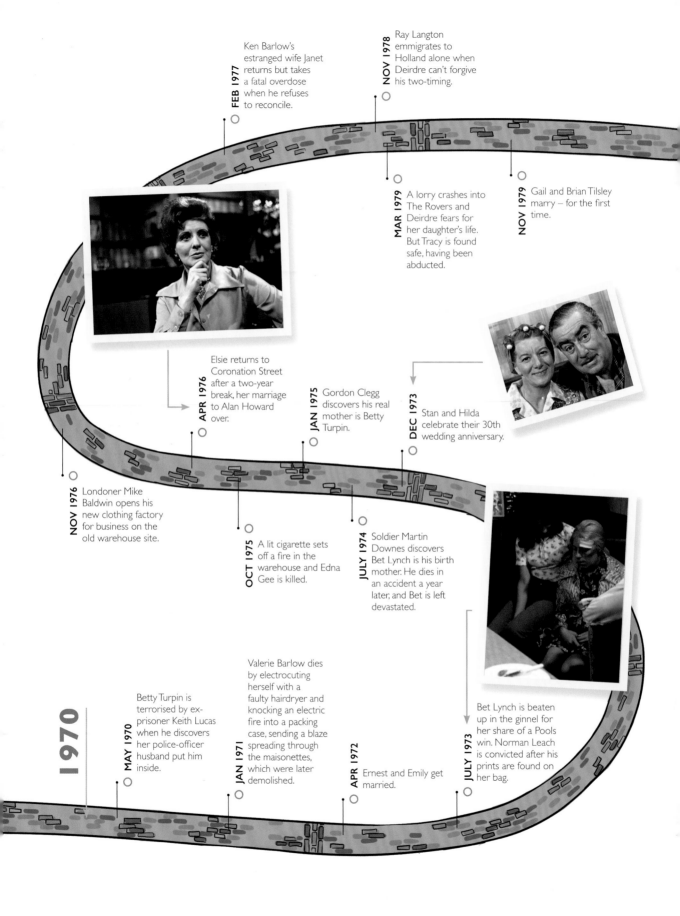

FEB 1977 Ken Barlow's estranged wife Janet returns but takes a fatal overdose when he refuses to reconcile.

NOV 1978 Ray Langton emmigrates to Holland alone when Deirdre can't forgive his two-timing.

MAR 1979 A lorry crashes into The Rovers and Deirdre fears for her daughter's life. But Tracy is found safe, having been abducted.

NOV 1979 Gail and Brian Tilsley marry – for the first time.

APR 1976 Elsie returns to Coronation Street after a two-year break, her marriage to Alan Howard over.

JAN 1975 Gordon Clegg discovers his real mother is Betty Turpin.

DEC 1973 Stan and Hilda celebrate their 30th wedding anniversary.

NOV 1976 Londoner Mike Baldwin opens his new clothing factory for business on the old warehouse site.

OCT 1975 A lit cigarette sets off a fire in the warehouse and Edna Gee is killed.

JULY 1974 Soldier Martin Downes discovers Bet Lynch is his birth mother. He dies in an accident a year later, and Bet is left devastated.

1970

MAY 1970 Betty Turpin is terrorised by ex-prisoner Keith Lucas when he discovers her police-officer husband put him inside.

JAN 1971 Valerie Barlow dies by electrocuting herself with a faulty hairdryer and knocking an electric fire into a packing case, sending a blaze spreading through the maisonettes, which were later demolished.

APR 1972 Ernest and Emily get married.

JULY 1973 Bet Lynch is beaten up in the ginnel for her share of a Pools win. Norman Leach is convicted after his prints are found on her bag.

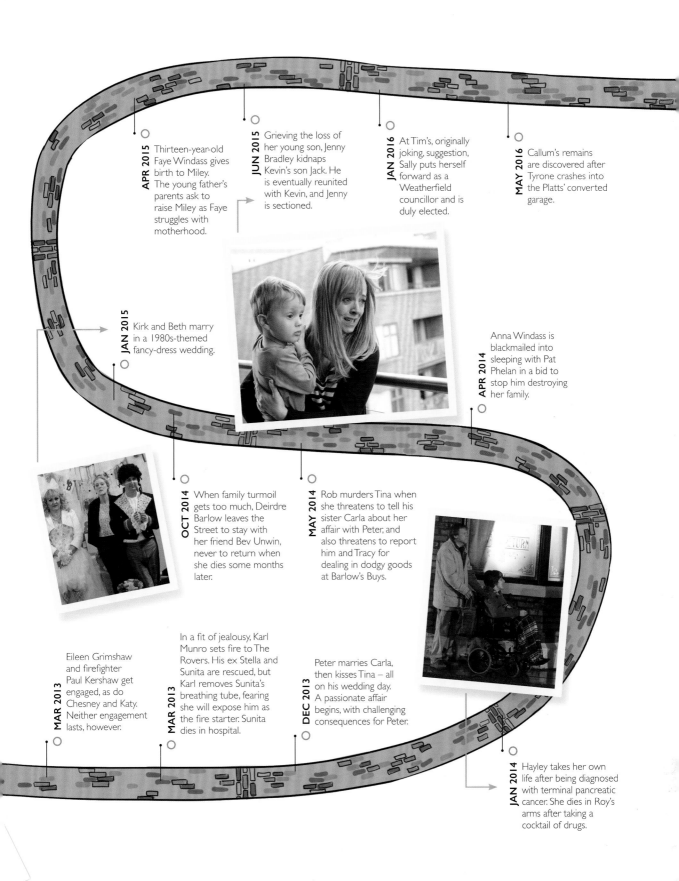

APR 2015 Thirteen-year-old Faye Windass gives birth to Miley. The young father's parents ask to raise Miley as Faye struggles with motherhood.

JUN 2015 Grieving the loss of her young son, Jenny Bradley kidnaps Kevin's son Jack. He is eventually reunited with Kevin, and Jenny is sectioned.

JAN 2016 At Tim's, originally joking, suggestion, Sally puts herself forward as a Weatherfield councillor and is duly elected.

MAY 2016 Callum's remains are discovered after Tyrone crashes into the Platts' converted garage.

JAN 2015 Kirk and Beth marry in a 1980s-themed fancy-dress wedding.

APR 2014 Anna Windass is blackmailed into sleeping with Pat Phelan in a bid to stop him destroying her family.

OCT 2014 When family turmoil gets too much, Deirdre Barlow leaves the Street to stay with her friend Bev Unwin, never to return when she dies some months later.

MAY 2014 Rob murders Tina when she threatens to tell his sister Carla about her affair with Peter, and also threatens to report him and Tracy for dealing in dodgy goods at Barlow's Buys.

MAR 2013 Eileen Grimshaw and firefighter Paul Kershaw get engaged, as do Chesney and Katy. Neither engagement lasts, however.

MAR 2013 In a fit of jealousy, Karl Munro sets fire to The Rovers. His ex Stella and Sunita are rescued, but Karl removes Sunita's breathing tube, fearing she will expose him as the fire starter. Sunita dies in hospital.

DEC 2013 Peter marries Carla, then kisses Tina – all on his wedding day. A passionate affair begins, with challenging consequences for Peter.

JAN 2014 Hayley takes her own life after being diagnosed with terminal pancreatic cancer. She dies in Roy's arms after taking a cocktail of drugs.

MAY 1995 Deirdre's husband Samir is attacked on the way to donate a kidney to Tracy, and subsequently dies of his injuries.

APR 1997 Don Brennan kidnaps Alma after realising he was scammed by her husband Mike. After a long feud, he dies in a crash as he attempts to run Mike over.

SEP 1999 After a prang in Terry Duckworth's 'cut and shut' car, Judy Mallett sustains fatal injuries and dies alone in her backyard.

2000

FEB 2000 Gail and Martin's teenage daughter Sarah is five months pregnant, and philandering Martin realises he has to stay with Gail and support his family.

FEB 1996 A drunk Jim savagely attacks wife Liz over a past affair with an army friend. Liz eventually files for divorce.

MAR 1998 Deirdre is jailed for fraud, set up by fiancé 'airline pilot' Jon Lindsay.

JAN 2000 Raquel briefly returns to the Street for the last time and tells Curly about his two-and-a-half-year-old daughter Alice.

JUN 2002 Bet Lynch is back for Betty's retirement party after seven years away from the cobbles.

MAY 2002 Richard Hillman cons the Street's residents out of their savings, and kills his second wife, under the nose of a blissfully unaware Gail.

MAY 2001 Alma is told she has terminal cervical cancer and dies one month later, with ex Mike, Audrey and Ken at her bedside.

FEB 2001 Susan Barlow dies in a car crash and Mike is awarded custody of their son, Adam.

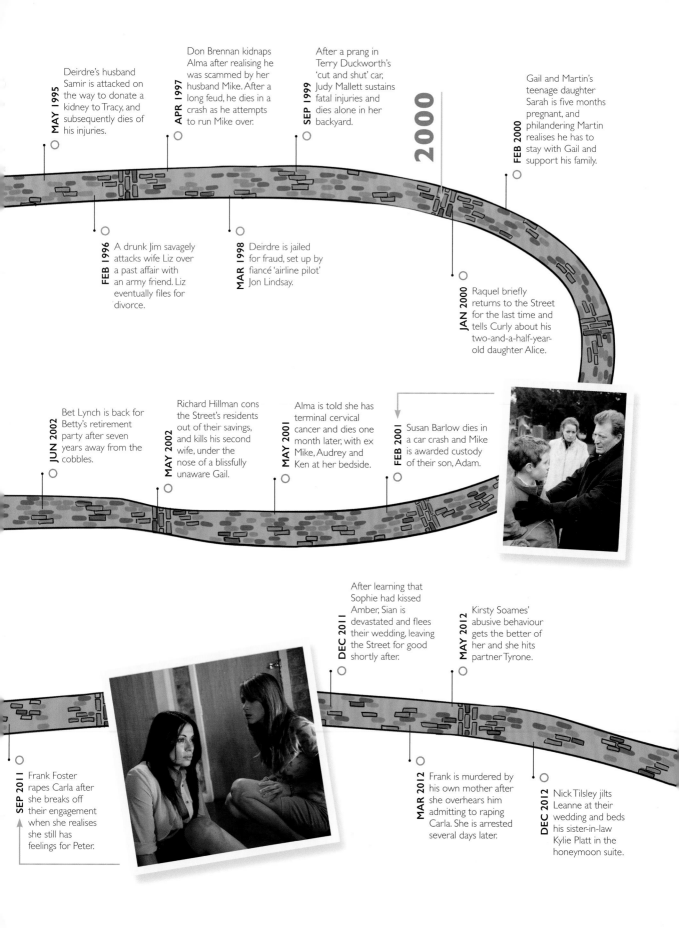

DEC 2011 After learning that Sophie had kissed Amber, Sian is devastated and flees their wedding, leaving the Street for good shortly after.

MAY 2012 Kirsty Soames' abusive behaviour gets the better of her and she hits partner Tyrone.

SEP 2011 Frank Foster rapes Carla after she breaks off their engagement when she realises she still has feelings for Peter.

MAR 2012 Frank is murdered by his own mother after she overhears him admitting to raping Carla. She is arrested several days later.

DEC 2012 Nick Tilsley jilts Leanne at their wedding and beds his sister-in-law Kylie Platt in the honeymoon suite.

1990

JAN 1990 Deirdre kicks Ken out following his affair and he moves in with his mistress Wendy Crozier.

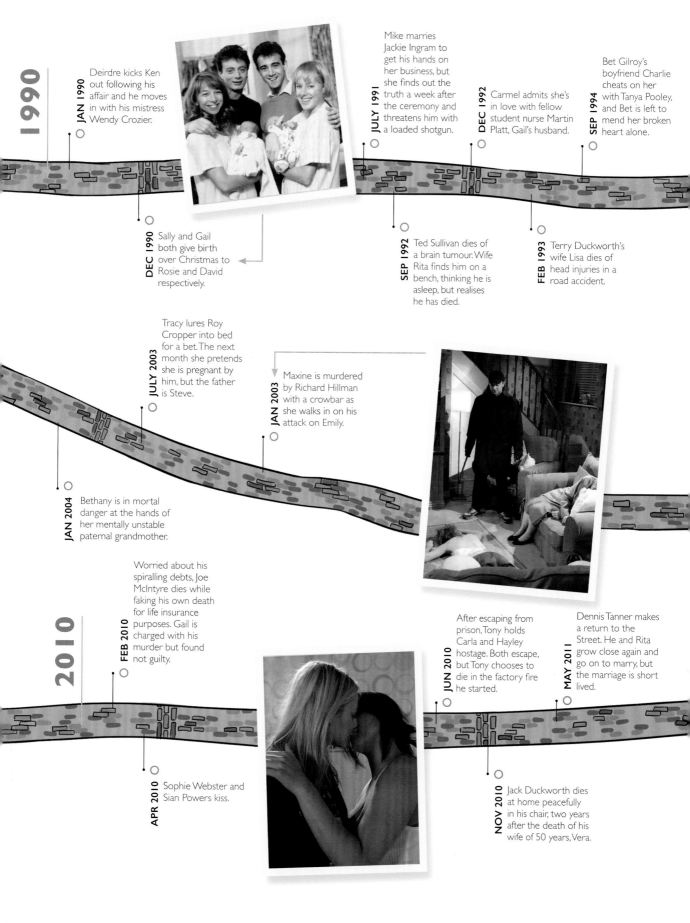

JULY 1991 Mike marries Jackie Ingram to get his hands on her business, but she finds out the truth a week after the ceremony and threatens him with a loaded shotgun.

DEC 1992 Carmel admits she's in love with fellow student nurse Martin Platt, Gail's husband.

SEP 1994 Bet Gilroy's boyfriend Charlie cheats on her with Tanya Pooley, and Bet is left to mend her broken heart alone.

DEC 1990 Sally and Gail both give birth over Christmas to Rosie and David respectively.

SEP 1992 Ted Sullivan dies of a brain tumour. Wife Rita finds him on a bench, thinking he is asleep, but realises he has died.

FEB 1993 Terry Duckworth's wife Lisa dies of head injuries in a road accident.

JULY 2003 Tracy lures Roy Cropper into bed for a bet. The next month she pretends she is pregnant by him, but the father is Steve.

JAN 2003 Maxine is murdered by Richard Hillman with a crowbar as she walks in on his attack on Emily.

JAN 2004 Bethany is in mortal danger at the hands of her mentally unstable paternal grandmother.

2010

FEB 2010 Worried about his spiralling debts, Joe McIntyre dies while faking his own death for life insurance purposes. Gail is charged with his murder but found not guilty.

JUN 2010 After escaping from prison, Tony holds Carla and Hayley hostage. Both escape, but Tony chooses to die in the factory fire he started.

MAY 2011 Dennis Tanner makes a return to the Street. He and Rita grow close again and go on to marry, but the marriage is short lived.

APR 2010 Sophie Webster and Sian Powers kiss.

NOV 2010 Jack Duckworth dies at home peacefully in his chair, two years after the death of his wife of 50 years, Vera.

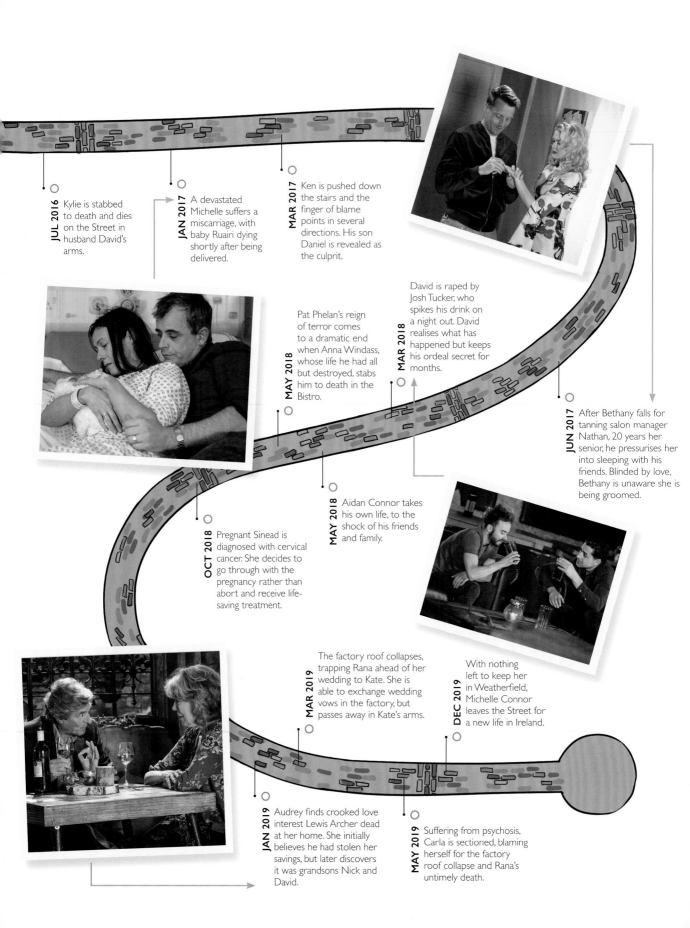

JUL 2016 Kylie is stabbed to death and dies on the Street in husband David's arms.

JAN 2017 A devastated Michelle suffers a miscarriage, with baby Ruairi dying shortly after being delivered.

MAR 2017 Ken is pushed down the stairs and the finger of blame points in several directions. His son Daniel is revealed as the culprit.

MAR 2018 David is raped by Josh Tucker, who spikes his drink on a night out. David realises what has happened but keeps his ordeal secret for months.

MAY 2018 Pat Phelan's reign of terror comes to a dramatic end when Anna Windass, whose life he had all but destroyed, stabs him to death in the Bistro.

JUN 2017 After Bethany falls for tanning salon manager Nathan, 20 years her senior, he pressurises her into sleeping with his friends. Blinded by love, Bethany is unaware she is being groomed.

MAY 2018 Aidan Connor takes his own life, to the shock of his friends and family.

OCT 2018 Pregnant Sinead is diagnosed with cervical cancer. She decides to go through with the pregnancy rather than abort and receive life-saving treatment.

MAR 2019 The factory roof collapses, trapping Rana ahead of her wedding to Kate. She is able to exchange wedding vows in the factory, but passes away in Kate's arms.

DEC 2019 With nothing left to keep her in Weatherfield, Michelle Connor leaves the Street for a new life in Ireland.

JAN 2019 Audrey finds crooked love interest Lewis Archer dead at her home. She initially believes he had stolen her savings, but later discovers it was grandsons Nick and David.

MAY 2019 Suffering from psychosis, Carla is sectioned, blaming herself for the factory roof collapse and Rana's untimely death.

Births, marriages and deaths

...or hatch, match and despatch. All aspects of life are represented on *Coronation Street* and just like any community, that includes the joy of new babies and weddings or saying farewell to a loved one. Here are *Coronation Street*'s arrivals, betrothals and departures.

By the start of 2020, a total of 56 babies had been born to current and former *Coronation Street* residents.

BIRTHS

DATE OF BIRTH	NAME	PLACE	PARENTS
14/06/1961	Paul Cheveski	Infirmary	Ivan and Linda Cheveski
06/08/1962	Christopher Hewitt	Infirmary	Harry and Concepta Hewitt
05/04/1965	Susan Ida Barlow	Weatherfield General	Kenneth and Valerie Barlow
05/04/1965	Peter Barlow	Weatherfield General	Kenneth and Valerie Barlow
20/11/1968	Darren Barlow	Australia	David and Irma Barlow
21/01/1976	Jayne Ogden	Chesterfield	Trevor and Pauline Ogden
24/01/1977	Tracy Lynette Langton	Weatherfield General	Ray and Deirdre Langton
31/12/1980	Nicholas Paul Tilsley	Weatherfield General	Brian and Gail Tilsley
13/04/1983	Mark Redman	Weatherfield General	Mike Baldwin and Maggie Redman
23/05/1984	Dawn Yeats	Bury	Eddie and Marion Yeats
25/03/1985	Peter Clegg	Wimbledon	Gordon and Caroline Clegg
16/02/1986	Paul Clayton	Unknown	Terry Duckworth and Andrea Clayton
03/02/1987	Sarah Louise Tilsley	Weatherfield General	Brian and Gail Tilsley
24/12/1990	Rosie Webster	Rosamund Street	Kevin and Sally Webster
25/12/1990	David Tilsley	Weatherfield General	Martin Platt and Gail Tilsley
01/01/1992	Katherine McDonald	Weatherfield General	Jim and Liz McDonald
09/09/1992	Thomas Duckworth	Weatherfield General	Terry and Lisa Duckworth
04/11/1994	Sophie Webster	Weatherfield General	Kevin and Sally Webster
04/01/1995	Daniel Albert Osbourne	Weatherfield General	Ken Barlow and Denise Osbourne
23/07/1997	Alice Diana Watts	London	Curly and Raquel Watts
14/02/1997	Brad Terry Armstrong	Rovers Return	Terry Duckworth and Tricia Armstrong

Fiona and Morgan

Gail, Sarah, Audrey and Bethany

BIRTHS

DATE OF BIRTH	NAME	PLACE	PARENTS
27/08/1997	Shannon Jade Tattersall	Weatherfield General	Liam Shepherd and Zoe Tattersall
16/02/1998	Morgan Middleton	Weatherfield General	Alan McKenna and Fiona Middleton
25/12/1998	William Mallett	Weatherfield General	Gary and Judy Mallett
25/12/1998	Rebecca Joyce Mallett	Weatherfield General	Gary and Judy Mallett
04/06/2000	Bethany Britney Platt	Weatherfield General	Neil Fearns and Sarah Louise Platt
05/06/2000	Jake Webster	Weatherfield General	Kevin and Alison Webster
19/02/2001	Laura Barnes	Cotswolds	Vinny Sorrell and Natalie Barnes
26/12/2001	Ben Watts	No 7 Coronation Street	Curly and Emma Watts
08/04/2002	Joshua Peacock	Weatherfield General	Matt Ramsden and Maxine Peacock
06/07/2003	Simon John Richards	Weatherfield General	Peter and Lucy Barlow
09/02/2004	Amy Katherine Barlow	Weatherfield General	Steve McDonald and Tracy Barlow
31/05/2004	Billy Platt	Weatherfield General	Todd Grimshaw and Sarah Platt
13/01/2006	Asha Alahan	Weatherfield General	Dev and Sunita Alahan
13/01/2006	Aadi Alahan	Weatherfield General	Dev and Sunita Alahan
17/07/2006	Frederick Thomas Peacock	No 4 Coronation Street	Ashley and Claire Peacock
22/02/2008	Dylan James Wilson	Rovers Return	Sean Tully and Violet Wilson
30/04/2008	Paul Connor	Weatherfield General	Liam and Maria Connor
01/07/2009	Liam Connor	Ainsdale Beach	Liam and Maria Connor
06/09/2010	Jack Dobbs	No 9 Coronation Street	Kevin Webster and Molly Dobbs
09/12/2010	Hope Stape	Weatherfield General	John and Fiz Stape
23/12/2011	Joseph Peter Brown	Weatherfield Community Hall	Chesney Brown and Katy Armstrong
09/09/2012	Ruby Soames	Rovers Return	Tyrone Dobbs and Kirsty Soames
26/05/2013	Jake Windass	Weatherfield General	Gary Windass and Izzy Armstrong
26/08/2013	Lily Platt	No 8 Coronation Street	David and Kylie Platt
01/04/2015	Miley Windass	Weatherfield General	Jackson Hodge and Faye Windass
21/03/2016	Harry Platt	Weatherfield General	Callum Logan and Sarah Platt
06/05/2016	name unknown	Jersey	Lloyd Mullaney and Andrea Beckett
11/01/2017	Ruairi McDonald	Weatherfield General	Steve McDonald and Michelle Connor
20/02/2017	Oliver Benjamin Battersby	Victoria Court	Steve McDonald and Leanne Battersby
30/04/2018	Susie Price	Lymm	Aidan Connor and Eva Price
25/05/2018	Zack Rubinstein	Weatherfield General	Gary Windass and Nicola Rubinstein
14/01/2019	Bertie Osbourne	Weatherfield General	Daniel Osbourne and Sinead Tinker
30/10/2019	Aled Winter-Brown	Cable car, Llandudno	Chesney Brown and Gemma Winter
30/10/2019	Bryn Winter-Brown	St Tudno's Hospital, Llandudno	Chesney Brown and Gemma Winter
30/10/2019	Carys Winter-Brown	St Tudno's Hospital, Llandudno	Chesney Brown and Gemma Winter
30/10/2019	Llio Winter-Brown	St Tudno's Hospital, Llandudno	Chesney Brown and Gemma Winter
20/12/2019	Sonny Jefferies	Heffernan Lodge Hotel	Robert Preston and Vicky Jefferies

MARRIAGES

DATE	BRIDE	GROOM	VENUE
08/03/1961	Joan Walker	Gordon Davies	St Thomas'
01/10/1961	Concepta Riley	Harry Hewitt	St Theresa's
20/06/1962	Christine Hardman	Colin Appleby	Register Office
04/08/1962	Valerie Tatlock	Ken Barlow	St Mary's
19/10/1963	Myra Dickinson	Jerry Booth	St Paul's
08/12/1965	Irma Ogden	David Barlow	Register Office
04/09/1967	Elsie Tanner	Steve Tanner	St Stephen's
29/05/1968	Jenny Sutton	Dennis Tanner	Register Office
15/07/1968	Audrey Bright	Dickie Fleming	Gretna Green
22/07/1970	Elsie Tanner	Alan Howard	Register Office
03/04/1972	Emily Nugent	Ernest Bishop	Mawdsley Street Chapel
29/10/1973	Janet Reid	Ken Barlow	Keswick
10/07/1974	Maggie Clegg	Ron Cooke	St Mary's
07/07/1975	Deirdre Hunt	Ray Langton	Register Office
20/04/1977	Rita Littlewood	Len Fairclough	St Mary's
20/03/1978	Renee Bradshaw	Alf Roberts	Register Office
28/11/1979	Gail Potter	Brian Tilsley	St Boniface
13/05/1981	Eunice Nuttall	Fred Gee	Register Office
27/07/1981	Deirdre Langton	Ken Barlow	All Saints'
20/01/1982	Caroline Wilson	Gordon Clegg	Wimbledon
31/10/1983	Marion Willis	Eddie Yeats	All Saints'
09/01/1985	Elaine Prior	Bill Webster	Register Office
23/12/1985	Audrey Potter	Alf Roberts	Register Office
14/05/1986	Susan Barlow	Mike Baldwin	St Mary's

Ken and Valerie Barlow

Alf and Renee Roberts

MARRIAGES

DATE	BRIDE	GROOM	VENUE
08/10/1986	Sally Seddon	Kevin Webster	Register Office
09/09/1987	Bet Lynch	Alec Gilroy	All Saints'
24/02/1988	Gail Tilsley	Brian Tilsley	Register Office
13/06/1988	Ivy Tilsley	Don Brennan	St Luke's
09/11/1988	Mavis Riley	Derek Wilton	Register Office
12/02/1990	Steph Jones	Des Barnes	Register Office
08/08/1990	Jessica Midgeley	Peter Barlow	Portsmouth
05/07/1991	Jackie Ingram	Mike Baldwin	Register Office
27/09/1991	Gail Tilsley	Martin Platt	Register Office
27/05/1992	Lisa Horton	Terry Duckworth	St Mary's
05/06/1992	Rita Fairclough	Ted Sullivan	Register Office
19/06/1992	Alma Sedgewick	Mike Baldwin	Register Office
29/09/1993	Olive Clarke	Edwin Turner	St Saviour's
26/01/1994	Maureen Naylor	Reg Holdsworth	St Christopher's
25/11/1994	Deirdre Barlow	Samir Rachid	Register Office
09/08/1995	Vicky Arden	Steve McDonald	St Lucia
20/10/1995	Betty Turpin	Billy Williams	St Mary's
08/12/1995	Raquel Wolstenhulme	Curly Watts	Register Office
29/12/1995	Angela Hawthorne	Norris Cole	St Christopher's
13/11/1996	Tracy Barlow	Robert Preston	Register Office
22/09/1997	Maureen Holdsworth	Fred Elliott	Register Office
30/01/1998	Leanne Battersby	Nick Tilsley	Kirkcudbright
23/10/1998	Natalie Horrocks	Des Barnes	Register Office
24/09/1999	Maxine Heavey	Ashley Peacock	St Christopher's

Eddie and Marion Yeats

Bet and Alec Gilroy

Fred and Maureen Elliott

DATE	BRIDE	GROOM	VENUE
01/11/1999	Sharon Gaskell	Ian Bentley	Register Office
23/01/2000	Alison Wakefield	Kevin Webster	Register Office
10/09/2000	Linda Sykes	Mike Baldwin	De Lisle House
30/11/2000	Liz McDonald	Jim McDonald	Strangeways Prison
24/12/2000	Emma Taylor	Curly Watts	St Mary's
30/05/2001	Karen Phillips	Steve McDonald	Register Office
27/07/2002	Gail Platt	Richard Hillman	Aston Manor and Park
09/12/2002	Sally Webster	Kevin Webster	Register Office
24/03/2003	Lucy Richards	Peter Barlow	Register Office
17/11/2003	Tracy Barlow	Roy Cropper	Register Office
14/02/2004	Karen McDonald	Steve McDonald	Walcot Manor
23/10/2004	Sunita Parekh	Dev Alahan	Register Office
25/12/2004	Claire Casey	Ashley Peacock	St Christopher's
08/04/2005	Deirdre Rachid	Ken Barlow	Register Office
26/11/2005	Cilla Brown	Les Battersby	Register Office
31/10/2007	Sarah Platt	Jason Grimshaw	St Christopher's
31/12/2007	Liz McDonald	Vernon Tomlin	Register Office
11/02/2008	Maria Sutherland	Liam Connor	Douglas Hall Hotel
03/12/2008	Carla Connor	Tony Gordon	Hotel
12/01/2009	Molly Compton	Tyrone Dobbs	St Mark's
14/08/2009	Becky Granger	Steve McDonald	Register Office
28/09/2009	Fiz Brown	John Stape	HMP Highfield
08/01/2010	Gail Platt	Joe McIntyre	Register Office
30/08/2010	Hayley Cropper	Roy Cropper	Shawbrooke Country House Hotel

Ashley and Maxine Peacock

Dev and Sunita Alahan

Gail and Joe McIntyre

MARRIAGES

DATE	BRIDE	GROOM	VENUE
09/12/2010	Leanne Battersby	Peter Barlow	Weatherfield General Hospital
08/04/2011	Xin Chiang	Graeme Proctor	Register Office
08/04/2011	Kylie Turner	David Platt	Register Office
23/01/2012	Tracy Barlow	Steve McDonald	St James'
04/06/2012	Rita Sullivan	Dennis Tanner	Register Office
11/01/2013	Leanne Barlow	Nick Tilsley	Dalebrook Hall
11/09/2013	Stella Price	Karl Munro	Register Office
04/12/2013	Carla Connor	Peter Barlow	Charston House Hotel
24/04/2015	Gail McIntyre	Michael Rodwell	Register Office
25/05/2015	Michelle Connor	Steve McDonald	Register Office
10/03/2016	Maria Connor	Pablo Duarte	Cyprus
22/05/2016	Carla Connor	Nick Tilsley	Nick's Bistro
20/01/2017	Eileen Grimshaw	Pat Phelan	Register Office
25/08/2017	Mary Taylor	Norris Cole	Register Office
18/09/2017	Jenny Bradley	Johnny Connor	Weatherfield General Hospital
17/11/2017	Rana Nazir	Zeedan Nazir	Register Office
08/10/2018	Tracy Barlow	Steve McDonald	Chariot Square Hotel
09/09/2019	Sinead Tinker	Daniel Osbourne	Register Office
07/11/2019	Shona Ramsey	David Platt	Viaduct Bistro
16/11/2019	Yasmeen Nazir	Geoff Metcalfe	Las Vegas
02/03/2020	Sarah Platt	Adam Barlow	Hotel

Sarah and Adam Barlow

David and Shona Platt

DEATHS

DATE	NAME	CAUSE OF DEATH
31/12/1960	May Hardman	Brain tumour
11/09/1961	Ida Barlow	Run over by a bus
12/10/1962	Colin Appleby	Car crash
27/01/1964	Susan Schofield	Run over by a lorry
13/05/1964	Martha Longhurst	Heart attack
15/09/1965	Robert Maxwell	Heart attack
11/01/1967	Vera Lomax	Brain tumour
10/05/1967	Sonia Peters	Crushed under rubble
04/09/1967	Harry Hewitt	Crushed under a van
28/09/1968	Steve Tanner	Pushed down the stairs
05/11/1969	Reg Ellis	Coach crash
08/04/1970	David Barlow	Car crash
09/04/1970	Darren Barlow	Car crash
30/06/1970	Jack Walker	Heart attack
21/12/1970	Joe Donelli	Shot himself
27/01/1971	Valerie Barlow	Electrocuted
02/05/1973	Herbert 'Jessie' James	Heart attack
25/02/1974	Cyril Turpin	Heart attack
29/01/1975	Lynn Johnson	Battered by her husband
09/07/1975	Martin Downes	Car crash
01/10/1975	Edna Gee	Died in a fire
10/11/1975	Jerry Booth	Heart attack
21/02/1977	Janet Barlow	Overdose
17/08/1977	Edie Riley	Old age
11/01/1978	Ernest Bishop	Shot
30/07/1980	Renee Roberts	Car/lorry crash
12/11/1980	Monty Shawcross	Old age
28/12/1981	Arnold Swain	Mental illness
04/07/1982	Frankie Baldwin	Heart attack
18/05/1983	Archie Crabtree	Stroke
07/12/1983	Len Fairclough	Car crash
16/01/1984	Bert Tilsley	Mental illness
14/05/1984	Albert Tatlock	Old age
21/11/1984	Stan Ogden	Old age
03/06/1985	Don Ashton	Drowned
23/11/1987	Joan Lowther	Heart attack
11/01/1989	Eddie Seddon	Lorry crash
15/02/1989	Brian Tilsley	Stabbed

DATE	NAME	CAUSE OF DEATH
08/12/1989	Alan Bradley	Run over by a tram
17/08/1990	Peter Ingram	Heart attack
18/02/1991	Amy Burton	Heart attack
19/07/1991	Sandra Arden	Car crash
19/07/1991	Tim Arden	Car crash
02/01/1992	Katherine McDonald	Premature birth
09/09/1992	Ted Sullivan	Brain tumour
12/02/1993	Lisa Duckworth	Brain damage
05/05/1993	Les Curry	Heart attack
20/08/1993	Brendan Scott	Heart attack
08/11/1993	Joss Shackleton	Old age
25/03/1994	Mandy Baker	Cardiac arrest
02/06/1995	Samir Rachid	Fractured skull
21/06/1995	Cliff Duckworth	Car crash
21/06/1995	Elsie Duckworth	Car crash
23/08/1995	Ivy Brennan	Stroke
21/02/1997	Joyce Smedley	Run over by a car
07/04/1997	Derek Wilton	Heart attack
08/10/1997	Don Brennan	Car crash
03/11/1997	Billy Williams	Heart attack
18/03/1998	Babs Fanshawe	Heart attack
17/04/1998	Shannon Tattersall	Meningitis
25/05/1998	Elsie Seddon	Stroke
09/10/1998	Anne Malone	Frozen to death
18/11/1998	Des Barnes	Heart attack
01/01/1999	Alf Roberts	Stroke
04/02/1999	Tony Horrocks	Attacked
07/02/1999	Walter Byford	Heart attack
06/08/1999	Sidney Templeton	Heart attack
24/09/1999	Judy Mallett	Embolism
25/12/1999	Simon	Knocked off his bike
05/06/2000	Jake Webster	Group B strep
07/06/2000	Alison Webster	Run over by a lorry
15/09/2000	Jez Quigley	Internal injuries after beating
12/10/2000	Dean Sykes	Gunshot wounds
11/02/2001	Susan Barlow	Car crash
17/06/2001	Alma Halliwell	Cervical cancer
19/09/2001	Edna Miller	Heart attack

DEATHS

DATE	NAME	CAUSE OF DEATH
02/01/2002	Dennis Stringer	Car crash
04/02/2002	Duggie Ferguson	Fell through the banister
20/05/2002	Patricia Hillman	Hit on the head with a shovel
13/01/2003	Maxine Peacock	Bludgeoned with a crowbar
11/03/2003	Richard Hillman	Drowned
03/11/2003	Preston King	Heart attack
28/11/2003	Cecil Newton	Heart attack
02/06/2004	Billy Platt	Premature birth
02/03/2005	Tommy Harris	Hit on the head with a wrench
08/04/2005	Ray Langton	Stomach cancer
20/04/2005	Katy Harris	Cerebral oedema caused by diabetic ketoacidosis
13/05/2005	Barney the Rabbit	Unknown
25/07/2005	Harry Baldwin	Suspected heart attack
01/01/2006	Lena Thistlewood	Old age
07/04/2006	Mike Baldwin	Alzheimer's, pneumonia and heart attack
09/10/2006	Fred Elliott	Stroke
15/01/2007	Charlie Stubbs	Hit on the head with an ornament
16/04/2007	Kasia Barowicz	Broken neck
06/06/2007	Paul Connor	Car crash
04/08/2007	Angela Hawthorne	Heart attack

DATE	NAME	CAUSE OF DEATH
03/10/2007	Frank Nichols	In his sleep
18/01/2008	Vera Duckworth	Heart attack
30/04/2008	Paul Connor Jr	Still birth
02/10/2008	Lucy Richards	Breast cancer
16/10/2008	Liam Connor	Run over by a car
30/01/2009	Mike Scott	Clot on a lung
18/05/2009	Colin Grimshaw	Stroke
26/08/2009	Ramsay Clegg	Brain tumour
08/02/2010	Joe McIntyre	Drowned
03/05/2010	Blanche Hunt	In her sleep
01/06/2010	Robbie Sloane	Shot
01/06/2010	Tony Gordon	Burned alive
30/07/2010	Colin Fishwick	Acute extradural haemorrhage
07/11/2010	Jack Duckworth	Heart attack (caused by non-Hodgkin's lymphoma)
13/11/2010	Luke 'Quinny' Quinn	Bomb explosion
09/12/2010	Ashley Peacock	Crushed by a collapsed viaduct
09/12/2010	Molly Dobbs	Blood loss
09/12/2010	Charlotte Hoyle	Brain damage
10/01/2011	Joy Fishwick	Angina attack
07/03/2011	Edna Hargreaves	Natural causes
28/10/2011	John Stape	Cardiac arrest as a result of a car crash
08/12/2011	Jonno Richardson	Liver failure

Michael Vernon Baldwin

1942 – 2006

Maxine Peacock
1975–2003

Sunita Alahan
Died 3rd April 2013
Aged 35 Years

Deirdre Barlow
Born 8th July 1955
Died 8th July 2015

Kylie Platt
Died 15th July 2016
Aged 28 Years

TINA McINTYRE
AT REST
2ND JUNE 2014
AGED 23 YEARS

Kylie Platt
22.08.1987 - 15.07.2016

St Edmond's Church
Monday 1st August 2016
at 2pm

DATE	NAME	CAUSE OF DEATH
06/01/2012	Sam Foster	Heart attack
05/03/2012	Frank Foster	Blow to the head
05/04/2012	Geoff Horton	Heart attack
16/04/2012	Betty Williams	Old age
11/05/2012	Lesley Kershaw	Electrocuted
23/09/2012	Meredith McGuire	Illness
25/02/2013	Eric Babbage	Heart attack
18/03/2013	Toni Griffiths	Pub fire
03/04/2013	Sunita Alahan	Inhalation of the products of combustion
06/11/2013	Jane Rayner	Pancreatic cancer
20/01/2014	Hayley Cropper	Morphine overdose
02/06/2014	Tina McIntyre	Head injury
22/10/2014	Lenny Baker	Unknown
13/03/2015	Gavin Rodwell	Cardiac arrest
25/05/2015	Kal Nazir	Burned alive
01/06/2015	Maddie Heath	Head injury
08/07/2015	Deirdre Barlow	Aneurysm
21/09/2015	Callum Logan	Head injury
20/04/2016	Tony Stewart	Heart attack
15/07/2016	Kylie Platt	Stabbed
18/11/2016	Michael Rodwell	Heart attack
11/01/2017	Ruairi McDonald	Late miscarriage
19/06/2017	Drew Spellman	Heart failure
02/10/2017	Lara Cutler	Jumped from a bridge
18/10/2017	Katy Armstrong	Car crash

DATE	NAME	CAUSE OF DEATH
27/10/2017	Vinny Ashford	Shot
27/10/2017	Andy Carver	Shot
05/01/2018	Luke Britton	Car explosion
09/05/2018	Aidan Connor	Suicide
28/05/2018	Pat Phelan	Stabbed
23/07/2018	Jackie Dobbs	Long illness
17/08/2018	Hassan Habeeb	Stroke
28/09/2018	Cormac Truman	Drug overdose
08/10/2018	Ronan Truman	Acute intra-abdominal haemorrhage
12/12/2018	Steff Mulvenney	Breast cancer (complications after contracting mumps)
14/12/2018	Archie Shuttleworth	Old age
01/01/2019	Lewis Archer	Heart attack
23/01/2019	Sylvia Goodwin	Heart attack
01/02/2019	Dane Hibbs	Overdose
19/03/2019	Rana Habeeb	Crushed by an iron girder
17/06/2019	Rick Neelan	Bludgeoned with a rock
12/08/2019	John Brooker	Stomach cancer
25/10/2019	Sinead Osbourne	Cervical cancer
18/12/2019	Richard Lucas	Pulmonary fibrosis
25/12/2019	Derek Milligan	Fell to his death
25/12/2019	Robert Preston	Shot
Jan 2020	Dennis Tanner	Dementia

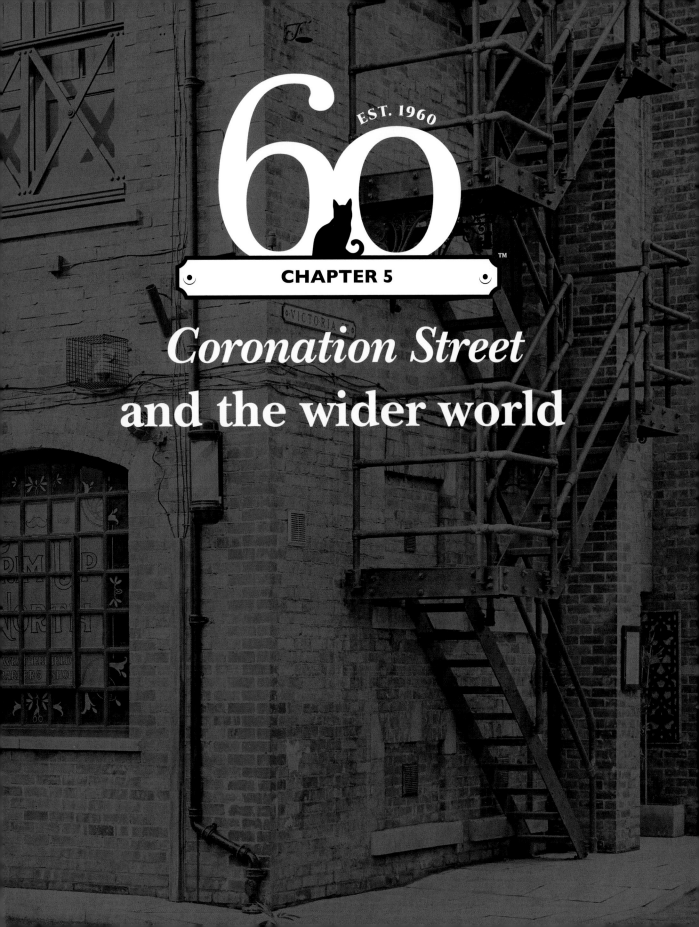

EST. 1960

60

CHAPTER 5

Coronation Street
and the wider world

Important issues *Coronation Street* has tackled

CORONATION STREET is known for its strong characters, its northern humour and its homely feel, but it has also addressed contemporary issues throughout its 60 years, in a believable and sympathetic way, thanks to the talent of its writers and the interpretation of those writers' words by the cast over the years. Its treatment of issues that, in some way, will touch us all at some point has been recognised not only with the awards it has amassed but also by the viewers, whose own life experiences have been echoed in the show.

Producer Iain MacLeod says that, latterly, what *Coronation Street* has become very good at is the big, socially important, state-of-the-nation storylines. 'My predecessor Kate Oates was extremely good at that. The storyline about Bethany's grooming for example was huge and important, and part of what soaps do when they're at their best is prompt conversations in people's living rooms about subjects that might otherwise be swept under the carpet.'

He adds that Aidan's suicide story was important for that and, more recently, the Sinead cancer story. 'I'm very proud of all the work we did on that. It's kind of the 20-something version of what we did with Roy and Hayley in the pancreatic cancer story.'

Patti Clare, who plays Mary, agrees: 'We go into people's homes several times a week and the show, I believe, creates massive value, such as with the Sinead storyline or Hayley's euthanasia story. It might be the first time some young people see things like this. That means something.'

Here are some of the storylines that made headlines and, sometimes, actually saved lives…

Teen pregnancy

When Sarah Louise Platt gave birth to Bethany in June 2000, at the age of 13, the storyline was seen as highly controversial and made headlines in the UK. The show's writers were able to go on to examine the life of a teenage single mum and the impact on the wider family.

Discussing the pregnancy storyline, Helen Worth said: 'When Jack and Tina (David and Sarah) came in and we did the pregnancy storyline, I think that's when I really felt I'd landed. I had two wonderful young actors to work with, they were so good. I hope we did a good job with that storyline.'

Sarah's experience was echoed in 2015 when Faye Windass gave birth to baby Miley (named, befitting Faye's young age, after pop star Miley Cyrus). In 2019 Amy Barlow had an abortion after getting pregnant at 14. In each underage pregnancy, the father was a schoolfriend.

Transgender issues

Ahead of its time, *Coronation Street* introduced the soap world's first transgender main character, when shy Hayley Patterson appeared in 1998. The writers explored the blossoming romance between Hayley and her future husband Roy Cropper, Roy's initial rejection when Hayley revealed that she had been born a male called Harold and the bigotry she initially encountered on the Street when her secret was revealed. Hayley proved immensely popular throughout her 16 years in the show, thanks in large part to actor Julie Hesmondhalgh's sympathetic portrayal, which went a long way to revolutionising the public's attitude to transgender people. Her storyline also contributed to a national debate ahead of the 2004 Gender Recognition Act, which granted transgender people legal status in their chosen gender. Roy and Hayley's story also covered civil partnerships and same-sex marriages.

Hayley Patterson, soap's first major transgender character

The right to die story remains one of the most memorable and influential storylines of which Coronation Street is rightfully proud.

The right to die

Again, Hayley was at the centre of the national debate over the ethical issue of the right to die. The character was diagnosed with inoperable pancreatic cancer in 2013 and, after treatment proved ineffectual and worried about the chance that she could, in the later stages of the disease and under the effects of high doses of morphine, regress into being Harold – she wanted to die as Hayley – she chose to end her own life. The show's researchers consulted The Samaritans among other experts ahead of filming and the view was taken that the storyline should not sentimentalise suicide in any way. The storyline coincided with the progress through the House of Lords of an assisted dying bill, which would have enabled terminally ill patients with fewer than six months to live to be prescribed a fatal dose of drugs if they demonstrated that they have reached a 'clear and settled intention' to end their life.

The episode in which Hayley swallowed a cocktail of poison to end her life, on the bed of their flat in the arms of a terrified but ever-loving Roy, not only explored the trauma of loved ones who struggle with such a decision, but also resulted in heart-breaking episodes that were highly praised by both viewers and critics, saw record viewing figures and contributed to the show winning a coveted BAFTA in 2014. It remains one of the most memorable and influential storylines of which *Coronation Street* is rightfully very proud.

Racism

Right from the early days *Coronation Street* has intermittently tackled racism. The first black character to appear was bus driver Johnny Alexander, played by Thomas Baptiste. He featured in several episodes in 1963, where the character was sacked following an altercation with Len Fairclough. His wife in the show was played by Barbara Assoon.

Over the years several storylines have examined the issue of racism. Interracial couple Curly Watts and Shirley Armitage experienced prejudice when they moved into the Corner Shop flat together, Samir Rachid encountered a gang of youths who mocked his ethnicity before fatally attacking him, while firefighter Paul Kershaw's use of outdated language offended Lloyd Mullaney and his daughter Jenna Kamara and sparked a debate among the residents.

Len Fairclough gets a bus driver unfairly dismissed in a racist row

Curly Watts and Shirley Armitage experienced prejudice against their relationship

Coercive control

When Yasmeen Nazir became involved with Geoff Metcalfe, the slow-burn introduction of his controlling nature proved compelling viewing. 'The writers were wonderful in creating Yasmeen's character,' says Shelley King who plays the grandmother, 'because she was ripe for the sort of coercive abuse she receives from Geoff. She was abandoned by her husband, so she feared abandonment. And he doesn't want people to leave him either. It's about co-dependency.

'The situation was drip-fed and then ramped up. I cannot emphasise enough the importance of the abuse storyline. The number of people who stop me in the street and begin to tell me about their experiences. How important it is and how they wish they could have had something to relate to. This kind of storyline lets them see that they're not alone.'

And Ian Bartholomew (Geoff) adds: 'The coercive control is one of those issues that a soap like *Coronation Street* has as part of their remit. If people see something on TV that helps them in any way, then that's an incredibly useful and proper thing to do. We spoke to people who work with victims of domestic abuse and coercive control. People said it was uncomfortable, it hit a nerve and that means we're doing our job. It was a terribly important issue that we were tackling and we had to do it properly.'

Cancer

Sinead Osbourne's 2019 death from cervical cancer, 18 years after the subject was covered with Alma Halliwell, contained scenes that were as accurate as they were moving, thanks to the research and collaboration undertaken with cancer charities. Actor Katie McGlynn says: 'The response we got to Sinead's storyline was overwhelming for me, I didn't expect it to be so big. I knew it was a big story because we all worked hard on it for 18 months, but I didn't realise how big it would be, so I just feel so lucky they gave me the opportunity to do it.'

Homosexuality, including within the Church

Coronation Street has embraced several gay characters over the years, from Todd Grimshaw and Sean Tully – the show's first regular gay character – to Billy Mayhew, a gay vicar, where the writers examined the issue of homosexuality within the clergy, Sophie Webster and, more recently, Kate Connor and Rana Habeeb, Gemma's twin brother Paul and footballer James Bailey. Gay characters such as Sean and Sophie are characters who are uncontroversial in their sexuality, but homophobia was covered specifically in a 2015 episode, where Sean and his then boyfriend Billy suffered homophobic abuse at the hands of a guesthouse owner.

Domestic abuse on males

When Tyrone Dobbs was shown suffering in silence at the hands of violent partner Kirsty Soames, it lifted a lid on a subject rarely discussed in public, and abuse charities saw an increase in men wanting to talk about the hidden problem.

Historic sexual abuse

2019's harrowing storyline covered Paul Foreman's childhood abuse at the hands of his mother Bernie's ex-partner and examined not only Paul's ordeal, but also the impact on family members. We also saw the repercussions of Bernie trying to out the paedophile on social media when arsonists targeted Gemma and Chesney's home.

Geoff and Yasmeen's coercive control storyline shocked audiences

'Calls to male rape charities went up 1,700 per cent after David's rape storyline.'

Sophie Webster with Maddie

Grooming

Bethany Platt's grooming and subsequent sexual abuse by an older man and his friends echoed recent news stories about organised grooming gangs. The issue was sensitively treated and went on to show the longer-term effects on Bethany.

Suicide

Although *Coronation Street* had covered suicide previously, it was Aidan Connor's that made the headlines. The writers shone a light on the issue of people, especially young men, being unable to discuss their mental health problems.

Coronation Street's chief publicity officer Alison Sinclair says that the Aidan suicide story really did make a difference. 'It saved lives, 100 per cent. I tweeted about it and a guy messaged me to say he was in the same position as Aidan, he was about to kill himself and he watched that episode and he realised the effect it would have on all his family, and a year on his life had completely turned around.

'That was one of those moments that we were able to make a massive difference. Handling the PR on that storyline was

really important. We worked with The Samaritans and CALM (Campaign Against Living Miserably) ahead of transmission, and that was one of those occasions where we didn't keep it a secret because it was so important, we had to tell people it was going to happen.'

Alison adds: 'Calls to male rape charities went up 1,700 per cent after David's rape storyline. Hayley's suicide resulted in a petition about assisted dying. A lot of people will sit in a doctor's surgery and see the leaflets for help with this or that and you don't take it in, you don't pick up a leaflet, but you get home and sit on the sofa with your family and whether it's Bethany being groomed, Sinead's cervical cancer, Alma dying of cancer, male rape or transgender issues, it gets people talking about things with their family like nothing else can.'

Casting director Gennie Radcliffe concludes: 'We have some phenomenal writers, they're really passionate about it. I love the stories that make people talk, like Aidan's suicide and the Bethany grooming storyline. We got letters from teachers and parents saying we'd given them a way to start a conversation with their daughters and even if that's just one person that you've helped not be groomed, then it's worth it. I feel proud to work on a programme that hopefully does some good.'

Johnny Connor tries to come to terms with his son's suicide

Coronation Street's crowning glory — royal (and VIP) visits to the Street

AS the nation's favourite soap, *Coronation Street* has hosted more than one royal visit over the years. In May 1982, the Queen and Prince Philip arrived to officially open the new outdoor set at Granada's Manchester studios. They walked along the Street, greeting excited cast members and production staff, and when the Queen asked Tony Warren where the real Coronation Street was, Warren is reported to have replied to the smiling monarch: 'It sounds a bit crowy Ma'am, but it's wherever you want it to be in your own heart.'

Cast members had met the Queen five years earlier when a *Coronation Street* sketch was specially written for a royal visit to a Manchester theatre, and there have been reports over the years that

Her Majesty is a fan of the show. To mark the programme's 40th anniversary live episode in 2000, Prince Charles appeared in a pre-recorded cameo and also visited the set, enjoying a quick 'drink' in The Rovers.

First assistant director at the time Dayle Evans-Kar recalls: 'For the 40th we had a live insert which was going to be Prince Charles, and the writers had thought, wouldn't it be great if Audrey could, as the local councillor, present Prince Charles with a plant for his garden at Highgrove? We were given the go-ahead from the Prince's office that this would be fine, so a small unit was going to go and meet Prince Charles at Piccadilly Station and it would be a snatched moment that would go out that night during the live episode.

'I had to go in and tell him to be quiet!'

'A couple of days before, we got a message that it wasn't happening, it wasn't possible. But then on the day, I arrived to be told it was happening after all! We had since lost Piccadilly Station as everyone had been stood down, so we had to decide what to do. He ended up meeting the cast and Audrey did the presentation. I was there to greet him, but I can't remember to this day what he said or what I said to him.'

Ten years later, at the time of the show's 50th anniversary, the Duchess of Cornwall paid a visit to the set and was presented with a brooch of Hilda's flying ducks. And in 2016, Princess Anne was welcomed to the studios as part of a visit to Manchester by dignitaries from the Commonwealth.

As well as members of the British aristocracy, members of Hollywood royalty have been welcomed onto the cobbles. Alfred Hitchcock, Dustin Hoffman and Howard Keel have all popped into The Rovers at some point.

And Dayle Evans-Kar once had to take Hannibal Lecter in hand. 'Anthony Hopkins was here once – he came to visit, he wasn't actually on the show, but I remember he was so excited coming in to the old studios. We were filming in The Rovers and he was in The Kabin taking photos – I had to go in and tell him off, tell him to be quiet!'

Alfred Hitchcock peers out of The Rovers Return

Queen Elizabeth II visiting in 1982

The Prince of Wales celebrates *Coronation Street*'s 40th anniversary

The Duchess of Cornwall drops in to celebrate the 50th anniversary

In the headlines
and in Parliament

CORONATION STREET'S stars and their storylines have made front-page news ever since the show began in the 1960s. When Pat Phoenix left the Street, acres of newsprint were devoted to her, and Violet Carson's death in 1983 was the front-page splash in the *Daily Express* with the headline 'Ena Sharples is dead'.

These days the show's younger actors feature heavily in newspapers, magazines and online. And the impact of some of *Coronation Street*'s storylines is such that they have even been discussed in Parliament.

Hayley's transgender story prompted an Early Day Motion to be tabled in the House of Commons in November 1998. It stated: 'This House congratulates the scriptwriters, actors and producers of *Coronation Street* for their sensitive and realistic portrayal of Hayley, a transsexual woman [...] gives special regard to Julie Hesmondhalgh, who has made so much effort to find out about what it is to be transsexual, and hopes that the Government will soon see fit to guarantee transsexual people full civil rights [...]

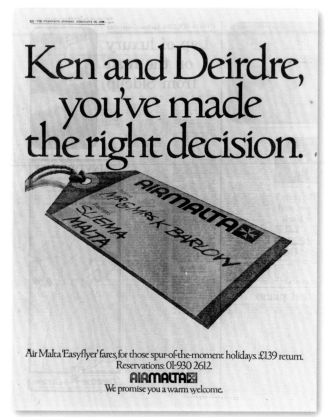

Air Malta celebrates the Barlows' holiday in 1983

The Daily Express, 27th December 1983

so that Hayley and Roy will, like any other couple, be entitled to make a state-recognised, lifelong commitment.' Eventually the law was changed and Roy and Hayley were able to marry in the show.

When Deirdre Rachid was wrongly jailed in 1998, the nationwide Free the Weatherfield One campaign even attracted the attention of Prime Minister Tony Blair who, in a tongue-in-cheek moment, asked his Home Secretary to intervene. Chief Publicity Officer Alison Sinclair remembers receiving a call in the press office. 'Someone said he was from the Downing Street press office and could I brief him on the Deirdre story because Tony Blair was going to talk about it and I said, yeah right, which radio station is this, because I thought it was a wind-up. But it really was No 10! That's one of those moments you go, this show is ridiculous, it's actually being discussed in Parliament!'

Patricia Phoenix with just some of the Street's press cuttings

Journalist Katie Fitzpatrick is a TV and showbiz writer for the *Manchester Evening News*. She writes spoilers, viewer reaction stories to the characters and storylines, and visits the set regularly for important episode screenings and interviews with the cast. Katie explains how important *Coronation Street* is to readers, not just in Manchester, but around the world. 'Online, stories about *Coronation Street* come second only to Manchester United news in terms of readership across the globe. There's so much love for *Corrie* we decided to set up our own *Coronation Street* Facebook page, which has members in New Zealand and Canada, and it hosts some strong discussions about characters, storylines as well as nostalgia.'

For the *Coronation Street* live episode to mark ITV's 60th anniversary, the newspaper set up a live blog on its website to cover every moment. 'As a journalist I love finding out future *Coronation Street* plots because I feel part of the team while keeping them secret, and then I love watching them all unfold again through the eyes of the viewer and their reactions to the storylines. It means such a lot to the people of Manchester and Salford because these familiar faces who we grew up watching on TV feel like our own neighbours. They hold up a mirror to our lives. Life without *Coronation Street* is unimaginable. It feels as though it will outlive us all.'

The future – 2020 onwards

AS the nation's favourite soap celebrates its diamond anniversary, viewers can be sure that its writers will continue to serve up dramatic, touching and humorous storylines long into the future.

Production may have been interrupted due to the coronavirus pandemic but, while scenes were hastily rewritten, screenings were reduced and the actors and crew spent time at home under lockdown, future storylines continued to evolve alongside planning for the 60th celebrations.

Producer Iain MacLeod says, 'We felt that the right way to begin and end our 60th year was to keep the core, long-running families in the middle of everything. We worked out which characters had been central to the show for the longest and put them front and centre.

'We wanted some big heart-breaking family sagas with some tragedy in the middle of them. We also planned some lighter, frothier stories. We have a very good cohort of younger actors now so we wanted something big for them that would start growing the stars of the next 60 years. We know we can't please everyone all the time but we wanted to have a really good try.'

When plans for the 60th anniversary were taking place, the team wanted to do something memorable but the coronavirus pandemic meant there was a limit to the number of technical, spectacular elements they could include.

'These days, when you've got a big anniversary the audience is expecting something meaty to get their teeth into. But coronavirus meant we simply couldn't have months of construction, with people working on top of each other to build all the sets for a big stunt, due to social distancing. Instead, we had to focus on what *Corrie* does best: character and storytelling.

'I think the week of our anniversary was destined to be no less memorable for having to strip out the customary spectacular elements. Necessity is the mother of invention and our new ways of working forced us to think creatively about how to mark the anniversary with something gripping and satisfying.'

Before filming was suspended in March 2020, one storyline in particular caught the public imagination and shone a spotlight on a highly important issue, that of domestic abuse in the form of gaslighting and coercive control. We saw Yasmeen, at the end of her tether following months of mental cruelty and belittling at the hands of new husband Geoff Metcalfe, lash out in desperation, putting Geoff in hospital and herself in a police interview room. The implications of this disturbing course of events, with many viewers commenting on social media that it was hard to watch, saw healthy viewing figures and would go on to inform episodes

towards the end of the year. It also saw the actors and storyliners actively support charities that had been consulted in the creation of the plot – another example of the soap trying to making a difference to people in real life.

Equally importantly, Gemma's battle with postnatal depression was explored, as was David's return to self-destructive behaviour following wife Shona's injuries in the Christmas shooting, while Leanne, Steve and Nick were among several favourite characters to suffer some traumatic events. We also saw Ken Barlow move back into the Street – where he belongs.

The start of the year witnessed another *Coronation Street* landmark that bears special mention – on Friday 7th February 2020 the 10,000th episode was screened. Harking back to that very first episode, it opened with young Ruby and Hope playing outside the Corner Shop, singing the same children's rhyme as the youngsters in its 1960 predecessor. The hour-long episode went on to honour *Coronation Street*'s tradition of trips to Blackpool and the story of Rita's bid to scatter Dennis Tanner's ashes was interlaced with humour, a gentle poignancy and plenty of nods to those great characters of the past. It united characters young and old and was a welcome reminder of everything we love about *Coronation Street*.

Antony Cotton who plays Sean Tully says: '*Coronation Street* is unique, truly the first of its kind. It created a genre and is to this day the flagship of a whole television network, watched all over the world. Our stories are important to so many people and have been over the years. It was the blueprint that all others followed. It's been groundbreaking in the way that most things want to be groundbreaking, but aren't.'

And as for the future? *Coronation Street* stalwart Helen Worth predicts an even longer and more successful one.

'People relate to *Coronation Street*. They've grown up with it, their mothers watched it probably when they were in the womb and their children continue to watch it,' she says. 'People know it, they get used to you. You can always sit down at the end of a hard day's work and relax and enjoy it.

'It feels funny when you think it's been on for 60 years and I've been here for more than 46, and it is an extraordinarily long time for a programme to have survived as well as it has. They're getting something right.

'The young ones coming in now are wonderful. They do different things, they work differently, they think differently and you just have to watch them and move along into new waters with them because they're the next generation of the *Street* and they'll take it forward. It's in safe hands!'

MAIN CHARACTERS

Elsie Tanner (Patricia Phoenix)
The original Street siren

Dennis Tanner (Philip Lowrie)
Elsie Tanner's son and talent scout

Linda Cheveski (Anne Cunningham)
Elsie Tanner's daughter, married to Ivan

Ena Sharples (Violet Carson)
Legendary battleaxe

Florrie Lindley (Betty Alberge)
Corner Shop owner

Frank Barlow (Frank Pemberton)
Ken Barlow's father

Ida Barlow (Noel Dyson)
Ken Barlow's mother

Kenneth Barlow (William Roache)
Street legend and Deirdre's widower

David Barlow (Alan Rothwell)
Ken's younger brother

Albert Tatlock (Jack Howarth)
Ken's uncle by marriage

Annie Walker (Doris Speed)
The original Rovers landlady

Elsie Lappin (Maudie Edwards)
Owner of the Corner Shop from 1945–1960

Susan Cunningham (Patricia Shakesby)
Ken's first girlfriend

Jack Walker (Arthur Leslie)
Annie's husband and Rovers landlord

Martha Longhurst (Lynne Carol)
Cleaner pal of Ena and Minnie Caldwell

Christine Hardman (Christine Hargreaves)
Early Street resident, briefly engaged to Frank Barlow

Harry Hewitt (Ivan Beavis)
Widowed father of Lucille Hewitt

Esther Hayes (Daphne Oxenford)
Civil servant and early Street resident

Ivan Cheveski (Ernst Walder)
Husband to Linda

Minnie Caldwell (Margot Bryant)
Jed Stone's landlady and pal of Ena

May Hardman (Joan Heath)
Christine's widowed mother

Leonard Swindley (Arthur Lowe)
Manager of Gamma Garments

Lucille Hewitt (Jennifer Moss)
Daughter of Harry Hewitt, and ward of the Walkers

Vera Lomax (Ruth Holden)
Ena Sharples' daughter

Concepta Riley (Doreen Keogh)
Coronation Street's first barmaid and second wife of Harry Hewitt

Dot Greenhalgh (Joan Francis)
Elsie Tanner's best friend

Sheila Birtles (Eileen Mayers)
Factory worker who lived above the Corner Shop

Joe Makinson (Brian Rawlinson)
Plumber boyfriend of Christine Hardman

Beattie Pearson (Gabrielle Daye)
Albert Tatlock's daughter

Doreen Lostock (Angela Crow)
Factory worker and later Rovers barmaid

Arnold Tanner (Frank Crawshaw)
Estranged husband of Elsie Tanner

Len Fairclough (Peter Adamson)
Builder friend of Elsie who married Rita

Emily Nugent (Eileen Derbyshire)
Long-standing Street resident and widow of Ernest Bishop

Billy Walker (Kenneth Farrington)
Annie and Jack's son

Joan Walker (June Barry, Dorothy White)
Annie and Jack Walker's daughter

Alf Roberts (Bryan Mosley)
Grocer husband of Audrey

Alice Burgess (Avis Bunnage)
Widowed sister of Harry Hewitt

Jean Stark (Renny Lister)
Factory worker and Christine Hardman's pal

Jed Stone (Kenneth Cope)
Minnie Caldwell's Jack-the-lad lodger

Tom Hayes (Dudley Foster)
Brother of Esther Hayes

Nancy Leathers (Norah Hammond)
Ken and David Barlow's grandmother

Valerie Tatlock (Anne Reid)
Ken Barlow's first wife and mother of Peter and Susan

Bill Gregory (Jack Watson)
Elsie Tanner's boyfriend

Stanley Fairclough (Peter Noone, Ronald Cunliffe, Jonathan Coy)
Len's son from his first marriage

Jerry Booth (Graham Haberfield)
Len Faircough's partner

Dave Smith (Reginald Marsh)
Weatherfield bookie

Neil Crossley (Geoffrey Matthews)
Manager of Gamma Garments

Walter Potts (Christopher Sandford)
Singing window cleaner

Myra Dickinson (Susan Jameson)
Typist married to Jerry Booth

Laurie Frazer (Stanley Meadows)
Manager of the Viaduct Sporting Club

Dave Robbins (Jon Rollason)
Teacher at Bessie Street School

Irma Ogden (Sandra Gough)
Stan and Hilda's daughter

Charlie Moffitt (Gordon Rollings)
Viaduct Sporting Club's resident comic

Stan Ogden (Bernard Youens)
Window cleaner and husband of Hilda

Hilda Ogden (Jean Alexander)
Legendary cleaner and wife of Stan

Trevor Ogden (Jonathan Collins, Don Hawkins)
Son of Stan and Hilda

Tickler Murphy (Patrick McAlinney)
Minnie Caldwell's lodger

Sandra Petty (Heather Moore)
Lionel Petty's daughter

Rita Littlewood (Barbara Knox)
Former singer and long-time Street stalwart

William Piggott (George A Cooper)
Unscrupulous butcher and businessman

Susan Barlow (Katie Heanneau, Wendy Jane Walker, Suzy Patterson, Joanna Foster)
Ken and Valerie's daughter, and Peter's twin

Peter Barlow (John Heanneau, Christopher Dormer, Mark Duncan, Linus Roache, Joseph McKenna, David Lonsdale, Chris Gascoyne)
Ken and Valerie's son, and Susan's twin

Lionel Petty (Edward Evans)
Corner Shop owner in 1965–6

Clara Midgeley (Betty Hardy)
Mission Hall caretaker

Nellie Harvey (Mollie Sugden)
Landlady of The Laughing Donkey

Jim Mount (Barry Keagan)
Boyfriend of Elsie Tanner

Jackie Marsh (Pamela Craig)
Local reporter

Ray Langton (Neville Buswell)
Deirdre's first husband and Tracy's father

Ruth Winter (Collette O'Neil)
Community social worker

Wally Tanner (George Betton)
Arnold Tanner's father

Bet Lynch (Julie Goodyear)
Iconic Rovers barmaid, then licensee

Paul Cheveski (Marcus Saville, Nigel Greaves)
Ivan and Linda's son

Gregg Flint (Bill Nagy)
Steve Tanner's pal

Gary Strauss (Callen Angelo)
American GI who dated Elsie Tanner

Steve Tanner (Paul Maxwell)
Elsie Tanner's second husband

Joe Donelli (Shane Rimmer)
American GI who killed Steve Tanner

Ernest Bishop (Stephen Hancock)
Emily's husband murdered in a factory robbery

Jenny Sutton (Mitzi Rogers)
First wife of Dennis Tanner

Miklos Zadic (Paul Stassino)
Demolition firm boss who romanced Emily

Les Clegg (John Sharp)
Alcoholic owner of the Corner Shop in 1968

Maggie Clegg (Irene Sutcliffe)
Les Clegg's wife and Betty Turpin's sister

Gordon Clegg (Bill Kenwright, Geoffrey Leesley)
Betty Turpin's son

Audrey Bright (Gillian McCann)
Dickie Fleming's wife who had an affair with Ray Langton

Dickie Fleming (Nigel Humphries)
Audrey Bright's husband

Effie Spicer (Anne Dyson)
Widow who lodged at No 1

Tommy Deakin (Paddy Joyce)
Rag-and-bone man

Alice Pickins (Doris Hare)
Albert Tatlock's fiancée

Edith Tatlock (Clare Kelly)
Valerie Barlow's mother

Betty Turpin (Betty Driver)
Longest-serving member of The Rovers staff

Cyril Turpin (William Moore)
Betty Turpin's police sergeant husband

Janet Reid (Judith Barker)
Ken Barlow's second wife

Bernard Butler (Gorden Kaye)
Elsie Tanner's nephew

Sandra Butler (Patricia Fuller)
Elsie Tanner's niece

Alan Howard (Alan Browning)
Elsie Tanner's third husband

Handel Gartside (Harry Markham)
Minnie Caldwell's friend

Mark Howard (Nicholas Jones)
Alan Howard's son

Ivy Tilsley (Lynne Perrie)
Mother of Brian

Edna Gee (Mavis Rogerson)
Fred Gee's wife

Mavis Riley (Thelma Barlow)
Rita's pal and wife of Derek Wilton

Wilfred Perkins (Wensley Pithey)
Headmaster of Bessie Street School

Norma Ford (Diana Davies)
Worked in the Corner Shop and pursued Ken Barlow

Jacko Ford (Robert Keegan)
Father of Norma Ford

Alec Gilroy (Roy Barraclough)
Talent agent, Rovers licensee and husband of Bet Lynch

Deirdre Hunt (Anne Kirkbride)
Coronation Street icon and late wife of Ken Barlow

Elaine Perkins (Joanna Lumley)
Ken Barlow's girlfriend

Tricia Hopkins (Kathy Jones)
Gail's best mate, daughter of Idris and Vera

MAIN CHARACTERS

Vera Hopkins (Kathy Staff)
Wife of Idris and mother of Tricia

Idris Hopkins (Richard Davies)
Foundry worker, father of Tricia

Megan Hopkins (Jessie Evans)
Idris's mother

Gail Potter (Helen Worth)
Much-married long-term Street resident

Vera Duckworth (Elizabeth Dawn)
Factory worker and wife of Jack

Blanche Hunt (Patricia Cutts, Maggie Jones)
Deirdre's mother

Eddie Yeats (Geoffrey Hughes)
Binman lodger of the Ogdens

Fred Gee (Fred Feast)
Rovers potman

Terry Bradshaw (Bob Mason)
Renee Bradshaw's brother

Derek Wilton (Peter Baldwin)
Mavis Riley's husband

Renee Bradshaw (Madge Hindle)
Alf Roberts' second wife

Mike Baldwin (Johnny Briggs)
Cockney factory owner and long-term Wetherfield resident

Suzie Birchall (Cheryl Murray)
Gail's pal and Elsie's lodger

Tracy Langton (Christabel Finch, Holly Chamarette, Dawn Acton, Kate Ford)
Deirdre's daughter and Amy's mum

Steve Fisher (Lawrence Mullin)
Van driver at Baldwin's Casuals

Ida Clough (Helene Palmer)
Machinist at Baldwin's Casuals

Janice Stubbs (Angela Bruce)
Waitress who had an affair with Ray Langton

Brian Tilsley (Christopher Quinten)
Gail's first husband

Bert Tilsley (Peter Dudley)
Ivy's first husband

Audrey Potter (Sue Nicholls)
Gail's mother and wife of Alf

Jack Duckworth (William Tarmey)
Vera's husband and Rovers potman

Arnold Swain (George Waring)
Emily's bigamist husband

Martin Cheveski (Jonathan Caplan)
Ivan and Linda's second son

Frankie Baldwin (Sam Kydd)
Father of Mike Baldwin

Nick Tilsley (Warren Jackson, Adam Rickitt, Ben Price)
Gail and Brian's son

Eunice Nuttall (Meg Johnson)
Second wife of Fred Gee

Alma Sedgewick (Amanda Barrie)
Gail's pal and third wife of Mike Baldwin

Chalkie Whitely (Teddy Turner)
Eddie Yeats' workmate and sometime owner of No 9

Marion Willis (Veronica Doran)
Wife of Eddie Yeats

Sharon Gaskell (Tracie Bennett)
Len and Rita's foster daughter

Maggie Dunlop (Jill Kerman)
Mike Baldwin's girlfriend and mother of Mark Redman

Phyllis Pearce (Jill Summers)
Purple-haired pensioner who pursued Percy Sugden

Victor Pendlebury (Christopher Coll)
Mavis's boyfriend

Curly Watts (Kevin Kennedy)
Reg Holdsworth's sidekick and husband of Raquel

Terry Duckworth (Nigel Pivaro)
Jack and Vera's villainous son

Percy Sugden (Bill Waddington)
Officious Community Centre caretaker

Shirley Armitage (Lisa Lewis)
Machinist and Curly Watts' girlfriend

Kevin Webster (Michael Le Vell)
Mechanic and Sally's first husband

Mark Redman (Thomas Hawkeswood, Christopher Oakes, Michael Bolstridge, Chris Cook, Paul Fox)
Mike Baldwin and Maggie Dunlop's son

Bill Webster (Peter Armitage)
Kevin Webster's father

Debbie Webster (Sue Devaney)
Kevin's younger sister

Elaine Prior (Judy Gridley)
Bill Webster's wife

Gloria Todd (Sue Jenkins)
Rovers barmaid

Martin Platt (Sean Wilson)
Gail's second husband and father of David

Connie Clayton (Susan Brown, Irene Skillington)
Wife of Harry Clayton

Harry Clayton (Johnny Leeze)
Milkman husband of Connie

Andrea Clayton (Caroline O'Neill)
Gave birth to Terry Duckworth's son Paul

George Wardle (Ron Davies)
Ivy's fiancé

Stella Rigby (Vivienne Ross)
Landlady of The White Swan and pal of Bet Lynch

Sam Tindall (Tom Mennard)
Percy Sugden's love rival

Jenny Bradley (Sally Ann Matthews)
Rita's foster daughter and Rovers landlady

Alan Bradley (Mark Eden)

Rita's violent partner

Sally Seddon (Sally Dynevor)
Long-time Street resident and one-time Mayor of Weatherfield

Ian Latimer (Michael Loney)
Gail's lover

Sarah Louise Tilsley (Leah and Lynsay King, Tina O'Brien)
Gail and Brian's daughter

Don Brennan (Geoff Hinsliff)
Ivy's second husband

Amy Burton (Fanny Carby)
Vera Duckworth's mother

Gina Seddon (Julie Foy, Connie Hyde)
Sally's sister

Sandra Stubbs (Sally Watts)
Rovers cleaner and wife of Ronnie

Tina Fowler (Michelle Holmes)
Rovers barmaid

Mark Casey (Stuart Wolfenden)
Kevin's assistant mechanic

Wendy Crozier (Roberta Kerr)
Ken's mistress

Maurice Jones (Alan Moore)
Property developer

Reg Holdsworth (Ken Morley)
Bettabuy manager and Maureen's husband

Kimberley Taylor (Suzanne Hall)
Curly's fiancée

Jim McDonald (Charles Lawson)
Ex-army sergeant, husband of Liz

Liz McDonald (Beverley Callard)
Jim's wife, Rovers stalwart and mother of Steve, Andy and Katie

Steve McDonald (Simon Gregson)
Much-married taxi firm boss

Andy McDonald (Nicholas Cochrane)
Steve's twin brother

Victoria Arden (Helen Warburton, Chloe Newsome)
Alec Gilroy's granddaughter and Steve's first wife

Peter Ingram (Tony Osoba)
Textile boss and husband of Jackie

Des Barnes (Philip Middlemiss)
Bookie husband of Steph, then Natalie

Steph Barnes (Amelia Bullmore)
Daughter of Maurice Jones and first wife of Des

Felicity Khan (Rita Wolf)
Student friend of Jenny Bradley

Dave Barton (David Beckett)
Joiner boyfriend of Deirdre

Jackie Ingram (Shirin Taylor)
Mike Baldwin's second wife

Phil Jennings (Tommy Boyle)
Deirdre's boyfriend

Angie Freeman (Deborah McAndrew)
Curly's lodger and co-founder of Underworld

Rosie Webster (Emma Collinge, Helen Flanagan)
Sally and Kevin's daughter

David Platt (Thomas Ormson, Jack P Shepherd)
Gail and Martin's son

Raquel Wolstenhulme (Sarah Lancashire)
Rovers barmaid and Curly's first wife

Brendan Scott (Milton Johns)
Corner Shop owner

Lisa Horton (Caroline Milmoe)
Mother of Tommy Duckworth

Ted Sullivan (William Russell)
Confectionery salesman and Rita's second husband

Carmel Finnan (Catherine Cusack)
Student nurse who pursued Martin Platt

Tommy Duckworth (Darryl Edwards, Joseph Aston, Chris Fountain)
Terry and Lisa Duckworth's son

Harold Potts (Russell Dixon)
Corrupt councillor

Denise Osbourne (Denise Black)
Ex-partner of Ken and mother of Daniel

Fiona Middleton (Angela Griffin)
Hairdresser, mother of Emma Brooker

Maureen Naylor (Sherrie Hewson)
Reg's wife who then married Fred Elliott and Bill Webster

Maud Grimes (Elizabeth Bradley)
Maureen's mother

Tanya Pooley (Eva Pope)
Troublesome Rovers barmaid

Colin Barnes (Ian Embleton)
Des Barnes' brother

Charlie Whelan (John St Ryan)
Bet Gilroy's trucker boyfriend

Jamie Armstrong (Joseph Gilgun)
Son of Tricia Armstrong

Tricia Armstrong (Tracy Brabin)
Mother of Jamie, also had baby Brad by Terry Duckworth

Norris Cole (Malcolm Hebden)
Nosy parker pal of Rita and Street favourite

Sean Skinner (Terence Hillyer)
Ran the betting shop on Rosamund Street

Samir Rachid (Al Nedjari)
Deirdre's third husband

Fred Elliott (John Savident)
Butcher father of Ashley

Sophie Webster (Ashleigh Middleton, Emma Woodward, Brooke Vincent)

Kevin and Sally's younger daughter

Daniel Osbourne (Lewis Harney, Dominic Holmes, Rob Mallard) –
Son of Ken Barlow and Denise Osbourne, widower of Sinead and dad to Bertie

Josie Clarke (Ellie Haddington)
Don Brennan's girlfriend

Ashley Peacock (Steven Arnold)
Fred Elliott's son, husband to Maxine, then Claire, and father to Freddie

Maxine Heavey (Tracy Shaw)
Ashley's first wife, murdered by Richard Hillman

Billy Williams (Frank Mills)
Betty's second husband

Roy Cropper (David Neilson)
Café owner and Hayley's husband

Anne Malone (Eve Steele)
Pursued Curly and died in a Freshco freezer

Gary Mallett (Ian Mercer)
Judy's husband and father of twins

Judy Mallett (Gaynor Faye)
Married to Gary and mother of twins

Tony Horrocks (Lee Warburton)
Natalie's criminal son

Stephen Reid (Todd Boyce)
Audrey's long-lost son from Canada

Joyce Smedley (Anita Carey)
Judy Mallett's mother and Rovers cleaner

Samantha Failsworth (Tina Hobley)
Rovers barmaid

Alan McKenna (Glenn Hugill)
Police detective who jilted Fiona Middleton

Robert Preston (Julian Kay, Tristan Gemmill)
Chef, Tracy and Michelle's ex

Janice Battersby (Vicky Entwistle)
Wife of Les and Battersby matriarch

Natalie Horrocks (Denise Welch)
Rovers landlady and Des Barnes' second wife

Chris Collins (Matthew Marsden)
Mechanic who had a fling with Sally

Zoe Tattersall (Joanne Froggatt)
Young mum who gave up daughter to the Malletts

Jon Lindsay (Owen Aaronovitch)
Conman who landed Deirdre in jail

Jez Quigley (Lee Boardman)
Violent drug dealer

Les Battersby (Bruce Jones)
Lazy husband of Janice, then Cilla

Leanne Battersby (Jane Danson)
Daughter of Les and Stella Price

Toyah Battersby (Georgia Taylor)
Daughter of Janice and stepdaughter of Les

Spider Nugent (Martin Hancock)
Emily's eco-warrior nephew

Hayley Patterson (Julie Hesmondhalgh)
Transgender Street favourite who married Roy

Greg Kelly (Stephen Billington)
Les's son who seduced Sally then terrorised her

Edna Miller (Joan Kempson)
Factory worker and pub cleaner

Jackie Dobbs (Margi Clarke)
Deirdre's prison cellmate

Linda Sykes (Jacqueline Pirie)
Mike Baldwin's fourth wife

Tyrone Dobbs (Alan Halsall)
Long-term Street mechanic, partner to Fiz

Alison Wakefield (Naomi Radcliffe)
Kevin Webster's second wife

Ravi Desai (Saeed Jaffrey)
Corner Shop owner

Nita Desai (Rebecca Sarker)
Ravi Desai's daughter

Ian Bentley (Jonathan Guy Lewis)
Married Sharon Gaskell

Vikram Desai (Chris Bisson)
Ravi Desai's son

Danny Hargreaves (Richard Standing)
Sally's fiancé

Vinny Sorrell (James Gaddas)
Natalie's boyfriend who ran off with her sister Debs

Duggie Ferguson (John Bowe)
Property developer and Rovers landlord

Candice Stowe (Nikki Sanderson)
Hairdresser pal of Sarah

Dev Alahan (Jimmi Harkishin)
Corner Shop owner and widower

Rebecca Hopkins (Jill Halfpenny)
Nurse who pursued Martin Platt

Debs Brownlow (Gabrielle Glaister)
Natalie Barnes' sister

Dennis Stringer (Charles Dale)
Biker who fell for Janice

Geena Gregory (Jennifer James)
Rovers barmaid and Dev's fiancée

Bobbi Lewis (Naomi Ryan)
Underworld machinist

Emma Taylor (Angela Lonsdale)
Police officer and Curly's second wife

Eileen Grimshaw (Sue Cleaver)
Street Cars operator and mum to Todd and Jason

Maria Sutherland (Samia Longchambon)
Widowed hairdresser and mother of Liam

Bethany Platt (Amy and Emily Walton, Lucy Fallon)
Sarah Platt's daughter

Sam Kingston (Scott Wright)
Mechanic and part-time stripper 'the Masked Python'

Karen Phillips (Suranne Jones)
Steve McDonald's second wife

Anthony Stephens (John Quayle)
Bookseller friend of Rita

Evelyn Sykes (Melanie Kilburn)
Linda's mother and bigamist wife of Fred Elliott

Kirk Sutherland (Andrew Whyment)
Maria's brother and partner of Beth

Molly Hardcastle (Jacqueline Kington)
Nurse who went out with Kevin

Charlie Ramsden (Clare McGlinn)
Troubled teacher married to Matt

Matt Ramsden (Stephen Beckett)
GP who slept with Maxine

Paul Clayton (Lee Booth, Tom Hudson)
Son of Terry Duckworth and Andrea Clayton

Wayne Hayes (Gary Damer, Adam Barlow)
Abused boy helped by the Croppers

Jason Grimshaw (Ryan Thomas)
Eileen's builder son

Adam Barlow (Iain De Caestecker, Samuel Robertson)
Mike Baldwin and Susan Barlow's son

Todd Grimshaw (Bruno Langley)
Eileen's youngest son

Sunita Parekh (Shobna Gulati)
Married Dev Alahan

Fiz Brown (Jennie McAlpine)
Tyrone's partner, mother to Hope, stepmother to Ruby

Shelley Unwin (Sally Lindsay)
Rovers manageress who married bigamist Peter Barlow

Richard Hillman (Brian Capron)
Street serial killer who married Gail

Archie Shuttleworth (Roy Hudd)
Undertaker friend of Audrey Roberts

Joshua Peacock (Benjamin Beresford)
Maxine's son, fathered by Matt Ramsden

Aidan Critchley (Dean Ashton)
Sarah Platt's boyfriend

Joe Carter (Jonathan Wrather)
Businessman who had an affair with Karen McDonald

Ciaran McCarthy (Keith Duffy)
Chef and Navy pal of Peter Barlow

Harry Flagg (Iain Rogerson)
Rovers and Underworld cleaner

Lucy Richards (Katy Carmichael)
Florist who married Peter Barlow, late mother of Simon

Mick Hopwood (Ian Gain)
Janice Battersby's police officer boyfriend

Angela Nelson (Kathryn Hunt)
Real name Harris. Moved with family to Weatherfield under witness protection scheme

Craig Nelson (Richard Fleeshman)
Rosie Webster's goth boyfriend

Tommy Nelson (Thomas Craig)
Angela's mechanic husband murdered by daughter Katy

Katy Nelson (Lucy-Jo Hudson)
Martin Platt's young girlfriend turned killer

Patrick Tussel (Trevor Dwyer-Lynch)
Cab driver

John Arnley (Paul Warriner)
Toyah's unfaithful lecturer boyfriend

Tony Stewart (Alan Igbon, Terence Maynard)
Jason Grimshaw's father

Bev Unwin (Susie Blake)
Shelley Unwin's mother and close friend of Deirdre

Claire Casey (Julia Haworth)
Married to Ashley Peacock, mother of Freddie

Wally Bannister (Bernard Cribbins)
Lothario who courted Blanche Hunt

Sonia Marshall (Tina Gambe)
Factory worker who went out with Martin

Sean Tully (Antony Cotton)
Knicker-stitcher and Rovers barman

Penny King (Pauline Fleming)
Mike Baldwin's girlfriend

Maya Sharma (Sasha Behar)
Solicitor obsessed with Dev

Brenda Fearns (Julia Deakin)
Bethany Platt's paternal grandmother

Cilla Brown (Wendi Peters)
Fiz and Chesney's mother who married Les Battersby

Charlie Stubbs (Bill Ward)
Abusive builder murdered by girlfriend Tracy

Chesney Brown (Sam Aston)
Fiz's brother and father of quads with Gemma

Karl Foster (Chris Finch)
Nurse, and Todd Grimshaw's first male lover

Amy Barlow (Amber Chadwick, Elle Mulvaney)
Tracy and Steve's daughter

Danny Baldwin (Bradley Walsh)
Mike Baldwin's son and half-brother of Adam

Frankie Baldwin (Debra Stephenson)
Danny's wife, mother of Warren and stepmother of Jamie

MAIN CHARACTERS

Jamie Baldwin (Rupert Hill)
Danny's son, had an affair with his stepmother

Warren Baldwin (Danny Young)
Footballer son of Danny and Frankie

Kelly Crabtree (Tupele Dorgu)
Machinist and Lloyd Mullaney's girlfriend

Rula Romanoff (Honor Blackman)
Old friend of Rita

Yana Lumb (Jayne Tunnicliffe)
Cilla Battersby-Brown's best friend

Violet Wilson (Jenny Platt)
Rovers barmaid and mother of Sean's son Dylan

Ian Davenport (Philip Bretherton)
Sally's car salesman boss and lover

Diggory Compton (Eric Potts)
Baker father of Molly Dobbs

Jessie Jackson (Nailah Cumberbatch)
Underworld machinist

Joanne Jackson (Zaraah Abrahams)
Jessie's illegal immigrant cousin, posing as her twin

Keith Appleyard (Ian Redford)
Father of Angela Harris

Nathan Cooper (Ray Fearon)
Mechanic at Webster's Autos

Mel Hutchwright aka Lionel Hipkis (Ian McKellen)
Conman and author of Hard Grinding

Carol Baldwin (Lynne Pearson)
First wife of Danny Baldwin

Lloyd Mullaney (Craig Charles)
Former co-owner of Street Cars

Freda Burgess (Ali Briggs)
Emily's niece engaged to Norris Cole

Phil Nail (Clive Russell)
Reflexologist boyfriend of Gail

Becky Granger (Amanda Tyrell, Katherine Kelly)
Third wife of Steve McDonald and sister to Kylie, Rovers barmaid

Molly Compton (Vicky Binns)
Daughter of Diggory Compton, married Tyrone and had a son by Kevin

Ronnie Clayton (Emma Stansfield)
Street Cars employee and love interest of Steve McDonald

Amber Kalirai (Nikki Patel)
Dev Alahan's daughter

Vernon Tomlin (Ian Reddington)
Musician married to Liz McDonald

Michelle Connor (Kym Marsh)
Steve's fifth wife, barmaid and mother to Ali, Ryan and Ruairi

Ryan Connor (Ben Thompson, Sol Heras, Ryan Prescott)
Raised as Michelle's son after hospital mix up

Liam Connor (Rob James-Collier)
Michelle's brother and father of Liam Jr, murdered by Tony Gordon

Paul Connor (Sean Gallagher)
Late brother of Michelle, married to Carla

Carla Connor (Alison King)
Four-times married co-owner of Underworld

Sonny Dhillon (Pal Aron)
Michelle Connor's bisexual boyfriend

Roger Stiles (Andrew Dunn)
Janice Battersby's plumber boyfriend

Jodie Morton (Samantha Seager)
Jerry Morton's daughter

Wilf Morton (Rodney Litchfield)
Ex-jailbird head of the Morton family

Doreen Fenwick (Barbara Young)
Old friend of Rita

Wiki Dankowska (Wanda Opalinska)
Factory worker

Casey Carswell (Zoe Henry)
Disturbed woman who stalked Claire and Ashley

Jerry Morton (Michael Starke)
Owner of Jerry's Takeaway

Darryl Morton (Jonathan Dixon)
Jerry's son

Mel Morton (Emma Edmondson)
Darryl's twin sister and trainee police officer

Kayleigh Morton (Jessica Barden)
Jerry's youngest daughter

Teresa Bryant (Karen Henthorn)
Mother of the Morton clan, dated Lloyd

John Stape (Graeme Hawley)
Teacher married to Fiz, father of Hope and Jade

Marcus Dent (Charlie Condou)
Midwife and boyfriend of Sean Tully

Tony Gordon (Gray O'Brien)
Killer businessman

Harry Mason (Jack Ellis)
Bookie

Dan Mason (Matthew Crompton)
Harry Mason's son

Alex Neeson (Dario Coates, James Burrows)
Biological son of Michelle and Dean

Tina McIntyre (Michelle Keegan)
Rovers barmaid, murdered by Rob Donovan

Helen Connor (Sorcha Cusack, Dearbhla Molloy)
Mother of Paul, Liam and Michelle

Barry Connor (Frank Grimes)
Helen Connor's husband

Graeme Proctor (Craig Gazey)
David Platt's pal, married Xin Chiang

Julie Carp (Katy Cavanagh)
Eileen Grimshaw's half-sister

Ted Page (Michael Byrne)
Gail's father

Natasha Blakeman (Rachel Leskovac)
Hairdresser and Nick Tilsley's former girlfriend

Joe McIntyre (Reece Dinsdale)
Tina's father and Gail's fourth husband

Tom Kerrigan (Philip McGinley)
Michelle Connor's cousin

Pam Hobsworth (Kate Anthony)
Diggory Compton's sister

Nina Mandal (Harvey Virdi)
Ex-Bollywood star who had a fling with Dev

Tara Mandal (Ayesha Dharker)
Nina's daughter who Dev proposed to

Simon Barlow (Alex Bain)
Son of Peter Barlow and Lucy Richards

Eddie Windass (Steve Huison)
Common-law husband of Anna

Anna Windass (Debbie Rush)
Mum of Gary and adoptive mum of Faye

Gary Windass (Mikey North)
Ex-squaddie turned loan shark, dad of Jake and Zack

Len Windass (Conor Ryan)
Brother of Eddie Windass

Minnie Chandra (Poppy Jhakra)
College friend of Amber Kalirai

Mary Taylor (Patti Clare)
Ex-wife of Norris Cole and flower-shop assistant

Colin Grimshaw (Edward de Souza)
Eileen Grimshaw and Julie Carp's father

Jesse Chadwick (John Thomson)
Children's entertainer

Poppy Morales (Sophiya Haque)
Assistant manager of The Rovers

Sian Powers (Sacha Parkinson)
Sophie's former fiancée

Martha Fraser (Stephanie Beacham)
Actress who had an affair with Ken

Ben Richardson (Lucien Laviscount)
Sophie Webster's first and only boyfriend

Luke Strong (Craig Kelly)
Businessman friend of Carla

Paula Carp (Sharon Duce)
Julie Carp's mother

Umed Alahan (Harish Patel)
Dev Alahan's uncle

Ramsay Clegg (Andrew Sachs)
Norris Cole's half-brother

Rick Neelan (Greg Wood)
Loan shark killed by Gary Windass

Aadi Alahan (Zennon Ditchett, Adam Hussain)
Dev and Sunita's son, Asha's twin brother

Asha Alahan (Tanisha Gorey)
Aadi's twin sister

Lewis Archer (Nigel Havers)
Conman who courted Audrey and Gail

Claudia Colby (Rula Lenska)
Hairdresser and Ken's partner

Trevor Dean (Steve Jackson)
Binman boyfriend of Janice Battersby

Cheryl Gray (Holly Quin-Ankrah)
Lapdancer friend of Leanne, girlfriend of Lloyd

Brian Packham (Peter Gunn)
Former headteacher now Kabin owner and Cathy Matthews' partner

Izzy Armstrong (Cherylee Houston)
Gary Windass's ex and mother of Jake

Liam Connor Jr (Ollie and Elliott Barnett, Charlie Wrenshall)
Son of Maria and Liam Connor

Owen Armstrong (Ian Puleston-Davies)
Builder father of Izzy and Katy, and Anna Windass's ex

Chris Gray (Will Thorp)
Cheryl's abusive ex who lured her back from Lloyd

Katy Armstrong (Georgia May Foote)
Owen's younger daughter, mother of Joseph

Matt Carter (Oliver Mellor)
GP at Rosamund Street Medical Centre

Kylie Turner (Paula Lane)
David Platt's first wife, mother of Max and Lily

Max Turner (Harry McDermott)
Son of Kylie and Callum, brother of Lily and Harry

Lawrence Cunningham (Linus Roache)
Ken's long-lost son

James Cunningham (James Roache)
Lawrence Cunningham's son

Jack Dobbs (Jaxon and Maddox Beswick, Kyran Bowes)
Kevin and Molly's love child

Paul Kershaw (Tony Hirst)
Firefighter partner of Eileen Grimshaw

Marc Selby (Andrew Hall)
Transvestite love interest of Audrey Roberts and Claudia Colby

Frank Foster (Andrew Lancel)
Carla's violent fiancé

Faye Butler (Ellie Leach)
Tim's biological daughter adopted by Anna

Jeff Cullen (Steven Houghton)
Rosie Webster's model agent boss

Xin Chiang (Elizabeth Tan)
Wife of Graeme Proctor

Sylvia Goodwin (Stephanie Cole)
Roy Cropper's mother

Stella Price (Michelle Collins)
Rovers landlady and mother of Eva Price and Leanne Battersby

Karl Munro (John Michie)
Stella Price's murderous husband

Eva Price (Catherine Tyldesley)
Leanne's half-sister, mother of Susie

Beth Tinker (Lisa George)
Machinist, aunt to Sinead and partner of Kirk Sutherland

Craig Tinker (Colson Smith)
Beth's police officer son

Anne Foster (Gwen Taylor)
Frank Foster's mother

Kirsty Soames (Natalie Gumede)
Tyrone's abusive ex

Lesley Kershaw (Judy Holt)
Paul Kershaw's wife, suffering from early-onset Alzheimer's disease

Danny Stratton (Jeremy Sheffield)
Hotel manager and Becky McDonald's partner

Milton Fanshaw (Robert Vaughn)
Love interest of Sylvia Goodwin

Rob Donovan (Marc Baylis)
Carla's brother who murdered Tina McIntyre

Gloria Price (Sue Johnston)
Stella Price's mother

Ruby Soames (Macy Alabi)
Daughter of Kirsty and Tyrone

Mandy Kamara (Pamela Nomvete)
Lloyd Mullaney's ex and mother of Jenna

Jenna Kamara (Krissi Bohn)
Daughter of Mandy Kamara and Lloyd Mullaney

Tim Metcalfe (Joe Duttine)
Faye's father who married Sally bigamously

Hope Stape (Faith and Nicole Holt, Isabella Flanagan)
Fiz and John's daughter

Eric Babbage (Timothy West)
Gloria Price's fiancé

Steph Britton (Tisha Merry)
Waitress and Luke Britton's sister

Toni Griffiths (Tara Moran)
Firefighter who died in The Rovers blaze

Sinead Tinker (Katie McGlynn)
Late wife of Daniel Osbourne and mother of Bertie

Pat Phelan (Connor McIntyre)
Eileen Grimshaw's husband, builder and serial killer

Kal Nazir (Jimi Mistry)
Leanne's partner and father of Alya and Zeedan Nazir

Andrea Beckett (Hayley Tamaddon)
Lloyd Mullaney's partner

Maddie Heath (Amy James-Kelly)
Sophie Webster's partner

Sharif Nazir (Marc Anwar)
Yasmeen Nazir's husband

Luke Britton (Dean Fagan)
Mechanic, romanced Maria and Alya

Michael Rodwell (Les Dennis)
Burglar who became Gail's fifth husband

Alya Nazir (Sair Khan)
Kal Nazir's daughter, sister to Zeedan

Yasmeen Nazir (Shelley King)
Kal's mother

Joseph Brown (Lucca-Owen Warwick, William Flanagan)
Son of Chesney and Katy

Zeedan Nazir (Qasim Akhtar)
Brother to Alya, married Rana Habeeb

Gemma Winter (Dolly-Rose Campbell)
Chesney's partner and mother of quads

Macca Hibbs (Gareth Berliner)
Callum Logan's dodgy mate

Callum Logan (Sean Ward)
Kylie's drug-dealing ex, father of Max

Andy Carver (Oliver Farnworth)
Waiter murdered by Pat Phelan

Billy Mayhew (Daniel Brocklebank)
Vicar and partner to Paul Foreman

Erica Holroyd (Claire King)
Liz McDonald's pal and Dev Alahan's ex

Cathy Matthews (Melanie Hill)
Brian Packham's partner

Jackson Hodge (Rhys Cadman)
Father of Faye Windass's daughter, Miley

Aidan Connor (Shayne Ward)
Johnny Connor's son and Carla's half-brother

Alex Warner (Liam Bairstow)
Cathy's nephew and café assistant

Johnny Connor (Richard Hawley)
Rovers landlord and husband to Jenny

Kate Connor (Faye Brookes)
Johnny Connor's daughter

Nessa Warner (Sadie Shimmin)
Cathy Matthews' sister, mother to Alex

Brendan Finch (Ted Robbins)
Mary Taylor's lover

Caz Hammond (Rhea Bailey)
Kate Connor's obsessive ex

Jake Windass (Seth and Theo Wild, Bobby Bradshaw)
Izzy and Gary's son born via surrogate

Rana Habeeb (Bhavna Limbachia)
Kate Connor's fiancée

Freddie Smith (Derek Griffiths)
Widowed friend of Kylie

Will Chatterton (Leon Ockenden)
Michelle's stalker ex

Lee Mayhew (Richard Crehan)
Billy Mayhew's drug addict brother

Lily Platt (Brooke Malonie)
David and Kylie Platt's daughter

Clayton Hibbs (Callum Harrison)
Teenage tearaway who murdered Kylie Platt

Sonia Rahman (Sudha Bhuchar)
Sharif Nazir's lover

Dr Gaddas (Christine Mackie)
Regular Weatherfield GP

Vinny Ashford (Ian Kelsey)
Associate of Pat Phelan, killed by Andy Carver

Seb Franklin (Harry Visinoni)
Abi Franklin's son

Shona Ramsey (Julia Goulding)
Mother of Clayton, married to David Platt

Nathan Curtis (Christopher Harper)
Groomed Bethany Platt

Jude Appleton (Paddy Wallace)
Mary's long-lost son

Mel Maguire (Sonia Ibrahim)
Friend of Nathan Curtis

Oliver Battersby (Emmanuel and Jeremiah Cheetham)
Leanne Battersby and Steve McDonald's son

Harry Platt (Freddie and Isaac Rhodes)
Son of Sarah Platt and Callum Logan

Neil Clifton (Ben Cartwright)
Police officer friend of Nathan Curtis who abused Bethany

Drew Spellman (Tom Godwin)
Billy Mayhew's ex and adoptive father of Summer

Nicola Rubinstein (Nicola Thorp)
Pat Phelan's daughter, mother of Zack

Summer Spellman (Matilda Freeman)
Drew Spellman's adoptive daughter

Moira Pollock (Louiza Patikas)
Rosamund Street Medical Centre practice manager

Angie Appleton (Victoria Ekanoye)
Jude Appleton's wife

Colin Callen (Jim Moir)
Marketing boss and newsagent

Abi Franklin (Sally Carman)
Mechanic and mother to Seb, Charlie and Lexi

Imran Habeeb (Charlie de Melo)
Solicitor, partner of Toyah Battersby

Josh Tucker (Ryan Clayton)
David Platt's rapist

Rosemary Piper (Sophie Thompson)
Bogus medium in league with Lewis Archer

Tyler Jefferies (Will Barnett)
Teenager who got Amy Barlow pregnant

Geoff Metcalfe (Ian Bartholomew)
Tim Metcalfe's father and Yasmeen Nazir's abusive husband

Emma Brooker (Alexandra Mardell)
Barmaid daughter of Fiona Middleton and Steve McDonald

Paul Foreman (Peter Ash)
Gemma Winter's twin brother

Duncan Radfield (Nicholas Gleaves)
Fraudster who charmed Sally Metcalfe

Paula Martin (Stirling Gallacher)
Sophie Webster's solicitor ex

Hannah Gilmore (Hannah Ellis Ryan)
Claimed to be Liz McDonald's deceased daughter Katie

Evelyn Plummer (Maureen Lipman)
Tyrone Dobbs' grandmother

Vicky Jefferies (Kerri Quinn)
Robert Preston's lover

Jan Lozinski (Piotr Baumann)
Eileen Grimshaw's partner

Bertie Osbourne (Rufus Morgan-Smith)
Son of Daniel and Sinead

Alina Pop (Ruxandra Porojnicu)
Romanian love interest of Seb Franklin

Corey Brent (Maximus Evans)
Asha's on-off boyfriend

James Bailey (Nathan Graham)
Weatherfield County footballer

Ed Bailey (Trevor Michael Georges)
James and Michael's builder father, husband to Aggie

Michael Bailey (Ryan Russell)
Ed and Aggie Bailey's entrepreneur son

Aggie Bailey (Lorna Laidlaw)
Nurse and mother to James and Michael

Kelly Neelan (Millie Gibson)
Rick's teenage daughter

Ray Crosby (Mark Frost)
Owner of Viaduct Bistro

Bernie Winter (Jane Hazlegrove)
Gemma and Paul's mother

Derek Milligan (Craige Els)
Gary Windass's crazed client

Kel Hinchley (Joseph Alessi)
Bernie Winter's ex

Jade Rowan (Lottie Henshall)
John Stape's daughter

Aled, Bryn, Carys and Llio Winter-Brown (Charlotte and James Holt, Arthur, Lily and Lucy Taylor, Harry and Harvey Thompson)
Gemma and Chesney's quads

Nina Lucas (Mollie Gallagher)
Roy Cropper's niece

Richard Lucas (Paul Bown)
Roy Cropper's half-brother and Nina's father

Arthur Medwin (Paul Copley)
Evelyn Plummer's former love

Scott Emberton (Tom Roberts)
Ghost from Johnny Connor's past

Index

Acknowledgements

Publisher's Acknowledgements

The publisher would like to thank the following for their expert knowledge and diligence on this project: Dominic Khouri, Abigail Kemp, Shirley Patton, Helen Nugent, Iain MacLeod, John Whitton, Sarah Tobias, Amanda-Jane Read, Nicola Gillham, Clare Cooper-Marshall and Helen Mills.

Author Acknowledements

This book could not have been written without the help of many people who work or have worked on *Coronation Street*, or are linked to it in some way, but especially the following people. Thank you to every single one of you. In no particular order:
The friends of Tony Warren, William Roache MBE, Barbara Knox MBE, Philip Lowrie, Helen Worth, Sally Dynevor, Beverley Callard, Alison King, Jack P Shepherd, Ben Price, Sally Ann Matthews, Antony Cotton, Daniel Brocklebank, Patti Clare, Dolly-Rose Campbell, Joe Duttine, Alexandra Mardell, Katie McGlynn, Shelley King, Ian Bartholomew, Rob Mallard, Lorna Laidlaw, Rula Lenska, Joanna Lumley, Amanda Barrie, Paula Lane, Connor McIntyre, Charlie Lawson, Roy Hudd, Denise Welch, Les Dennis, Iain MacLeod, Jan McVerry, Martin Sterling, Billie Williams, Helen Nugent, David Nugent, Dominic Khouri, Alison Sinclair, Lee Rayner, John Friend Newman, Judi Hayfield, Gennie Radcliffe, Katy Scully, Caroline Campbell, Ally Nolan, Dayle Evans-Kar, Alex Hatzar, Margaret Wood and everyone in the costume department, Jacquelyn Walker, Jane Hatch, Tina Lyons and the whole makeup team, Andy Ashworth, Marc Hough, Sophie Byrne, David Williams, Patrick Henshaw, Paul Sparrow, Stephen Polack, Angie Ryan, John, Karen and David (from coronationstreet.fandom. com/wiki/Corriepedia, I could not have done this without your incredible knowledge and help), Katie Fitzpatrick, Derek Hornby, Louis and Isobel Kemp, the whole team at Octopus, and the entire *Corrie* family – cast, crew and all the staff behind the scenes – what an incredible team!